Dear Reader:

The book you are about to read is the latest bestseller from the St. Martin's True Crime Library, the imprint the *New York Times* calls "the leader in true crime!" Each month, we offer you a fascinating account of the latest, most sensational crime that has captured the national attention. St. Martin's is the publisher of bestselling true crime author and crime journalist Kieran Crowley, who explores the dark, deadly links between a prominent Manhattan surgeon and the disappearance of his wife fifteen years earlier in THE SURGEON'S WIFE. Suzy Spencer's BREAKING POINT guides readers through the tortuous twists and turns in the case of Andrea Yates, the Houston mother who drowned her five young children in the family's bathtub. In Edgar Award-nominated DARK DREAMS, legendary FBI profiler Roy Hazelwood and bestselling crime author Stephen G. Michaud shine light on the inner workings of America's most violent and depraved murderers. In the book you now hold, BLOOD JUSTICE, Tom Henderson examines the trail of a serial killer gone cold . . . and how one person got the case going again.

St. Martin's True Crime Library gives you the stories behind the headlines. Our authors take you right to the scene of the crime and into the minds of the most notorious murderers to show you what really makes them tick. St. Martin's True Crime Library paperbacks are better than the most terrifying thriller, because it's all true! The next time you want a crackling good read, make sure it's got the St. Martin's True Crime Library logo on the spine—you'll be up all night!

Charles E. Spicer, Jr.
Executive Editor, St. Martin's True Crime Library

# BLOOD
# JUSTICE

Titles by Tom Henderson

*A Deadly Affair*

*Blood Justice*

from the True Crime Library
of St. Martin's Paperbacks

# BLOOD JUSTICE

## Tom Henderson

St. Martin's Paperbacks

**NOTE:** If you purchased this book without a cover you should be aware that this book is stolen property. It was reported as "unsold and destroyed" to the publisher, and neither the author nor the publisher has received any payment for this "stripped book."

BLOOD JUSTICE

Copyright © 2004 by Tom Henderson.

Cover photograph of house by Mary Steinbacher/Photonica. Photos of Mark Eby and Margarette Eby courtesy Mark Eby. Photo of Jeff Gorton courtesy Dan Snyder.

All rights reserved. No part of this book may be used or reproduced in any manner whatsoever without written permission except in the case of brief quotations embodied in critical articles or reviews. For information address St. Martin's Press, 175 Fifth Avenue, New York, NY 10010.

ISBN: 0-312-99087-1

Printed in the United States of America

St. Martin's Paperbacks edition / September 2004

10  9  8  7  6  5  4  3  2  1

With special thanks to my wife, Kathleen, for putting up with a spouse who makes his living from murder and mayhem and who, though she tires of the too-many gory details long before I'm done recounting them, graciously serves as my sounding board during the months of research and again during the writing and editing.

"I've prosecuted serial killers before, and they didn't scare me. HE scares me. He's the man your mother warned you about as a little girl. He's the bogeyman who jumps out in the night and grabs you."

—Betty Walker, Wayne County, Michigan's, star prosecutor.

# Preface

I had a small, vested interest in the murder of Nancy Ludwig, one of the two murder cases this book details. I thought one of my acquaintances might have killed her. There is a chapter in the book recounting the night some of us, members of a downtown Detroit running club, decided we had to turn in one of our fellow runners as a suspect in the brutal rape and slaying of this Northwest flight attendant.

That was in the winter of 1991. We never knew if the police followed up on the tip and, if so, what the outcome was. Had "Rick" been cleared? Or did he do it but they just couldn't prove it? In any event, he continued to run with us, and we continued to give him a wide berth when we could.

Nancy Ludwig's murder touched a nerve in a city you would think would have been inured to murder. Detroit was considered the nation's Murder Capital then, and residents used to take a perverse pride in being from such a tough place. You'd even see T-shirts proclaiming: "DETROIT—WE EAT OUR YOUNG."

But Ludwig's murder—the savage butchery and rape of an attractive woman who had just arrived at the Airport Hilton from a long day of flying—was huge news. And it stayed huge news as it went unsolved. Over the years, on the anniversary date of her murder, TV and radio stations and the city's two daily newspapers would invariably run look-back stories on her death and update listeners or readers on what was new, if anything.

It seemed, alas, her murder would never be solved.

There was another equally notorious, older case that had dominated the headlines in Flint, seventy-five minutes north of Detroit. Margarette Eby, an attractive music professor who was one of Flint's leading citizens, and who traveled in the highest social circles, was brutally raped and murdered in 1986.

I must have read about the murder, but I don't remember anything about it from the time. Detroit and Flint are just far enough apart that big news in one city isn't necessarily big news in another. Flint has its own TV stations and its own daily newspaper. Eby's death seemed as if it would go unsolved, too.

And then early in 2002 came the dramatic announcement that both cases likely had been solved and an arrest made. The same killer had raped and murdered both women and now was in custody.

The accused killer was not our running buddy. Guilty till proven innocent in our eyes, we now owed him an apology.

I had written my first true crime book for St. Martin's Paperbacks in the summer and fall of 2000. Titled *A Deadly Affair*, it told the tale of Michael Fletcher, a suburban Detroit defense attorney who was convicted of murdering his pregnant wife so he could continue his affair with a prominent and beautiful local judge.

Despite his conviction, and much to my surprise, by the time I was finished with my research, I was pretty sure Fletcher was innocent of the charges for which he was sentenced to life in prison without parole. I wasn't sure of his innocence, but I was sure that there were so many doubts about his guilt that he should never have been convicted.

It was a frustrating way to end a year of my life, not knowing if the subject of the book had committed murder or not. Did he deserve his punishment? Or was he the unluckiest person on earth? There was no middle ground. And, for me, no resolution.

This book, thankfully, has no such ambiguities. The bad guy did it. Good work by a Michigan State Police cold-case squad eventually caught him.

As I awaited word from my faithful agent, Jane Dystel, on whether St. Martin's wanted me to write a book on these old Michigan murders, I began compiling a list of people I'd need to contact. It eventually grew to more than seventy names. Some people refused to be interviewed. Most were willing to talk on the record. Some of them I interviewed many times, and I thank them for their patience, and for bearing with me when I proved to them that it is, indeed, possible to ask a dumb question.

Nothing in this book is made up. The excellent fact-checkers at St. Martin's, and my equally excellent editor, Joe Cleemann, have kept errors to a minimum. Any that do occur are mine, and entirely inadvertent.

None of the conversations are made up of whole cloth. They come from court testimony, police records or from those involved. Obviously I wasn't at either murder scene with a tape recorder. When I quote people at those scenes, or any of the other scenes depicted in the book, I do so based on, at the very least, what they remember having said, and, at best, what others at the scene also remember.

A few names have been changed. The runner whose name we phoned in I have changed, since he turned out to be merely weird and not a killer. I also changed the name of the children and the wife of the man convicted of the murders—out of common decency, first of all, since they, too, were victims, and second of all because it was a condition set in advance of our getting together.

There are many dozens of people to thank. Most of them will have to be satisfied with my personal thanks. Here, though, I must thank and acknowledge debts to the following:

Lieutenant Dan Snyder, the best cop in the history of the Romulus police force. He opened his house to me and graciously suffered through more than a dozen interviews, counting the times I bugged him by phone, too. That, just two weeks after the conclusion of the biggest case in his career, he was given the choice between early retirement or a reduction in rank, speaks volumes.

Detective Lieutenant Mike Larsen, who was gracious and accommodating from the start. His work with the Michigan State Police cold-case squad helped solve this case. His work with me was invaluable. He provided photos and copies of all the reports and evidence that had been compiled over the years, and heartfelt encouragement. I wish I could have taken him up on his offer to join him for his weekly pick-up hockey games.

Betty Walker, the dynamic star prosecutor for the Wayne County Prosecutor's Office. She's one of the good guys, laboring for a fraction of what she could make in private practice, sharing a tiny office with two others, so she can put the bad guys where they belong. She's got her own chapter, and deservedly so. She made room in her busy schedule for several long interviews and, more important, saved me the hassles and expense of going through bureaucratic hoops. Instead of making me fill out a Freedom of Information Act request to get copies of exhibits and evidence, which would have likely ended up costing me a small fortune, she just gave me the huge footlocker she'd crammed full of stuff, told me to take a week to copy it all and to get it back when I was done. "Lose it, and you're dead," she said. I'm alive.

Dan Loga, a hero to his family, a huge help to me in convincing his sister-in-law to meet with me on the record, to discuss what it was like finding out the man she loved had been a serial murderer, torturing, raping and killing women both before and after their marriage. Dan became a surrogate father for his niece and nephew, was instrumental in helping the police conduct their post-arrest investigation, and stuck by his brother-in-law, too, meeting with him in prison for prayer sessions and to catch him up on what was going on with his family. Those who know Dan will be forever touched by his generosity of spirit.

Wayne County Circuit Judge Maggie Drake, who's got a chapter of her own, too, but whose life story deserves a book. A great judge, a great interview, and a bigger-than-life pioneer for both women and blacks.

Gordie Malaniak, Snyder's partner, a quiet, no bull, suffer-no-fools cop's cop who, like Snyder, was forced into retirement by office politics after closing out the biggest case in his city's history. Reading the volumes of reports he and Snyder put together in the days and weeks after Ludwig's murder told volumes, too, about their tenacity.

Bryn Mickle of *The Flint Journal*, a terrific young reporter, who was very helpful and non-territorial in helping guide me through events he knew more about than I. The librarian at the *Journal*, Dave Larzelere, was a saint, saving me a fortune in money, a huge amount of time and a lot of eyestrain by copying huge amounts of back stories instead of sending me off to the microfiche at the public library.

The State Police Crime Lab folks, who were extremely helpful, both in solving the case and in helping me understand the science behind what they do—Jeff Nye, who made the DNA analysis that led to an arrest, and Lynne Helton, who worked the Ludwig case and whose passion, and ability to express it so wonderfully, I'll never forget.

Colonel Robert Bertee, the second in command at the state police, who helped start the cold-case squad and who offered to pull all the strings I needed. Just mentioning his name and telling people the colonel was on board suddenly made more than a few folks willing and able to meet.

Flint Police Chief Brad Barksdale, who was a godsend for a writer, wonderfully blunt and quotable, and without whose support the cold-case squad would never have gotten off the ground.

Flint Prosecutor Art Busch, Barksdale's nemesis and, surprisingly enough, frequent critic of the state police, who was equally quotable and frank; and his able assistant, Randy Petrides, who was of much value in our single extended interview.

Retired Flint homicide cop Dave King, a truly nice guy and good cop. He knew it would be easy for me to potshot him for mistakes made in the biggest case of his career. But he never once ducked a question, inviting me into his house and into his office in his new job at the state police training center and spending hours aiming me in all the right directions. Too bad the FBI hadn't done nearly so well in aiming him. For their sins, he has taken much of the blame.

The other good cops who helped with the investigation and were, if not happy, at least willing, to sit down with me, often more than once—Mike St. Andre, Greg Brandemihl, Gary Elford, Dan Bohnett, Mark Reaves, Mike Thomas, Ken Kraus, Rudy Gonzalez and Hal Zettle.

Nancy Schultz, the legal assistant for Flint attorney Philip Beauvais, who let me look at the transcripts of the first trial, which saved me a fortune, to which anyone who has had to buy documents from a court reporter can testify.

Finally, special words of thanks to some of the living victims.

Mark Eby and Lynn Rimer, two of Margarette Eby's children, welcomed me into their homes and were gracious and considerate and hugely helpful, even though I was the guy making a buck writing about the long-ago but still dreadfully painful death of their mother in Flint in 1986. Thanks to Mark for taking me through the family photo albums and bringing his mother to life for me.

Art Ludwig is a saint. He welcomed me into his home in suburban Minneapolis and opened up his heart and his memories for me and was patient through a long series of e-mails clarifying one point or another.

Marie Gagliano is the one happy ending in all of this. She welcomed me into her home in Georgia and told me how this long, sorry tale began. I just wish I could have seen her shoot an armadillo.

# BLOOD
# JUSTICE

# PART ONE

## End Game?

# 1
## THE SNATCHER

It had been a very snowy February of 2002 in mid-Michigan. Snow was piled up in walls along the Gortons' driveway in Vienna, north of Flint. It was barely 6 p.m., but it had long since been pitch black when the Gortons—Jeffrey, Brenda and their two kids, Wally, 10, and Jenny, 7—loaded into the station wagon and slowly eased out onto the busy two-lane highway, Tuscola Road, that ran in front of their house. Jeff made sure the coast was clear before he made his right turn. Speeders were notorious here, a constant complaint of area residents.

It was February 7, the first Thursday of the month, which meant it was their kids' elementary school's monthly roller-rink party at Skateland, a couple of miles away on N. Dort Highway in the small city of Mount Morris.

Jeff was too busy to go in the fall and spring, putting in long hours in his parents' lawn-sprinkler installation and maintenance business, but in the winter he was happy to go.

He liked doing things with Brenda and the kids. He'd volunteer at the school's Fun Fair each year, when the school rooms masqueraded as a carnival. He'd help decorate, pitch in with whatever needed to be done, same as he'd volunteer at the school's Haunted House each Halloween, hanging lights and whatnot. He volunteered at functions at their Baptist church, too, which he attended each Sunday, and was active in Boy Scouts.

Jeff loved holidays. The Gortons' neighborhood had modest, low-slung homes on very large lots, some several acres or more, and there was nothing Jeff liked more than spending hours decorating his house and grounds in the theme of the season. Not just the usual, Halloween and Christmas, but others, too, Thanksgiving, Easter, Fourth of July.

Brenda took pride in her husband's interest in holiday decorating. "The house'd be done up like crazy. People drove by in awe," she says.

They drove the three or four miles to the rink. As usual, the place was jammed. And loud. Music playing, kids laughing and screaming. Everyone knew everyone. The kids would skate till they were hungry, grab a slice of pizza and a soda pop in the adjacent grillroom, and skate some more. Some of the parents skated, too, or they'd sit up in the bleachers or chat over some food in the grill or step out for a smoke.

Jeff was a bit of a flirt. Always had been. Brenda didn't mind as Jeff, as usual, circulated, chatting up the other moms. They didn't seem to mind, either. Again, everyone knew everyone.

Well, this Thursday, not quite.

One guy stood out like a swollen thumb. Everyone knew everyone, but no one knew him. He was very stocky, broad-shouldered, big bellied, had his head shaved, wore big hooped silver earrings and grungy blue jeans and a flannel shirt. He looked like he belonged in a biker bar, not at an elementary school function. There was another stranger in the rink, too, but the bald guy was the one they noticed.

"We seen a stranger walking around. You don't know how many times I wanted to say to him, 'Who you here with?' " recalled Brenda months later. "You do all these school functions, you know everyone. We thought there was gonna be a child-snatching. I'll never forget him. I'll never forget what that man looked like."

There was going to be a snatching, all right. But not the kind Brenda feared. It wouldn't be a kid. But if it went the way the stranger hoped, it'd be worse than anything she ever imagined.

He wasn't there looking for kids. His name was Mike St. Andre, and he *would* have fit right in at a biker bar. In fact, he fit right in at biker bars all the time. He was an undercover narcotics cop from the hardscrabble blue-collar downriver Detroit suburb of Romulus, whose chief downtown attraction is a topless joint known as the Landing Strip and whose major employer and taxpayer is the sprawling Metropolitan Detroit Airport, which sits smack dab in the middle of the city's thirty-six square miles.

There are a lot of felons serving time in Michigan prisons who got the shock of their lives when they found out St. Andre wasn't who he appeared to be.

This night, St. Andre wasn't interested in kids and he wasn't interested in drugs. He was there to keep an eye on Jeff Gorton. He wanted to watch him, to see if he ate or drank anything. He wanted to see if he sucked out of a straw, put a cup to his lip, wiped his face with a napkin, used a fork or a knife, went outside to puff on a cigarette and toss the butt to the ground.

St. Andre wanted to keep an eye out for any of that stuff, and snatch it if he could, and get it to the Michigan State Police Crime Lab in Lansing. They needed to see if Gorton's DNA matched semen the state police scientists had kept frozen for more than fifteen years in one Flint case and nearly eleven years in a Romulus case.

Both crimes had involved almost unspeakable savagery—slow torture ending in the near-decapitation of victims who were raped and murdered. Both cases likely involved necrophilia, too. Not counting Jimmy Hoffa, they were the two highest-profile unsolved murder cases in Michigan in the last fifty years. If this was the guy who did it, was responsible, and something with his DNA on it needed snatching, St. Andre wanted to be the one who snatched it.

His adrenaline barely under control, sure he was working the case of a lifetime, St. Andre watched and waited and followed Gorton around as he chatted up the wives, went in the rink to watch his kids and then—here it comes!—returned to the food area, got in line and picked up some pizza. Good old messy pizza. He watched Gorton chow down. He watched the sauce grease accumulate on Gorton's lips and the corner of his mouth. He watched Gorton wipe his mouth, eat some more, then wipe it again. Gorton went through one napkin. A second. He did St. Andre a favor by twisting his used napkins into strings so there'd be no mistaking which were his. St. Andre watched Gorton drink his pop. He watched and watched. And then he snatched.

## 2
## "WE GOT HIM"

Like many kids growing up in the suburbs of a city that calls itself "Hockeytown, USA," Mike St. Andre wanted to be a professional hockey player. He was pretty good, and worked hard at it, too.

He had a job as a paperboy, in the early 1970s, when papers were still delivered by kids with bikes instead of adults with cars, the way they are now. When he was 12, he started delivering the afternoon *Detroit News* to his neighbors in Trenton, a middle-class community across a channel of the Detroit River from affluent Grosse Ile and its mansions. Factory workers lived in Trenton, factory owners on the island.

St. Andre's district manager was a guy named Dan Snyder. Most managers had reputations as tyrants, gruff guys who scared their kids into showing up on time, day after day, and scared them into being accurate with their accounts and collecting on time.

But Snyder "was the greatest guy in the world," recalls St. Andre. Snyder was his boss for a year, then left the newspaper business.

"That was the last I saw him. Until he showed up at my door," says the burly St. Andre. Snyder came to his house in 1984. About the time that he was in the 10th grade, St. Andre gave up on his dreams of playing hockey and decided to become a cop. After graduation from Trenton High in 1979, he paid his own way through the Metro Detroit Police Academy, then got a job patrolling the area Huron-Clinton Metro Parks that ring Detroit, pretty much the bottom rung of law enforcement.

In 1984, he applied for a job in Romulus, and, to his surprise, Snyder, his old boss, now a cop in Romulus, too, was the one who showed up at his house to interview him. Snyder remembered him as a hard-working, reliable kid on his paper route—and hired him.

In 1989, St. Andre was assigned to a DEA task force at Metropolitan Airport, working undercover to ferret out drugs, smugglers and people illegally carrying large sums of money. With its proximity to Canada, Metro was a major transit point for couriers.

Mostly St. Andre worked tips from airline personnel, evolving out of overheard conversations or educated hunches. Usually, St. Andre had no probable cause when he approached a suspect coming off a plane. The tips would never have stood up in court. But there's no law against asking people if they will submit to a search, and no law against them being stupid enough to agree. All they had to say was "Nope," and they'd have been able to keep on going.

St. Andre was amazed by how many said "Okay" instead, and within minutes he'd find pounds of cocaine, or bags of pot, or bundles of cash in suitcases, in some instances more than $1 million.

When the 1991 case of a murdered flight attendant made headlines for weeks in the Detroit papers—and, in the if-it-bleeds-it-leads department, dominated local TV news night after night—St. Andre had been one of the guys who worked the airport hard. Armed with composite sketches made by eyewitnesses, he spent many hours scanning faces, looking for a traveler returning to the scene of the crime, or, more likely, some airline employee who had used a uniform to avoid raising the suspicions of his victim.

His surveillance at the airport was futile.

Nearly a decade later, in 2000, he was assigned to Romulus' special investigations unit, which mostly did undercover narcotics work. But now, at the behest of the Michigan State Police, he was taking a break from drugs and up in the Flint area trying to catch the same perp he'd been looking for in 1991.

Snyder, newly promoted to the head of the detective bureau, had been told early that morning by the MSP that a suspect had finally emerged, and Romulus' help was needed for round-the-clock surveillance.

Within twenty minutes, Snyder and his partner, Gordie Malaniak, were on their way to the state police post on Corunna Road, just west of the city of Flint. Four other Romulus cops—St. Andre, Greg Brandemihl, Jeff Hlinak and Mike Ondejko—would later join them. After getting briefed, accompanied by State Police Sergeant Mark Reaves, Malaniak, St. Andre, Brandemihl and Hlinak went out to relieve state troopers who'd been watching the Gorton house all day.

Instead of the tedium that a crew of state police had suffered through all day—cold, nothing happening, time dragging by—less than half an hour into their shift, out came the Gorton family, piling into a blue 1993 Pontiac station wagon and heading out.

Driving separate cars scattered around the area, one by one the police pulled in behind Gorton. Soon, they were at the rink. St. Andre and Brandemihl saw kids and parents lined up at the door and worried they wouldn't fit in, but there was nothing to do for it.

St. Andre went in first, paying $5 admission.

"Where are your kids?" asked the attendant, expecting to be collecting more money.

"They're already in."

Brandemihl waited a few minutes, then followed him inside.

Brandemihl, the son of a cop, spent four years in Army Intelligence in Germany before joining the Romulus police in 1987. He was an evidence tech for the department at the time of the 1991 murder, but ironically was not called to the scene. Snyder, the detective in charge of the crime scene, knew the case was going to be a big one and, no disrespect to his own people but wanting the best help he could get, had chosen to call in a state police evidence team instead.

Brandemihl was a member of SIU. Inside the rink, he and St. Andre pretended they were old friends who, coincidentally, had run into each other.

"Hey, how you doing?" said Brandemihl.

St. Andre spotted Gorton. His kids and his wife were putting on skates. They went into the rink. Gorton followed, taking a spot in the bleachers. St. Andre, on an adrenaline rush and acting the cowboy, sat behind Gorton, close enough to touch him. He got out the Nextel and called Snyder, who was back at the Flint post.

"You won't believe what's going on. I'm sitting behind your best friend. I could tap him on the shoulder." If it seemed a foolish thing to do, well, St. Andre will admit to being brazen. The rink was very loud, music and the screams and hollering of what seemed like hundreds of kids covering up his conversation.

Later St. Andre would say, "Brandemihl was looking at me like, 'I don't believe you.' Hey, Gorton didn't know who I was. I was just fitting in. Talking on a cell phone."

Gorton got up and left the rink. St. Andre moseyed out after him, into the adjoining entryway, where Gorton circulated from woman to woman. St. Andre was surprised by how easily Gorton seemed to fit in. The women knew him. They seemed to like him, and he had an ease with them that seemed odd for a suspected serial killer whose brutality had been so vivid in the crime-scene photos. Who had playfully tortured his victims for quite some time before trying to decapitate them with a serrated knife. Who had posed his victims after death. Who had taken the time to clean up and, in one case, had been so cool as to make several trips to his car, hauling off the woman's belongings.

But although Gorton seemed at ease with the women, he was nervous, too. Fidgety. Looking over his shoulder. Did he suspect something?

"In our mind, he doesn't know anything. He'd gotten away with what he'd done all these years. But it was odd he'd act so nervous," said Brandemihl. "He didn't know we were there. Then we realized, he'd done so much over the years, he was always nervous."

Gorton circulated for twenty minutes. Finally his kids came back out. They wanted to eat, and the Gortons went into the snack bar.

The room was filled with long tables. St. Andre and Brandemihl sat two tables away from the Gortons. Jeff's wife and kids stayed at the table, and he got in line to get food. St. Andre got in line behind him.

Gorton picked up some Styrofoam cups, and ordered pizza and a pitcher of Mountain Dew. St. Andre ordered two pops and took his seat. A spot opened up at the table next to the Gortons and the two cops slid over.

Gorton wiped his greasy mouth with a napkin then twisted it into a string. First one, then a second.

"You know what? We got you," said St. Andre to himself.

The Gortons put their refuse on their trays and pushed them aside, in front of an empty seat. Someone came up, asked if the Gortons were done, then pushed the trays farther down the table to make room.

"Watch this," said St. Andre to his partner. It was 7:25 p.m.

His next move was brazen. St. Andre would counter that what seems brazen really wasn't, that the bolder you are, the more invisible you can be. Or so he thought. He walked over, tapped Gorton on the shoulder: "Are you done with your tray? If you're done, I'll take it."

Gorton nodded and St. Andre picked it up and walked to the far end of the room, where Brandemihl had gone. Making sure the Gortons weren't looking, Brandemihl quickly opened up a manilla evidence bag and St. Andre dumped in the tray's contents.

But they still didn't have Gorton's cup, and they were determined to get it. Piece of chewing gum would be nice, too. Or a cigarette butt.

A few minutes later, the two kids went back into the rink to resume skating. Gorton remained seated. There were Styrofoam cups all over the table, and one right in front of him. St. Andre eyeballed it.

Gorton reached out, poured Mountain Dew into it from a pitcher, took four or five swallows, set it down and got up. St. Andre walked over, picked up the half-filled cup and set it inside a larger size cup so he wouldn't have to touch it any more than necessary.

He noticed people looking at him. "It was like, 'Hey, if you want a pop that bad, we'll buy you one.' "

Little did he know that Gorton had looked back and seen him grab the cup, too. He told his wife, "That guy just took my pop."

"Yeah, right, Jeff," said his wife skeptically. She was willing to believe the scruffy guy with the earrings was a child-snatcher, but who steals someone's half-empty cup of pop?

St. Andre passed the cup to Brandemihl. He went outside and gave the evidence bag and the cup to Malaniak, then returned to the rink, hopefully to get more DNA evidence. Malaniak went over to Reaves' car and gave the bag and cup to him. Reaves poured the pop out on the ground, put the cup-inside-a-cup in another evidence bag, started his car and headed for the Flint post. The plan was: He'd give the stuff to fellow state trooper, Hal Zettle, who would drive it west on I-69 to the small town of Perry.

Jeff Nye, a chemist and DNA specialist at the crime lab in Lansing, lived in Perry. He'd been alerted that a team was going to try to get something with Gorton's DNA. When and if they did, they'd call Nye, no matter what the time, and he'd meet someone in the parking lot of a Burger King at exit 105 to Perry then take the evidence to the lab to be analyzed.

St. Andre and Brandemihl got on the Nextels to Snyder. "We got him! We got him!"

And then they talked to each other about the same thought they'd independently had.

"It was kind of sad," said St. Andre months later. "We were looking at his kids. Beautiful kids. Two beautiful little children. And we're thinking, 'You know what? If this goes right, this is going to be the last night you're ever going to spend with your father.' We talked about it, being parents, thinking the things these kids are going to have to go through. They're going to pay for it. His wife's going to pay for it."

If it went right.

### 3
### BAD NEWS BY PHONE

Hal Zettle grew up in northern Michigan, in West Branch, a pretty town surrounded by forest and lakes. He had been with the state police since getting out of high school. At 18, as part of a federal grant, he was hired as a service trooper, helping out with sobriety-check lanes and school bus inspections.

In 1976, when he was 21, he joined the academy and became a full-fledged trooper. In June of 2000, he was assigned to a new cold-case, violent-crimes task force in Flint and was one of four troopers assigned to a series of ten prostitute murders. As it turned out, there were at least two serial murderers killing the prostitutes. Zettle helped take 450 DNA swabs on the case, with one of them finally leading to the arrest and conviction of Keith Cummings for murdering two women and leaving them in abandoned houses.

Two weeks after Cummings' arrest, Zettle was assigned to the unsolved 1986 murder of a Flint woman. To everyone's surprise, a DNA test using new technology had linked it to a 1991 case in Romulus. Zettle spent hundreds of hours going through old files, re-interviewing witnesses, taking

DNA swabs, tracking down people who hadn't been interviewed but should have been way back when.

On February 6, 2001, a long-overdue FBI report that the cold-case squad had requested came back with startling news. A partial print found at the Flint homicide scene—a very partial print, one long thought to be impossible to work with—had come back with a positive identification. Not only that, but the guy it identified still lived in the Flint area.

A print at a scene is hardly evidence of murder—most crime scenes contain hundreds of prints of innocent people—but this had been a bloody print. Those, you don't find too many of.

Zettle was part of the surveillance team quickly assembled the afternoon of February 6. The next morning, an MSP team out of Lansing took over surveillance duties for the day shift. Zettle and other members of the cold-case squad—Greg Kilbourn, Mike Larsen and Dennis Diggs—scrambled to amass as much data on the suspect, Jeffrey Gorton, as they could. Employment history. Known addresses. Checking out his time spent in Florida. Running down his military record.

The time flew by. Zettle started early in the morning "and the next thing I knew, I got a call at the post that they had a Styrofoam cup he'd been drinking from and a couple of napkins."

About 8:10 p.m., Reaves arrived at the post, handed the evidence to Zettle and off he went. "I had a little Corsica, a state-issued rattletrap, and I pushed that thing all the way there."

A forty-mile drive to Perry took less than half an hour. As planned, he met with Nye at the Burger King. No Whoppers for Zettle, though. "Food didn't sound interesting. The adrenaline was pumping. When things broke, it was like, 'Hang on, we're going for a ride.' "

He'd worked thirty-six out of the last forty-four hours and was still going strong.

Nye was a former entrepreneur turned happy civilian state employee. He has two master's degrees—in soil science and toxicology—and had worked for seven years at the Michigan Biotechnology Institute in Lansing, an incubator trying to spin Michigan State University research into for-profit companies.

The job involved a lot of spinning, very little profit. Most of the companies there struggle to find real products to sell to real markets, and suffer through a kind of hand-to-mouth existence, surviving, if they did, on a series of small research grants from various federal agencies.

Tired of the insecurity, never knowing if the next grant would be awarded in time to meet payroll, Nye had left the world of entrepreneurship for the nice pay and benefits that accrue to civilian employees at the State Police Crime Lab, which moved into a new state-of-the-art facility in 1999.

Nye was in the biology unit at the lab, analyzing semen, blood, and footwear impressions. He worked crime-scene investigations, too.

Nye had already played a crucial role in the reopened investigation into the Flint homicide of 1986. Semen and blood samples had been collected at the time. But technology had taken quantum leaps since then—something called PCR, for polymerase chain reaction, had drastically reduced the amount of DNA needed to identify a suspect, and a computerized system called CODIS allowed DNA samples to be matched both to known individuals and to unsolved cases where the DNA had been typed but not linked to a known perpetrator.

Nye, as part of his ongoing work updating stored evidence, had run the samples from the Flint case through a PCR and entered the results into the CODIS system.

CODIS couldn't link the DNA to a known individual, but did link it to another unsolved case, that of the rape and murder of the flight attendant in Romulus in 1991.

Linking those two high-profile cases had put the MSP cold-case investigation on a front burner, and quieted criticism from Flint police, politicians and prosecutors that the state was meddling in the city's business.

So when Nye had been called about 2 in the afternoon to ask if he could conduct a rush test on Gorton's DNA—*if* evidence could be gathered—he said he'd be happy to, any time of the day or night. Just give him a call. "I'll shortcut all chain-of-command issues," he said.

At 8:10 p.m., Nye got his call. About 9 p.m., he was meeting Zettle in the Burger King lot. By 9:15 he was at the lab.

He opened up the large manilla envelope. A Styrofoam cup was wedged inside a larger Pepsi cup. He could see Mountain Dew residue on the sides. There were two soiled napkins, twisted, pizza sauce evident.

It wasn't a good start. Napkins are porous. So is Styrofoam. Liquids don't leak through it, but they do absorb into it. It acts as a sponge. It's tough to work with. He would have preferred something glass or ceramic, a metal or plastic fork perhaps.

Nye took cuttings from the napkins and wiped the rim of the cup with a sterile swab. He put the cuttings and cotton swab tip into tubes, then added a liquid solution, something called a protenase K enzyme, which breaks open cells, chews up everything but DNA. He then washed off the cellular debris and what was left was some yet-to-be-determined amount of DNA in a clear liquid.

He got nothing off the napkins, despite the presence of sauce that had been on Gorton's face and lips. He got just the tiniest of bits from the cup. He eyeballed the dew-drop speck of liquid, guessed it would be about 15–20 microliters. DNA would only be a small fraction of that.

In the old days of something called RFLP testing of DNA samples, which produced bands of varying widths to be compared with other samples to see if the bands lined up, you needed at least 300 nanograms of DNA. Now, you normally needed at least one nanogram, preferably more, a nanogram being just a billionth of a gram—or, one billionth of one twenty-eighth of an ounce—an incomprehensibly small amount. Nye figured he had 0.5 nanograms at best.

Nye was crestfallen. He didn't have enough. He'd go through the motions and run the sample through his equipment to see if he could still get a match to the semen samples on hand, but it was doubtful. Highly doubtful.

About midnight, he called Greg Kilbourn.

"Greg, we don't have enough DNA. I'm going to run the tests, anyway, but it doesn't look like we have enough. Sorry."

Kilbourn called Snyder, who was back home for the night. No go, he said.

Snyder called Malaniak and Brandemihl and St. Andre at their homes.

The bad news weighing heavily on them, they went to bed.

# PART TWO

## Bogeyman, 1983–86

# 4

# A SCREAM IN THE NIGHT

Florida has long been a place for second chances. People sick of winter, sick of their lives, sick of their spouses, sick of their jobs—sick of whatever—have been heading there for decades for a new life. Swamps have been drained and turned into gated communities for the rich, or trailer parks for the poor or retired, into golf courses, condos, apartments, strip malls, shopping centers, amusement parks and freeways to satisfy the needs of the millions of lives that headed there to start anew.

Marie Gagliano was one of them. A native of Asbury Park, N.J., the place made famous by Bruce Springsteen, she was married at 21, divorced at 29, stuck in a rut as a paralegal at 32 and more than ready and eager for something different in 1982 when her best friend, Donna Smith, phoned, and convinced her to move to Orlando and join her in *her* new life.

Marie was a tiny thing, girlish-looking but pretty, short, fashion-model thin, dark brown hair. She was lively, spirited, an animated talker by nature who regained her animation with the move. Florida energized her, got her back to being herself after the marriage had gone sour and the inevitable post-divorce funk. She was fun to be around, and she and Donna fit right in with the mostly single crowd at their Grove Park Apartments on Curry Road.

With her new life came a new car, a 1982 Volkswagen Rabbit, a present to herself for starting her new life. It was the first major purchase she made after divorcing her husband. "My pride and joy," she called it.

Marie had tired of what she termed the "dirtbags" she dealt with in New Jersey in her role as a paralegal for a public defender. A new life meant just that, and though she'd gone to school to be a paralegal and was good at it, it had been time to end that chapter in her life, too.

In Orlando, she'd found a job as a sales clerk in cosmetics at Burdines in the Fashion Square Mall, one of the seemingly endless series of malls that was built up in the 1970s and '80s on the highways spoking out from the central city as Disney World and Epcot and the other theme parks opened and lured tens of thousands of workers and millions of visitors. She liked meeting new people all day. She liked selling them things.

It was April 29, a Friday night, a big night, as usual, for many of her new friends in the apartment complex. For her, though, it was supposed to be just a routine night. Stop on the way home for a few groceries, kick back from a week on her feet, get a bite to eat, go to bed. Donna'd likely be out, on a date or partying. Maybe down the hall from their second-floor apartment with some of the other Friday night partiers, maybe off somewhere else in town.

Burdines closed at 9 p.m. and Marie headed out to her Rabbit about 9:30. It was a warm, clear night. She stopped at the Albertson's around the block from her apartment complex for bread and milk and a few other staples, set her single brown bag in the back of the car and headed home. A car followed her out of the lot. Whether it had been following her from Burdines or just started at the grocery store, she'd never know.

Her apartment building had two entrances. She pulled into the first one. The other car drove past, then entered the driveway on the far side of the building and pulled into the large parking lot out back, still unnoticed. It was 10 p.m. The lot was pretty well lit with mercury vapor lights. It wasn't one of those lots you felt you had to scurry out of.

Marie got out, and as she walked behind her car, she noticed off to the right a man heading her way. She immediately thought: Guy walking his dog. She turned to face the rear of the car, put in the key, opened the hatchback and lifted the brownbag, and as she did, her subconscious mind flashed a warning. She wouldn't necessarily have seen a dog, given the cars in the lot, but something about the way the man was walking meant *no dog*.

A jolt of fear hit her and as she straightened up, the bag still in her arms, she turned to her left. By then, given his rate of speed, he would have been past her. Ten yards? Twenty yards? Somewhere to her left and receding. But the man wasn't walking, and he wasn't past her. He was standing *right there*, his face filling her vision, a foot from hers.

In a slasher movie, it would have been one of those moments where the audience jumped. A tight shot of a woman and a car. Woman turns. Man's head enters shot from left. Audience gasps en masse.

Marie screamed as the man reached down, lifted her skirt, grabbed her lower legs and flipped her over backwards. She landed on her left wrist and butt, groceries flying through the air and scattering across the pavement. He grabbed her ankles and lifted, and she went flat on her back.

She screamed one long scream. And he held her tightly by each ankle and dragged her toward the nearby Dumpster.

## 5
## A PROVOST COMES TO TOWN, 1981

After a nationwide search and a review of several finalists, officials at the Flint campus of the University of Michigan announced in the spring of 1981 that they had chosen Margarette Eby to fill the post of provost and vice chancellor for academic affairs, the second-highest administrative position at the university.

A picture of Eby greeted readers of *The Flint Journal*, at the right side of a story that spread across the entire top of page 6. It showed a woman with sparkling eyes, dark bangs swooping down over her forehead, a huge smile and dimples. The headline would be just her first of many.

Eby had been serving as dean of the College of Humanities and Fine Arts at the University of Northern Iowa in Cedar Falls. But she wasn't just an academician—she was also a talented musician who had given harpsichord, organ and piano recitals throughout the Midwest, and she was also named a full professor of music with tenure at the Flint campus.

It would be a triumphant return to her home state for Eby, a Detroit native who got her Ph.D. in musicology from the University of Michigan's main campus in Ann Arbor after many years of part-time studies while raising her four children.

After getting her doctorate in 1971, Eby headed the humanities department at the University of Michigan's Dearborn campus in suburban Detroit, where she founded the school's music-history and applied-music departments.

In 1977, she joined the faculty at Northern Iowa as a music professor and dean of humanities and fine arts.

Even before her arrival in Flint, eager to show she would be an active booster of the arts and culture, she became a sponsor of the Flint Institute of Arts.

Upon her arrival, Eby proved herself to be energetic, even vivacious, a supercharged dynamo who said she "play[ed] music for [her] soul," swam at the school pool on her lunch hour instead of eating and walked to work every day. She was a widow nearing 50 but didn't act or look it. She was trim and attractive and seemed younger. A product of her times—the '60s, the Pill, the sexual revolution—and now single, she was happy and willing to catch the eye of men she came into contact with.

On August 2, the *Journal* ran its next story about her, a lengthy feature that quoted past colleagues as praising her for her talent, friendliness and conscientiousness. "It feels like I have come home," she said of Flint.

As provost, she had been given the mission of bringing more discipline and accountability to a growing faculty in twenty-three departments, a faculty that was perceived by some as generally lax and soft. But she told the paper, "I don't intend to just storm in making changes right and left. Nor do I intend to sit alone in judgment of the quality of education. That would take colossal ignorance. It is inconceivable for one person to have all the necessary knowledge in all the different program areas to make that kind of judgment."

Eby soon began enlisting support in a project that at first seemed like tilting at windmills in the factory-dominated city of Flint. In Iowa, she had begun planning a three hundredth birthday bash/festival for J. S. Bach, who had been born on March 21, 1685. Now, she'd still put on a festival, but she'd do it in Michigan, instead. Slowly, she got others in her growing social and civic circle to commit time and money.

Eby recruited a cadre of twenty-five Flint boosters to help organize the festival, which was to begin in January of 1985, reach its zenith on March 21 and then taper off with a variety of events through June 1.

"Margarette Eby's 'crazy dream'—a festival to put Flint

in the front aisle seat for Johann Sebastian Bach's 300th birthday party—moved into the real world this week as the group planning the event received word of a $20,800 grant," read a story in the *Flint Journal* on August 25, 1983.

The grant had come from the National Endowment for the Humanities in Washington, D.C., for the full amount requested by Eby in her role as president of the Flint Community Cultural Festivals, Inc.

The festival ended up a roaring success, four months of jam-packed culture in a town more known for its six-pack approach to recreation. The forty-event festival did the unheard of—it raised $48,000 more in revenue than projections called for. In April, Goetz von Boehmer, the American consul general from West Germany, awarded Eby with the German-American Friendship Medal. The day the festival concluded on Saturday, June 1, with an evening of music and fireworks on the Flint River, the *Journal* named Eby its Winner of the Week.

But not everyone was enamored with Eby. She had been brought in to whip the faculty into shape, and those getting whipped didn't much appreciate it. Eby could drive others to distraction, whether it was faculty at the Flint campus or workers on the festival committee.

"She likes perfection," Margaret Struble, who was hired to work for the festival in January of 1984, told a *Journal* reporter. "She doesn't hesitate to ask you to do something over if it's not right. I've had to do that, and I think it would drive other people bananas. But when I've done a job over again, I could see that she's right.

"She's the most stimulating female I've ever worked with. She has lots of ideas, and she knows what to do with her ideas. She can do things at the spur of the moment. She doesn't have to hide behind an organizational chart."

But universities are all about organizational charts, hierarchies, and pecking orders. They are also internecine battle grounds, with raging egos and dirty fighters. As her festival approached, as it was held, as she triumphed in the media, some of her colleagues sharpened their knives—a metaphor that police would soon think might have crossed the boundary into the world of literal action.

Eby was again in the *Journal* on March 17 of 1986, in a story that detailed a successful "Viennese Evening with Schubert," organized by Eby at the University of Michigan–Flint theatre.

The next story in the *Journal* on Eby, accompanied by pictures of her in her Bach Festival T-shirt and the house she rented on an estate not far from campus—and big, bold headlines—ran on November 10, 1986.

By then, the woman who could do no wrong in her career had run afoul of her enemies. Carping and complaints had led to her losing her post as provost. She could be silly, charming and engaging with her friends, but hyper-demanding, caustic and verbally abusive with those she worked with. Smart enough to negotiate tenure before she left Iowa, she still held the single title of music professor.

But despite the loss of her provost position, life was still good. She was doing good work, she had a lot of friends, she was a lay minister at the First Presbyterian Church downtown, she was close to her children, and she had a dream place to live, a two-story gatehouse on the biggest estate in town that was a steal at $375 a month, including utilities, and which was just a walk from campus.

Eby constantly entertained on the grounds of the estate, hosting parties that included gifted students, corporate bigwigs, academics, intellectuals and artists. She held annual yule-log parties and arranged croquet matches and lawn bowling tournaments and any manner of cocktail parties and barbecues.

# 6
# PHOTO ALBUM

It was the fall of 1986 and Mark Eby, a civilian employee of the U.S. Army Tank Command, had been on assignment in Germany for a year. His wife, Cindy, was there with him. One project he'd decided on before he left home—to sort of keep him in touch with his tight-knit family—was to organize and catalog the thirty-six years of family photos that traced out the history of the Ebys, from the time of his mother's marriage to his dad in 1950.

He put the last photo in the first book. It told the first nine years of the family's tale. It also chronicled the parallel tales of the burgeoning Baby Boomer Era and of the growth of the American suburb.

There was another tale, too, hidden behind the shots of young babies, growing children, new houses, new cars—it was the story of a typical young American housewife doing the not-so-typical: going to college part-time, first for her bachelor's, then her master's, then her Ph.D., a woman who wouldn't harness her ambition or her mind just because she'd married at age 18 and started a family.

Margarette Fink was the second of five children whose mother was a strict, God-fearing German immigrant. Her younger sister, Ruth, would later spend most of her adult life as a missionary in Brazil. Margarette quit Wheaton College in Illinois to get married to Stewart Eby and delayed her bachelor's till she was 23. She was a woman determined to go places, figuratively and literally. A woman who would make her mark. A woman, who, like many others of her generation or the one to follow, would ultimately explore a sexuality beyond the limits of her conservative upbringing.

*Open the front cover of the album and two six-by-twelve black-and-white, torso-and-head-shot portraits greet you. On the left is Stewart Eby, a handsome boy in glasses, and Margarette Fink, a pretty girl with dark hair combed forward and clipped in very short bangs. They'd met in a Christian musical group. He sang, she was an accompanist. She has large eyes and is very pretty. Both strive mightily to look older than they are. She is perhaps 18, but carries off an air of sophistication. She leans toward her left. She wears a sleeveless, somewhat low-cut dress, its single strap going around the back of her neck, a hint of a knowing grin on her face, large costume-jewelry earrings clipped to her earlobes. Had you been able to see behind the grin, you would have seen the flaw that either added to her cuteness, or detracted from her beauty—depending on how you view such things— a noticeable gap between her two front teeth, which she always attributed to blowing woodwind instruments as a young girl.*

*Turn the page: A wedding. August 1950, Margarette walking down the aisle with her dad.*

*Turn again: Dayle, July 1951, a newborn. The first born.*

*Then: Mark, September, 1952, the second born.*

The Ebys lived in Detroit then, on Faust Street. He'd taken a job in the business office at John E. Green Plumbing and Heating in Highland Park. And worked his way to the top, too, treasurer of the company when he died of a heart attack at age 46, but that's getting ahead of the tale the album tells. Margarette was gregarious, outgoing, witty, charming. Stewart was shy, quiet, reserved. They were the opposites that attracted, personalities meshing just so.

*Possibly 1954, at a lake for summer vacation, Dad on a teeter-totter.*

*Florida, 1955, at the Tropical Hobbyland falls in Miami. Mom, Dad, cheesy backdrops, no kids. The Disney World Florida had yet to be born.*

*A big glossy black-and-white. A swank dinner at the Conrad Hilton in Chicago. Another shot, same dinner, wider angle, a married couple who made the weekend trip with them.*

Margarette and Stewart clearly love to travel.

*Undated shot in 1955 of Mom after getting her bachelor's from Wayne State.*

*A shot of Dad, looking dorky in argyle socks.* At least Mark thinks so. He tapes on a hand-written caption: "Nice socks!"

*Mother's Day, 1956. A suburban shot, this, a new house at 23820 Glencreek Drive in Farmington Hills. A tiny maple sapling has been planted in the front yard, recently dug up at a state park up north when no one was looking.*

The summer before, the family had moved to Farmington, Mich., a place that, as its name suggests, had once served as a marketplace and town for the surrounding farmers. The house is in Old Farm Colony, in what has been marketed as a subdivision, brick ranch houses with little saplings planted in what have recently been cornfields.

Mark and his friends in the neighborhood—lots and lots of friends in those Baby Boom days, dozens of kids within a short bike ride who were his age or a year older or a year younger—would go crawdad-catching in the nearby streams. Or play baseball, no adults in sight, no umpires, no organization needed, no uniforms, just kids in blue jeans with cuffs rolled up, and T-shirts, bikes lying on their sides nearby, picking up teams from scratch each day.

Or going off into nearby fields that wouldn't be subdivisions for another year or two and shooting arrows at pheasants but never, not once, not ever in hundreds of shots actually hitting one.

*Dayle's first day of school, 1956, waiting for the bus.*

*Jonathan, newly arrived home, January 1957, the third born.*

*Dayle's birthday party, 1957.* Like all birthday parties in those days, the scene is filled with kids, all looking to be the same age. They are crammed around a picnic table, wearing birthday hats that look like little dunce caps, affixed under the neck with rubber bands.

"If you didn't live through that Baby Boom, you can't explain it. How many kids there were. Everywhere," says Mark.

*A shot of a passel of neighborhood kids crammed on to a porch.*

*Niagara Falls, 1957. Mom smiling at the camera, the falls raging behind her.*

*Christmas portrait, 1957, Stewart sitting on a stuffed chair in a dark suit, white shirt and tie, dark-rimmed glasses, a bit of a proud smirk on his face. Infant Jonathan on his right thigh. Mark at the left edge of the photo, wearing a light*

*checked sport coat, looking off to the right. Dayle, in dress
and patent leather shoes standing at her dad's right shoulder. Margarette leaning on the chair at the back, staring at
the camera, her slightly bulging pregnant belly hidden from
view.*

*Lynn, last born in May of 1958, has just arrived home.
Blond bedroom furniture behind her.*

*Summer 1959, Grandma and Grandpa's house in St. Clair
Shores, another farmland turned suburb, financed by the
Veterans Housing Administration. The fins of a 1957 Ply-
mouth are visible out in the street, by the driveway.*

Margarette always loved fast cars. The Plymouth was an
art deco beauty, two-tone, with big fins, a big V-8 engine and
a push-button transmission. In 1965, she'd get one of the
hottest, coolest cars on the market, a yellow convertible
Chevy Malibu SS with bucket seats up front, a 327-cubic-
inch engine and a power roof.

Three years later she'd get a still-hotter car, a Chevy Ca-
maro SS with a 350.

Then came a 1971 Mustang Mach 1, "mach" of course
referring to the speed needed to break the sound barrier, a bit
of hyperbole to be sure, but the car could fly.

"I inherited her dislike for wasting time," said Mark many
years later. As a young man, he bought his mom's Malibu.

*A last family shot: Christmas, 1959.*

That was the first, thick album Mark compiled. There were
two decades' worth of photos to go into other albums. The
first book showed the family's first two homes, but not the
last. In 1964, the Ebys moved to Bloomfield Hills, one of
the most affluent of Detroit's suburbs, and soon to be a rival
with the blue-blood Grosse Pointe to the east as *the* place to
live.

This scene wasn't captured in a photo, but it makes for
one of the family memories the kids share. Their mom loved
the smell of clothes after they dried out on the line in the sun
and the wind.

She soon found out sensibilities were different in Bloomfield Hills, a place of much pretension. It was illegal in Bloomfield to hang clothes up on a line in your back yard, and when her neighbors saw her stuff fluttering the breeze, they went nuts. The authorities were summoned in.

There is another scene that Lynn, Dayle and Jonathan remember, too, captured in their minds but not on film.

They are in Germany. It is 1970, and Margarette is there doing research for her thesis, *The Vocal Concertos of Johann Dilliger (1593–1647)*. It is a return trip for her; in 1968 she'd won a Rackham Grant for music research in Europe. Mark can't join them because he's on his senior class trip to South America. (There were pluses as well as minuses to life in Bloomfield Hills.)

Margarette is notoriously thrifty. They are touring some castle. There is an orange-juice machine next to a vendor selling peanuts. Margarette puts in a coin, the equivalent of a dime. What she doesn't know is that she is supposed to take a cup from the stack of empty plastic cups next to the machine and hold it under the spout.

So orange juice starts pouring down, instead of the container of juice Margarette expected. She thrust her hands under the juice to catch some of it and drink it from her hands. No sense wasting the whole dime.

The kids roared with laughter and still laugh when they talk about it.

Some of the photos that didn't fit in the first album include:

*Summer of 1960, a beach in Oscoda, an up-north Michigan vacation destination on Lake Huron. Margarette, ever trim, lies on the sand in a two-piece bikini, a sailboat cruising by in the background.*

That was the summer Mark shot himself with a b-b gun just before the trip. The b-b lodged itself under the skin in his arm and had to be dug out by a doctor. Mark was worried about who was going to take the stitches out when the family was up north. "Don't worry. I'll do it," said his mom. Sure enough, when she decided they were ready to come out, she

got out a small pair of scissors, snipped the threads and carefully pulled them out.

The other kids at Spain's started calling her Dr. Eby. "How
do they know I'm working on my doctorate?" she asked.

"No, mom, it's because you took my stitches out," said
Mark. It became one of those endearing family stories all
families have, or should have: The time Mark shot himself
with a b-b gun and mom took the stitches out; the first time
she was called "Doctor."

*One labeled Christmas, 1977. Tony, a black man from Mar-
garette's church, is hugging her from behind as they both
face the camera. From their body language, even without
reading the caption, it is clear they share more than a
church. The caption says: "With Love Unspeakable." By
then, Stewart has been dead of a heart attack for two years,
leaving her a widow at age 44. But Margarette still wears
her love for him, literally. On the index finger of her right
hand is his wedding band. On her wrist, the large watch she
had given him for a gift just months before his death.*

"Mom was diverse. A very interesting person," says Mark
many years later, entirely nonjudgmental about the black
man in the photo.

*Thanksgiving, 1978. A rare shot of all the kids together, re-
united around the dinner table in Cedar Falls, Iowa, where
their mother is dean of humanities and fine arts at the University of Northern Iowa.*

"That had to be the last time we were all together," says
Mark.

Before he could start a second photo album, he got a call.
He was on vacation and had just arrived after a long drive by
car at a lodge owned by a friend and former Green Beret in
Viet Nam, right on the Austria border. He was there to hunt.
The call ended his vacation.

Seventeen years later, Mark has yet to start book No. 2.
Decades worth of photos sit in bags, the rest of their lives
waiting to be sorted out and laid out horizontally and verti-
cally.

"Someday I may get motivated to finish it," he says.

# 7

# BOGEYMAN, 1986, PART I

Toni Trombley met the Bogeyman in the summer of 1986. He was just back in the area from Florida, and his brother and sister-in-law lived next door to the house where Toni rented a room from her cousin in a house in Flint.

He was quiet, smart and enjoyed talking to her. Pretty soon he was stopping by every day to chat. Nothing romantic. Just friendly conversation.

One day, Toni came home to find he had been there. He had gotten in somehow and left a bouquet of flowers and a note for her. She looked around. Nothing was as she or her cousin had left it.

He had completely cleaned the house. It was spotless. He had also washed the laundry, folding it and putting it away before he left.

Toni freaked out. She confronted him later and told him to stay away from her. And she got a padlock for her bedroom door. One day, she came home to find the padlock broken off. She soon moved out, and that was the last she heard of him for more than fifteen years.

# 8

# BOGEYMAN, 1986, PART II

Margarette Eby's calendar was always busy. It would have been busy just with demands at school. She was also a director of the classical radio station WFBE. And she had a wide circle of friends, running the gamut from lovers to gay artists to fellow churchgoers to musicians she played with in various ensembles. At 55, she showed no sign of slowing down.

Whether it was her schedule or her natural high-energy metabolism, Eby still had the petite figure of a schoolgirl. She was 5 feet, 1 inch tall and weighed 123 pounds. The only concession to age was her dyed-brown hair, which she wore in a loose perm that was then fashionable.

The weekend of Friday, November 7, through Sunday, November 9, was typical. At 4 p.m. Friday, she was supposed to meet with a woman friend, but got out of that engagement so she could accept an offer to attend a dinner party at the home of Richard and Mary Newman in nearby Clio.

The Newmans were fellow members of First Presbyterian Church, a grand old stone edifice on S. Saginaw Street in downtown Flint. Also attending were John Hyde, an assistant principal at the Ottawa County Vocational Center; Soden Smith, a teacher at the Flint Academy who sang with Eby at the church; and William Renneckar, the church's chief organist and choir director.

Saturday, she had to go down to Detroit to pick up her 3-year-old granddaughter, Jessie, then it was off the Detroit Institute of Arts with her, and then, that night, to a concert at Hill Auditorium on the University of Michigan's Ann Arbor campus.

Sunday, she had a 2 p.m. concert to attend in Flint, and at 4 p.m. Hyde and Smith were stopping by the two-story Tudor gatehouse she rented on the Mott Estate. Eby had some geraniums she prized, and Hyde was going to transplant them to his greenhouse before a killer frost did them in. This time of year, a frost was overdue.

Friday's dinner was a quiet affair. The night before, at choir practice, all four of the guests had agreed to meet at Eby's at 6:15 and make the short drive to Clio in one car. Eby brought a cold seafood salad.

Eby told everyone she was upset at having recently received a letter from an attorney for the Mott Estate saying she might soon have to leave her beloved gatehouse home, that the estate planned to hire a full-time gardener and his contract might require that the estate provide him a place to live.

At one point Eby asked the group if anyone thought it was possible for someone to have a full social life and still be lonely.

"I wondered if it was a question of a professor to stimulate conversation, or if she was talking about herself," Smith would later recount.

At 11 p.m., the four headed back to Flint. At the gatehouse, all three men got out of the car and walked Eby to the front door of the gatehouse. But her key wouldn't work the lock. "It's schizophrenic," she said. "Sometimes it works and sometimes it doesn't."

The four then walked to a side door, where Eby used the same key to get inside. Before she closed the door, she turned and gave all three men quick, friendly pecks on the cheek goodnight.

Sunday afternoon, Hyde, a meticulous type, noticed when he pulled into Eby's driveway in his Buick Regal that he was eight minutes late. Eby's Chevy was in the driveway.

He went up to the front door, the schizophrenic one from Friday night. This time, it was a few inches ajar. He pulled it shut and then knocked loudly with the big brass knocker. When there was no response, he went back to his car, got out a windshield scraper and used that to pry the geraniums loose from the pots. He then returned to his car with the plants.

Smith arrived a few minutes later in his Honda Accord. He and Hyde were planning to drive to the city of Holland on the western side of the state later that evening.

The two men went up to the door and clanged the knocker, again. Still no answer.

They then opened the door and cautiously stepped in. It was dusk outside, and the dim light inside the house added to a sinister ambience. Smith thought they were out of line for walking in, but Hyde prevailed. Eby's purse and keys were visible on the dining room table. They called out. No response.

Smith and Hyde talked about what they should do, that it seemed odd the door would be open and her purse and keys there, but that she wouldn't have heard them by now. Of course, after a long weekend, she could have been taking a nap. Hyde said he'd go upstairs and take a peek.

He walked up the stairs. As he reached the top, he could see her through the open bedroom door, see her as he looked into a scene of unspeakable carnage and depravity. She was lying on her stomach, her right arm on the floor, her left arm bent behind her. There was a small puddle of congealed blood under her right hand, and a huge pool of it next to her head on the mattress. Her head had been nearly severed from her torso. She'd been tied up and raped. She'd been stabbed repeatedly.

Hyde thought he was going to throw up, but the feeling passed and he stumbled downstairs. "Margarette's up there and there's a lot of blood," he said, panicked.

Smith dialed 911.

The dispatcher wanted a house number. They didn't know it. Hyde went out to look and couldn't find one. *It was the gatehouse at the front of the Mott Estate, for God's sake.* The dispatcher didn't seem to be able to work around the lack of an address. *They didn't need an address, damn it. They needed to get there.*

Hysterical, Smith later remembered thinking they needed to hurry up because he had a long drive to make and needed to get going. Of course, he'd be going nowhere.

## 9
## A CALL AT HOME

Gary Elford had been a Flint cop for eleven years and a sergeant in the homicide bureau for a year when he got a call at home at 4:50 p.m. on Sunday, November 9, his day off.

It was Sergeant Harvey Beaucamp, back at the downtown headquarters. There was a body at the Mott Estate and he needed to get there ASAP.

Flint in the mid-1980s was, as it is today, a city of enormous contrasts: sprawling estates lining forested golf courses just blocks from some of the toughest urban terrain—dope-dealing, gangs, murder and mayhem—in America.

It was even worse in 1986. Flint—not Detroit seventy-five minutes south on I-75—was the epicenter of the Rust Belt. Foreign imports had cut into the Big Three's share of the domestic auto market, plants were being shuttered and those still open were going from three shifts to two to one. In 1986, unemployment was way up in double digits, triple the national average. At unemployment offices, lines ringed the building, and in winter they'd burn scraps of wood and garbage in garbage cans to keep warm while waiting to get inside for their checks.

On a per capita basis, there were more homicides in Flint than there were in Detroit, which was nationally known as the Murder City.

At 4:50 came the call from Beaucamp, a gruff desk sergeant who growled at Elford to get to the Mott Estate. A white female was in an upstairs bedroom and had been murdered.

Elford, surprised, turned to his wife. "I've got to go to the Mott Estate."

"Who's dead?"

"I think it's Mrs. Mott."

Elford would soon find out that it was Margarette Eby. Mrs. Mott, the 76-year-old matriarch of the estate, was away on vacation.

Elford got lots of calls at home. In 1986, there were sixty-three murders, not counting the justifiable homicides, in a city of about 150,000 residents. "We were out a lot that year," says Elford, who retired from the Flint police force in 2000 and is now captain in charge of detectives of affluent Grand Blanc in suburban Flint.

He may have been out a lot, but never to the Mott Estate. The Mott Estate and the half-mile-long cultural center it anchored just east of downtown were an oasis of civility, and immune to murder and mayhem. Or so it seemed. They were just a few miles and a few light years from the troubled north side.

A murder at Mott was nearly incomprehensible to Elford, a Flint native who had graduated from Flint Southwestern High in 1968. And it was, Elford knew, going to be a big deal. A very big deal. TV, newspapers, relentless attention and publicity.

"I knew it was huge as soon as I heard it was the Mott Estate . . . Mr. Mott *was* Flint," says Elford. "Everyone in Flint was touched by the Mott Foundation sooner or later."

Charles Stewart Mott was one of a handful of pioneering industrialists who had helped give birth to General Motors and what would become the most important, vibrant industry on earth.

Born in 1875, in 1906 he moved the family business—Weston–Mott Co. made wire wheels and axles—from Utica, N.Y., to Flint. In 1913, he sold his company to GM in exchange for stock, which would eventually make him a multi-millionaire.

He served three stints as Flint's mayor, the first beginning in 1912. In 1926, he established the C. S. Mott Foundation, which in 2002 had more than $3 billion in assets and made nearly $110 million in grants.

Mott died in 1973 at the age of 97. His widow, Ruth Rawlings Mott, still lived at Applewood in 1986. The estate's name has a double meaning—there is a pretty apple orchard on the property, and Mott was from the New York Motts made famous by their apple juice.

Elford got to the scene at 5:20 p.m. It was a cloudy day, getting dark, the temperature in the mid-30s. The first thing he did was call the Michigan State Police and request a crime-scene team to be sent down from the crime lab in Bridgeport, thirty miles to the north. "I didn't have confidence in our own people," he admits. The Flint PD was always fighting budget troubles. The state police would be able to send in more—and better-trained—crime-scene investigators.

Already there were Flint officers Alan Edwards and Julie Ringlein, who had secured the scene, and his boss, Lieutenant Joseph DeKatch. Most murders, the boss wouldn't have beat him to the scene on a Sunday—but this wasn't most murders.

DeKatch's boss, Captain Fay Peek, arrived at 5:40 and Dave King, another homicide sergeant, at 5:45. Elford served as the scene detective, meaning he would preserve the scene, get things organized, assign duties, direct the taking of photos and drawings, and later type up a detailed narrative report for whoever would lead the subsequent investigation.

Not wanting to contaminate the scene, the Flint cops waited outside till the state police arrived. Meanwhile, they worked the perimeter, checking windows and doors for signs of forced entry or for footprints leading up to or away from the house. The house sat just behind an eight-foot cyclone fence that surrounded the estate. It was just off the curving driveway that went from the entrance about fifty feet away to the eighteen-room Mott Estate a couple of hundred yards to the east. There was a gate at the driveway entrance, but it was never closed, and there was no security guard to check on who came and went.

Except for the front door, the doors were secured with deadbolts; the windows were locked, none of them broken. There were no footprints. There was an outdoor cement stairway on the south side of the house, which led down to an aluminum door at basement level. It, too, was dead-bolted.

At 6:25 the medical examiner, Dr. David Congdon, arrived. He was allowed to enter the house and make the pronouncement of death.

At 7:55, the state police team, which had assembled in Bridgeport before driving down in a large work van, arrived. The team of James Silva, Mike Thomas, John Wilmer and Michael Wolner would be assisted by Flint's evidence tech at the scene, Larry Safford.

Elford's six-page, single-spaced narrative report is rich with detail. Years later, state police investigators would be struck by the difference in quality and quantity of the detail in Elford's report and what would later be added to the file by others working the case. It would be an irony lost on no one.

From his report, one learns that:

The large estate is surrounded by a tall wire-mesh fence topped by barbed wire. The gatehouse was just inside the northwest corner of the fencing, south of one of two entrances to the estate and a few yards on the other side of the fence and a barrier of vegetation and trees from a theater parking lot.

A 1980 two-door Chevy registered to Eby sat parked in the driveway.

The cops went in through the front door into an entrance hallway. On one side was an archway to a dining room, on the other an archway to the living room. Elford was struck by how neat the place was. Everything tidy and clean, no sign of a struggle.

On the dining room table he found an unzipped gray purse and a key ring with fourteen keys. Under the purse was a flyer from the First Presbyterian Church of Flint for a noon luncheon four days earlier. There was a flyer for the U.S. Air Force Band for a show on November 21. There were several photos of Eby and her family and friends. In the top left drawer of the dresser were Eby's driver's license and several credit cards.

There were two windows in the room. Neither had curtains.

In the kitchen, an empty bottle of wine, Chateau Cantenac, 1970, sat on the top of a cupboard. Next to the bottle was a cork, an empty plastic cup and a clear glass wine decanter about a quarter filled with red wine. The windows above the sink had no curtains.

A grand piano dominated the living room, which faced a brick fireplace. The window on the north wall was curtainless.

The northwest bedroom upstairs was in sharp contrast to the mayhem across the hall. It had the one curtained window in the house, two twin beds, a small round table with a collection of children's books on top and a TV stand and TV. The room was undisturbed and tidy. Investigators would later find out that Margarette had made it into a room for her grandchild.

The bathroom seemed perfectly ordinary except for two things: a small jackknife on the top of a small plastic shelf next to the sink and a small dab of red next to the cold-water faucet.

There would be nothing small about the dab's eventual impact.

And then Elford's report gets to the southwest bedroom, where nothing was normal. The nearly two pages devoted to the bedroom speak both to the horror of the scene and to Elford's skilled attention to detail.

## 10
## A BLOODY BEDROOM

On first reading, the dry, clinical tone of Elford's report of Margarette Eby's bedroom masks the ghastliness of what he saw. But on second reading, the style seems to convey almost a cinematically chilling sweep as the reader pans across the bedroom, seeing the things of everyday life—laundry receipts, partially burned candles, gray socks, unopened pantyhose, bubble gum—and, between them, or on them, things of horror: large pools of blood on the carpet, drops of blood on a skirt hanging on a doorknob, a gold chain half buried in a gaping neck wound, a clown figure on top of a dresser that held earrings, below it, on the front of the dresser, more blood. The routine and the unimaginable.

Elford wrote:

*The victim's bedroom was located west off the upper hall in the southwest corner of the upstairs of the house. The bedroom door opened inward and was hinged on the north. Hanging on the outside of the bedroom doorknob was a black/gray wool skirt. This skirt had two small drops of blood, one being on the folded edge toward the west and the other was on the back. Hanging on the inside of the doorknob was a white plastic bag containing two pair of women's underwear. There was a bed located approximately in the middle of the room from south to north. The headboard was on the west wall and the bed extended to the east. On the bed was the body of a white female, later identified as Margarette Eby. She was lying on her stomach, nude, with her head at the northwest corner of the bed and her feet extending southeast to the middle of the bed. The victim's head was turned and facing south. The right arm was hanging over the north side of the bed and the hand was touching the floor. Under the hand was a dried pool of blood measuring 10 inches north to south and five inches east to west.*

*The victim's left arm was bent at the elbow and the left hand was at the lower back. Both wrists showed signs of being bound. Both were reddish color with the right wrist showing a very definite impression, where the left wrist was more red. The left exposed side of the victim's face was blood covered, along with the back of her head and hair. The blood also covered the top half of her back from the neck down. There was a massive wound to the victim's neck and around the neck and partially in the wound was a gold neck chain. Next to the victim on the south side under the left arm was a leather watchband.*

*Also next to the victim to the south was a yellow bath type robe. The robe's shoulder and neck area were lying in a pool of blood. A large concentration of partially wet and dry blood was on the mattress and under the victim. The concentration measure three feet north to south and two and a half feet east to west. The victim appeared to have been moved from a position of lying on her back in the middle of the bed to the position she was found. Folds on the blood-covered robe matched bloody areas on the victim's back . . .*

*The bed the victim was laying on consisted of a mattress and box springs and a metal frame. The frame was not attached to the headboard. The top blanket on the bed was a brown, white, tan and green striped, with fringed edges. The second blanket was a white electric type. This blanket was in the on position and turned to number seven. Controls for the electric blanket were slightly under the north side of the bed. There was a blue sheet on the mattress and two pillows on the head of the bed against the headboard. The pillowcases were blue in color with yellow flowers. Both pillow-cases were blood splattered. On the southeast bottom corner of the bed was a purple skirt. Draped over the edge on the top of the bed was a beige tan women's suit still on a hanger. The wall above the headboard and the headboard itself had several small blood spatterings.*

*On the bedroom's east wall extending south from the bedroom door was a dresser. Above the dresser just to the south of the door was located a light attached to the wall in the off position. Attached to the top of the dresser were two mirrors. On the top of the dresser was a laundry receipt for Pro-Clean Laundry, photos of the victim, partially burned candles, 10 pieces of different colored candy, two pieces of bubble gum, a large correspondence envelope from U of M addressed to Raymond Roth, Flint Music. There appeared to be a small blood drop on the envelope. Also on the envelope was a piece of yellow cloth material matching the yellow robe on the bed.*

*On the carpet in front of the dresser was a pair of*

*gray women's shoes. Next to the shoes on the carpet was a white plastic or rubber covered wire approximately seven inches long. The wire had three insulated inner strands of red, green and yellow. The south wall of the bedroom had a window covering approximately one half east to west. There were no coverings on this window. West of the window was another dresser and on top of the dresser was a clown figure that held earrings. On the front of the dresser two feet three inches off the floor were several small blood drops.*

*Just north of the bed in the northwest corner was a glass-topped wood table being used as a nightstand. On top of the table was a clock radio, two crumpled yellow tissues, a jar of moisturizing cream, two books, No. 1 being "Special People." Written on the first page was a note from Lynn Roberts dated 10-28-86. The No. 2 book was "Falcon and the Snowman." The bottom shelf of the table had a white telephone, another jar of moisturizing cream, a box of yellow tissue. On the floor between the table and the wall was a plastic fly swatter.*

*The victim was later turned over by Michigan State Police Crime Lab personnel Wolner and Thomas. The wound on the victim's neck was approximately two inches wide and covered approximately an area from ear to ear under the chin. The right side of the victim's face was blood covered. The victim was wearing post-type earrings, along with the aforementioned gold necklace, and a ring on the index finger of her right hand. The mark on the right wrist appeared to match the wire found on the floor. There also appeared to be a dried white substance in the vaginal opening of the victim. The victim's chest was also blood covered. The yellow robe was moved and the face of the watch was found on this robe. The yellow robe was missing the cuff on the left sleeve.*

The medical examiner would later report that the gaping wound to Eby's neck was so deep it nearly reached the spinal cord, that the murderer had used a serrated knife and would have had to use it like a saw to inflict the damage he did. And that she had also been stabbed in her chest and left breast.

Almost lost in the detail of Elford's report was something that would prove crucial—that Eby had an electric blanket and that it was turned up to seven. Lab tests would later show that the time between Eby's murder and the point when samples could be taken from her vagina, combined with the heat of the blanket, degraded the semen to the point where it could tell nothing about the killer. Not his blood type, not his sub-groupings.

If the samples taken from Eby were to yield any treasures, they would have to be frozen and stored away, waiting for breakthroughs in DNA technology.

The report was the last one Elford would write on the case until 2002. It finished with one simple, but scary, declarative sentence:

> It should be noted that during the search of the victim's home, no wallet or cash could be found.

The killer might have been a thief. But he was not a simple thief. If he'd taken Eby's ID, he might be a collector, too.

## 11
## KING GETS THE CASE

Gary Elford was in charge of the crime scene Sunday night. He knew from the start that Sergeant Dave King would be in charge of the case. But to his surprise, two days later, he was pulled off it altogether. His boss, Lieutenant DeKatch, wanted to take his place—highly unusual, but, then, so was the case. Some of it was DeKatch wanting the spotlight. Some of it was that Elford hadn't worked homicide very long. He went to work typing up his meticulous notes.

Today, King is retired from the Flint Police Department and is a civilian employee of the Michigan State Police, with a division called the Michigan Commission on Law Enforcement Standards.

MCOLES publishes a 470-page training manual that serves as a guide for Michigan police and sheriff's departments. As communications coordinator, King helps update the manual and gives presentations about it and proper police procedures around the state.

He loves police work. He loves the idea that he can help define and communicate standards that can teach young cops how to do things right.

King is extremely quiet spoken and mild mannered. He is the antithesis of what you'd expect from a homicide detective who's spent twenty years working some of the meanest streets in America.

He was never a tough guy, not one of those cops who commanded respect with his fists or his guns. A college graduate before that was common on the Flint PD—he graduated in police administration from Michigan State University in 1969—he always prided himself on a reasoned, cerebral approach to solving crime.

His dad was a parole officer for the state, and King, a Flint native, made the *Journal* in 1947 when he was born on the seventh day of the seventh month of 1947 in room 711 of the hospital. His dad even bought lunch that day for 77 cents.

When King graduated from Flint Southwestern in 1965, the plants were running three shifts a day, seven days a week. There was no end to overtime or the Buicks cranking off the assembly line and onto semis. Through most of King's career, though, Flint was a city in despair.

King married his high-school sweetheart, is a regular church-goer and sometime Sunday school teacher. He is a former marathon runner and many times has run the local ten-mile road race known as The Crim. It is the one bright day each year in the city, the biggest economic day of the year, when 15,000 runners and walkers come to town. *Runner's World* magazine and ESPN come, too. Until his knees got funky, King was thrilled to be part of his city's big day.

He was a popular cop, and a good one. He made it to lieutenant before he retired. But no matter how many cases he solved, no matter how much of his ingenuity sent large numbers of bad guys to Jackson Prison, King will always be associated with the one case he couldn't solve, by far the biggest case of his career.

And he'll always be haunted by the what-ifs and the hindsight criticisms that shine so clearly on the mistakes he made.

King graduated from MSU on a Saturday, moved his stuff back to Flint on Sunday and Monday and started work with the Flint PD on Tuesday. He spent four days in training and was in a uniform and a scout car on Saturday.

King spent a year writing traffic tickets and hated every minute of it. He spent three years on general patrol and then was moved into something new called the Special Operations Bureau. They were called, in a euphemism most cops would die for, the SOBs.

Despite his self-ascribed sobriquet, "I wasn't the kind of big, hulking cop going in knocking doors off hinges."

He then moved up to the first tactical operations unit in Flint's history. "We were going to solve Flint's crime problems. We were pretty optimistic. We juggled our hours. We'd do anything to catch the bad guys."

He was, he says, still enthusiastic, gung ho and naïve.

Tactical ops meant working Flint's north end, and no one stayed naïve there for long.

It was a place riddled with drunks, druggies, stupidity and meanness. Heroin addicts were doing a lot of home invasions, and they always had the same MO: they busted in, grabbed as much they could, then ditched it in some field or behind the nearest vacant house. Later, they'd come back for it.

King and his crew wouldn't bother trying to track down the perps. They'd just scout out the nearest fields and abandoned houses, invariably find the stash of stuff within minutes, then sit around waiting for the thieves to come back and pick it up.

From 1977 to 1980, King worked homicide. His first case was one of those easy ones where you know from the start who did it, and it takes you a couple of hours to prove it. He got the call and they had the suspect in custody before he even left the house.

The second case was a double-homicide execution, two dudes shot in the head in a car. It was an intractable case that got to him. He started dreaming one of the dead guys was alive. He'd come to King in his sleep, talking to him. It got so bad, King took a week off and visited his in-laws out of town.

"You need to build barriers, but you can't build them too high or you're no good," he says. The case never did get solved.

Procedure then was to rotate out of homicide after three years, so he moved over to the B&E squad as a supervisor, then into narcotics for five years and, in 1985, back to homicide.

King got the call Sunday late afternoon about the call at the Mott. It should have gone to another sergeant—King had picked up the most recent unsolved murder two weeks ago and another sergeant was due up in the rotation, but in those pre-pager, pre–cell phone days, the other guy hadn't answered his phone.

Elford answered his. King answered his.

Elford was already at the scene when King got there. So were his bosses, DeKatch and Peek.

The scene was unusual in several regards. Number one, of course, was that it was the most famous piece of land in Flint. But on a practical level, it was unusual because unlike most murder scenes Flint cops go to, it didn't offer a neighborhood. The main house was at the other end of the estate. There were no neighbors to canvass about what they might have seen or heard.

Ironically, as new a world as the Mott Estate proper was to the detectives, many of them in one way knew it very well. The gatehouse stood next to the fence. On the other side of the fence was a large parking lot, part of the Cultural Center. It was a favorite spot for Flint cops to duck into, to grab a coffee or a doughnut or even a snooze.

Like his fellow cops, King had been there many times. Also like them, he'd never noticed the house tucked in the shrubbery and trees just on the other side of the fence.

"I grew up in Flint. Any kid growing up in Flint knew Mr. Mott. But oddly enough, I wasn't familiar with the Mott Estate," says King.

Though the estate was fenced in, there was no guard at the entrances and nothing to prevent anyone from driving or walking in. The estate's caretaker was supposed to double as a security guard in theory, but in reality he had little to do with protecting the grounds or the estate's inhabitants.

After the state police crime-scene crew arrived, King entered the house. He was impressed by how homey it was. Not elaborate or pretentious. Like Elford, King was struck by the lack of curtains, blinds or shades.

It would have been easy for some peeping Tom to climb a tree and look inside. Had some pervert crossed the line from voyeurism to violence?

King left the crime scene while the state police were still working it heavily and went back to headquarters nearby to interview Hyde and Smith, the two guys who'd found the body. They were suspects, of course, simply because they had found the body, but were soon cleared.

The phone on his desk rang. It was Jonathan Eby. He was irate the police hadn't called him to tell him about his mother's murder. A friend had heard something on the news and had called him. King told him that while they suspected the body was his mother, no official identification had been made, yet. Moreover, he didn't have a phone number for him, didn't know his name, had no way of contacting him so quickly. He tried to calm him down and said they'd be doing everything they could and would be in touch.

## 12
## "WHAT ARE YOU TELLING ME?"

Margaret Lynn Rimer, Margarette Eby's youngest child, has always gone by her middle name. (Though the spelling on the first name is different, the pronunciation is the same.) Today, she is an emergency-room nurse at the sprawling Beaumont Hospital in the Detroit suburb of Royal Oak. "I'm an adrenaline junkie," she says when explaining her choice of professions.

She and her mother had plans for Saturday afternoon, November 8, 1986. Lynn was working then as a waitress at Restaurant Douglass, a posh suburban eatery in Southfield owned by one of the first nationally popular TV chefs, Douglass Douglass, the Emeril of his day.

Lynn and her husband had been having marital troubles off and on, and shortly after her mom moved to Flint, Lynn had moved into the gatehouse with her mother for six months. She had reconciled with her husband, though, and they had just moved into a rented bungalow on the west side of Detroit.

Her mom was an avid grandmother. As soon as Jessie was born in 1983, Margarette had redone Lynn's old bedroom upstairs at the gatehouse into a kid's room, and she frequently took Jessie on weekends. When Margarette was taking Jessie, she and Lynn generally would meet halfway between the two cities, at the I-75 exit at Joslyn Road near the city of Pontiac.

Margarette was supposed to take Jessie this weekend, but plans this time were a little different. She'd pick Jessie up at home around noon, take her to the Detroit Institute of Arts downtown, then out to eat. And then the two would go back to Flint for the rest of the weekend.

Lynn left early for the day-shift at the restaurant, leaving Jessie with her husband. When she returned from work early in the evening, to her surprise, Jessie was still there.

"Mom didn't come?" asked a surprised Lynn.

"No."

"What did she say?"

"She didn't call, either."

"Maybe she forgot," said Lynn, though it wasn't like her mom to miss out on a day with her granddaughter.

"You have to understand my mother," says Lynn years later. "She always had things going on three burners. She was the opposite of a couch potato. It wasn't like her not to take Jessie, but knowing her schedule, I wasn't that much concerned about it. I figured I'd hear from her, that maybe she had called and Ted had been in the shower or something."

She called her mom and left a message. She and her husband had dinner and went to bed.

There was no word from her mother Sunday.

Sunday night, the phone rang.

"Is this Margarette Eby's daughter?"

"Yes."

"Are you alone?"

"What's this about?"

"Are you alone?"

"Quit beating around the bush. What's going on?"

"Someone has been found dead at the Mott Estate."

Today, Rimer says of the rest of the conversation: "He just dragged it out horribly. He went on and on. Finally I said, 'Are you telling me my mom's dead?'

"Well, we don't know.'

"I knew it was her. Who else would it be? They found a woman in her bedroom and my mom is the only one who lives in the Mott Estate? Come on. It's my mom."

She told the caller, Sergeant Dave King, that she'd be in Flint as soon as she could make arrangements. Lynn had been living with her parents eleven years earlier when her father died of a massive heart attack at home. Her reaction now was the same as then. "It was surreal. This can't be happening. This cannot be real. This is a bad *Miami Vice* show. It's not real."

She then called her older sister, Dayle, who was a lawyer in Indianapolis.

"Dayle, Mom's dead. You gotta get on a plane and get here."

Dayle had already gotten the news from her brother Jonathan, upon arriving home from an Indianapolis Colts football game.

"Lynn, when we go through Mom's things, we're going to find a bag of tulip bulbs."

"Tulip bulbs?"

"Yep, tulip bulbs. She was going to surprise you and plant them this fall and when they came up in the spring, you'd say, 'Where did they come from?' "

Nearly two decades later, when Lynn would recount the tulip anecdote, tears would well up, her voice would break and her boyfriend would need to hold her hand while she regrouped. "That's the kind of woman my mother was. Someone who had five hundred things to do, and she'd take the time to plant my garden for me so I'd have a surprise in the spring."

Dayle caught an early flight to Detroit in the morning, was met at the airport by Jonathan, and they drove directly to Flint to identify the body.

# 13

# ANOTHER RIDE TO FLINT

Today, Mike Thomas is a captain with the Michigan State Police, one of its highest-ranking officers. He is the director of the forensics science division, which includes seven regional crime labs around the state and three DNA labs.

Back in November of 1986, Thomas was one of a four-person crime-scene crew working out of the Bridgeport post half an hour north of Flint up I-75. He was watching TV in his home in Bridgeport, just down the road from the State Police Crime Lab, when the phone rang. He got called out a lot, which meant rendezvousing at the lab with the rest of the team to pick up their specialized van, so it didn't make sense to live too far away.

Thomas was one of the new breed of cops when he joined the state police in 1978. He graduated from Madonna University in Livonia in just three years with a degree in criminal justice and had been accepted to grad school at Eastern Michigan University.

But when word came he'd been accepted to the eighty-fifth recruiting class of the MSP, grad school was quickly forgotten. He was assigned to the Bridgeport post as a trooper in January of 1979, across the driveway from the crime lab.

As a uniformed trooper, he worked various crime scenes with the lab folks, got intrigued by what they did and applied when a position opened up. In 1982, he moved across the driveway to start a two-year training program.

By the time of the Eby murder, Thomas was a crime-scene vet, working 35–40 major scenes a year, many of them called in by the Flint PD. His crew knew the Flint cops by name, and after working together there, they would often all head over to the White Horse, a cop hangout in Flint, for burgers and beer.

The dispatcher said there'd been another murder in Flint, this one of a woman in a cottage at the Mott Estate. James Silva, John Wilmer and Michael Wolner met him at the lab, gathered up their stuff, and drove down to Flint, arriving at 7:55 p.m. The Mott Estate meant nothing to Thomas. He was surprised when he got there that the cottage was a mansion by his standards. Not your typical Flint crime scene.

Silva and Thomas were fingerprint specialists. The other two would concentrate on serology and trace evidence. They entered the house and worked slowly through it toward the body. They took photos of everything, from every angle. They used contrasting powders to look for prints. When they found them, they put tape on the powder and lifted it. The impression of the print would remain on the tape. There were a ton of prints, which didn't mean much. Most houses have a ton of prints. The trick is to link one of them to a bad guy. As suspects would evolve, they'd check their prints versus the prints from the house and see if any matched.

They used high-intensity lights and a magnifying device known as a linen tester to help find prints. As the lights burned, the house got hotter and hotter.

Wilmer and Wolner picked up bits of fiber, hair and other trace evidence and put them in evidence bags. Once they got to the bedroom, they had lots of serology to deal with. There was blood everywhere and obvious semen stains on the victim.

Thomas was struck by the lack of curtains in her bedroom. "A peeping Tom?" he wondered. He was shocked, too, that her head was nearly severed. He'd seen lots of ugly scenes, lots of crimes of passion, but usually it was an angry stabbing or slashing. Something done quick. This one had taken a while.

Playing the role of plumbers, they pulled the trap from the bathroom sink. They'd search through its gunk later. While it was usually a long shot, sometimes the detritus normally found in the trap would contain a trace of the killer's blood.

It might not be such a long shot this time. There was a bloody partial print on the porcelain near the cold-water handle. Obviously the killer had washed up. Thomas photographed the print and lifted it.

Now it was time to roll the body over, look for other trace evidence that had been under it and check for lividity, the pooling and bruising of blood next to the skin, which can help fix the time of death.

As they were getting ready to roll her, King entered the bedroom, back from interviewing Hyde and Smith. When they turned her over, a stench hit them all.

Since Margarette had died on top of a heating blanket that was turned up, the heat had helped hasten the decay. There was a lot of lividity and she was rigid. King blurted out: "Holey moley, she's been dead awhile."

The body was then lifted onto a gurney by attendants from Life Line Ambulance and at 12:02 a.m. left for the Hurley Medical Center, which served as the county morgue. Its pathologists performed autopsies on a contract basis for the county. This one would be done by Willys Mueller, considered by the cops to be brilliant at his work with the dead.

Thomas was sweaty, and fingerprint dust caked his face and arms. He went into the bathroom downstairs and washed up.

The cops then secured the scene at 12:40 a.m. and left.

Monday morning, Elford and a crew from the Flint PD searched the estate for evidence. They found nothing unusual. King and Elford reentered the gatehouse and gathered up some of Eby's personal papers, including a list of sixteen men's names and one woman's name.

All day Monday, the Eby murder dominated the Flint TV news. Thomas was surprised to see himself during one Eby segment. He was caught on camera washing his hands and face, and the camera had zoomed in on him. There had been a TV camera outside the fence, and with all the leaves long blown off all the trees, they had had a clear shot at him.

A peeping Tom? he wondered again. If the TV crew could see him so clearly, maybe some nutball had seen Eby just as well and the sight of her in her bathroom had set him off. Soon, Mott employees were telling police that she liked to walk around her house nude, that they'd seen her numerous times through her curtainless windows, naked as a jay bird. And she used to like to sunbathe nude out behind the gatehouse, too.

### 14
### "DEATH AND THE MAIDEN"

The autopsy was conducted Monday morning. King was there, along with John Wilmer, Bob Avery and Mike Thomas of the state police crime lab, who would take samples for toxicology and serology purposes, and Mueller's assistant and a photographer. First the body had to be formally identified, with Jonathan and Dayle Eby taking on that horrific task. The last time Jonathan had seen his mother was when they'd driven to Stratford, Ontario, six weeks earlier to see a play.

Officials only let them see her face and the top of her head. They wanted to keep as much of the horror hidden from her children as possible. Dayle wanted to stroke her mother's hair but they wouldn't let her.

Jonathan and Dayle left and the rest went about their grim tasks. Eby's neck had been sawed with a serrated knife, going left to right. The murderer was right-handed. Her carotid artery and jugular vein were severed. The gaping wound was the result of two separate slashings, one across the top of the neck on an upward angle and the other horizontal at mid-throat. There was another stab wound in the neck.

There were three stab wounds on her chest, going into subcutaneous tissue and stopping at the sternum, but they showed no signs of bleeding, which meant they'd come after death. There was a diagonal stab wound on the inner portion of her left breast, a diagonal cut that perforated her left atrium, just above the mitral valve.

There was bruising inside her labia, a blue-black discoloration about twelve millimeters in length. There were visible semen stains, but the rectal area tested negative for sperm.

Mueller went to work with his bone saw, a sound no witness to an autopsy ever forgets, to examine her organs.

A Y incision was cut down the front of her chest and her rib cage was pulled back. An incision was made in the back of her scalp from one ear to the other and her scalp was pulled down over the front of her face. Her brain was pulled out and weighed, as were her organs. Tissue samples were taken.

Food, much of it undigested, uncooked vegetables, was taken out of her stomach and photographed. It would turn out they'd come from her last meal at the dinner party Friday, which was replete with an array of vegetable munchies and dip.

Mueller's conclusions? Manner of death: homicide. Cause of death: incised neck wounds.

Later King would show the photos of Eby's stomach contents while seeking out advice from Dr. Warner Spitz, the nationally renowned medical examiner in Wayne County, where Detroit ruled as the nation's Murder Capital.

"Well, that's fresh food. She just ate that and her digestive processes just stopped," said Spitz. "What stops the digestive processes? Extreme fear."

It raised the hackles on King's neck, the image of a woman coming home from a dinner party with friends, and immediately finding herself in such horror that her stomach juices stopped digesting food.

When King got back to his office from the autopsy, the media circus had clearly started. His desk was covered in pink "While You Were Out" notes from every radio and TV station in town, and from many of the state's daily newspapers.

One was from the editor of *The Flint Journal*, the first time the editor had ever called him. "I had worked forty previous homicides in Flint, and he didn't even know who I was," says King.

Early on, he and DeKatch made a tactical decision. Michigan sunshine laws made it a legal obligation for police to turn their reports, minus some deletions, over to news reporters. But if King and DeKatch didn't file very many, there wouldn't be much to turn over. They stopped typing up official reports. They took to scribbling things down on scrap paper and sticking them in drawers. Years later, the lack of decipherable reports and the excess of badly written scribbling, often in some sort of shorthand, would drive other investigators nuts. But that would be then.

After the autopsy, King met with Lynn Rimer.

That evening, he went back to the scene for a slow, detailed walk around the house.

He missed something interesting, though there was a good reason. It was inside the CD player, and in 1986 not many people had heard of CDs or CD players. Certainly not King. He didn't recognize it for what it was, and had no way of knowing there might be something of interest in that little slot on the front.

Her family would soon discover it and give him a call.

What popped out was a CD of a Schubert piece titled "Death and the Maiden." Eby had recently put together something she had billed as a "Schubertiad."

It gave King a jolt. A single woman is killed and inside her music player is something called "Death and the Maiden"? A weird coincidence? What were the chances? Or a clue from her killer, deliberately and diabolically planted? What were they dealing with, here?

## 15
## STRANGER IN THE HOUSE

Things got worse for Lynn Rimer, if that was possible, when she met with King. She hadn't been able to get to Flint in time to join her siblings in identifying the body. She says almost the first thing King asked was what her mom was involved in. He said that it looked like a gang hit. Why would she be involved in gangs? What was she up to? Was she into drugs?

"He said the FBI was being brought in. The whole thing went from bad to worse. Gangs? Drugs? My mom? It had all been strange enough, but when the Flint police started adding in all those fun facts, it got even more surreal.

"I remember being in a fog. Not enough of one, though, because I can remember the pain and terror of everything."

Lynn gave King something to ponder, in turn.

When she was staying with her mom during her separation several years earlier, she got home late one night, about 3 a.m., having worked the late shift waitressing at Patty McGee's, then a popular Flint eatery.

Her mom routinely worked fourteen-hour days then. "She loved her job. I'd call her at the office at ten p.m. and say, 'Mom, you've been at work for fourteen hours, it's time to come home.' And she'd said, 'Oh, I just lost track of the time.'"

So, in walked Lynn at 3 a.m. and the place was a mess. Nothing too bad, but messy for Margarette, who was an immaculate housekeeper, everything in its place. Lynn thought maybe she'd worked one of her fourteen-hour days, didn't have time to straighten up, and decided for once to go to bed with the house untidy.

At 7 a.m., Margarette woke her, yelling at her to get up, how dare she come in and make such a wreck of the house? "I think you can clean up your mess," she said.

"My mess? What are you talking about?"

They soon realized it was neither's mess. An intruder had been there. Lynn's underwear drawer was open. So was Margarette's. Since the house had been tidy when her mom came home at 11 p.m., that meant the intruder had been there, in her mother's bedroom, going through her underwear drawer while her mom slept just a few feet away.

They called the police, who found a window ajar and footprints leading up to it. The back door was open, the means of egress.

King scribbled notes as Lynn told the tale.

A week after her body was discovered, a memorial service for Eby was held at the First Presbyterian Church. As the body had been cremated, there was no public viewing.

The huge church was packed. In attendance were her children; her three brothers, John, George and Sigfried Fink; her mother, Martha Fink, who was now living in Texas with Sigfried; her sister, Ruth Decker, the missionary in Brazil; and her granddaughter, Jessie.

Also there was the entire staff of Restaurant Douglass, where Lynn worked. It was the first time the restaurant had ever shut its doors on a day it was scheduled to be open.

The family asked that instead of flowers, contributions be made to the Margarette F. Eby Keyboard Scholarship Fund at the U-M Music Development Office in Ann Arbor.

Reverend Donald McFerren, her pastor, praised her as a musician, as a member of his choir, as a community activist and as a friend.

"She was the best thing that ever happened to us," he said.

After the service, the family gathered at their Aunt Pauline's house in Milford and traded stories about the strong-willed woman they'd lost.

Over the years, Lynn had thought off and on of having her name legally changed, dropping the "Margaret." No more. They'd still call her Lynn, but she'd be Margaret forever.

# 16

# AFRAID FOR HER LIFE?

Old-time Flint cops had a saying: "If you got a case on the come, you gotta ride it till it's done."

King rode this one. For the next few weeks the days would start with a meeting at 8:30 a.m. to see where they stood and what the day's plan of attack was. He'd rarely go home before 11 p.m.

DeKatch, big, burly-looking but sharp, who got on well with the local media, was the point man for the press. Politically savvy, his role was also to keep the local politicians at bay. Eby's social circle was the very highest in Flint. Lloyd Reuss, the head of the Buick Motor Division, was a friend. So were many of the local luminaries, and they wanted to know what was being done to solve the crime.

Every day they'd come to the station and have a stack of messages from media folks who wanted to know the latest.

"The media appetite in this case was just insatiable," says King. TV reporters and *Flint Journal* reporters worked the case hard, too, and DeKatch and King often found themselves chasing angles they saw on TV or read in the paper, many of them dead ends, or flat-out wrong.

The hours were long, but they were a relief from the hours he was used to working on the north side. Ghetto crimes are committed by people who get up late and stay up late. You want to solve those crimes, you learn to work that schedule. One redeeming thing about the Eby case was that all the suspects were respectable folks. They kept respectable hours.

A week after Eby's murder, one of her students, Pamela Kostizen, reported a terrifying encounter. Pam had taken her dog to an obedience class and when she returned to her car, a man who had been hiding in the back seat put pruning shears to her neck and told her to drive off.

He told her he would cut off her ear and mail it to her parents if she didn't cooperate, and he told her he had killed Margarette Eby and would kill her, too, if she didn't do as he said. At some point driving down I-75, the woman's dog bit the man and he told her to pull over on the shoulder so he could kill her dog.

She pulled over, the man dragged the dog out of the car and Kostizen accelerated away. The dog then broke free of the man and chased after the car. She stopped, let the dog in and they took off, leaving the man on the side of the road, holding his shears.

The FBI and Flint PD investigated but didn't make an arrest, and couldn't conclusively link her abductor to Eby's killer.

Meanwhile, King and and DeKatch started at the beginning, with known friends and associates. Smith and Hyde were soon cleared, but you'd have to be blind not to see the clues aiming at someone who might be a lover or friend, or if not either of those, at least part of her social circle.

For one thing, there was no sign of a forced entry.

Until you got to the bedroom, there were no signs of disturbance in the house. Did she invite her killer into her room, thinking one thing was going to happen and then finding out something else entirely was about to take place?

For another, there was that list of men's names in her bedroom. "I had a hunch what that list was going to be," says King, and his hunch was right. It soon became clear that it was a chronological list of Eby's sexual liaisons, beginning with her deceased husband. Some of the men were even married to friends of hers, and many of them still lived in the area.

Was Eby hassling one of her ex-lovers? Was someone desperate to break off a relationship? Was there some spouse mad enough at having found out about an affair that she went over to Eby's for a confrontation, lost control and killed her in a rage?

A story in *The Detroit News* seemed to give credence that it was someone she knew. "Slain Prof Feared for Life" read the page-one headline. In it, Margaret Struble, one of the rare co-workers who had also become a friend, said Eby had told her over a recent breakfast at the gatehouse that she had suffered repeated break-ins. Her home was burglarized just weeks after she moved to Flint in 1981, and thieves hit her two more times, once when she was at home the previous January.

One time they grabbed her purse, which was later found on the grounds of the estate. Another time they made off with a cassette player.

More ominously, Struble told the reporter, Eby had awakened one night the month before her death to see a man standing there. She had screamed and the man had fled. Eby hadn't reported the incident to police, and Struble thought the reason was that the man was someone Eby knew and didn't want to get into legal trouble.

Struble said, melodramatically: "I lived in her shoes all through the month of October. I told my husband four times in October that she would not live through another month, through November."

Yet Struble's account was in contrast to a quote later in the story, when she recounted Eby's response to a suggestion that she move. " 'I grew up in Detroit,' " she quoted Eby as saying. " 'This is safe here. God is my umbrella. Nothing bad will come to me.' "

Police and Eby's other friends discounted Struble's comments. The friends, in particular, told reporters they thought she was just relishing her chance for five minutes in the spotlight a bit too much. Moreover, what they knew but the reporter didn't was that Struble had had a falling-out with Eby—she had been a paid employee of the Bach festival, quit, then gotten mad when Eby refused to rehire her when she asked for her job back. Later, she accused Eby of keeping her out of a master's program at U-M. Eventually they had patched up their differences, but things had remained strained.

Yet, Struble's story jibed with Lynn Rimer's report of someone coming into the gatehouse one night years earlier and going through their underwear drawers. And with no sign of a forced entry and no sign of a struggle, perhaps a person she knew had come to kill her. Perhaps the same man she'd shooed from her room the month before, or who'd been there the night Lynn came home late from Patty McGee's.

# 17

# WHITTLING THE LIST

The list of lovers was extremely promising, but was, after weeks of leg work and initial interviews and follow-up interviews, of no ultimate consequence. It did keep King in a higher circle of folks than he normally traveled while on homicide investigations.

One was a dean at the U-M–Flint.

One was a former Detroit cop with an affinity for jazz who later moved to Flint and opened a book and music store. He had met Eby in 1983 while trying to organize a three-day jazz festival in the city. They shared a passion for Miles Davis and Anita Baker and had had a one-night stand following one of their committee meetings.

One was a tenured professor of history at U-M's Ann Arbor campus, the husband of one of Eby's friends. He was the only one on the list who denied an involvement with her. But King had more than just a name on a list. He'd found a packet of erotic letters the historian had written, using scalable fonts on his Apple computer to describe different things he wanted to do with the music professor in Flint.

"I have these letters," said King.

"Oh, those, eh?"

Overall, "I was impressed by their brilliance," says King of Eby's lovers. And convinced by their alibis. "We couldn't develop anything."

The lovers described Eby as strong willed, even demanding, someone who seemed to immerse herself in the relationship, then just as quickly end it and move on.

One early suspect was a woman, a Detroit psychologist and lesbian named Carol Premo, with whom Eby had once had a serious affair after Stewart's death in 1979. Eby had broken off the affair about the time she moved to Iowa, leaving the psychologist very angry and upset. But they had remained friends and continued a non-sexual relationship until Eby's death.

Premo told King she'd met Eby soon after Eby's husband had died in April of 1975, a particularly traumatic death because it had happened during sex. She told him of Eby's mood swings, that she could be happy and child-like or angry and shrew-like. She told him Eby was extremely well liked by her friends and equally disliked by colleagues at the school.

Eby was open enough in those free-wheeling mid-1970s to even go on vacation with the psychologist to the Canary Islands, accompanied by Eby's daughter Lynn. There, Eby had turned the psychologist on to her first taste of marijuana and even talked her into smuggling a small amount of hashish back into the U.S.

Eby could be reckless, always driving fast, almost always leaving her doors unlocked, often walking around nude in her uncurtained gatehouse. When asked about such things, Eby would reply that God would protect her.

What Premo told King resonated with what Struble had told the *News*. About a week before her death, Eby had shown up unannounced at Premo's and told her that she was very upset, that she'd had a recent intruder, that she was worried someone was trying to kill her.

King would dismiss the psychologist as a suspect. Later he would say: "There was speculation all over Flint that Margarette Eby was a wild-ass lesbian into all sorts of wild-ass stuff. But I didn't find any evidence of that. Margarette Eby lived in a different world, a very liberal world. This was just a dalliance she tried after her husband died. From seeing the list of men, it seemed clear women weren't her preference."

King was beginning to feel as if he now knew Margarette Eby. He found himself growing to like her. She had a frankness he admired. He admired her spunk, too, her sense of self. "She was a very complicated woman. Driven to succeed. Eccentric. Pushy. She didn't behave the way women were expected to behave in that place and time."

A strong family man, he liked that she had clearly loved her children and her grandchild, that there was so much evidence of her family in her life.

And he got a big kick out of this anecdote he came across: When she had a deposit to make at the local bank, she didn't do what you'd normally do. "She was definitely not a person to stand in line," says King.

No, Margarette Eby, who traveled in his social circles,

would go straight to the bank president's office with her check and deposit slip and leave it for him.

They cleared the lovers and they cleared the family, Eby's children submitting to fingerprinting and temporary status as suspects until the results came back that none of them matched the bloody print in the bathroom. They cleared her colleagues at the college, too, though they confirmed that Eby could be abrasive, even demeaning, and was particularly disliked by the clerical staff.

They investigated a mentally ill man who claimed his thoughts were controlled by a machine at the Mott Estate. He'd first been caught on the grounds of the estate four years earlier but had escaped from Flint police. In the ensuing car chase, he crashed into a car and killed a woman. But they cleared him of killing Eby.

King and DeKatch moved on to the various, and numerous, Mott employees. Compounding the problem was the laxness of security at the Mott Estate. A large key ring was kept in plain sight in the main building. If you needed a key, or wanted one, you just took the ring.

The caretaker was a retired cop with a reputation for toughness when he was on the force, and he and Eby had argued frequently over the years. But he was cleared. So were the others. That end of the investigation quickly went nowhere, too.

Could it have been a stranger, then? Was it time to move on to the third category of possible suspects—all the contractors and sub-contractors, their employees and the various visitors to the estate around the time of the murder? That was surely a headache waiting for an already overworked department.

But, no, it wouldn't need to come to that. It wasn't a stranger, after all. A month and a half after Eby's death came word from the feds that King's suspicions were correct. It was a friend, or at least an acquaintance, said a team of FBI profilers. King and DeKatch just hadn't found out which one yet. The FBI report came along about the time King had started focusing in on someone whose name hadn't shown up on Eby's list of friends, who hadn't been a Mott employee, but who knew Eby well enough to visit her at her office and at the school's swimming pool.

# 18

# AN FBI PROFILE

Just before Christmas, three of the FBI's fabled profilers gave the Flint police a detailed profile of Margarette Eby's killer to work with. The Flint PD, not playing territorial games with this case, had asked the FBI back on November 11 if its behavioral-science experts could lend a hand.

The FBI team included Jim Harrington, the bureau's Michigan coordinator of the Behavioral Sciences Unit; William Hagmaier, from the FBI's headquarters in Quantico, Va.; and John Douglas, also of Quantico and internationally recognized as the FBI's leading profiler. Douglas was the inspiration for the profiler in Thomas Harris' famous novel, *The Silence of the Lambs.*

Douglas and Hagmaier flew to Michigan and held meetings over a two-day period with King, DeKatch, Harrington and John Morley, the head of Flint's FBI office, before coming up with their profile.

It wasn't just some vague description, the psychological equivalent of saying to look out for someone of medium height, medium weight and sandy hair. *This* had detail, and lots of it.

The profile said that the killer had known Eby and was in her home on more than one occasion prior to the night of her killing. He was experiencing financial and job-related stress before the killing, and after it, had undergone a major personality change.

The killer was drinking and may also have indulged in light drugs before going to her home to talk to her. Once in her home, he realized he wasn't welcome. He may not have intended to kill her, but he may have acted out of anger and frustration, his inhibitions lowered by the alcohol.

After the killing, he went to a local bar to establish an alibi. He wanted to leave town, but needed to wait until after the body was found two days later, probably watching media reports to see when the discovery had been made.

After the body was found, he became withdrawn and nervous. He underwent his personality change, growing very rigid. He likely began feeling remorse and may have confided in someone what he had done, or given hints of it.

Of the profilers' meetings with Flint police, DeKatch told *The Flint Journal*: "The meetings went extremely well. Some initial findings and suspicions were confirmed."

If a recent high-profile case in Michigan was any clue, the Flint cops, Eby's family, her wide circle of friends, the community at large—all could be assured, said the Feds, that this profile would help move this case along. And probably dramatically.

The year before, said the Feds, another profile done by Harrington, of another serial killer in Michigan, had cracked a chain of unsolved murders wide open.

## 19
# THE 90-PERCENT PROFILE

It was 1985, and there was a serial rapist and killer of teenage boys on the loose in metropolitan Detroit.

Kenneth Meyers, 14, was kidnapped on July 16, 1984, from a parking lot near his home in Ferndale on Detroit's near north side. Two days later, his body was found in Hines Park, in the Westland portion of a greenbelt park along the Rouge River that ran for forty miles, from Northville in far western Wayne County, to Dearborn, near the Henry Ford Estate.

Shawn Moore, 13, was abducted on August 31, 1985, while riding his bike in Green Oak, west of the Detroit urban area. His body was found thirteen days later in the woods near a cabin outside Gladwin, a small town at the south end of Michigan's vast tourist area of lakes, beaches and woods known as "up north."

Other boys had reported being kidnapped and sexually assaulted.

Moore's abduction resonated particularly hard with one Redford teen, who had been kidnapped from the Livonia Mall and assaulted in June of 1984.

The kidnapper had driven him to Hines Park, made him drink two beers, then performed oral sex on him. His assailant then released him unharmed after warning him that if he told anyone, he would come back for him and kill him and the members of his family.

The boy kept quiet about the assault until the widespread publicity generated by the discovery of Moore's body. The boy told his mother, who convinced him to call police. The boy was so fearful of his attacker that it took Livonia police hours to convince him that it was okay, they would protect him. He finally gave a detailed description of his assailant.

On September 10, police in Brighton, the nearest city to Green Oak, grilled Ronald Bailey for twelve hours, but he was released after witnesses to Moore's abduction failed to pick him out of a lineup.

On September 12, an arrest warrant was issued for Bailey, but he had flown to Florida the day before. FBI agents got a tip he was in a trailer park in Ocala in central Florida, but as they were about to serve it, he fled into the dense, snake-infested woods nearby. He spent two days hiding in the woods before he was captured without incident seven miles away and returned to Michigan.

Bailey was a 26-year-old who looked more like 16. He was neatly groomed, with sandy hair cut on the long side and parted in the middle. Hidden by his boy-next-door exterior was a troubled past and a tortured present. When he was 13, he assaulted an 8-year-old and received counseling. In 1976, he had been charged with the kidnapping, sexual assault and attempted murder of a young boy and was committed to Northville State Hospital. Three years later, doctors at the psychiatric institution said Bailey was ready to rejoin society.

Later, one of Bailey's psychiatrists at Northville, Jose Tombo, was fired for allegedly having sexual relations with patients. It was alleged, but never proven, that Tombo had sexually abused Bailey numerous times.

Bailey moved to Florida from 1980 to 1983, where he was charged twice with contributing to the delinquency of minors by furnishing them with alcohol.

In September of 1986, Bailey was convicted of Moore's murder.

At his second murder trial in Wayne County in November, Bailey, as part of his insanity defense, took the stand and in graphic testimony admitted to having kidnapped at least fifteen boys in Michigan and Florida "for companionship and friendship. They were my friends . . . I'm a good, caring person but I have some bad problems."

He told a stunned courtroom that he killed Kenny Myers so "I'd be the last person he'd ever have sex with. I didn't want him to have normal sex with anyone else. He was so good looking. I was a little sexually excited because I knew he was dead."

After the mood of sexual excitement passed, Bailey said he cried "because my friend was dead."

On November 20, 1986, less than two weeks after Margarette Eby's rape and death in Flint, Bailey was sentenced to life in prison without the possibility of parole.

Jim Harrington's profile was just about a perfect match for Ronald Bailey. Harrington not so modestly claimed his profile to have fit Bailey to an accuracy of more than 90 percent. Another law-enforcement official said the profile was so thorough, it "contained everything about him except his name."

A month later, the FBI would trumpet Bailey's arrest and conviction as proof of the science behind their profiling. And trumpet Harrington as one of their stars.

"I feel we can quite easily paint a portrait of the killer," Douglas told the Flint media. The Feds had taken aim and woe be to Margarette Eby's murderer.

## 20
## A CHILDHOOD FRIEND

In the early days of the investigation, Dave King stopped by Eby's office at the University of Michigan–Flint campus. He went through the stuff on top of her desk, looked through its drawers, rummaged through her file cabinet, looked at the photos and odds and ends of decoration that go into personalizing one's office space.

The list of lovers from Eby's home was a good start, but

he wanted more to work with. If nothing else, her office would at least give him more of a feel for who she was.

He wasn't there long before Ray Roth, an associate professor in the school's music department and one of Eby's colleagues, walked in. It was one of those small-world-isn't-it? things. Roth had been the band director at Flint Southwestern when King went to school there, and the professor remembered the name and the face.

"One of your old classmates was in town visiting Margarette just before she died," said Roth, not passing on a tip so much as just chatting with an old acquaintance about mutual friends.

"Who?"

"Chuck Stone."

No kidding, thought King. To say he and Stone went back a long way was to put it mildly. They'd grown up in the same neighborhood and knew each other as far back as King could remember, though they'd gone their different ways after high school.

They'd gone to school together from kindergarten right on up. They went to Longfellow, a neighborhood K–9 school, then had ridden the bus together to Southwestern High for three years.

Everybody else called him "Chuck." For some reason, King had always called him "Charlie." Roth and King talked a bit about Stone and then King went back to his work.

Soon after, though, that casual conversation became anything but. King got a call on the Eby case from a tipster.

"Please don't tell anyone I'm calling," he implored. And went on to say that he thought the police ought to take a good look at his nephew, that he might have been involved in Eby's murder.

His nephew had been in town for two weeks and he'd had some contact with Margarette Eby. And his nephew was strange, too. Very strange. So much so that when he asked his uncle if he could stay with him while he was in town, his aunt put her foot down: "No!"

Some friends of his at the college ended up finding him some place to stay.

His nephew's name? Chuck Stone.

# 21

# JEFF AND BRENDA

It was Friday, November 21, two weeks to the day after Margarette Eby's murder. Brenda Fleming couldn't wait for her afternoon shift to end at the medical lab, where she worked as an office assistant, receiving specimens and routing them to the appropriate lab people to work on them. She and a co-worker were heading a few blocks over to the Nightingale bowling alley in Burton, outside of Flint, where her favorite local band, "In the Red," was playing.

The band performed top-40 covers and some of its own stuff, and a kick-butt female lead singer who got the place hopping separated it from the herd of cover bands on the weekend bar and lounge circuit around town.

They got off on time, no last-minute specimens to worry about, and hurried over to the bowling alley, ordered drinks and sat back to listen to the band.

Almost immediately, Brenda caught a good-looking, younger guy glancing her way.

"That guy's staring at me," said Brenda. She was short and chubby, but cute, too, cuter when she laughed her frequent laugh and her face lit up. But she wasn't the type guys usually stared at minutes after she entered a room.

The young man was playing a bar game called "quarter bounce" with his friends, the object being to bounce a quarter into a glass of beer. Between bounces, and sips of his beer, he kept looking at her.

Finally, near closing time, he walked over and asked her if he could have the last dance. She was happy to oblige.

After the dance, they talked. The guy—Jeff Gorton—was young, younger than she'd thought. She was 29, he was just 24. The five years' difference, though, took some of the pressure off in the game of singles-meet. Brenda felt herself relaxing a bit when he told her his age. Too young to be a prospect for anything more than a nice guy to talk to and dance with.

They seemed to hit it off.

"You going to be here next week?" he asked before leaving.

"No. My sister's coming in from out of town for Thanksgiving and we'll be busy all weekend," said Brenda.

The Friday after Thanksgiving, Brenda and her co-worker returned to the Nightingale. Jeff was there. Waiting for her. "And we've been friends ever since," says Brenda, emphasizing the word "friends." She enjoyed his banter, his sense of humor, the ease he felt with her and she with him.

Brenda, the youngest of three sisters, is a daughter of Flint, too. Her father worked the line at GM his whole adult life, turning out Buicks by the thousands. Her mother had an office job with the company. Growing up, Brenda always worked. She cleaned houses, sold make-up, worked in a furniture store and a pharmacy, went to tech school, then started her career as a medical assistant.

The Flemings were uncomplicated folks elevated to middle-class status by union pay and the overtime that often rolled in during Flint's heyday. There was usually a nice car in the driveway and even a summer cabin up north.

The family didn't pay much attention to current events. World affairs and the latest news were of little interest.

Less than a month after that second meeting, Brenda and Jeff were close enough that she brought him to Christmas dinner at her brother-in-law Dan Loga's house in suburban Grand Blanc. Though the family naturally thought something was up, what with Brenda bringing a guy she'd just met to the family Christmas dinner, to her, "We were still just friends. I thought he was too young for me, but he kept on pursuing me."

To Jeff's surprise, Brenda's mom had bought him a gift, so he wouldn't feel bad being the only one not having something to open. He seemed stunned at the generosity, and pleasantly taken aback by the camaraderie and loud byplay that accompanied a Fleming family dinner. Brenda would later learn that his family wasn't much for presents, not much for family celebrations, not much for loudness and laughter.

Dan, who'd met Brenda when she was in the fifth grade and he, a tenth-grader, had followed her sister home from school one day, regarded the young suitor a bit wistfully—he was young, unmarried, good-looking, no obligations. "He has the world by the gonads," Dan thought.

Jeff was a charmer, and Brenda wasn't necessarily some-one used to being charmed. Or pursued. She liked it, and she found herself liking Jeff more and more.

On New Year's Eve, they met again at the Nightingale, which was decorated for the big night. There were flowers at each table. Jeff grabbed a batch and presented them to her.

The circus was coming to town and at some point Brenda mentioned it'd be nice to go. Next thing you know, there's Jeff, tickets in hand. "That's the way he was. Anything I ever wanted, I got. It wasn't a relationship I had to work at," says Brenda.

It didn't hurt, either, that he thought she was sexy. He wanted her with a passion that was flattering. It wasn't long before everyone, Brenda included, considered them an item. He was no longer just a friend. His age hadn't mattered one whit.

Soon, they were living together in Brenda's mobile home. Jeff was happy to have settled down. Happy to stop hanging out in the bars so much with the guys after work, where it wasn't unusual for them to pound down ten or twelve beers in a night.

They were sure enough of their relationship that, though they weren't married, they bought a house together on a large lot on Tuscola Road in Vienna, north of Flint. They bought it for $36,000, closing the deal on February 25, 1988. That was another plus to the guy. He was young and fun, but serious, too, and doing well in the family business. Able to qualify for a mortgage, smart enough to know that renting didn't make much sense. Though one thing seemed odd—he hadn't been interested in looking at houses. Brenda had picked it out on her own and decided it was the one for them, and he'd agreed, sight unseen.

In February of 1989, Jeff was the best man at his brother Greg's wedding. It was a simple affair, with a justice of the peace, and the reception at Greg and Jeff's parents' large house next door to the family sprinkler business.

Brenda caught the bouquet.

After the good-natured cheers and huzzahs from the crowd, Jeff said, a big smile on his face: "Go get a calendar." It was time, he said, to get married themselves.

She got a calendar and they started flipping through the

months. They settled on September 22, 1990 for their wedding day.

On Sweetest Day in October of 1989, Jeff had a surprise. It was a holiday, and Jeff was big on holidays. He took Brenda's hand casually, and while talking to her, diverting her attention, he slipped an engagement ring on her hand. "He'd picked it out and got it on my hand without me knowing it," says Brenda.

Her friends threw her a bachelorette party and hired a male stripper. One of her gifts was a pair of white lace G-string underpants.

One of her friends at the party was Marci, a co-worker at the medical lab. In the small world that Flint could be, she had known Jeff before she knew Brenda. Brenda confided in her that Jeff had told her he'd been in a little trouble when he was in the Navy in Florida. The manager of his trailer park had accused him of window-peeping, but he and the manager had worked it out and the police hadn't been involved.

Like others, Marci thought Jeff was very smart. One thing that stood out was that he couldn't stand still. He was always swaying.

At the wedding reception, at a hall down the road from the family business, Brenda's brother-in-law, Dan, was struck by the contrast between Brenda's family and Jeff's.

Brenda's side of the family was loud, gregarious, full of noise and laughter and joy. Dan's wife, son and daughter were all in the wedding party—Brenda's sister was maid of honor—and Brenda's clan in general came dressed to the nines, tuxedos, gowns, the works. Gorton's father refused to wear a tux and came in a business suit.

Jeff's parents, Laurence and Shirley, kept to themselves at the reception, didn't seem to Dan to be having much fun, ate their dinner and left early. "They just disappeared," says Dan. He remembers thinking then, and being reinforced in the belief over the years, that Jeff's mother, a small woman, was dominated by his father. When not with him, Shirley was intelligent, generally quiet but nonetheless a good conversationalist. When Laurence was there, silence.

"She bent to his will and that was it," says Dan.

Jeff and Brenda's honeymoon was as traditional as Jeff could make it. He wanted everything just right. He took her to the Oakes Hotel at Niagara Falls, where he sprang a surprise on her. What she'd thought was just going to be a two-day stay there—fall was a busy season for the sprinkler business, and he couldn't spare much time away from work—was a five-day honeymoon, instead.

That surprise was so he could cover up another surprise, which needed the extra days. For generations, Flint area residents who wanted something special in the way of furniture shopped at a store called Peerless. It said something about you if you had a Peerless dining room set or a Peerless bedroom suite.

Over Labor Day, Brenda and Jeff had window-shopped at the store. It was closed, but there was a top-line bedroom suite in the showroom window and Brenda had pointed it out. "Isn't that cool?" she'd said. But it was $3,000, and who in the world could afford that much?

Jeff, that's who. As Brenda found out when they returned to Flint from Buffalo. While they were gone, Peerless had delivered the suite and his dad had coordinated his schedule so he could be there to let the delivery crew in.

When Brenda walked into the bedroom, there it was, the exact one she'd pointed out. And she hadn't even been sure he'd been paying attention. They'd only been window-shopping. But that's the kind of guy Jeff was, always full of surprises. Always considerate. They didn't wait long to see if the bed was as comfortable as it looked. That's the kind of guy Jeff was, too. Interested in sex, and interested in Brenda. A few months later, she was pregnant.

Their first child, Wally, was born on Oct. 18, 1991. Jenny was born May 6, 1994. Jeff was in the delivery room for both births.

Jeff grew close to Brenda's family. He was the master of ceremonies at the annual fireworks show at the family cabin in Hersey, outside of Clare, the city that denotes the demarcation between the farmland of central Michigan and the tourist mecca of "up north."

The cabin was a retreat her parents had owned for thirty-five years, and each summer her siblings, in-laws, nieces and nephews flocked there to see if Jeff could top last year's show.

Fourth of July seemed to last a month. Gorton would collect $20 a head from members of the extended family and go to Indiana to buy as much cool stuff as he could. Fourth of July was the big day, of course, but for days before and after there'd be fireworks going off at the cabin.

Father's Day was also a big deal in Brenda's family. Different family members would host it each year and sixty or more would show up for a full day of eating and drinking and shooting the bull. Jeff loved the day, would happily man the video camera and film away.

And each year, either after Thanksgiving or near Christmas, fourteen or so members of the extended Fleming clan would go to the Midland Valley Plaza Hotel in central Michigan for a weekend getaway, playing in the pool and going out for dinner, and Jeff was always included.

Jeff was active in church, and at school. He rarely drank—rum and Coke once in a while, or a beer. He'd never smoked cigarettes. Did a joint once in a while if someone offered it, but that was about it. He helped his kids with their homework. When Brenda's best friend got divorced, and was wracked with depression and stress, Jeff was there for her, offering a shoulder to cry on and lots of good advice. He'd help Brenda plan showers for her girlfriends.

He was a good husband and a good father. It was a good marriage, though he'd confided in his best man at the wedding, Kevin Bosh, an old friend from high school, that it bugged him that Brenda wasn't much for cleaning house or cooking. Jeff, a compulsive neatnik, was always picking up after her.

If there was one thing about Jeff that Brenda could have changed, she'd have done it in a heartbeat. Jeff was so nervous it'd drive you crazy if you let it. He didn't like to sit. At family functions, you'd never see him sitting. He'd always be standing. Or pacing. If he did sit, he rocked. And standing or sitting, he bit his nails.

"He rocked twenty-four/seven. And he bit his nails twenty-four/seven," says Brenda. "We'd watch TV at night and he'd rock, and he'd bite his nails."

She got used to it. It wasn't so big a deal that she couldn't ignore it. No one's perfect.

Brenda wasn't the first woman Jeff had charmed. She wasn't the first woman to bear his child. She wasn't the first woman to think he had strange habits worth overlooking. There was the girl he'd met at Rollerworld in 1981, Dawn Thierbach. He charmed the heck out of her, too, got her pregnant in her sophomore year in high school, and did the right thing and married her.

## 22
## AN ANGUISHED DIARY

Gorton's 1980 high-school yearbook credited him as being one of the "outstanding players" who contributed to the chess club's third-place finish in the regional tournament and a seventh-place finish at the state tournament. He was the number-2 man on the team and his best buddy, Joe Contreras, was number 3.

A photo in the 1981 yearbook, the year he graduated—coincidentally, he attended Flint Southwestern, the same school as Dave King, Gary Elford and Charlie Stone—shows Jeff leaning over a typewriter. "Jeff Gorton, expert typist, keeps his eraser close at hand," reads the caption.

Contreras met Jeff in the ninth grade, when they both tried out for and made the freshman football team. Neither of them played much. Neither were what you'd call in with the in crowd. Jeff had horrible acne, just an excruciating complexion that made him very, very self-conscious. Quiet by nature, he was extra quiet when it came to girls. Jeff had many acquaintances, few close friends. He had good connections for obtaining pot and beer, which made some of the acquaintances act as if they liked him more than they really did.

Joe, though, was a legitimate best friend, and Jeff spent a lot of time at his house. Once, Jeff confided in Joe that he felt jealous at how warm and close Joe's family was. Jeff's parents impressed Joe as being cold and aloof, anything but warm.

Jeff got to be friends with Joe's younger sister, Nora, too.

Nora never let boys in her bedroom, but Jeff was the exception. He'd come in and they'd talk. Nora never said anything to Joe about it, but one time after Jeff had been in visiting, she couldn't find a pair of black-and-white underwear.

Jeff had a crush on a girl named Tina their junior year. She and some other friends attended one of their chess matches and Jeff was supposed to drive them all out for pizza after. When it came time to pile in the car, Tina got in the back seat between Joe and Greg, instead of in the front with Jeff. Jeff got so mad, he took her straight home instead of stopping for pizza. Later that night, she committed suicide by overdosing on drugs. No one blamed Jeff, they thought it was just a coincidence. Still, if they'd gone out for pizza, who knows?

Most of the kids they knew smoked pot and drank frequently, Jeff less so than most of them, and a lot less than Joe. Jeff didn't study much and used to impress his friends by pulling down A's and B's anyway.

Jeff also ran track briefly, but decided he'd rather have gas money and spending money than a letter sweater, so he quit sports to work part-time. His dad, stern, old-fashioned, a task-master, was much happier having his son work than waste time playing sports.

In 1978 and 1979, Jeff worked as a stock boy at Sears. In 1980 he helped his dad in the new company business, installing lawn sprinklers. And in 1980 and '81 he was a stock boy at the Big C Market in Flint.

Two months before he graduated, Jeff met Dawn Leigh Ann Thierbach at Rollerworld. Dawn was there with Dawn Gach, her best friend since they were 8 or 9. Gach knew Jeff from hanging around the rink and had something of a crush on him. She introduced him to her friend. Jeff wasn't Dawn Thierbach's type—he had bad acne and seemed kind of geeky—but he was charming, paid her a lot of attention and basically swept her off her feet. She didn't just think he was smart, she thought he was brilliant. Part of it was that he was 18 and a senior and she was just a 16-year-old sophomore at Ainsworth High. And he had a cool teal-and-white 1974 Buick Regal, too.

Figuratively and literally she was swept off her feet. By June, she was pregnant.

The first few attempts at sex, she would later recount, Jeff hadn't been able to get an erection. But finally, in the parking lot of the Genesee Valley Mall, they succeeded. From then on, they had sex on a daily basis. He would park down the street from her house in Flint and wait for her father to leave for work. Then they'd have sex before going to school.

Gorton and Contreras were both accepted for the fall term at U-M–Flint after graduating from Southwestern. Jeff signed up for introductory anthropology, college rhetoric, U.S. history since 1987, math and computer use 1, thirteen credits in all. In August, shortly after Dawn returned home from summer Bible camp, he broke up with her, and in September he started school.

But on October 23, both Jeff and Joe had withdrawn from school and on October 30, they enlisted in the Navy, signing up in a buddy program that would allow them to go to basic training together. Meanwhile, panicking over her advancing pregnancy, Dawn was frantically trying to get back together with Jeff. She left him notes, she called him, she begged and pleaded. She would later acknowledge that she'd continually hounded him on her mission to get married.

Her junior year of high school, Dawn kept a diary in a daily planner. Her entries for December of 1981 and January of 1982, printed in the tiniest cramped letters, maybe an eighth of an inch high, show a frantic, lovesick girl.

Sunday, December 27, she wrote: "I don't know if Jeff had to work or not. I haven't talked to him since yesterday. I do miss him a lot. Hopefully I'll get to see him tomorrow. Jeff never called me today."

Monday she had an appointment with her pediatrician. Jeff came home from work early and they were together from 5–10 p.m. She told Jeff she hated the baby but admitted in her diary that she was lying. It's her way, she said, of not getting attached. She seemed to be thinking of giving the baby up when it is born.

Tuesday, she called Jeff, who promised to call her back, but didn't. So Dawn went to see him at work. He told her, again, that he'd call. Again, he didn't. She was scared he was out partying with Greg and Randy.

Wednesday Jeff came by, an hour later than she was expecting, and they went to a friend's so Jeff could work on his car. They had a big fight when he dropped her off because he didn't want to see her on New Year's. "It really does hurt to know that I can't get to spend the New Year with the father of my child. I really do miss him. It never works out my way."

Thursday, New Year's Eve, her parents had a party. Everyone having fun made her feel extra lonely. At midnight she held Jeff's bracelet and picture and "had a dance . . . It was so lonely and the worst New Year's ever."

Saturday, January 2, she went to see Jeff at work. They had had a talk and she concluded, "I don't think he believes that it's his baby." If she couldn't get Jeff back, she wrote, she was going to give up the baby because it's not right to have just one parent. "Maybe because I love him so much I have to let him go and forget about him. He's giving me pity and I want love."

Day after day it went on. She really did love him. He didn't call. He didn't stop by. She went to his work. She called him at home. She kept track of when he got in. She stayed up calling him until he got in, no matter the hour. If he got in late, she wrote that he told her they hadn't been partying, or that he'd only had one joint.

On his day off, she went over and woke him up, demanding answers for why he didn't come by the day before. He promised they hadn't been partying. They were just playing cards. "We promised each other to talk things over. I also made him a bet that he couldn't go without partying for two days," she wrote.

One day he promised to come over the next day at 2 p.m. for three hours. She wrote that it wasn't enough, they had so much to make up for. So the next day she called first thing and asked him to come over earlier. He said he would try. He showed up at 2:10 smelling of pot and she blew up. She apologized. He accepted. "We were just holding each other. It was terrific," she wrote.

January 11, Dawn went to the doctor. She'd gained ten pounds. After, Jeff came by and he held her and told her he cared about her, and Dawn wrote she wished every day could be like that. Jeff had been awfully friendly lately and maybe he was changing his mind about marrying her, but she doubted it.

January 13, she was going to drive over to his house in the morning but the car had a flat and that got her crying. So she called Jeff and asked him to come by. He said he would at noon, but didn't. She called at 1 p.m. He was shoveling snow and said he'd call back. He didn't. He did stop over, though. Dawn came to the door crying, and he wanted to know what was wrong. He left at 2:30 a.m. "Everything's perfect," she wrote. "Everything's solved."

The 14th, she'd decided Jeff didn't care, after all. His brother was saying mean stuff about her and she worried Jeff believed it. It seemed like it'd be an eternity before she could see him.

She saw him the next day. He said he'd come over from 1 to 5, but he got there at 1:50. He wanted to feel the baby kick. He promised to call that night but never did. Was he out partying with Joe? She's going to insist the next day that he stay with her till he goes to work.

Sunday, the 17th, she called Jeff in the morning but he'd already left for work. He called her at 7:30 p.m. "It greatly shocked me. It must mean that he cares a little about me," she wrote.

Monday, her car battery wouldn't turn over. She called him crying. She said she didn't want to be trapped in the house and he said he wouldn't come over and they had a fight. She called him before he left for work and apologized, though she told her diary she knew she wasn't wrong.

Tuesday, Jeff said he'd come over because she missed him so much but he never showed up. So she went looking for him and found him at Joe's. He said he'd call at 9:30 a.m. She was in night school and had her final in history and then hurried home but he never called.

Thursday, the 21st, her birth classes started. Jeff went with her. The class started at 6 p.m. and they showed movies till 8 and then handed out gift packs. Then they went to Playland South, but she couldn't go in because the last time they were there was when she told Jeff she was going to have an abortion, so it was gonna hurt too much to go back in, again. Jeff understood and took her for an ice cream instead, and then they had an argument about the next day when Dawn said they were supposed to go out with Joe and Michelle. And then Jeff had to go to Big C to get some money from a

friend. "I do love him and tonight he proved that he cares
about me. It was perfect."

According to Dawn, victory occurred on February 22, 1982,
the day she says they finally got back together as boyfriend
and girlfriend and, parked in a car near the Humane Society
in Flint, he promised to marry her. The two of them drove to
her house to break the news to her mom.

On the 28th, Gorton and Contreras left for Detroit. They
officially began their tour of duty the next day, and they arrived in Florida on March 2.

Dawn would tell friends that Jeff joined the Navy because Flint was going through one of its periodic downturns.
Weren't any good jobs to be had for a high-school graduate.

But Gorton told his friends another story. When he joined
the Navy, he had no intention of marrying her. He was getting the hell out because Dawn was knocked up and he
didn't think the baby was his. Hell, they'd been broken up
when she gave him the news. What kind of crap was that?
She was putting the pressure on, putting the pressure on, putting the pressure on. "It was a crazy time," he would say
years later. "I was trying to get away from a kid. She was
pregnant and trying to make me think it was mine. I told her
I didn't think it was mine."

On March 28, their son, Jeffery—same pronunciation as
the dad, different spelling—was born in Flint. Jeff had
promised to call and write, but hardly ever did.

On May 14, Dawn, little Jeffery and her mother all flew
to Orlando for the weekend and met with Jeff. Whatever they
said worked. Jeff finished basic training on June 11, flew to
Flint and they were married on June 12. Greg DeDolph was
the best man.

However it had come about, they were man and wife.
Dawn was about the happiest person on earth. She was des-
perately in love and she'd landed her man, who was the father of her child. That she knew for a fact.

She didn't stay happy for long. The day after their marriage,
Jeff started training at the Navy's Great Lakes Training Facility in Chicago. Dawn and little Jeff moved to Chicago,
too. Things went downhill fast. After his day of training was

over, he'd stay out who-knew-where till all hours. In July, saying she was lonely in Illinois, Dawn returned to Flint for two weeks. Jeff didn't seem the least upset to see her go.

By September, all was seemingly well again. Jeff was transferred back to Orlando, accompanied by his family, and began training in the nuclear program at the Orlando Naval Base. The last day in Chicago had been odd though. Jeff had rented a U-Haul and they'd packed their stuff. But their last night in Chicago, Jeff said he had pulled guard duty and would be gone all night, which struck Dawn as odd since he'd never had guard duty in his summer of training. He rolled in at 7 or 8 a.m., and they got in the car and headed to Florida.

Once in Florida, living in a trailer park, she began to feel lonely again. Jeff was gone all the time. Things were nice at Christmas, though, with her family down to spend the holidays with them. They all managed to get out of Orlando for a few days, traveling down the West Coast to stay a couple of nights at her aunt's house in the Naples–Ft. Myers area.

All in all, things were going well. Jeff's training at the nuclear power school was going well, his skin was clearing up, and the Navy regimen had taken off a few pounds and trimmed him up. In high school he smoked a little pot, drank a little beer. Now, though, he was Mr. Clean, a non-smoker, non-drinker, non-drug user. He was quiet, didn't argue or raise his voice with Dawn. The only thing that made him mad was a mess around the house. He liked things ship-shape, a pretty good trait for a guy in the Navy. Their life was looking good.

## 23
## BRILLIANT BUT TROUBLED

Charlie moved right to King's front burner. He was a hot suspect, and the more King dug, the hotter he got.

Stone had, in fact, been in town for two weeks, and was in town when Eby died. He had known Eby through church and through the Basically Bach festival. Then, Eby had held out hope that Stone would become a major contributor through a rich aunt. But others told King they thought the aunt was just a fiction by Stone, and Eby had been angry when she found out he'd been stringing her along.

While in town in the fall of 1986, Stone had not only stopped by Eby's office, but had been at the school's swimming pool when Eby was doing laps one day. Word was that, by then, Eby considered him harmless, nothing more.

Soon after the murder, Stone left town, presumably returning to his home near the campus of the University of Delaware.

From their days of growing up together, King remembered Stone as being absolutely brilliant. His father was a professor at the General Motors Institute, a world-class engineering school where GM groomed its best and brightest. His father had always pushed Chuck to academic excellence. King remembered Stone was always taking what they called "intensives" in high school, accelerated courses reserved for brains.

Slight and short, Stone had been social enough when they were playing together in the neighborhood as 6- and 7-year-olds, but by high school he had developed a bad stutter and seemed to have regressed socially. He turned into a loner.

Stone went to the University of Michigan in Ann Arbor and was accepted into its prestigious medical school, where he was a brilliant student. But he had lost most of his ability to interact socially, and did so poorly during the clinical rotations at the end of medical school, where he was required to interact with doctors and patients in hospital settings, that he was washed out of the program.

Stone, possessor of a master's degree in biochemistry, eventually left Michigan and ended up in Delaware, where he took a job delivering pizzas for Domino's. The University of Delaware had the same basic school colors as the University of Michigan, blue and gold. A coincidence? Or some weird psychological sign? Brilliant med student ends up on another campus with similar colors and logos as his alma mater, delivering pizzas to students.

There was no end to Stone's quirkiness. He was the kind of guy who'd write to the CEO of Nabisco asking for a job, then for years carry around in his wallet the form letter that came back saying they didn't have any jobs for someone of his qualifications. It wasn't a sign of rejection; on the other hand, it was proof of his contacts, a letter from upper management at Nabisco, for God's sake. And he'd carry a note in his pocket detailing future phone conversations he hoped to have with people.

About the time Stone had become a focus of the investigation, and not merely a name on a list, the FBI released its profile.

The killer knew Eby well enough to be in her home? Well, Stone knew her well enough to visit her in her office and at a swimming pool. The killer was experiencing financial and job-related stress? Well, delivering pizzas in your thirties couldn't be lucrative, or fun. The killer had undergone a major personality change? Stone had gone from affable nerdiness to stuttering social misfit. Perhaps he had crossed the line from misfit to madman. And, the Feds said, the killer would wait until Eby's body was found, then leave town. Stone had been in town before her murder, was in town over the weekend of her death, and had left shortly thereafter.

There was one other thing. Stone's dad had accumulated a collection of World War II knives over the years. Stone had recently pawned them in Lansing. What was the Eby murder weapon? A knife. And why would you drive an hour to Lansing to pawn a set of knives when there were dozens of pawn shops right in Flint?

Early in February, they decided it was time to pay Stone a visit.

## 24
## A CHASE

It was a long and boring drive. Stone's uncle gave them his address, in Landenberg, Pa., near where Delaware, Pennsylvania and Maryland converge. There wasn't a lot of travel budget in the Flint PD. DeKatch and King drove there in a black unmarked vehicle that screamed "COP CAR!"

DeKatch talked the whole way there—and back—about

his marriage, how he had screwed up by having an affair, how it was falling apart, how sorry he was.

(DeKatch would have lots more to talk about in coming years. Once Flint's most quotable, and quoted, cop, by the mid-1990s he had become an object of derision and pity. He retired from the Flint PD, took a job as chief of police in Flint, then went to work for a company that sold law-enforcement software to police departments. His wife went through with their divorce. While trying to pay his daughter's private-school tuition, DeKatch stole some of his landlord's checks and forged them, was caught and prosecuted. He avoided jail time with a guilty plea and got two years' probation in 1996. Later he took a job as a greeter at Brown's Funeral Home on Flint's east side.)

Stone was renting a room in an upscale neighborhood of elaborate three-story homes. The subdivision had one exit out onto the highway, so it would be easy to do a stakeout. They parked at a good vantage point when it was still dark and waited for Stone's car to go by.

"The plan was to follow him, see where he went, how he behaved," says King. "We knew he had a drunk-driving conviction on his record. Maybe we'd tail him to a bar and DeKatch would go in and strike up a conversation."

Early on the first morning of their stakeout, Stone drove past them in his junky Citation. There was a rise on the highway just after the exit from the subdivision, and they let him go over the rise before they pulled up. They crested the rise, too and . . . they couldn't see him. They were sure he hadn't spotted them, or, if he had, could not have known who they were, but in any event, he must have floored it. "He was hauling ass," said King later.

King floored it, too, getting the big cop car up to 90 mph. Soon, they had him in sight. He was pulling into Newark. They saw him turn right at a light, which they made, too. They pulled up behind him at the next light. He looked left, then right, then floored it through the red light.

That gave King a jolt of adrenaline. What was up with that? Why was he in such a hurry? Had he made them?

Stone pulled into a gas station. King decided it was time for Plan B. King pulled the cop car in, blocking Stone's car, and got out.

Stone recognized him right away. "Oh, Dave King!" He was clearly surprised. He hadn't made them.

King introduced DeKatch, told him who they were and asked if they could buy him breakfast at a restaurant across the street while they explained what this was all about.

Over breakfast, DeKatch played bad cop, King played good cop, their usual roles.

Stone admitted visiting Eby, saying he knew her through the First Presbyterian Church. He denied any knowledge of her murder. He denied any involvement. But, then, he also denied running a red light twenty minutes earlier.

Stone seemed happy to talk with them. There was this conspiracy they ought to know about. Remember that series of killings years ago at the VA hospital in Ann Arbor? Filipino nurses did it, remember? There's this guy that flunked me out of medical school and he's the same guy who got those nurses to kill those guys. Somebody oughta do something about him. Same guy flunked me out of school. Conspired against me. Made stuff up. Now he's killing people.

King got him back on track. He and DeKatch took a formal statement from him and asked him if he'd be willing to take a polygraph. To their surprise, he agreed.

They made hasty arrangements to have a polygraph test at a nearby Pennsylvania State Police post, and Stone met them there at 6 p.m. that night.

What happened next is open to debate. Stone took the polygraph, administered by one of the Pennsylvania State Police polygraph experts. King and DeKatch were not allowed in the room while the test went on.

Officially, Stone passed it, meaning he didn't seem to be lying when asked questions about Eby's murder.

But in King's mind, Stone flunked the test. The expert administering it told King that Stone had exhibited "indicators of deception." To this day King isn't sure what that meant and wishes he'd asked for more of an explanation.

Actually, King did have an explanation. Fitting the facts to his theory—a no-no in detective work—or, more accurately, fitting the facts to his long-held impression of Stone as some sort of genius, King figured his chief suspect had merely outwitted him.

He'd had most of the day to get ready for his test, right?

King thought he'd probably gone over to the university library and looked up all there was to look up on polygraphs. He'd probably read about how you can beat the test. And then he'd shown up at 6 and beat it. Well, not exactly. He might have gotten the big questions right, but he'd been nervous enough to give the examiner pause.

Stone signed a consent form, and they took back samples of his pubic hair, scalp hair, blood and saliva on their long drive back to Michigan. They also took hair samples from his cats, Sam and Tigger, and his dogs, Akita and Samson.

DeKatch wouldn't stop talking and King couldn't stop thinking that Stone was their man. Sooner or later, one way or another, they were going to prove it.

They turned in Stone's hair and blood samples and his animals' hair samples on January 12. Michael Thomas reported back on January 23 that Stone's prints did not match the bloody print in the bathroom.

Other reports, reflecting the glacial pace of the technology of the time, came back in late May. On May 26 came the report on hair and vaginal samples taken from Eby's body. She was blood type O. Swabs from her vagina showed the presence of sperm, but the only typing they could get was also O. Either the killer was type O, or his semen had been degraded by time and heat from the blanket to a point where it was useless and the O in the sample was Eby's. Sperm was hardier than seminal fluid, but it was the fluid chemists needed to run their tests. No conclusions could be drawn.

The same day, the report came in telling King that none of the hairs from Stone's animals matched hairs found at the murder scene.

On May 27 came the report on Stone. None of his hairs, scalp or pubic, matched the hairs found at the scene. His blood type was O, with a phosphoglucomutase (PGM) subgrouping of 1+2+.

With the vaginal samples from Eby being inconclusive, Stone was still a suspect. What was one reason for Eby's samples to test as O, no other blood type present? That her killer was an O, too. And what was Stone? An O.

Never mind that everyone who knew Stone told King he might be a total fruitcake, but no way was he a killer.

# 25

# THE PRIVATE EYE

King and DeKatch weren't the only ones on Stone's trail. The Ebys were, too. Or, rather, the private investigator they hired.

It was a somber Thanksgiving for the Eby children, less than three weeks after their mom's murder. They gathered at their dad's parents', who had been devastated by the news.

One of their relatives asked what they were going to do about the murder. The kids hadn't been planning to do anything. It was in the cops' hands.

The relative said if it had been her mom, she'd do more. She'd hire a private investigator and get to the bottom of things.

Lynn disagreed, but that planted the bug. Her siblings eventually decided to hire a PI out of Ann Arbor named Thomas Reed. Jonathan had his first meeting with him on September 20, 1987.

"We ended up spending a fortune on him," says Lynn. The money came out of the proceeds from their mother's estate. The PI talked to the Flint cops. He filed report after report, mostly in log form: "11/4/87 at 9 a.m., returned J. Eby's phone call; 11/4/87 at 10:30 p.m., spoke with J. Eby; 11/4/87 at 10:35 p.m., spoke with D. Eby; 11/5/87 at 10 p.m., left message for D. Eby; 11/6/87 at 8 a.m., spoke with D. Eby." And so on.

"He just kept sending us these reports. I couldn't stand the guy," says Lynn.

Unlike some PIs, Reed seemed to enjoy the limelight, not hanging back in the shadows. He managed to alert the Flint reporters who he was and was quoted in the paper nearing the first anniversary of Eby's death that even if he were fired he'd keep working the case because it was so unusual.

"I'll work on this until I reach a conclusion," he said in an article on November 7, though there is no evidence that he continued to work it once he was fired.

In another article on November 19, he said he was work-

ing numerous new leads and might soon release a composite
sketch of a new suspect. He never did.

In his log, the PI would note things like: "11/6/87 at 1:30
p.m., spoke with Todd Seibt of *The Flint Journal* and gave
him details of how we were going to proceed with the investigation"; and "11/6/87 at 3:10 p.m., spoke with newscaster
Barb Schroeder from TV 12 concerning the investigation";
and "11/13/87 at 3 p.m., talked with Barb Schroeder, who
wanted to know if, in fact, we were meeting the following
Tuesday at 3 p.m. with the Flint Police Department."

He traveled to Boston and Florida, conducting interviews
with former friends and colleagues of their mother and,
though he told King he disagreed with him about Stone being a viable suspect, he traveled to Pennsylvania, too.

For his visit to Stone, he flew to Philadelphia and rented a
car on May 31, 1988, and stayed till June 6. On June 1, he
found out from the Newark, Del., police that Stone had recently been in trouble with them. He'd been hanging around
the library at the University of Delaware, trying to strike up
oddball conversations with women, some of whom were
frightened and called police. The cops asked him not to return to the library.

Other than that, he'd had no trouble with any police
agency in the tri-state area.

Except for his brief conversation with police, the first
three days of the detective's trip were fruitless, uneventful
and expensive for the Ebys. He recorded sixteen hours of
billable time the first day, eleven the second, fourteen the
third. In three days of trying, he never even saw Stone,
couldn't verify that he still lived where King and DeKatch
found him, couldn't find the car he thought Stone was driving, a Chevy Citation of 1974–88 vintage. He went to the
place where he thought Stone worked, but he hadn't worked
there for a year.

On the fourth day, things improved. They were still fruitless, still expensive, but at least they got comedic. Reed
staked out Stone's supposed residence in Landenberg from
5:20 a.m. to 4:30 p.m., apparently just staring at the house,
waiting to see Stone or his Chevy. His report to the Ebys of
the day is unintentionally funny. "I simply couldn't take the
chance of wasting additional time . . . I decided to contact

one of the neighbors," he wrote. A brainstorm! "As it worked out, this was the best thing to do. I went to the residence next door to Mr. Stone's residence and spoke with a lady at the household at 4:30 p.m. She indicated that she knew Charlie Stone quite well but didn't feel comfortable going into specific detail and asked that I come back at approximately 5:30 p.m. to speak with her husband."

The husband, he reported, provided a wealth of information. Such as, Stone was still living next door and occasionally took trips out of town for two or three days. He delivered pizza for Domino's in downtown Newark and used to deliver pizzas in New Castle, Del. And—what a surprise, given that he delivered pizzas—he generally worked afternoons and evenings.

He also told Reed that Stone hung out after work at Klondike Kate's, a bar popular with University of Delaware students. So, the detective decided to stake out Klondike Kate's, from the inside, and await Stone's post-midnight arrival. "I hoped to run into him," he wrote in his report to the Ebys. "Mr. Stone ended up not showing up, and I called Domino's Pizza and found out that he ended up working late. This happens to be a very busy franchise . . . Note: This was approximately a 16-hour day."

June 4 was a Saturday. The detective wrote that he decided not to try to talk to Stone at his house before going to work but would wait till he got to work. "In conducting limited surveillance at this particular establishment, I was able to verify that it was not unusual for individuals to stop by the Domino's Pizza and pick up their own pizzas," the detective duly reported. Surveillance has its rewards.

Hence, a plan. At 7:45 p.m., the detective went into Domino's and ordered a pizza. While waiting, he would look for the opportunity to strike up a casual conversation with his quarry. Only one problem. The quarry was on a delivery. Timing is everything.

The detective got lucky, though. Stone came back before Reed started arousing suspicion by not carrying out his carry-out pizza, and the detective did, indeed, strike up a conversation. He was going to be in town for a week, wondered what was a good place for some action. Stone told him about Klondike Kate's. The detective thanked him and said he'd try it, and if Stone wanted to stop by later, he'd buy him a drink.

Back to Klondike's, on the Ebys' dime. Where Stone did not go after work. The best laid plans . . .

Sunday, the detective called Stone's neighbor at 2:20 p.m. and verified that Stone was home. He got there twenty minutes later. Stone's car was gone. Just missed him, said the neighbor. He left and pulled onto Route 896 just in time to see Stone driving by in the opposite direction. Reed pulled a U-turn and followed Stone to a rural cemetery, where he got out and started taking photographs of headstones.

"I drove by him based on the fact that it would have been very unusual for me to run into him out in the country after meeting him at the pizza establishment," he wrote in his report. No wonder Lynn Rimer was pulling her hair out.

That night the detective had a plan. He'd go back to Domino's, order another pizza and strike up a conversation with Stone. The déjà-vu plan, you could call it. He ordered his pizza and thanked Stone for the tip on Klondike Kate's, but said it was too young a crowd and did Stone have any other suggestions for a cool place to hang out?

Bennigan's, Stone replied. Lots of women there.

"I stated that I would be in town for approximately one more week, and I asked him to join me for a drink. I again stated to him that I knew no one in town. Mr. Stone was very polite and seemed somewhat excited about my conversation with him. He indicated that he wouldn't mind at all having a drink with me," the detective wrote.

"Somewhat excited" must be a relative term. For Stone also told him that since he was working late each night for the next week, he was going to have to pass on that drink offer.

At least it was only a six-hour day.

In six days, Reed had talked to Stone twice, about places to hang out in Newark—maybe he was hoping to get Stone drunk before he mentioned the reason for the trip, Margarette Eby—learned that Stone still lived where he used to live, still drove the car he used to drive, still delivered pizzas and still worked late. There'd been the pizza, though, and he'd gotten to watch college kids getting hammered at Klondike Kate's, so the trip wasn't without its rewards.

The detective had one day left. He made it through all of it without surveilling the Domino's or ordering another pie.

The report of his final day reads: "On Monday, June 6, 1988 I ended up contacting an individual I believe to be a reliable informant. I would be glad to give you more detailed information concerning this individual and how he may be contacted. I ended up taking a late flight out based on the fact that it was the most inexpensive fare. Note: This was approximately a 14-and-one-half-hour day. Please do not hesitate to contact me if you have any questions concerning the information stated in this report."

Spencer, he wasn't. Questions, there were none. What was to question? Deep dish or regular?

On September 15, 1988, on behalf of the Eby family, Reed offered a reward of $25,000 for information leading to an arrest and conviction in the murder.

Finally, Lynn confronted her siblings: "I've had enough. Cash me out. From now on, you're paying it three ways."

Shortly thereafter, they terminated his services. Nothing came of it except Stone was more convinced than ever that there was a conspiracy to get him, one that involved the Flint police, the FBI, the Veterans Administration and, now, some suspicious guy hanging around Domino's.

Stone was proof: Just because you're paranoid doesn't mean they're not out to get you.

## 26
## ANOTHER CASE

In February 1987, King got his next homicide case. He didn't need a bigger caseload, but this one worked out well. He needed a sense of accomplishment.

A call came into the PD, saying there was a guy beaten to death with a baseball bat in a house in Flint.

King was out running that morning, about 5 a.m. It was snowing up a storm and when he got back home, he had icicles hanging from his mustache. His wife said to call the desk, they had a body he needed to look into.

The whole thing ended up a comedy of errors, and after working Eby non-stop, King was in the mood for comedy. The body had been taken to the wrong hospital. Instead of going to the Hurley Medical Center, where it was supposed to go, some rookie cop had dispatched it to an osteopathic hospital, instead.

By the time King tracked it down, the nurses there had cleaned the body and stitched the wounds so they could send it nice and neat to the funeral home. Destroyed all the evidence in the process.

Turns out there had been white trash folks, two men and a woman, boozing it up big time at a house in Flint. The two survivors were sitting at the PD. They told King that they'd been partying with the dead guy before he was dead, then they'd left the house to get something to eat, and when they came back, there he was, all smashed up.

No eyewitnesses, two suspects telling a story that's stupid but hard to refute, a body that's been all cleaned and fixed up and is nearly useless from an evidentiary point of view.

King puts the two in separate rooms. He talks to the man, gets the same story. Talks to the woman, she's telling the tale when suddenly she starts crying and in twenty seconds spills out an entirely different story.

She was going to have sex with the one guy, the second guy wanted to have sex, too, so the first guy beat him up with the bat.

King goes back to the guy's room and he looks at King and says, "She talked to you, didn't she? Okay, I'll talk to you."

"It was one of those dramatic confessions. You never get dramatic confessions. Boy, I needed that one," says King.

But King was still back where he started from: a dead end on Eby.

Three months had gone by. The list of sexual partners he thought surely would lead to a quick arrest hadn't. The Mott employees had come up clean. Stone did it, but how to prove it? The mad genius had outwitted King so far—heck, he'd been outwitting him since they were 5 and showed no signs of stopping, now.

# 27

# "THE TWO MRS. EBYS"

In April, the Eby family was devastated once more, this time by a peculiar profile in a monthly city magazine called *Metropolitan Detroit*, one of those slick city magazines more often given to features on the five best pick-up bars or the ten best pizzas in town than to serious journalism.

But *Metropolitan Detroit* was locked in an ad and circulation war with another city monthly—a war it would soon lose—and was trying to beef up interest in what had once been a fat, well-read magazine. Maybe it could beef up readership and sales by shedding its image as a dispenser of puffery, and what was less puffy than sex and murder?

The Ebys thought they were participating in what would be both a tribute to their mother and a way to generate publicity about the case.

Publicity, they got. A tribute? Hardly.

As its name implied, the magazine rarely, if ever, dealt with things or events outside the metropolitan Detroit area. Flint was far off its normal radar screen. If it was going to send one of its associate editors to Flint, if it was going to be able to grab attention back home with any subsequent story, well, its goals wouldn't be served by being reverential.

The article, titled "The Two Mrs. Ebys," was not only cruel, it was dead wrong. How wrong would take years to find out.

The article approached Eby's life, and death, the way an investigative reporter might report the death, and secret life, of a national figure. Eby was a public figure of sorts in Flint, to be sure. The writer, Cynthia Shaw Glascock, and the magazine seemed to take pride in rooting out the secrets of her life, though the secrets amounted to little more than revealing that the gatehouse was a bit run-down, that—shock of shocks, given the knife-in-the-back nature of academia—Eby hadn't been liked, had even been despised, by some of those who reported to her when she was provost. And that she liked men.

Glascock quoted a real-estate agent who said that when Eby met with her about a place to live, the first question she asked was about the city's eligible bachelors.

Margarette Eby, said the story, was a woman who appeared to move in Flint's highest circles, was gifted, attractive, energetic. But, intoned the article melodramatically,

> *there was also something else. A question of who this woman was, really. In the days and weeks following her own death, investigators discovered that there was more to know—that, in fact, she was not a person easily known. That, like a planet in orbit, there was a side of her in sunshine, and a side in darkness.*

Read between the lines, the article early on seemed to hint of a willing participant in fetishist sex gone awry.

> *Police say there was no sign of a break-in. There was no sign of theft . . . There was no sign of struggle, nor any indication that she was drugged or assaulted sexually against her will. While police will not comment . . . one hears, though this, too, is unconfirmed, that her wrists had been bound and then released.*

Later, a woman identified only as "an acquaintance," tells Glascock:

> *"You had the feeling that the well-dressed provost could become a different Margarette Eby—dress wildly, maybe, and attend functions, let's say, not normally attended by a university provost."*

One pictures, as Glascock seemed to suggest, orgies and wild carryings-on. How an editor let such rank speculations remain in the story is hard to imagine. The source clearly had no idea what Eby did in her spare time. All she had was a "feeling" that the well-dressed Eby might be someone who could dress wildly. Clearly, Glascock hadn't been able to get sources who knew if there were orgies or if Eby had wild clothes. Worse is the unspoken implication that event A—dressing wildly and going to abnormal functions—if true, somehow made event B—getting her head nearly severed off with a serrated knife—her fault.

Glascock wrote that Eby had expressed concern for a lack of a security alarm at the gatehouse and had asked Mrs.

Mott, without result, to install one. It was Eby's fault, then, that she didn't pay for a system out of her own funds. "Others wonder why, if Margarette was so scared, she didn't buy her own system," she wrote, quoting the real-estate agent once more: " 'I had the feeling she was penurious.' "

Ooh, wild *and* cheap.

The agent went on to say that three months before Eby's murder, she had called Eby to tell her that a Tudor had come on the market if she were interested in buying instead of renting. The article says she told the agent: "I don't believe I'm interested because I'm so happy here."

"But she wasn't happy," wrote Glascock. "By then she apparently believed she needed the gatehouse and the status it conferred."

Eby had resigned as provost and was difficult to work with, said Glascock. She treated those above her reverentially and those below her with cruelty and disdain. The "bad" Margarette Eby was arrogant, abrasive, aggressive, and insensitive. One woman who used to report to her had been treated for stress. After the Bach festival was over, Eby had to go back to being an ordinary music professor, not a powerful administrator.

"All she had left, Margarette Eby feared, was the gatehouse," wrote Glascock, a dramatic overstatement that overlooks her rich social life, family involvement and granddaughter. The gatehouse was hardly the only thing in Eby's life, as her calendar for the weekend she died proves.

The gatehouse was all she had, though, wrote Glascock, and the house itself, like Eby, was not what it seemed. Glascock found it tacky and in bad taste. It had, she said, green shag carpeting throughout, wood trim on the exterior that seemed to show spots of rot and a tiny kitchen that "looked like it hadn't been updated since the Forties, and the basement leaked."

One can barely imagine.

Or, maybe one can, considering Eby was paying $375 a month, including utilities.

Glascock also told of the FBI's involvement, of those sharp, all-seeing, all-knowing profilers. And that the word on the street—meaning the word she was getting from police or FBI on a not-for-attribution basis—was that the cops

knew her killer but were forced to play a waiting game for
more evidence. To wait for the killer to make a mistake.

By now, late in the article, there was no need to read between the lines to see the victim being blamed.

"Imagine this," wrote Glascock.

> A slightly inebriated male of indeterminant age goes
> to Margarette Eby's house to talk. Exact time of day or
> night uncertain. Financial and occupational stress
> weigh heavily on his mind. Mrs. Eby lets him in, they
> talk and, though he hadn't intended it, a rage is un-
> leashed and he kills her—slashing her delicate throat.
> Afterward, the man remains in the Flint area, despite
> his desire to leave. He also undergoes a personality
> change.
>
> The above scenario is fact, according to FBI behav-
> ioral science experts. Using the same method employed
> in tracking down Ronald Bailey, the man recently found
> guilty of the abduction and slaying of Shawn Moore,
> the FBI last December released a profile of the killer.
> The agency concluded that the assailant not only knew
> Margarette Eby, he had been in her home before.

Glascock went on.

> Late Friday night or very early Saturday morning,
> Margarette Eby is at home after a quiet, entertaining
> evening with friends. There is a knock at the door. Sur-
> prised, she calls for identification and a familiar voice
> responds. A very familiar voice.
>
> Together, the two go upstairs . . . Once in her bed-
> room, both parties undress, Margarette neatly hanging
> her clothes, as is her habit. Then she readies the bed,
> pulling back the covers and turning on the electric
> blanket she uses in place of a bottom sheet. She will-
> ingly gives him her wrists; it's a game they've played
> before. He fastens them tightly. Passion follows. Then,
> before he frees her, he gets up.
>
> She, so calm now, doesn't notice. Perhaps her eyes
> are drowsily closed. Then the cold steel of the blade

*presses against her skin. Death comes quickly. He unties her hands.*

What Glascock didn't know—or didn't write about if she did know—was that the woman who served as a main source, Margaret Struble, the same woman who had once told *The Flint Journal* how wonderful her boss was, and who later claimed to reporters to have told her husband that Eby would never live through the month of November, had, in fact, been a suspect, herself.

Eby's other friends had told King that the relationship had soured when she quit the Bach festival and Eby wouldn't rehire her. Struble had later bad-mouthed Eby, claiming, erroneously, that she had blocked Struble's admission to a graduate program at U-M.

At one point during what King described as a hard interview with Struble, the woman broke down and began crying. Briefly, King thought she was about to confess to Eby's murder. She was eventually cleared.

Glascock also had no way of knowing that Struble had, according to private investigator Reed, told him that she once considered her *husband* a suspect in Eby's death, that he had hated Eby and acted very suspiciously the weekend of the slaying.

Adding a final odd touch to the story, Struble claimed that Glascock had never interviewed her, but had pulled quotes of hers out of various *Flint Journal* and *Detroit News* stories.

## 28
## THE TRAIL GOES COLD

The Eby murder was Flint's most prominent unsolved homicide in 1986, but hardly its only one. There were sixty-one murders for the year, an all-time record for the city, and as February 1987 rolled around, eighteen of them were still unsolved.

King's case load was brutal, as was the entire homicide squad's. Even so, its clearance rate for homicides in 1986 was 71 percent. The state average was 46 percent. In Detroit, it was just 40 percent. According to FBI figures, the national average was 74. Given its case load, given its budget woes and resources, the Flint PD more than held its own.

"Police Still Seek Clues to 1986 Homicides," read a *Flint Journal* headline from the Sunday paper of February 8, 1987. The Eby case was most prominent in the roundup of unsolved murders. The others were more what you'd expect—Robert Fordham, stabbed to death days after being indicted on cocaine charges; Victor Arteaga, shot somewhere else and dumped in front of a stranger's house; Sammy Sanders, a 15-year-old boy stabbed next to his home for his tennis shoes; Eric Gibson, wanted on an armed-robbery charge, shot with a large-caliber handgun in the back.

Reading between the lines, it was bad news. The Eby case had moved, in the editors' minds, from the category of breaking news to the category of a looking-back feature.

In June, it was time for the paper to take another look back. "Eby Slaying Investigators Still Making Progress," read the headline for June 22.

As usual, DeKatch was quoted prominently: "It remains a case that still generates a great deal of interest, not only in the community, but when it was presented last month at the Homicide Investigators' Conference at the Michigan State Police Academy in Lansing," he said.

DeKatch told the reporter that while there had been no startling developments in the case, detectives were still working on it and making progress. He declined to elaborate.

"The shopping list of things that had to be done was immense at the beginning of the investigation," he said. "It is still long, and we're continuing to do things on the list."

In fact, they were out of to-dos and had been for some time. But DeKatch was hardly about to tell a reporter looking for an angle that they had given up, that there seemed to be no chance they'd solve the case, that Charlie Stone was home free.

Ironically, DeKatch continued to plug the FBI. "The general profile provided by the FBI limited the number of possible suspects," he said.

Another big Sunday feature on November 1, 1987: "Who Killed Eby? One Year Later, Questions Still Outnumber Answers" read the headline.

"We think about it all the time," said DeKatch. "That is still the number one topic of conversation: 'What are you doing on the Eby case?' "

He told the reporter he got asked the question at the supermarket, at football games, at social gatherings. King got the same question from his neighbors and the folks at church. Rarely a Sunday went by without someone at church asking King what progress they were making.

Again, DeKatch praised the FBI.

"We know that the profiling technique works, and we still remain confident that we will solve this case," he said.

## 29

## ABOUT THAT PROFILE . . .

Jim Harrington may have conjured up some magic when he worked up Ronald Bailey's profile. The press and Flint police had every reason to believe he'd conjured up some more with the profile of Eby's killer.

It certainly helped set the course of events for years to come. It helped put Charlie Stone directly in King's metaphorical crosshairs. It helped keep him there. It kept the Flint PD from expanding its investigation. It served as the basis for *Metropolitan Detroit*'s devastating profile of Eby and the article's image of a woman inviting a lover to tie her up and have sex with her.

There was only one thing wrong. Harrington's profile as a factor in solving the Bailey killings seems to have been worthless. That such a profile even existed can't be discerned from reading any of the thousands of inches of newspaper clippings on the case, which commanded headlines in *The Detroit News*, the *Detroit Free Press* and the suburban *Observer & Eccentric Newspapers* for months.

Not once is the profile even referred to. Nowhere is it quoted by the papers as a means to solicit tips. Harrington's name never comes up. That's not to say Harrington didn't do a bang-up job or that it wasn't distributed to police. But no one at the time seems to have paid the least bit of attention to it, including the police involved. The cops never credited it. The papers never used it.

According to the *Livonia Observer*, which gave the Bailey murders blanket coverage for more than a year, the first time Bailey's name came to the attention of the local police was on September 6, 1985, when his name turned up on a list of owners of gold 1985 Jeeps, which witnesses had seen at Moore's abduction. Bailey got caught, not because of the Feds, but because he was stupid enough, and frantic enough, to grab a kid in broad daylight while driving a car that stood out a mile away.

The first description to match Bailey was on a WANTED flyer put together by those same witnesses. Reporters covering those cases have no memory of any involvement by FBI profilers. But the Bailey murders were off the radar screen in Flint. If the FBI wanted to brag about how they'd helped solve the case, how they did everything but name Bailey in their profile, who was to dispute it?

There was another thing wrong about the profile of Eby's killer.

It didn't have a shred of truth to it. Not a bit of real insight. It was the wildest sort of inaccurate, hocus-pocus malarkey. The FBI couldn't have been more wrong about Eby's killer if it had said Benjamin Franklin had come back from the dead to electrocute her.

The profile gave the Flint police some direction, though, a direction they followed as faithfully as a ship's captain eyeing a compass in a fogbank.

They believed in Harrington. They believed the profile. They would believe it for years, despite any lack of results, despite eventual evidence to the contrary. It was their story and they were going to stick to it: Margarette Eby had been killed by someone she knew. And when it came time to exclude a whole category of possible suspects—the estate's various contractors, sub-contractors and vendors who might have had access to the gatehouse grounds, or even to the house, itself, but who did not know Eby personally—the FBI profile provided one excuse. The workload for police, and manpower and budget problems provided three others.

# PART
# THREE

## Bogeyman, 1991

There was no sign in the summer of 1954 that Art Ludwig would become a pioneer of the fledgling TV industry. Or that it would make him wealthy. Little to show anyone, least of all his exasperated mother, that he'd become much of anything as he partied his nights away and wasted the mornings in bed.

"I thought life was going to be one long party," he says today.

A Korean War vet who had enlisted in the National Guard when he was still in high school, he spent his tour of duty stateside at Fort Rucker, Ala. Art showed leadership skills in the service. He was a tank commander, then a platoon sergeant and finally a company first sergeant before his discharge just before Christmas of 1953. He would later rise to the rank of colonel in the Army Reserves.

He returned to Brainerd, Minn., and was happy to be part of the post-war ebullience of the times. Brainerd, a town of 4,500 that is 125 miles north of Minneapolis, is the self-proclaimed "Heart of the Lake Country" and long a tourist mecca for those hoping to fish or swim or get sunburned on or near one of Minnesota's 10,000 lakes.

Art was from a large family—four sisters and two brothers, one of whom died as a baby. His dad, Arthur, had owned a local grocery store, but went broke during the Depression when he continued to sell on credit to his friends and neighbors. The family moved north to Duluth for a while, where his dad found a job as a machinist, but the lure of Brainerd soon brought them back.

Art graduated from Brainerd High in the class of 1949. During high school, he worked as a busboy at the Land O'Lakes Bar and Café, one of just two real restaurants in town, and the only one with a liquor license. On summer weekends it did a big business and closed too late for Art to avoid breaking the curfew laws then in effect for kids, so he and another busboy would sleep in cramped quarters reserved for them over the restaurant.

Smart, witty, sharp with the patter, good with the girls,

Ludwig was content to just let the days and nights roll by when he returned to Brainerd after his stint in the Army.

Christmas came and went, New Year's came and went, with not much to distinguish one night from the next. There was always a party somewhere, or a gathering of friends at one joint or another.

Early one night in January of 1954, Art was drinking with some friends and one of them said they were leaving the next day.

"Why?" asked Art.

"We're going to college."

"Where?"

"The University of Minnesota."

"Sounds like a good idea to me," said Art.

The next morning Art was brutally hung over, but he managed to get out of bed and pile himself into his friend's car for the drive south. When they got to Minneapolis, Art went to the registrar's office.

"Where are your transcripts?"

"What are transcripts?"

Normally that would have been the end of it, but the post-war days were boom times for American colleges, as they enrolled classrooms full of ex-soldiers taking advantage of the GI Bill and raked in millions of Uncle Sam's dollars. The registrar's office worked around the immediate lack of transcripts and sent him to a counselor to figure out how he could take the requisite fourteen hours required by the GI Bill when nearly every class was already filled. Somehow the counselor found the hours—including courses in English literature, history and speech—and he was in.

Art enjoyed life as a college student and, returning to Brainerd for the summer, vowed to enjoy life as a college student on break, too. It was back to a routine of long nights, short mornings.

The summer was broken up by two weeks of what was then called AT, for active training, as part of his ongoing military obligations. While at AT at Camp Ripley, Minn., Art ran into a friend from his days at Fort Rucker, Walter Butler. Butler's father owned a new TV station, WTCN.

There had been two stations in the Twin Cities and the Federal Communication Commission said there could be two more. In its infinite wisdom, it had assigned both of them the same channel, 11. St. Paul's new station, WMIN, would sign on and present two hours of programming, then sign off. WTCN would then sign on, run two hours, and sign off. And so it went throughout the day.

When Art ran into Butler at AT, Butler shook his hand enthusiastically and immediately offered him a job at the station: "Hey, why don't you go to work with me? We need a switchboard operator."

"Yeah, sure," said Art unenthusiastically, having no intentions of ruining his summer by taking any sort of meaningful employment.

After AT, Art went back to Brainerd and forgot all about TV.

"I hadn't spent an hour watching TV in my life. I know I'd never even turned one on or off in my life," he recalls many years later.

A few days later, he was lying in bed, deciding when and if to get up, when his mother, Delores, came to his room.

"There's a man on the phone."

"Who is it?"

"Walter Butler."

"I don't want to talk to him. Tell him I'm not home."

A couple of days later, on another late morning, his mom came to his room again.

"It's Walter Butler, again."

"I don't want to talk to him. Tell him I'm out."

A few days later, his mom came to his room once more, this time poking him in the ribs with a broom handle.

"It's Walter Butler, again. Why does he keep calling you?"

"He wants me to go to work with him."

"And . . . ?"

"I don't want to."

"Well, what are you going to do this summer?"

"Nothing. I'm a veteran. I'm going to stay home with you." Left unsaid was the important part: *And party till I have to go back to school.*

"Where are you going to stay?"

"Here."

"No, you're not. No son of mine is going to lay in bed when he's wanted for a job."

And she poked him harder in the ribs, got him up and sent him to the phone.

Art drove to the Twin Cities. Butler had told him he'd mostly be needed on the switchboard on weekends but there'd no doubt be other hours.

As he was filling out the application, someone walked into the office, asked him what he was doing, told him he wasn't going to be a switchboard operator, after all, grabbed him and led him to the nearby sound stage.

A stagehand had failed to show up for work, and in those days of live TV, stagehands were the glue that held the shows—with their cheesy backdrops—together. It was also the TV era of on-the-job training. Everyone in the business was new to it. If you walked into the station and applied for a job and that's the day a salesman quit, you were a salesman. If a stagehand stayed home with a hangover, you were a stagehand. Art was a stagehand.

In their alternating two-hour blocks of time, the crew at WTCN put on cooking shows, clown shows, the *Accordion School on the Air*, church shows and evangelists. It also put on the number-1 rated show in Minnesota TV, *The Casey Jones Show* at noon. The half-hour began with a filmed black-and-white opening shot of the local rail yard, then broke to the studio and a cheap plywood set, with Casey the train engineer leaning out the window of his make-believe engine. He'd get out of the train and do his lunch-time shtick for those kids lucky enough to live within walking or running distance of school.

The special effects were such that the stage crew would chain-smoke furiously leading up to the show so the smoke enveloping the engine would look like steam.

One of the stock-in-trade bits of business for those shows, whether it was Casey Jones in Minneapolis or Soupy Sales in Detroit, was to have the star go to a door at the edge of the set, open it and engage in a wide variety of interactions with imagined off-camera characters.

Or, in some cases, real off-camera characters. Art and his co-workers constantly tried to throw Casey off the script by planting surprises on the other side of the door, surprises he could see but the audience at home could not. The goal was to fluster the star. And flustered Casey was one day when he went to the door during one live commercial—as he always did at the same time each show—to accept a glass of the sponsor's cold, delicious milk.

Instead of a stagehand passing him a glass, there stood the station's biggest-bosomed female employee, stark naked with the full glass of milk lodged firmly between her breasts as she pushed them together. He had to pry the glass loose and drink it down without choking, and nearly failed.

They were heady, wild days as TV invented itself, and its pioneers prided themselves on being heady and wild themselves. "There were a number of bars in close proximity to the station," recalls Ludwig. "You got paid for eight hours, you worked four and you partied four."

**31**
# ART AND NANCY

In that pre-ESPN era, WTCN carved out a niche as a sports station, covering everything from high-school basketball games to Big Ten football to pro sports.

In time it was *the* sports station of the area. It handled local coverage and all of the feeds for the visiting teams of the Minnesota Twins of major league baseball, the National Football League's Minnesota Vikings, and the National Hockey League's North Stars. And it branched well beyond the Twin Cities, contracting to send its truck and crew out to send feeds to other stations for games out of Kansas City and Milwaukee.

Art, whose early duties included chain-smoking to make a mock train engine look like it was steaming, quickly worked his way through the ranks. Just two years after hiring on, he was directing and producing live sporting events.

His family grew as quickly as his career. He met an attractive waitress named Barbara at a restaurant not far from the station, started dating her and they were married in 1956. The next year, his first of seven daughters, Laura, was born. His youngest, Julie, was born with Down syndrome in 1969 and died from related complications two years later.

By then, WTCN, which would be bought and have its call letters changed to KARE, was the acknowledged giant of local sports, and Art was production manager of its sports telecasts and vice president of programming.

The frequent road trips, and the ongoing socializing and drinking inherent in those days in the TV business, began to take a toll on his marriage. By the early 1970s, he says, "my marriage was going south fast," and by 1973, Art was separated from his family, living with a male friend, and going through the usual guilt a parent undergoes when he leaves his children.

Art went to the office Christmas party that year. It was at the Park Terrace, half a mile down Excelsior Boulevard from the TV station, an upscale bar and restaurant that was across the street from the staff's normal hangout at Jennings' Red Coach. He found himself talking to, and being intrigued by, the last woman he would have thought would pique his interest. Not that she wasn't attractive. Nancy Jean LaPole was trim—5' 2", 108 pounds, with brown hair and striking green eyes—and pretty, even beautiful if you caught her at a certain angle. She was working at an ad agency, then, but she had once worked at the station and Art hadn't much liked her. Something about her rubbed him the wrong way.

"I didn't particularly care for her. She was very efficient in everything she did, in her approach to her job. I interpreted that as—I don't know—well, coldly efficient. In a business where a lot of people goofed off a lot," he says. In other words, she could seem a bitch.

But at that party they found themselves standing alone when people they'd been with wandered off to get a drink or chat someone else up. They started talking and to Art's surprise, the Teutonic persona of the office was gone and in front of him was this funny, charming, witty woman.

Office Christmas parties have a way of exaggerating people's charm and wit, and in the light of the next day, Art didn't think much more about it.

Until a couple of months later when, as was standard operating procedure for many at the station, he popped into the Red Coach after work. "When you left work, you didn't go home, you went down the street," he says. "Drinking was the number-one hobby in those days."

It was the birth-control, pre-AIDS, pre-herpes, pre–Mothers Against Drunk Driving era, and you never knew what kind of action or energy level you'd walk into, but chances were you wouldn't be bored at the Red Coach. If nothing else, there'd be other sharp, funny, high-energy people there slinging lines and trading banter and bitching about bosses.

Nancy was at a table with some of her old friends from the station. Art sat down. The drinks and conversation flowed. One by one, people drifted off. Suddenly it was just Art and Nancy.

Again, they hit it off. It was funny the way the right person can make you funnier, glibber, more interesting. They made each other very funny, very glib, very interesting. A week later, they went out to dinner on their first date. Not quite love at first sight, it was nonetheless quickly clear to both that something special was going on.

Though he was eighteen years her senior—she was born the same year he graduated from high school—the age difference never bothered her. "She totally loved him," recalls her best friend, Patti Alt, now a professional photographer with a studio specializing in commercial advertising in Eden Prairie, Minn.

Alt had met Nancy in 1971, on her first night as a waitress at The Five, a downtown Minneapolis nightclub. The boss told Nancy to show her the ropes and they hit it off from the start.

"They were meant to be together," she says of Art and Nancy. "They were one of those unique couples. When she met him, she thought, 'That does it.' "

Art, worried about his kids and what they thought of him—"at first they thought I had deserted their mother"—was in no hurry to get divorced and remarried. Nancy didn't pressure him, but she made it clear that's what she wanted.

When she started flying with North Central Airlines in 1976, she had a T-shirt made up that said: "Marry me and fly free."

In 1977, the same year he got a divorce, they moved in together, in an apartment in the Minneapolis suburb of St. Louis Park. On June 2, 1978, they were married in Mount Olivet Lutheran Church, where her parents, Samuel and Gladys, were members. It was a big wedding in the largest and most impressive, ornate church in Minnesota.

The wedding was one to remember and so was the honeymoon. She lived up to the T-shirt, and they flew free to Rome, Greece and Egypt, where Luxor had just been opened to tourists, and the sight of two Americans was enough to solicit a crowd of the curious who politely followed them around.

They continued to fly free, at least one big trip a year. They rode a boat through Aberdeen Bay in Hong Kong, where thousands of junks were tied together in a sort of Oriental version of a trailer park. Laundry hung everywhere. Kids played on most of the boats. There were puppies on each boat, too.

"Isn't that nice? They have nothing, but they all have pets," said Nancy to Art, referring to the poor residents of the junks.

Art didn't have the heart to tell his animal-loving wife—who thought nothing of berating strangers if she saw them being unkind to their pets—that the boat-owners weren't raising pets, they were raising dinner.

On another trip, to southern China, they toured a 2,000-year-old open-air market, with food of every kind hanging up—dead rats, songbirds still singing, hundreds of puppies in cages. By then, Nancy knew they were being offered as food, not pets. "She wanted to buy them all and set them free. It killed her to see people walking home from the market with puppies and cats on ropes," recalls Art.

They visited Europe repeatedly, including tours behind the Iron Curtain before it fell. They went to Australia, to New Zealand, to Kenya.

Usually the trips were with little or no planning, reflecting Nancy's spontaneity. "She'd come home and say, 'We're going.' She'd think nothing of going to Europe for two weeks with just our airline passes. No hotel reservations, nothing," says Art.

At first they'd argue about it. Art did a lot of traveling in his job and preferred things a bit more structured, or a bit more upscale, accustomed to staying, say, in the Plaza in New York on his expense account. But she'd say: "I don't tell you about TV, don't tell me about travel."

Neither spoke a foreign language, but it didn't stop Nancy, once they'd cleared customs somewhere, from going up to strangers and coming back with recommendations on places to stay and things to do.

One time they stayed in a shabby pensione with a crack under the door so big a cat squeezed under it and into their room. Another time, in Paris, they stayed on the third floor of a third- or fourth-class joint with an elevator only big enough for one, and a room so small you had to stand sideways to close the door. It was just after a series of terrorist attacks by Muslim extremists, and they came back to their hotel one night after dinner to find fifteen Middle Eastern types sitting in the lobby chain-smoking.

"I was sure we were going to be murdered in our sleep," says Art. Nancy was nonplussed.

They rarely rented cars, preferring to walk for hours, wandering through art galleries and museums. As at home, what one liked to do, the other invariably liked to do, too. The only significant disagreement seemed to be in the area of hotel choices.

Back in Minneapolis, they bowled in a mixed-doubles league. They were avid fishermen. "You mentioned fishing and she was the first one down to the boat," says Art, referring to The Frontier Lodge on Lake Kabetogama up by the Canadian border, where he kept a boat and a 32-foot trailer.

When they weren't on the boat fishing for walleye, northern pike, bass and crappies, they were canoeing through the boundary waters area. One photo shows Nancy beaming a huge smile, holding aloft a twenty-two-pound salmon she caught on Lake Michigan.

In the winter, they'd ski, either on weekend trips north of Minneapolis, or on day trips to Salt Lake. His schedule permitting, it wasn't unusual for them to pick up the Saturday morning paper, drive to the airport, park in the employee lot of Republic Airlines, take the employee shuttle to the terminal and, in those pre–9/11 days, quickly clear security, get on a plane and—it was also the days when airlines fed you—enjoy breakfast while they read the paper and flew west.

They'd arrive in Salt Lake, catch a shuttle bus to one of the many ski resorts west of the city, ski till mid-afternoon, catch a shuttle back to the airport, pick up an evening paper and read it while eating dinner on the flight home.

They'd have dinner with friends Saturday night, then repeat the process on Sunday. And, depending on Art's work schedule, again on Monday. They loved to fly, it didn't cost them a dime, and they loved to ski, and what better way to spend two or three days in the winter?

Art, well off financially, took an early retirement from the TV station in 1989. By then, Republic had merged with Northwest and Nancy's seniority was such that she could bid for the flights at the beginning or end of her schedule that left her with plenty of time for recreation. She could catch a trip to Seoul, say, that would mean six or seven days on the job at the beginning of a work cycle, catch another long trip at the end of the month, and have ten or twelve days in the middle to do whatever they wanted.

"She'd look at the social calendar, then look at the bid sheet and bid flights so she could attend every party, every fishing trip, every family function," recalls Art.

Patti Alt had stood up in Nancy's large wedding. Not long after, Patti got engaged, but she was having a small wedding. Typical of Nancy, outgoing, fearless and brash, she called Patti up and announced: "Patti, I want to be in your wedding."

Other words Patti uses to describe her are: confident, persistent, caring, honest, humorous, witty, playful and spontaneous.

"When I think of Nancy, I think of *I Love Lucy*. That was Nancy, always full of surprises. She was always coming up with surprises and doing weird things to make you laugh."

And Nancy and Art would banter back and forth like Ricky and Lucy, giving each other digs but in a way, it was clear to the observer, that was always loving, never malicious.

"The two of them were our entertainment. They were so funny together. They were perfect. I loved Art. He was like her. The same personality. Usually in a marriage, there's a quiet spouse and a loud, lively spouse. Not them. They were both the same."

By 1989, after eleven years of marriage, "things were idyllic," says Art. And they remained so. By then, his daughters had grown to accept Nancy, even love her. A couple of them were particularly close to her.

The couple had their fishing, their bowling, their frequent

trips to exotic locales, boating, skiing, parties, a big house in Minnetonka, an affluent suburb of Minneapolis, that she'd picked out and decorated, her beloved cockapoo, Snuffy, and each other.

"There was no question about me wanting to go off with my buddies, or her going off with her friends. We did everything together. We had reached a plateau in life where everything was perfect."

"They lived life. Nancy lived every second of her life on earth," says Alt.

## 32
## TWO TRIPS TO VEGAS

In late January of 1991, Art and Nancy took a quick trip to Las Vegas. One day they returned to their room and Nancy had to fumble at the door for her key, which was buried somewhere in the collection of stuff in her purse.

It ticked off Art and he chastised her for it. It was one of his pet peeves, hotel security or the lack thereof. He was always nagging at her to have her key ready so she could make a quick entrance. Don't be a target, he'd say. Don't waste time at the door.

She thought he was a bit phobic on the topic. After all, this was a guy who, when he was still working and on the road, would deadbolt his hotel room door, then put the waste basket underneath the handle and put a glassful of water balanced between the edge of the basket and the door.

Several times he'd awoken in the morning to see that someone had tried to come in, the glass knocked over.

"By my own experience, hotels are not safe places," he says. "You act like you're at home, but you aren't. Hotel security is horseshit, no matter the name of the hotel or where you go."

Art also nagged Nancy about working as an add-on flight attendant. As an add-on, you pick up crews in the middle of a trip, or drop off a crew in the middle. Where most flight attendants traveled in groups to and from hotels, add-ons often traveled alone.

"I didn't like the idea of her going into hotels by herself, but she said I was old-fashioned. 'I can handle myself. I'm a world-traveler,' she'd say."

She had agreed to curtail her add-on duties, though. One battle won, thought Art.

The morning of Sunday, February 17, 1991, as was their practice since he'd retired, Art drove Nancy to the airport. She had a busy day ahead of her. On the way, she told him that she was flying this trip as an add-on. Earlier in the month she'd been scheduled to work a troop charter for Northwest, ferrying troops on civilian aircraft to Saudi Arabia. At the last minute, the trip was canceled. To pick up the hours she'd need to fill out her month's requirements, so she and Art could take a planned vacation ski trip to Lake Tahoe, Nancy had signed on as an add-on for a flight to Las Vegas, then was joining another crew for a filled plane, where she'd help out with the dinner rush, then leave that crew when it continued on from its stopover in Detroit.

Art was ticked off, but what could he do? It was just this one last time, anyway. Nancy kissed Art goodbye and got out of the car at about 7 a.m. She'd overnight in Detroit, then pick up a third crew Monday morning and continue on to Ft. Lauderdale, Memphis and Indianapolis. Tuesday, she was doing Indianapolis, New York, Memphis and Minneapolis, scheduled to finish three killer days when she touched down at her home base at 5:06 p.m.

Art would pick her up at the airport, it'd be a couple of days of R&R, and then they'd be off to Lake Tahoe to ski.

Art went home to finish reading the paper, have some coffee and watch news of Desert Storm on CNN. He was coming down with something, too. He never got sick, but he could feel a cold or worse coming on.

Monday, Art woke up feeling terrible. He'd stayed in the day before, tried to soak the cold out in a long, hot bath, but the rest and hot water hadn't done a thing.

He was an active guy in his retirement. If he had nothing else to do, he'd often go for a run in the neighborhood. But this day he felt so lousy, he decided to sit in and do nothing. Not a thing, which was very unusual for him. He'd sit back, nap, read, watch TV and hope things didn't get worse.

They would.

# 33

# A FACE IN THE HALL

Ann Johnson, a Northwest flight attendant, had a long lay-over in Detroit during the day on Sunday, February 17. The airline had a contract with the Hilton Airport Inn, which was across I-94 from Metropolitan Airport, on Wick Road. Large blocks of rooms were reserved for use by flight attendants and pilots on layover, with anywhere from 50–100 North-west employees checking in each day. Between Northwest and three other airlines, about 90 percent of the hotel's 268 rooms were reserved for flight personnel. Most layovers in-volved spending a night, but some were just for the day.

Johnson was on what was called a "sit." She was with a crew on a DC-10 out of Minneapolis, and since they were laying over for five hours, the company was required to pro-vide a hotel room for them to rest in.

Her crew of four got off the airport shuttle van and en-tered the lobby. At the front desk they didn't find a clerk, but they found their keys easily enough. A sign-in sheet was sit-ting on the counter. The day clerk had prepared the sheet, listing a job description, flight number and estimated arrival and departure times. The first-shift clerk also assigned room numbers.

The Hilton used Vanguard door locks, which required plastic cards that were the predecessor to today's swipe cards. They had holes punched in them instead of a strip along one side. The Northwest employees were supposed to show their badges, sign in and get their room keys. But on the morning of the 17th, the keys were just sitting there for the grabbing, next to the sheet.

Johnson's crew joked about the lax security. Well, didn't joke, exactly. Called it a joke.

On overnight stays, for security purposes, Northwest pro-hibited the Hilton from assigning employees rooms on the first floor. It was too easy for a thief to get in by a window. But first-floor rooms were okay for daytime "sits" and that's what Johnson's crew got.

Johnson didn't feel like sitting around the room with the

other three. She wanted to get a workout in, but it was a lousy, blustery winter day out. She went to the hotel's workout room, but it was packed, so she decided to go for a run on the hotel's four-story stairwell. Nothing like running stairs to get the heart pumping and the pulse elevated. She'd stayed at the hotel many times and was well versed with its stairwell.

She ran up the four flights, walked them back down to save the pounding on her knees, then ran back up. She did this repeatedly. About 1:30 p.m., near the end of her workout, she started what she called her cool-down phase. She finished running on the top floor and planned to walk the two hallways of the L on the fourth floor to the opposite stairwell, walk down to three, then walk the hallways to the opposite stairwell and continue in that fashion until she got to the ground floor.

Something cut her cool-down short. She opened the doorway on the third floor and came face-to-face with a young man. He was near the concession/vending area and carrying a canvas bag. He had sandy hair and was wearing jeans and tennis shoes. Something about him, beyond his just suddenly being there on the opposite side of the doorway, startled her.

She walked past him and instead of continuing as planned, she went straight to her room. "Something felt wrong to me, and I quit my workout," she says.

When she entered her room, one of her co-workers said: "Oh, you're done early."

"Yeah. I ran into something and I felt uncomfortable."

Lynn Ellisworth checked in with Martha Houk and both flight attendants went up together to their rooms on the third floor. They both put their things in their rooms, then walked down the hallway to the ice machine.

There was a guy acting odd at the candy machine. He had sandy hair and was wearing blue jeans and tennis shoes, holding a duffel bag close to his body. He didn't seem to be looking at candy choices, it was more like he was hiding his face. He was almost pressed to the machine, his back to them.

They got their ice and walked back to their rooms. Ellisworth could hear the man walking down the carpeted hallway behind them. When she got in her room, she looked out through her peephole. The man was standing with his back to her door, staring at Houk's door across the hall. And then he moved on.

Monday night, upon arriving home in Minneapolis, Ann Johnson got a call from her father. He wanted to know: Did you hear what happened in Detroit?

## 34
## THE MAN ON THE SHUTTLE

Lynn Nelms, like Nancy Ludwig, was an add-on flight attendant for Northwest. She wasn't part of a regular crew, but was added to full flights to fulfill staffing requirements or added to flight segments at meal times. In industry lingo, she would be either a meal chaser or an aircraft chaser. Like Ludwig, she was the only crew member of her flight staying over in Detroit. Like Ludwig, about 8:45 p.m. Sunday night she made her way by herself through the terminal to the driveway out front to await the Airport Hilton's shuttle van.

The van pulled up to the curb. The driver got out, put her bag in the storage area in the rear of the van and Nelms got on, sitting directly behind the driver's seat. She was the only one on board. Then Ludwig got on and sat directly behind her. Nelms knew her but didn't recognize her because Ludwig had stooped over to avoid hitting her head as she entered the van.

"Is that you, Lynn?" said Nancy from her seat.

"Yes. Who is it?" said Nelms, turning to look. It was dark in the van.

"It's me. Nancy."

"Hi."

A man came on board and, though the van was nearly empty, sat next to Nancy. On the ten-minute drive to the Hilton, Nelms and Ludwig caught each other up on recent flights and how things were going. Nancy's day had been a bitch. Weather delayed her flight out of Minneapolis. She got to Las Vegas late. Too much racing around. She was whipped. At 41, maybe she was getting a little old for this add-on business. They talked about a mutual friend.

The man sat silent. Nelms thought it odd he would sit

next to someone on a nearly empty van, especially if he didn't know who he was sitting next to. Since he didn't join the conversation, it was clear he didn't know Nancy.

Nelms thought he looked stern. He had a look on his face she'd remember for years. "He just looked mad and he looked intense and he was just so focused," she would say more than a decade later.

And he kept looking sideways at Nancy.

Lynn was sure of one thing: he was not an airline employee. Even given a bad day—a bad flight with demanding passengers—no attendant would have sat there silently. He would have had something to contribute to the conversation.

At the hotel, the three passengers got out. Nancy and Lynn got their bags from the rear of the van and wheeled them into the lobby. As Nancy and Lynn walked to the front desk to check in, chatting on the way, Lynn forgot about the man. Later she'd remember he didn't check in.

David Bennett, the front-desk and night-audit clerk from 3–11 p.m., asked them which flights they came in on and passed them a sign-in sheet and their plastic key cards.

Nancy and Lynn rode the elevator together. A hotel employee with a room-service cart rode with them to the second floor and they went on to the third.

They were no longer just engaging in idle chatter. Nancy told her about the death of both of her parents recently, and about the added stress of two tubal pregnancies she'd suffered through.

That wing of the Hilton was laid out in a long L. The elevator opened on to the longer hallway. As they walked down it, Lynn asked if Nancy wanted to meet her at 8 a.m. in the lobby so they could ride back to the airport together. Nancy's flight left a little later and she thought briefly about trying to catch a little extra sleep, but then agreed to meet her.

Lynn's room, 341, was at the end of the first hallway. They said goodnight at the door. Nancy's room, 354, was at the end of the shorter hallway, to the right. Just past 354 was the doorway to the emergency-exit stairwell.

Lynn was in the lobby the next morning at 8. Nancy was supposed to get a 7:30 wake-up call and meet her in the lobby. Nancy was late. Lynn talked to another flight attendant she knew as they waited for the van. When it pulled up,

Lynn told the attendant to go on without her, she wanted to wait a bit more for Nancy.

For the next van, there was a handful of attendants waiting. Still no Nancy. Lynn decided she'd better get going.

## 35
### "LIKE A SORE THUMB"

Frederick Roybal was also a Northwest flight attendant. He got to the Hilton about fifteen minutes before Nelms and Ludwig. He, too, was an add-on attendant and he had to be out early in the morning. He dropped his stuff off in room 353, the second-to-last room on the left-hand side of the corridor.

Roybal got a bucket of ice at the machine down the hall and returned to his room, not sure yet if he'd read for an hour or watch TV before turning the lights out.

He opted for TV and at 9 exactly he turned it on. Moments later, he heard two high-pitched noises, the first higher and louder than the second. Screams possibly, or kids squealing. Maybe a TV in a nearby room. In most hotels, it's not unusual to hear odd noises at 9 p.m. But this wing of the Hilton was reserved for airline employees and, Roybal knew from past experience, usually very quiet. People were there to sleep and relax, not party.

Alarmed, he went to his door and looked out the peephole. He saw nothing in the hall. He heard no further sounds. He returned to his bed and called down to the front desk for an early wake-up call. He needed to be gone by 6 a.m.

Phil Arcia's flight from Boston had gone smoothly, but his check-in at 10:15 p.m. hadn't.

The heater didn't work in the room he was assigned on the second floor—it was freezing in there—and the only room they had left was on the first floor, room 129. The Hilton wasn't supposed to give Northwest employees first-floor rooms, but Arcia didn't feel like making an issue of it.

Ironically, the heat was blasting in that room. It hit him in the face when he opened the door, and he set his luggage down and went straight over to the controls to shut it off.

The heater was under the window and the curtains were

open, and outside, in the big parking lot between the hotel and the freeway, he could see a man carrying a burgundy suitcase, a color required by Northwest. The parking lot was well lit and a new snowfall was thick on the ground, turning night nearly into day.

The man went to the trunk of a brownish-gold Monte Carlo. Arcia was a car buff and he'd recently had a roommate who owned a Monte Carlo, so he was sure of the make. Briefly, Arcia assumed the man was a flight attendant. But only briefly. Arcia would consider himself a typical male flight attendant—very well groomed, prideful in dress and appearance, whether in or out of uniform.

"After flying for so many years, you can tell a flight attendant when they're out of uniform. We have a look—the way we dress, the way we present ourselves. We are always dressed differently and groomed differently. He didn't have the look. He stood out like a sore thumb," Arcia says.

The man's hair was messy. He wore sneakers, a definite fashion no-no. He had a hooded sweatshirt with the hood down. Moreover, his pants were rolled up at the cuffs, way up, like maybe five inches' worth. A look if there ever was one. Dressed like that, he couldn't even be a pilot, thought Arcia.

"Pilots are the worst. They have no sense of fashion. They're hicks when it comes to dressing. And he was one step below that."

And a flight attendant would be rolling his luggage, not carrying it under his arm. Then there was the way the man just threw the luggage into the trunk, instead of setting it in.

The man left the Monte Carlo and headed back across the parking lot. Oddly, he left the car trunk open. "That's stupid. That's a good way to lose something," Arcia thought. He stood by the window, being the Good Samaritan, making make sure no one came by to steal anything. The man walked to Arcia's right and around the corner of the building. Arcia's room was on the long hallway of the L.

Around the corner of the building, at the far end of the shorter part of the wing, the emergency exit opened up onto another part of the parking lot. The door was locked at night, but no alarm sounded if someone opened it from inside. Guests routinely propped the door open if they planned on returning right away, saving themselves a long walk to their rooms from the lobby entrance.

Arcia stood at the window watching the Monte Carlo until, a few minutes later, the man returned, this time carrying what looked to be a bundle of clothing—and what was clearly flight attendant stuff, including a beige overcoat with a burgundy lining.

The way the man just threw the clothes into the trunk caught Arcia's eye. No concern for them whatsoever. "Our uniforms then were the most hideous uniform we ever had, but you wouldn't crush it into a ball and throw it into a dirty trunk."

A lot caught Arcia's eye. The way the man was dressed. His height—5 foot 11. His weight—175–180 pounds. His hair—light and cut short. His race—white. His age—no more than 30.

The man made three more trips to the hotel and back to the Monte Carlo, always with something bunched under his arm.

The man closed the trunk. Just then another car pulled into the parking lot. The man seemed to freeze. He stood there motionless. After the car passed him, he got in the Monte Carlo and drove off.

Despite all Arcia had seen, there were logical explanations. Detroit is a major hub for Northwest and many attendants either live in the area or rent cheap rooms to use as a home away from home. Perhaps he was a spouse or a friend of an attendant and was picking him or her up, or helping exchange dirty clothes for clean. You couldn't very well call the front desk and complain about the way someone threw clothing into a car.

Arcia went to bed. He had an early flight to Boston. When he got there, someone asked him if he'd heard the news.

## 36
## ROOM 354

It was a busy morning for Joann Sweet, one of the Hilton's maids. The hotel had had a busy night, which meant a lot of rooms to clean for the next round of check-ins.

She had a list of check-outs and did those rooms first.

While she was working those, others checked out, opening up more rooms for cleaning. Finally, at maybe 12:40 p.m., she was down to the last few. Room 354 was scheduled to be empty. Its occupant had left a 7 a.m. wake-up call and was supposed to be gone by 8, but she hadn't checked out, and the "Do Not Disturb" sign hung from the door's exterior handle.

She probably had been in a rush this morning and just caught the shuttle van without bothering to wait in line for check-out. As for the sign, it didn't mean much to Sweet. Most people who put them out never bothered to bring them back in.

She knocked on the door. No response. Knocked again. Nothing. "Hello, maid," she said. She opened the door a crack and said again: "Maid."

There was silence. The room was very dark, just a glow from the TV. She flicked the light switch on by the wall near the door. The room remained black. She felt her way to the heavy drapes, pulled them partially open and turned around.

At first she thought she had screwed up, that she had walked in on the woman sleeping on the far bed. That she hadn't been loud enough at the door.

And then she realized she was surrounded by blood. Blood everywhere. On the walls, the floor, the bed next to her, the furniture. And that the woman must be dead.

She fled from the room.


Paul Janiga, the Hilton's chief engineer, was in his office on the ground floor when he got a call from the third-floor maid. She was frantic. There was a body on the bed in room 354. Janiga's first thought was heart attack. Something natural and peaceful, a placid body on the bed. "She's been killed," said the maid.

Janiga hurried to the room. The "Do Not Disturb" sign was still on the handle. He opened the door and flicked the switch nearby, but the light didn't come on. The lamp that it worked had been unplugged and the cord sat on top of the wall counter. The room was gloomy despite the light coming in from the windows and the glow from the TV, which was tuned to CNN. Desert Storm was on.

Soon, there'd be other, non-war news for the cable and network folks to talk about.

He went to the windows, fully opened the curtains and turned around. He saw a lot of blood on the bed closest to him. On the far bed, he saw bedding bunched up into a pile. A foot stuck out of the pile. At the opposite end, he saw a head, and a gaping wound on the neck.

He went over to the body and touched the heel. Part of him said: This is a prank; it's not a real body. But the heel was real. He touched the neck, looking for a pulse. There was none.

He left the room, closed the door and went down to tell his manager. The manager called the police. Janiga went back up to the room and waited outside the door so he could open it for them as soon as they arrived. It was Presidents' Day, but the holiday would soon be over for the Romulus PD.

## 37
## THE HOLIDAY ENDS

Michael Giroux didn't have much seniority with the Romulus Police Department, which was why he was working February 18, Presidents' Day.

When the call came in from the Hilton at 1:02 p.m. that there was a body in room 354, he was sent to the scene. Several hotel employees were in the hallway and one of them let him in.

The TV was on, giving an eerie light to the otherwise darkened room. He saw a woman lying face down, propped up at the waist by a stack of pillows. There was blood everywhere. He called for other officers to join him at the scene and began taking 35-millimeter and Polaroid photos.

Dan Snyder, quiet spoken, calm and methodical, had an unlikely background for a homicide detective. He'd worked seventeen years in the circulation department for *The Detroit News* and was vested for a Teamster pension before he decided to try his hand at police work.

He started as a paper boy at age 12 in the downriver Detroit suburb of Southgate and worked his way up to district

station manager. In the '50s and '60s, when newspapers
made their profits on the labors of young boys pedaling their
Schwinns around the neighborhood with canvas bags of papers strapped to the handlebars or fenders, station managers
were some of the gruffest guys in capitalism.

Not Snyder. The kids actually liked him, including young
Mike St. Andre. St. Andre thought the world of his boss,
enough so, in fact, that years later he'd go to work for him as
a rookie cop in Romulus.

Among other jobs Snyder had with the paper was as a
jumper on a truck, throwing out bundles of papers at stops. A
fellow jumper was Ken Cockrell, who would go on to become something of a Detroit legend, a black activist in the
turbulent '60s who later became a prominent Detroit attorney and then a city council member.

Snyder worked his way up to driver, then to station manager, making good wages with great fringe benefits. He'd
married his high-school sweetheart, started a family and
bought a house in a new subdivision in Southgate. The future
seemed set. Except, for some reason or another, he'd always
wanted to be a cop. And a neighbor down the street from his
new house was a Wayne County sheriff who told him they
were hiring.

Snyder went down, took a test, passed it, got on a list and
two years later, on March 15, 1976, at the age of 29, started
his new career at the county jail downtown.

In 1981, he was assigned to the sheriff's office at Metro
Airport, but was laid off soon after. Romulus was a young
city, then, not a lot of residents, mostly just a bunch of farmland surrounding the airport. For ten years, Wayne County
sheriffs had patrolled the city. But about the time Snyder was
laid off, the county commissioners decided it was time for
the city to hire its own police force.

Snyder applied and started working in Romulus in November. On February 18, 1991, he was a detective sergeant.
As Romulus had grown and its cornfield turned into subdivisions, so, too, had its police force, to fifty members. But just
two detective sergeants handled all the investigations, from
bad-check cases to felonious assaults to embezzlement to
robberies to murder.

Snyder was a good dresser, favoring tweed sports coats

and coordinated slacks. With his neatly groomed sandy hair and trimmed mustache, he looked, wrote one reporter, "more like a literature professor than a detective."

Snyder and his wife, Jean, were putting the day off to good use, meeting with someone to put a down payment on five acres of land in nearby Huron Township. At 1:20 p.m., Snyder got a page. He asked the people selling the land if he could use their phone and called in to the station.

"We got a body at the Airport Hilton, Dan," said the dispatcher.

He and his wife raced to the Romulus station, where he picked up a police car and drove to the hotel, arriving at 1:45 p.m.

Giroux led him into room 354. The first thing he saw was the body, covered by a bedspread, her rear thrust up in the air, her feet sticking out. And then he saw the blood. Everywhere he saw blood. There was a partial bloody footprint just inside the door, a bloody washcloth by the sink in the bathroom, and a pool of bloody water in the bathtub where it looked as if the perpetrator had taken a shower to clean up.

Snyder moved farther into the hotel room. There was no blood between the entryway and the first bed. Between the far bed and the window, and on the three walls surrounding the bed, and on a chair, a table and a dresser, there was a lot of blood.

It looked as if she'd bled to death on the bed by the window, then been picked up, bedding and all, and carried to the other bed. The way she was propped up, Snyder thought the killer might have had sex with her after she'd died.

He went back to the body and looked at it closely. Her head was nearly severed. Her face was severely beaten and bruised, with what looked to be numerous knife wounds and pinprick-type holes in her skin. Her hands were lacerated from the fight she'd put up against the knife; some of her fingers nearly severed, too.

Snyder knew this was bigger than the Romulus PD. He had his own crime-scene investigator he could have called in, and there might be noses out of joint if he didn't. But he made an immediate decision to call the Michigan State Police Crime Lab. His people had plenty of experience dealing with lowlifes, mostly drunks and druggies and prostitutes

working the airport hotels and city bars. But something this
bad, at a Hilton, at the airport, where the killer could have
fled by now to any place in the world? No, for this case,
they'd need all the help they could get.

The state police would have a team of crime-scene veterans to work the scene. He called their Northville crime lab
and told them what he had. It was a decision that would pay
off, but not for more than a decade.

He also called in his partner, Gordie Malaniak. Malaniak's pager went off as he and his wife were coming out of
an afternoon movie. His holiday was over, too.

## 38
## "BY FAR THE WORST"

Snyder had told him it was a bad scene, but nothing prepared
Malaniak for what he saw when he arrived about 2 p.m. Dan
was waiting for him in the hall and when he got there, they
did a walk-through before the state police arrived.

"Dan had said she had severe wounds to the neck, but *that*
was an understatement," says Malaniak. Blood was splattered all over the walls, the bedding, the furniture, the floor.
It was like nothing he'd ever seen, or would see. "It was by
far the worst."

From the blood on one bed, it was clear she'd been killed
there and moved to the second bed. She was face down, buttocks propped up in the air on a bunch of pillows and bedding. You could see dried semen that had run out of her
vagina, had run out while she'd been on her back on the
other bed, and dried. So now when you looked at it, it looked
as if it had run up, not down. It struck Malaniak that the
killer had posed her to look that way, was making a statement by leaving her in that position.

Malaniak looked at the TV. Desert Storm.

There was blood around the sink, and there was a pool of
pink water in the bottom of the bathtub, a ghastly residue of
the room's last shower. There was a bloody washcloth on top
of the vanity by the sink. So, the killer had been cool enough
to clean up.

There wasn't any luggage, no clothes, no ID.

Snyder and Malaniak backed out of the room.

Malaniak went knocking on doors, to see who was still there and who had heard anything. By now, chances were that most people had checked out and headed off who knew where. Anywhere in the world.

They had a name from the hotel manager, Nancy Ludwig, but that was about it. No ID, no confirmation of anything.

Malaniak had little luck finding guests and moved on to employees. He talked to the maid who'd found her. He talked to two persons at the front desk.

About 2:45, the state crime-lab folks arrived. It was time to back to room 354.

## 39
## "VIOLENCE HUNG IN THE AIR"

Lynne Helton had reasons to smile as she put away her groceries at her home in Wixom, a suburb northwest of Detroit, whose rapid change from farmland to city had been sparked by a sprawling Ford Motor stamping plant that was no longer out in the middle of nowhere. It was a holiday, for one. For another, she was two months pregnant with her second daughter, and thinking about breaking the news at work now that those risky first few weeks had passed.

Wixom was a convenient place to live for those at the auto plant, and a good place for others to buy what the realtors called "starter homes." Helton and her husband, Tom, couldn't afford to live where he worked, as a cop in the nearby, very affluent suburb of West Bloomfield. They could afford Wixom, and it was just up I-96 from Northville, where Helton worked as a crime-scene specialist and serologist for the Michigan State Police.

The phone rang. It was her lab director, Jim Hauncher, ending her holiday. In those pre–cell phone days, he'd been having a tough time reaching his crime-scene crew, who were out enjoying their day off, and was relieved to find Lynne at home. There'd been a homicide at the Airport Hilton, and he filled her in on what little he knew—a flight attendant on layover from Minnesota, found by the housekeeper, pretty nasty scene.

She drove the few miles over to the State Police Crime Lab on Seven Mile Road, one mile south of the road that Eminem would later make famous. Hauncher had been able to reach one other crime-scene tech, fingerprint expert Detective Sergeant John Terry, and the two of them got in the state-issued rattletrap silver van and headed south on I-275 to I-94. The two freeways intersected just west of the airport.

There were no seats in the back of the van, the space loaded with gear.

Helton had graduated from Detroit's Mercy College in 1982 with a BS in chemistry, then got her master's in forensic chemistry a year later from the University of Pittsburgh.

Pitt has one of the best forensics programs in the world, and its graduates are highly recruited. Helton was offered a job doing drug screening and analysis in Dade County in southern Florida, the very definition of job security in one of the drug-trafficking centers of the world, but she was engaged to be married to Tom and wanted to return home.

Her heart set on the state police, while she waited for a job to open up, she worked first as a waitress—"a noble profession; everything you learn in life you can learn from waitressing," she says—then with the federal Food and Drug Administration in downtown Detroit, inspecting everything from potato chips to soy-based infants' formula to penicillin. She also did drug screening for the medical examiner's office in suburban Oakland County.

After two and a half years, in 1985, she was hired as a civilian serologist with the state police and assigned to the Northville lab.

Her first murder scene had its darkly comical moments. "I remember being scared stiff. Not because of what I'd see, but because of how I'd react. I didn't want to be anything less than professional. I didn't want to get there and cry or throw up." This latest one would be far too gruesome for humor.

She did neither. She worked the scene. Each crime-scene investigator has a specialty, but they all pitch in on other tasks, too—shooting videos, taking Polaroids and 35-millimeter shots, making sketches.

The evidence at the scene didn't require much forensics detective work. Police found a baseball cap and a pair of glasses, both belonging to the murderer. They found something else he left behind, his hearing aid.

Turns out, it was the father-in-law. His daughter had long been physically abused by her husband, something his wife and daughter had kept secret from him. The daughter had been hospitalized for a hysterectomy, and within hours of the operation, the husband had shown up, demanding sex in the hospital bed. The wife turned him down, then, fearing a beating when she got home, told her mother. This time, the mother told her husband.

He had gone over to confront his son-in-law, an argument ensued and he'd shot him dead. Finding the hearing aid might not be slap-your-thighs uproarious, but when you make your living at violent crime scenes, you take your humor where you can find it.

At the Hilton, a uniformed Romulus cop led them to room 354. The door was open. Snyder gave them an overview and then he and Malaniak went in with them. The hotel manager and two Northwest Airlines officials remained out in the hall.

As Helton looked in through the open door, she could see part of the body on the bed to the right.

The procedure was, she and Terry would work the scene, gathering blood, semen and fingerprint and fiber evidence, then shoot a video and take rolls of photos, but leave the body undisturbed. After the several hours or so it would take them to do that, they'd call the county medical examiner's office in downtown Detroit, one of the busiest ME's offices in the world. The ME's crew would arrive within an hour, at which point they'd roll Nancy Ludwig onto her back, gather whatever evidence presented itself, let the ME people make their preliminary determination of manner and cause of death and then have them take the body back to the morgue for the next day's autopsy.

That was the procedure. They had that part of it down. What Helton didn't have down, and would never get over, was the violence that filled the room, literally and metaphorically.

Helton's first task was shooting a video of the scene, seven minutes of silence that screams its violence.

*It starts benignly, a long shot from the outside hall-way of the open door to room 354, then, the camera slowly enters the room and peers into the bathroom, on the immediate right, door half open, light on. There are drops of red on the bright white tile floor. The room is tackily decorated, green floral wall paper, bright yellow counter, bright drops of blood in the sink.*

*Looking down the short hallway, now, from the door to the room, proper, on the left a long, narrow, wall-mounted desk, lamp, hotel stationery, small white plas-tic ice bucket, TV on in the corner. To the right, a right foot sticking out.*

*Walk in, zoom toward first bed. Right arm hanging off the right side, body on one bedspread, covered by a second green floral bedspread now half red with big blotches. Pan to other bed, rusty orange blanket balled up, white sheet stained red. Behind it, a window with gauzy, sheer drapes pulled shut, heavy drapes pulled open.*

*Zoom in on window and wall. Two orange chairs to the right surround a round Formica table. Thick blood drops on the wall, on the table, on each chair, hurled out and around the room during the mayhem.*

*Pan to wall behind the beds. Zoom in on painting be-hind the bed nearest the window. Numerous blood drops on the glass.*

*Pan back to the bed with the body and zoom in on blood-saturated white bathmat that covers her face. There is a large gag in her mouth.*

Helton, ever meticulous, turns the camera off, leaves the room, does another take to make sure she hasn't missed any-thing.

*Shot of door, zooming in on the number 354. Slowly enter room, turn to the right, zoom in on white tile and drops of blood. Zoom in on drops of blood on the yel-low counter and in the sink.*

*Down the short hallway, right foot sticking out, pan to bed and zoom in on right hand, fingers nearly severed in her furious fight to avoid death. Zoom in on bloody bathmat over her face. Zoom in on the small wall-mounted table between the two beds. Drops of blood on it and the wall behind it.*

*Zoom in on blood on the glass on the painting over the other bed, on the wall next to it, on the two orange chairs, the table, the wall next to the window, on the front of the wall-mounted heater to the left of the window. Blood everywhere.*

*Some guy is driving a car on the TV, big head in profile.*

*Pan to the long wall-mounted desk. Drops of blood next to the white stationery, along the front and top of the desk. Fade to black.*

Next, Helton took numerous Polaroids and several rolls of 35-millimeter film. Then, as she took dozens of samples to be tested later back at the lab, taking swabs from Ludwig's buttocks and vagina with a sterile cotton swab, and cutting fibers from various surfaces, Terry went to work, painstakingly shining a laser light about the room to highlight otherwise invisible fingerprints. They'd be dusted and photographed.

If evidence was wet, they needed to get it dry—the quicker it dried, the less degradation to any DNA it contained. They didn't put samples in plastic, which degrades materials, but in permeable paper envelopes.

Bedding was put in large paper bags, as was the bathmat that had been wrapped around her nearly severed neck. Back at the lab, the bedding would be laid out in the drying room on large clean sheets of butcher paper pulled off huge rolls. The cotton swabs would be broken off their sticks and placed into cryovials, plastic tubes about 1.5 inches tall that were labeled and frozen to be used as evidence when, and if, the murderer was ever caught.

Helton did her work calmly and methodically, no trace of how disturbed she really was. She'd work other nasty crimes with Snyder, one involving the rape of an 18-month-old girl by the mother's boyfriend, which ripped the girl open so badly she had to have a colostomy, and other murders without him, one of a woman beaten to death so violently by her grandson because she wouldn't give him drug money that he broke a cast iron pan into pieces on her skull—but nothing would approach the violence she felt, now, and her reaction to it.

"It wasn't until all the aspects of the scene came together, and you really looked at the body and realized everything that had happened to her that you could feel the violence in an overpowering sense," she would say later. "The violence hung in the air. It shouted at you. It was the only crime scene *that* ever happened to me.

"You'd have to be a monster to do what he did to Nancy Ludwig. The whole process he put her through."

A long, thick heavy men's athletic tube sock of considerable volume had been stuffed into her mouth, forcing her lips to distend. Her hands had been bound with twine. She clearly had put up a ferocious fight, and the defensive wounds on her hands went to the bone. "The degree to which she fought was so striking," says Helton. "Just seeing the wounds on her hands, it was impossible to avoid reliving what she went through." She inflicted some of her own facial wounds, scratches made while trying to remove the gag that was suffocating her while she aspirated on her own blood.

There was bruising all over her face, and her eyes had been blackened from her beating. There were pinpricks on her face where the killer had lightly jabbed her with the point of a knife, playing with her after having gotten her gagged and bound. There was an elongated Z, almost like the mark of the old TV character Zorro, above her left nipple. Once the killer had gotten her under control, he had played with her. "She was tortured over a period of time. There were so many controlling wounds, the knife marks on her face, all the scrapes," says Helton.

And then there was the wound that killed her, a slashing of her throat that would have decapitated her but for her spine. "Cutting her through wouldn't have been a quick and easy process. It was more sawing than cutting," she says. The killer used a serrated knife, and you could see the saw marks it made on Nancy's flesh. There was blunt force trauma to her left temporal and mid-forehead areas.

There was so much blood that even though she'd been killed the night before, much of it was still wet around the neck.

It was clear she'd been raped while on her back on the far bed. Semen had drained out of her vagina. After a period of time long enough for the semen to dry completely, the body had been carried over to the other bed, turned over and propped up by four pillows so that the buttocks were in the air, her arms dangling off the bed, and she'd been raped again. Afterwards, the killer had smeared his semen on her buttocks. Though Helton had no doubt what she was looking at, a test at the scene confirmed it was semen.

They found bits of human fecal matter on the floor between the beds, four raisin-sized pieces. What to make of that?

At some point, Northwest officials faxed over Nancy Ludwig's fingerprints. Terry confirmed that the dead woman was, in fact, Ludwig, though they would wait for her husband to make an official identification of the body the next day before releasing her name.

More semen stains were found on the pillows used to prop Ludwig up. Helton cut these and bagged them, too.

This second sex act and the second set of semen stains occurred well after Nancy Ludwig had died. The murderer was also a necrophiliac.

Helton could tell because Ludwig's vagina was distended. Instead of regaining its shape as it normally would have after the penis was removed, it remained wide open. "I had never seen that before," Helton would say later. "It was so unusual, I almost photographed it, but out of trying to protect her modesty, I didn't."

The two-person crew from the county medical examiner's was finally called after hours of painstaking work, and arrived about 8 p.m. The body was rolled over. Not much examination was needed to reveal the manner—homicide—and cause—the slashed neck—of death. At 8:30, the body was placed on a gurney and wheeled out of the room. TV crews outside filmed the body as it came through the fire exit. It is particularly true in Detroit that if it bleeds, it leads, and the murder and rape led the news that night and for several thereafter.

Helton and Terry wrapped up their work in the room, though their day was hardly over. They would have to start processing the evidence and write reports once they got back to Northville.

Adding to the bloody mystery, and the chills the murder gave them, was that the room was nearly devoid of Ludwig's things. Her clothes were gone and so, too, were her flight attendant's rolling suitcase, her purse, her ID. Her Seiko watch was gone and her wedding and engagement rings had been pulled from her bloody fingers. The only things that remained—found rolled up in the bedding and overlooked by her killer—were a burgundy button from her blazer, a thin belt and a small gold charm that had broken off her bracelet, a little goose that was a memento from her days flying with North Central.

The killer was a collector, too.

## 40
## THE DAY FROM HELL

Art Ludwig still felt like crap. He wasn't sinking fast, but he was sinking. When you're never sick, it seems to hit you so much harder when you are.

About 3 p.m., the phone rang. "I was lying on the couch reading, on top of the world, leading a perfect existence, thinking now and again about the ski trip to Tahoe and hoping I licked my cold by then. I had no inkling at all my world wasn't perfect," he says.

It was Nancy's supervisor, Linda Bowman.

"Is Nancy there?"

"No. She's at work. She won't be back for a few days."

"Are you sure?"

"Yeah. I dropped her off at the airport yesterday."

"Art, Nancy did not make the connection with her flight this morning. Can you do me a favor? There's a policeman at your door. Can you go let him in?"

He went to the front door and sure enough, there was a Minnetonka cop on the porch. Apparently he'd been in communication with the supervisor at her office.

Art let the cop in and went back to the phone.

"They found a body in a Detroit hotel, and they're afraid it might be Nancy. Can you make it out to the airport tonight? There's a flight to Detroit and they want you to come."

The rest of the day was a dark, horrid haze. Time frozen. Panic ebbing and flowing. Nothing to do. Everything at stake.

The cop never said anything, apparently had been there just to make sure Art didn't kill himself or something. When he saw that Art seemed to be composed, he left.

Art called his best friend from the TV station, Art Kintop, an ad salesman who lived nearby, explained the situation and asked for a ride to the airport. There was a blizzard raging outside and it took them forever to get there slogging and sliding their way at a few miles an hour. They got there at 7.

Bowman met Art and sat with him in a private Northwest lounge. The blizzard would delay, maybe even cancel, the flight out. They sat in the windowless room, waiting out the storm for nearly four hours. If there was anything Art wanted to do less than fly to Detroit right now, it was to be told the flight was canceled and have to drive home, then come back again in the morning and sit through this with Bowman one more time.

The silence was crushingly loud. "It was absolutely horrible," recalls Art, both for him and for Bowman. "I thought later, 'What an experience for that woman.' It must have been equally horrible for her."

While he was sitting there, Detroit's Channel 4, WDIV-TV, went on the air with a report that a flight attendant named Nancy Ludwig had been raped and murdered at the Airport Hilton. The body hadn't been ID'd yet, and standard practice in the industry is to withhold the victim's name until immediate relatives had been identified, but someone at the hotel had leaked the name to a reporter and the station went with it.

The story was picked up by Minneapolis TV stations. Nancy's six stepdaughters got the word that way, watching television, as did many of her family and friends.

Finally, the storm abated a bit and they were cleared for takeoff. At 2 a.m., Art arrived in Detroit and was taken to an airport hotel, not the Hilton. The worst day of his life was finally over.

The next day would be worse. Much worse.

# 41

# THE MORGUE

In his hotel room, Art stared at the ceiling and hoped against hope. He didn't have much. He didn't delude himself. "I knew they wouldn't have called me without being pretty sure it was Nancy."

Finally, mercifully, at a time of the year when night clings selfishly to its existence in Michigan, light broke the darkness.

Malaniak picked him up and they drove to Northwest's flight services office at Metro Airport. There were a handful of FBI agents waiting. Desert Storm was at its height, and since Ludwig was a flight attendant and her ID, passport and uniform were missing, the Feds were worried her death might be the act of terrorists plotting something worse. They put out a nationwide bulletin asking security agents at airports to watch for her stolen Northwest ID.

The Feds had a few questions for him. Malaniak had a lot and started in at 9:25 a.m. You always look at the husband first, for good reason. Lots of them have killed their wives. Or hired someone to do it. They wanted to solve this fast, and when you solve a murder quickly, it's usually because you've taken immediate and careful aim at the spouse. Art would be guilty until proven innocent.

There was no easy way to proceed. Malaniak needed to clear Art, and to do that he had to ask some pretty pointed questions.

Was there anything wrong with the marriage?

Had they been fighting?

Was she seeing anyone?

Was he?

Was there anyone he knew of who might want to do this?

Could he account for his whereabouts?

It went on for half an hour.

"If he hadn't been a cop, I would have tried to punch him out," says Art today. "I understood shortly thereafter he was just doing his job. The husband is the first guy you suspect. It starts with a small circle and works out. But you resent getting asked those questions."

Malaniak wanted to polygraph him. Not on your life, said Snyder. No fricking way. He didn't see him as the killer. He'd been through enough. He wasn't going to have him hooked up to a machine.

And then things got really bad. They drove for twenty minutes up I-94 to the county morgue in downtown Detroit. The morgue, which has since been replaced, was an old, creaky building, not far from the even creakier police headquarters on Beaubien Street. All the bleach in the world couldn't get rid of the stench of death and embalming fluid that punched you in the nose when you walked in the front door.

An employee led Art to a wide curtained-off window. Someone on the other side wheeled the body to the window and pulled the curtain.

Art started in horror at the mutilated, purple-bruised and bloodied face of his dead wife. Being told someone has found a body in a hotel room and it might be your wife is one thing. To see *that*, to see her face and a neck nearly severed from its shoulders, was beyond imagining. Art nodded that it was Nancy, and they pulled the curtain and led him outside, to air he could breathe.

"To this day I don't know why it was necessary to have me look at her. I would have thought they'd be able to do it with fingerprints," he says. "My last image of her is the four or five seconds of looking at her face. It was so badly beaten. You can't imagine going through it. It was the worst thing in my life. And the rage that I felt afterward, that someone could do that to another human being."

They told him they wouldn't be able to release the body for a few days. They told him the clichéd "Don't leave town without telling us."

At 5 p.m., Art called Snyder. He was leaving town. He'd be in Minnetonka if anyone needed him.

A few hours earlier, back in Minneapolis, Patti Alt had been feeling ill. Though it was the middle of the day, she went into her bedroom and tumbled onto the bed. Seconds later, or maybe minutes or hours—she had no idea how long, she was *that* dead asleep—she was aware of someone shaking her. She groggily came back to consciousness. It was her husband. Still sick, she struggled to sit up. He told her there was bad news. It was on TV. Nancy had been murdered.

"It pretty much killed me," said Alt, breaking into tears twelve years later when asked about it. "It was one of the hugest things that ever happened to me. It put me into a tail-spin that was transforming. I just stayed depressed. It was one of those shocking things. People die of cancer, or in car wrecks, and you get over it. But this, it was so senseless. That someone who didn't know her would do this. For no reason. You never get over it."

Art Ludwig went home in a blind rage and depression that lasted for months. Every time he tried to sleep, Nancy's face shocked him into consciousness. He thought of suicide. "The first six months were really terrible."

He started grief counseling, "but I decided the grief counselor needed more help than I did."

He'd fantasize for hours about getting a gun and moving to Romulus, hanging out in the bars and strip joints and hotels and motels until one day, sooner or later, he'd come across Nancy's killer. And shoot him dead.

His family, like good families do, helped save him. They had resented Nancy at first, but had grown to like, even love her in the years of their marriage.

"My kids took turns babysitting me. I was getting daily calls. Something like that, if you don't have great family support and great friends, I don't know what you do. They spent a lot of time with me."

Art hated living in the big house Nancy had picked out and decorated. Her keys and her ID had been stolen, and he kept dreaming the killer was coming for him, too. Eventually he sold it.

## 42
## NEVER A DULL DAY

Romulus is like a big square doughnut, six miles on a side, with a huge square hole in the middle. The sprawling Metropolitan Airport is the hole. The airport dominates the geography of the city and its tax base.

There is no real downtown in the city. What people call downtown is more like an intersection at Shook and Goddard roads, with a couple of old buildings to show that at least something in the city is more than thirty years old, and that at least something here predates the airport.

Romulus is a city, technically, but not the way you'd picture one normally. It has little culture, no movie theaters, no real place for people to congregate. The major business downtown is the Landing Strip, a cavernous topless joint that, says a sign on the building, offers "Non-Stop Live Entertainment."

The city is an odd mix of cornfields, trailer parks and a smattering of new subdivisions of large homes.

Romulus has always been an interesting place to be a cop. The city has more than its share of cheap bars and motels that cater both to the transients passing through the airport and to those passing through life, looking for cheap prostitutes or a cheap place to smoke their crack or snort their coke.

As tens of thousands of Southerners flocked to Detroit's auto factories in the early and mid–20th century, each blue-collar community that sprung up seemed to have a need to look down on its neighboring blue-collar community, to feel that *it* somehow was a cut above. And the way it did it was the unique southeastern Michigan regionalism of taking the "tucky" ending of "Kentucky" and affixing it to the beginning of whatever city or town was in need of denigration.

So people in the downriver city of Southgate would refer to the neighboring city of Taylor as "Taylortucky." And those in Ferndale to the north would call Hazel Park "Hazeltucky." Romulus made a perfect "Romutucky."

In 1991, the city was in sharp contrast to many others in the county. Where average density in the county was more than 3,000 per square mile, there were just 477 per square mile in Romulus, thanks in large part to the huge chunk in the middle given over to the airport.

While it had just 17,165 residents, the city was known for having far more than its share of weird crimes, drunken brawling, drug dealing, mayhem and murder. Boredom was not a peril of a cop's job.

Mayhem and murder? For instance, Dan Snyder had worked the cases of:

The girl who was set on fire on her nineteenth birthday and thrown out of a moving car.

The mom who poured Drano down her daughter's throat while she was sleeping.

The grandma who called the cops about a drive-by shooting that had just killed her son-in-law. Cops arrive, she's sitting on the couch on the front porch with her two grandkids. Police ask her to step inside. She says her and the kids are staying put, ain't leaving the couch. She tells them about this van that had driven by, someone shot a rifle out the window. There was a van all right, and the police soon found it and the rifle. Only one thing wrong, the body of the son-in-law was riddled with shotgun pellets.

The police come back with a search warrant, find Grandma passed out on the couch on the porch, an empty fifth on the floor. They rouse her, get her up, find the shotgun under the cushions. She and the grandkids had been sitting on it when the cops showed up the first time. Kids claim she shot him on the way out the door, a screwdriver in his hand as he went to fix his car. Lawyer got her off on self-defense, claiming she thought he was coming at her with the screwdriver.

Then there was the teen-ager who was yelling on the phone at 4 a.m. His dad, who owns a doughnut shop and has to get up at 5, wakes up, tells the kid to get off the phone. The kid keeps yelling. The dad rips the phone out of the wall. The kid goes to his bedroom, gets the 30-30 his dad bought him for Christmas, loads it and starts firing through the wall. One bullet hits his dad and kills him instantly. The kid walks in, sees his dad lying there, tells his mom to give him the car keys. Freaking out, she hands over a set of keys. He leaves, comes back in screaming: "You gave me the wrong God-damned keys!" Gets the other set, steps over his dad again and leaves.

Or the unsolved string of prostitute murders.

Or the suicide who checks into a motel, drinks half a fifth of booze, slits his wrists but doesn't do a good job, finishes off the fifth while he slowly bleeds out. Runs out of booze, gets in the car, trailing blood, goes to the liquor store, buys another fifth, leaving red stains on the counter, goes back to the motel, starts working on that fifth and finally dies.

Because of his expertise working weird homicides in Romulus, nearby Van Buren Township asked for Snyder's help on a case of a gutted hooker. Not only had she been gutted, but both breasts had been cut off, with one of them left over her face. While they were working the crime scene, a guy drives up in his van. A cop looks in the window, sees a bloody ax and a machete on the back seat and arrests him. True to the cliché, he'd returned to the scene of the crime.

Later in the 1990s, Snyder would work one of Dr. Death's cases. Malaniak worked a lot of them. Jack Kervorkian, the famous, or infamous, advocate of assisted suicide, left a bunch of bodies in Romulus. His "patients" would fly in from around the country. He'd meet them at a hotel near the airport and help them do the deed, then call police.

So, it was always something in Romulus. Snyder had seen it all, or thought he had till he stepped into room 354.

## 43
## "DID YOU SEE THE PAPER?"

There was one major complication with the Ludwig case that set it apart from other murders Snyder had worked. This murderer wasn't some drunken grandmother passed out sleeping on a shotgun, or some trailer trash who knifed a neighbor and is still covered in blood when the police show up, or some crank-addled junkie pulling a gun on a clerk while the video camera films away.

By the time the body was found, chances were most of the witnesses were time zones away. And the murderer could literally have been anywhere on earth.

They interviewed the hotel employees, but didn't learn much more than they already knew.

They got a list of Northwest Airlines employees who'd been at the Hilton and started putting out the word they needed to talk to them. It helped that Metro was a Northwest hub. One by one, as their schedules allowed, Phil Arcia, Frederick Roybal, Lynn Nelms and the others came back to town to give statements. The picture of the badly dressed stalker began to emerge.

The all-news radio stations trumpeted the story for days. The daily newpapers played it big for a week.

Mark Eby, who was living in Michigan in 1991 between assignments in Germany, was having his morning coffee and reading the *Free Press* the day after Ludwig's body had been found. The Ludwig story caught his eye. The details struck him as awfully similar to his mother's death. He called Snyder at the Romulus police station and left a message that they ought to check with the Flint police and look into a possible connection to the murder of Margarette Eby in 1986.

He then called his brother, Jonathan.

"Did you see that article in the *Free Press* this morning?"

"Yeah, I just got off the phone with the Flint police. I told them they had to talk to the Romulus Police Department. As far as I can tell, it looks like the same MO."

A dozen years later, Mark would say: "It went beyond the similarities of rape and murder. We were both hit by it at the same time. 'Somebody needs to look at this.' "

On March 8, 1991, Jonathan Eby wrote Arthur Ludwig a letter, which said:

> Please accept my deepest sympathy on the terrible loss of your wife. You have been in my thoughts and prayers since the news hit the papers here in Detroit, and I wondered then if I should write to you. Given the lack of substantive progress in the investigation and your personal appeals in the Detroit area for information, I decided to bring to your attention a similar situation to allow you to respond as you consider appropriate. My mother, Margarette Eby, was murdered in Flint in November of 1986 in the gatehouse of the Mott mansion and the police have failed to solve the case. She had been bound, gagged, possibly raped and her throat had been cut. And there was no signs of a forced entry. When the news about your wife was aired, we were struck by the similarities of the crimes, and we alerted police both in Romulus and in Flint.
>
> In our experience, however, we were assured early in the investigation that they believed that the case would be rapidly solved, and we were advised not to become involved or post a reward, and basically to allow the police to handle it. We did, and I regret not having done more earlier. We did post a reward and hired an investigator about 10 months later to no effect.
>
> I bring this before you not to cast aspersions on the efforts of the police, but to encourage you to continue

*to personally do all that you can to move the case
forward. While they certainly want the case solved, they
have other agendas as well, and lack the motivation of
those whose lives have been so significantly affected by
the crime. It is a long shot, I'm sure, that our cases are
connected, particularly if the perpetrator in your case
is a very young man.*

*But I wondered if publicity of the sort you are doing
in Detroit might yield results if the situation and the
man's picture were shown in Flint. The officer who
handled our case was Sgt. David King. If I can be of
any other use to you, I can be reached at . . . My prayers
for God's grace, peace and strength continue to be with
you and your family.*

*Sincerely,*
*Jonathan S. Eby*

Ludwig turned the note over to the Romulus police. He was
getting a lot of crank mail and calls and didn't know if this
was another one, but it seemed worth passing on.

Neither one of the Ebys heard back from the cops in either city. King didn't follow up on his tip. The Romulus PD
did. Ludwig's further efforts at publicity, including posting
and mailing flyers, buying ads that displayed composite
drawings and offering a reward, did not extend to Flint.

**44**
# THE MICHIGAN MURDERS

They were Michigan's most famous serial murders, before
the term had entered the lexicon.

Mary Fleszar was the first to die, in July of 1967. A pretty
co-ed at Eastern Michigan University in Ypsilanti, she van-
ished from campus. Two teen-age boys found her body on
August 7, stabbed to death and decomposing, her hands and
feet hacked off.

Joan Schell was abducted on July 1, 1968. Five days later,
her body was found in Ann Arbor. She'd been raped and
stabbed forty-seven times. Cops soon learned she'd been
seen with a fellow EMU student, John Norman Collins, the

night she disappeared. Collins was a square-jawed, handsome, personable young man, and police believed his alibi and dismissed him as a suspect.

Eight months later, a third co-ed, Jane Mixer, went missing. She was discovered in a cemetery in Ypsilanti on March 21, 1969. She'd been strangled with a nylon stocking and shot in the brain at point-blank range.

The first killing had been news for a few days. The second killing seemed mere coincidence. The third killing screamed that a madman was on the loose. His doing was dubbed "the Co-Ed Murders." News accounts of the day, hard as it is to believe now, did not call him a serial killer. Serial killing was something Jack the Ripper did, or, more recently the Boston Strangler, but such monsters were rare and there wasn't a handy name for them or their work.

Or, maybe it wasn't that rare after all.

On March 25, construction workers found the body of 16-year-old Maralynn Skelton. She'd been killed with massive blows to the head. A stick had been jammed into her vagina. She'd been badly flogged with a belt or strap before she was killed.

A fourth body sent the media of southeastern Michigan into a frenzy, and young women started staying home, or going out only with trusted friends, or enrolling in self-defense classes.

Three weeks later, the half-naked body of 13-year-old Dawn Basom was discovered. She'd been strangled with an electric cord. Her sweater was found in an old abandoned farmhouse nearby, about a mile from where Fleszar's body had been abandoned at the beginning of this horrid sequence.

Things got even weirder. Police went back to the farmhouse where the sweater had been found to do another search, looking for clues they might have missed. Lying there were several articles of Dawn Basom's clothing that had not been there the first time. The killer was now taunting them.

In May, someone torched a barn on the property, where police had found electrical cord identical to that which had bound Basom. Across the driveway from the burned-out barn were five freshly-cut lilac blossoms, one, police speculated, for each of the dead women, who also had been cut down in full bloom.

On June 9, 1969, other teen-age boys found the body of Alice Kalom, a recent EMU graduate. She'd been raped and stabbed repeatedly. Her throat was slashed. A bullet had been fired into her brain at close range.

The final victim, Karen Beineman, disappeared from her dorm room at Eastern on July 23. Her body was found three days later in a wooded gully, another victim of unimaginable rage. She'd been beaten and strangled. Her stomach and breasts had been burned with some caustic liquid. Her panties had been balled up and stuffed into her vagina. Mysteriously, the panties contained short bits of hair that had been cut from someone else. Other victims, perhaps?

As it turned out, no. The hair came from innocent children.

Three days after Beineman's body was discovered, State Police Corporal David Leik returned to his home in Ypsilanti from vacation. He found a big splotch of black paint in the basement and assumed it had been spilled there by his wife's nephew, John Collins, who had taken care of the family dog while they were gone.

Thinking nothing of it, Leik went to work, where he was told that Collins had been questioned as a suspect in the co-ed killings. Suspicious now, Leik spent that night scraping off the paint. Beneath it was a brown stain that he feared might be blood. He pushed a washing machine aside and under it were bits of brown hair, remnants of hair-cutting sessions with his sons.

He turned samples of the hair over to investigators, and they took samples of the brown stain, too. The stain turned out to be harmless, just varnish. The hair, though, matched the hair in Beineman's underpants.

Subsequent investigations revealed that Collins had led an active and exotic sex life. Past partners told police he was over-sexed and sometimes a violent lover who was into bondage. He was also repulsed by women who were menstruating, as several of his victims had been.

Apparently, Beineman had been tortured in Leik's basement, where her panties had come in contact with the children's hair. Later, Collins must have mistaken the brown stain for blood and hastily painted over it.

Collins was convicted of murdering Beineman and sentenced to life in prison. A book on the case, *The Michigan Murders* by Edward Keyes, was published shortly thereafter. An ironic title: *THE Michigan Murders*. Alas, they would turn out not to be so unique. "Serial killing" was slowly entering the national vocabulary, and Michigan would have others after Collins was locked away.

State Police Detective Ken Kraus worked the Co-Ed Murders. He was mentioned prominently in Keyes' book. He assumed when he retired from the state police to help start the new Romulus police force that the Collins case would be his first and last serial killing. He would be wrong. But he wouldn't know it until more than a decade after Nancy Ludwig's murder in 1991.

### 45
## HOLDING DOWN THE FORT

Ken Kraus is a Yooper, the term people born in Michigan's vast and underpopulated Upper Peninsula, or "the UP" as it is commonly called, used to refer to themselves. Trolls are those who live in the Lower Peninsula. "Trolls" as in those who live beneath bridges in the old Grimms' Fairy Tales. The two peninsulas are connected by the Mackinac Bridge, an engineering miracle when it was built in the 1950s. If you come from south of the bridge, or below it, you're a troll.

Kraus grew up on a farm outside the city of Menominee, graduated high school in 1952 and married his high-school sweetheart. He worked the family farm and in a factory in town, making TV cabinets for the fast-growing industry for 50 cents an hour.

In the fall of 1955, Kraus heard that the state police were recruiting. In the UP, where unemployment was triple or quadruple the state average, government jobs were something to aspire to, not quite a godsend, but close.

Kraus got lucky. The state police were and are a paramilitary organization. Until the mid-1950s, they only recruited single men. The rules were changed just in time for Kraus to join the academy in East Lansing for the graduating class of May 1956.

He spent his five years in the far western Upper Peninsula town of Wakefield, was assigned to the Flint post in 1961, and in 1967 was assigned to Ypsilanti and promoted to detective.

He worked anything and everything, from kidnappings to rapes to robberies to murders. "Anything and everything" took on new meaning with the Co-Ed Murders.

He was quickly appointed to a task force of area police agencies, a force that would grow to include fifty members before Collins was caught. In those pre-computer days, Kraus became something of an expert in managing tips, and collecting, organizing and cross-referencing them.

In 1981, Kraus retired from the state police to start and head up the detective bureau at the new Romulus Police Department. The PD was set up in one long room in an old school, with a bunch of phones on a table. No switchboard, no switchboard operator. The phone rang, you ran over to the table and listened to see which one you should pick up.

Dave Early of the Detroit PD and Dan Snyder of the Wayne County Sheriff's Department, were his first recruits.

February 18, 1991, Kraus was enjoying the holiday, futzing around in the garage when he got the call saying there'd been a murder at the Airport Hilton. He wasn't a micromanager. He knew Snyder and Malaniak could handle things, so he didn't rush to the scene.

The next day, Kraus went in and took control. He told them they would likely be swamped with tips. He'd set up the tip file, get it organized and cross-referenced. The PD was computerized by then and they'd keep a paper tip file and a computerized file. The computer file would make it easy to cross-reference tips and bits of information.

Kraus, who always prided himself as a hands-on lieutenant who didn't mind getting out from behind his desk, told Snyder, Malaniak and the rest of the DB to work the Ludwig case. He'd take care of other stuff that came up that they normally would attend to. He'd also, if they needed him, interview witnesses, make phone calls, whatever.

"Ken Kraus pretty much held down the fort," says Malaniak.

Eventually the line they set up would generate 2,300 tips. Each one would be addressed, some in a matter of seconds, some with a great deal of deliberation.

# 46

# A HYPNOTIC COMPOSITE

While Kraus held down the fort, Malaniak and Snyder and a handful of others put in their long days of double shifts. Malaniak and Snyder spent some nights on the floor in the detective bureau, too tired, or pressed for time, to bother driving home.

The investigation spread out quickly from ground zero. They began with hotel employees and guests. Right away they hit upon one of the best leads they'd get. "We thought we cracked it the first day," says Snyder. A Hilton shuttle bus driver had been fired a few days earlier for screaming at a Northwest flight attendant. He'd vowed revenge when he was fired. But he had an alibi and was quickly cleared.

The desk clerk who said she'd checked Ludwig in gave them a couple of hot leads. She said Ludwig had been at the hotel several times previously, as recently as the week before. This might mean she'd had the opportunity to meet someone on previous trips, someone she'd invited into her room this time. That seemed particularly credible because the clerk said that about 9:45 p.m. the night of the murder, a male had called the front desk and asked for Nancy Ludwig's room. The clerk had patched him into room 354. A friend from past trips about to pay a lethal visit?

There was only one problem. Malaniak quickly found out it was Ludwig's first trip to Detroit. She hadn't even known how to catch the shuttle to the hotel. The clerk hadn't seen her before. In fact, while the woman had been working the desk that night, it was a male clerk, David Bennett, who had checked in Ludwig and Nelms.

As for the call? Malaniak and Snyder quickly discounted that, too. Art Ludwig hadn't called her. Michigan Bell had no record of a call coming in to the hotel at that time. Hotel equipment couldn't confirm a call had been transferred. And the timing made no sense, given that Arcia had seen the killer at 10:30, already done raping, torturing and murdering Ludwig, already done with his lengthy clean-up, and already dressed and packing up the Monte Carlo.

"She was wrong on every statement," says Snyder. "If

you believe a call was made to the room, it had to come from the killer. Given the evidence that Nancy was immediately attacked upon entering the room, there was no time or need for the killer to call." According to Snyder, "She made the whole thing up. Why? I have no idea."

So much for eyewitnesses. It's a law of police work: Eyewitnesses are notoriously unreliable. You might be an eyewitness, but that doesn't mean you saw what you think you saw. Juries love eyewitnesses, prosecutors rely on them, and defense attorneys and cops share one thing in common: they hate them.

Things got weirder. The clerk who had claimed to have checked Nancy in? Her boyfriend drove a gold Monte Carlo, and he had driven her to work the night Ludwig died. The boyfriend, briefly a suspect, was later cleared.

One Romulus crew went out to the landfill nearby to see if they could find any clues in the garbage that had been carted off from the hotel before the body had been found.

Literally wading through refuse, one of the cops found a piece of paper that had "Nancy Ludwig" written on it. It gave a momentary thrill, but it wasn't the murderer who had written it; it turned out to be something jotted down by a hotel employee.

They got copies of room charges run up by all the guests at the Hilton the night of the murder, seeing who was accounted for—in a restaurant or bar or getting room service—during the time in question.

They gathered the names of all 8,000 guests who had stayed at the twenty-one airport hotels and motels that weekend, from high-end places like the Hilton to $20-a-night motels with peeling paint and bedspreads stained with who-knew-what, and began entering them into a database, looking for people convicted of crimes or wanted by police.

They learned of a big party thrown over the weekend by a group known as the Tri-County Singles. Maybe some lonely single took out his frustrations on a pretty flight attendant. They got a list of members and started tracking them down.

They started calling all the pilots and flight attendants who'd been at the Hilton. One flight attendant had stayed on the other side of the wall from Ludwig. Malaniak was sure she must have heard something. The way Ludwig had fought back, it must have sounded like all hell breaking loose.

Malaniak reached her by phone. She sounded like she didn't want to be bothered. She said she hadn't heard anything. Malaniak didn't believe her, but was polite.

A little while later, the attendant's husband called him back, hot as hell, screaming that Malaniak had upset his wife. What was he calling her for? And so forth.

"Hey, it could have been your wife," said Malaniak, hot himself.

Phil Arcia made a return flight to Detroit from Boston on Wednesday. He got to the Hilton about 8 p.m. and asked the desk clerk if they had arrested anyone. No.

Arcia went to his room, and then, suddenly, it hit him: the guy in the parking lot. The guy with the Monte Carlo.

The next day, he was checking out and asked again if anyone had been caught. Still no. "I think I saw something," he told the desk clerk. "I don't know if it would help. Is there anyone I can talk to?"

The hotel manager called Snyder. Snyder rushed to the hotel. Northwest officials pulled Arcia off his flight out. And then he told the story of the guy with the bad haircut and bad fashion sense stuffing Northwest luggage into the back of a gold Monte Carlo.

He seemed remarkably sure of what he'd seen, was very precise in his details. Snyder sent for a state police sketch artist, who came to the hotel. They put two composites together, both profiles, one with glasses, one without.

"If we need anything else, we'll let you know," said Snyder, handing Arcia his card. That was the last he heard from Snyder for eleven years.

Two other composites would come out the first week in March. Lynn Nelms was put under hypnosis at the St. Paul, Minn., police department and a drawing was made by police artist Paul Johnson while she was under. That showed someone about 40, with some wrinkles. While under, Nelms told the artist the suspect had what seemed to be acne scars, but they were left off the composite. They would have looked too pronounced in a drawing and might have caused people to look for someone more scarred than he really was.

Johnson then met with Ann Johnson. The composite

made from her recollection—and she had seen the suspect face-to-face in broad daylight, while Nelms had seen him in a dark van—showed a man with similar features but much younger, 28–30 or so. Two versions of this composite were ultimately released, one with glasses, one without.

Both Nelms' and Johnson's versions showed the same hair as Arcia's, but the nose was shortened a bit.

Many years would pass before police, including Dan Snyder, who himself was trained to make composite drawings, would pronounce Ann Johnson's composite the most accurate—stunningly accurate—they had ever seen.

## 47
# HOT LEADS, COLD TRAIL

The Romulus PD had a limited budget for travel. With so many prospective witnesses spread around the country, the department turned to the FBI for help. FBI agents agreed to help out interviewing out-of-state residents who might not be coming back to Michigan soon.

Friday, February 22, the police released the first composite drawing.

"Mystery Man With Luggage Sought in Attendant Slaying," read the headline in Saturday's *Free Press*. The Saturday paper was traditionally very thin, without much of a news hole. The five-day-old story made page 2.

Deputy Chief Dave Early was quoted: "We're not saying this is the killer or the main suspect. If he wants to come in and say, 'Hey, that was my luggage and I had a legitimate reason to be there,' we'd sure love to hear from him."

Arcia's information sounded good, but like Snyder and Malaniak, Kraus didn't put a lot of store in it. What, after all, had Arcia's information amounted to? He saw a guy putting luggage into a car at an airport hotel. How common was that? Still, it was the best thing they'd come up with so far. The composite was generating tons of tips, which would keep them busy. And they had men at the airport, passing the composite out to employees and eyeballing passengers as they came and went.

They turned to the secretary of state in their search for

late-model Monte Carlos. They thought they might get another 80 or 100 leads that way. Wrong. They got a list of more than 2,600 in the state of similar colors in the right range of model years. They started running the names through LEIN (the Law Enforcement Intelligence Network, a computerized system) to see if anything turned up. The Monte Carlo was built on the same platform as other, very similar-looking GM cars. What if it wasn't a Monte Carlo, but one of its first cousins, another Chevy, Pontiac or Buick? You could never run them all down.

Arcia had said the car had white plates. Many of the leads in this case either went nowhere or to too many places. That year, thirty-eight states and the province of Ontario had white or mostly white plates.

Before they were done, they had more than 20,000 names in their database. Names of pilots. Names of Romulus hotel guests. Names of flight attendants. Names of Monte Carlo owners. Names of singles. Names off tip sheets. Eventually 200 of the names were deemed important enough to run lab tests on.

In 1991, running DNA profiles was very expensive and slow, with results taking six months or more. Snyder had a lab report from Helton that the perp was blood type A, which was very common, but secreted in his semen a rare enzyme, called PGM 2-1+, the PGM standing for phosphoglucomutase, a water-soluble molecule found in perspiration and in vaginal and seminal secretions. Less than two percent of the male population has that PGM grouping, which drastically narrowed down the field.

They'd start with a blood sample and a saliva sample. If the blood came back as type A and the saliva sample showed that he was a secreter, meaning blood-type molecules were present in water-soluble fluids other than blood—80 percent of the population are secreters—then a follow-up blood test would determine if he was a PGM type of 2-1+. If he was, then they'd run a DNA profile. Of the 200 suspects they tested, only one was a PGM 2-1+, and his DNA cleared him.

Snyder asked the Minneapolis police to videotape Nancy's funeral. Maybe the killer would get his kicks by showing up. One person caught their eyes, someone hanging out at the fringes snapping pictures, but he was just a free-lance photographer.

Hopes of an early capture faded as the long hours came and went.

"It was dead end, dead end, dead end," says Malaniak.

As the first week ended, "hope faded for a solution," said Kraus. "There was nothing surfacing."

They kept plugging away. They compiled a list of all fired Hilton employees and started looking them up. On March 8, they interviewed a cook who had been fired the previous March for smoking marijuana in a room with a maid. He had a record of arrest for indecent exposure. Saliva samples cleared him.

Snyder was determined to track down every lead possible. The piece of twine at the scene, that had been used to bind Ludwig's wrist—where did that come from? Who sold such twine? Who made it? In April he and Malaniak visited a local distributor of rope and twine and showed them the piece of twine used to bind Ludwig's hands.

It was something called, in the twine trade, a two-ply nature jute, and it had only one distributor in Michigan and Ohio. The distributor sold large reels of it to four companies, large balls of it to four companies and small balls of it to seven companies.

A solid lead came out of it, something to cross-reference: the particular twine the killer used was often used by landscapers. So, they went back and checked to see if anyone they'd talked to so far was a landscaper. Another dead end.

Mostly, they seemed to be compiling lists and files. They had 47 pages on the Tri-County Singles; 120 pages of Monte Carlos; 167 pages of airline passengers; 88 names of sex offenders; 5 pages of pilots who'd been attending a Northwest seminar in Detroit the weekend of the murder; 10 pages of Hilton employees.

All of the names and lists and pages had to be checked out. None of the information went anywhere.

For weeks that became months, Malaniak seemed to see gold Monte Carlos everywhere, at work, out with his wife, in his sleep. He'd jot down the license number and hurry back to the station to run it through the computer. Nothing.

# 48

# ANOTHER TRIP TO VEGAS

On Thursday, February 21, as Mike St. Andre wandered the concourses of Metro Airport four days after Nancy Ludwig's murder, keeping an eye out for someone of the killer's description and interviewing airport employees, Brenda Gorton was walking the concourses, too, trying to contain herself.

One of the suppliers for the family business, Century Rain Aid, organized yearly trips for people in the sprinkler trade. This year, it was to Vegas. There were 146 making the trip in all, including Jeff, Brenda, his brother, Greg, and Greg's wife, Sarah.

Because Buckler had done so much business with Century, the company was picking up the tab for a trip for two. At Christmas, Jeff's dad, Laurence, had put each brother's name in a hat and pulled one out to see who'd get the trip. Jeff won.

And what could be better in mid-winter in gloomy Michigan than a four-day trip to sunny Las Vegas at the Flamingo?

If Brenda saw St. Andre, it didn't register. She knew nothing about his mission or the death of the Northwest flight attendant. It had made the papers in Flint, though it wasn't big news or anything—nothing like it had been, and still was, in Detroit—but even if it had been big news, she probably wouldn't have paid attention, anyway. She didn't read the papers and didn't watch much TV news.

Because she had this coming weekend off, she had had to work the previous weekend, pulling the second shift at Flint Osteopathic Hospital and working late both Saturday, the 16th, and Sunday, the 17th.

It was the second of four trips the Gortons would take out of Metropolitan Airport. They'd gone to Cancun in 1989, before they were married; later they'd taken a trip to Disney World with their two young kids; and in January of 2001 they'd have a particularly odd start to their trip to Costa Rica. On the airport grounds, just short of the terminal, a merging truck from Alvan Motor Freight sandwiched into Gorton's 1993 Pontiac. Police arrived and took a report.

Gorton's car had to be towed away. But, miraculously, he, Brenda, his brother, Greg, and Greg's wife still made— barely—their flight.

They got the car out of the impound lot when they got back, unbent a fender enough so the car was operable, and were able to drive it back to Flint.

Hard to imagine a more memorable airport experience.

Or, maybe not.

The flight for Vegas in 1991 left at 9:20 a.m. on Continental Airlines. As Brenda anxiously awaited takeoff, she went over their itinerary. It was going to be a crazy, jam-packed four days. There were a lot of decisions to be made, too.

They were due to arrive in Vegas at 10:20 a.m. and due to depart on February 24 at 6:30 p.m., a flight that would get them into Metro at 1:25 a.m. on the 25th and back to their house in Flint by about 4 or so.

The itinerary had been arranged by Nevada Host Inc. Thursday and Friday were you're-on-your-own days. She and Jeff—neither of them were much for gambling—could take their choice of a tour to the Hoover Dam; an in-city tour of museums, stars' homes, the Chocolate Factory and Glitter Gulch; or a tour to Red Rock Canyon and Old Nevada.

Their literature said they could take their choice of big acts—Tom Jones was at Bally's, Julio Iglesias was at Caesars Palace, Frank Sinatra Jr. was at the Four Queens Hotel, Siegfried and Roy were at the Mirage, Paul Anka was at the Riviera, and Wayne Newton was at the Hilton.

One thing good and bad about Jeff was that he was so laid back. He'd be happy to do anything, but she'd have to decide.

Saturday morning, they had a breakfast with other Century Rain Aid trip winners, and Saturday afternoon there was a bowl-a-thon at Arizona Charlie's.

Sunday, they'd have to check out by 11:15 a.m., but they'd have the afternoon free.

Since Brenda wasn't much for gambling, something else she could read on the flight might come in handy. Century Rain Aid had provided some basic tips on gambling. They told her to always split a pair of aces or eights if she was playing blackjack, and to never split a pair of fives or ten-count cards.

That was easy enough. The other stuff? Forget it. Who could remember all that "with ace–seven, double down if the dealer shows three through six; draw if his up card is nine or ten; stand if he shows two, seven, eight or ace" malarkey? They were there to have fun, not study.

The day after Jeff and Brenda's flight left for Vegas, St. Andre was back at the airport. This time he was armed with two composite drawings to pass out, done by the state police sketch artist and based on Arcia's description. They showed a profile of a studious-looking young man with tousled, shortish hair; one version had him wearing big round glasses, the other had him without.

Just after the Gortons returned from Vegas, Brenda got good news. She was pregnant with their second child, had been since January.

## 49

# TIP NUMBER 1

After the first week's flurry of sixteen- and eighteen-hour days, of tracking down witnesses near and far, of working the area hotels, Malaniak and others started putting in more time on the tips that were pouring in.

One early tip seemed to corroborate fears by the FBI that the killing might somehow be related to Desert Storm, a plot by terrorists to steal a flight attendant's uniform, passport and Northwest ID, using rape and murder as a cover-up.

With as many as a quarter of a million Arab Americans in southeastern Michigan, certainly some of them had ties to Saddam's regime and were angry enough about the war to take desperate measures.

This tipster said that the murder had, in fact, been part of a terrorist plot, that a passport from a slight, dark-haired woman was needed to carry out the assassination of a top U.S. government official.

Snyder discounted the tip but passed it on to the FBI. The tipster somehow got Ludwig's home number and called him. Ludwig, against Snyder's wishes, agreed to fly to Detroit and meet the tipster at the Big Boy Restaurant across I-94 from Metro Airport.

The man showed up as scheduled, carrying twenty-eight pages of paper scrawled with anti-Arab rhetoric. Two of Snyder's undercover cops watched from a nearby table as the man ranted and raved at Ludwig about the Arabs.

Ludwig got the man's name and the police later ran it, without result. He was ultimately dismissed as a bigot and a nut, and his so-called terrorist scheme as merely a fantasy.

Ludwig's meeting with him was reminiscent of a weird rendezvous Lynne Helton had later on in the case. Only on TV shows do crime-scene investigators take an active part in investigations. Their work is done collecting samples at the scene and analyzing them back at the lab. But Helton, who had been quoted at length on the case in various media outlets, got a call from a woman who was fearful a close relative of hers might have been involved in the Ludwig killing.

He had recently died and she wanted for her own piece of mind to find out one way or another if he had done it.

Helton agreed to meet with the woman in the parking lot of the state police headquarters in East Lansing. Helton talked to her outside her car, in view of the guard booth, took an article of clothing from her that for some reason or another had been substantially bloodied by the man in question.

As the woman pulled out, Helton scribbled down the license plate number, Snyder ran it but nothing suspicious turned up.

Helton tested the clothing and it came up clean.

"We were like spies exchanging clandestine information. I couldn't believe what I was doing, and I wasn't sure I was safe. It almost smacks of the ridiculous," says Helton. "But it shows there was no length I wouldn't go to to solve this case."

State Police Detective Dan Bohnett called in a hot tip. He'd been working a case of a wife who suspected her husband of trying to murder her.

He was a lawyer in a posh Detroit suburb. Twice his wife had been hospitalized, violently ill. Both times before she got sick, her husband had brought dinner home from Mc-Donald's.

His wife brought the state police a book she had found at

home, on how to make poison. They got a warrant and paid him a visit at his office. Growing on his window sill at work they found castor beans, which can be very deadly if prepared properly.

Police took tissue samples from the attorney and ran them through U.S. military labs, but the enzymes they were looking for break down quickly and the samples tested negative. While Bohnett was convinced the attorney was guilty, there wasn't enough to charge him.

Of interest, though, was something the attorney's secretary told him. That one day in February, she recalled, about the time of the Ludwig murder, the attorney had come to work all scratched up and bruised. When she asked him what happened, he said he fell on his bike, February in Michigan being an unlikely time to ride a bike.

Bohnett called it in. The attorney was cleared of Ludwig's murder.


Snyder passed another early tip on to Malaniak to chase down, this one from a Mark Eby about some similar murder of his mother in Flint. Neither Snyder nor Malaniak had heard of the Eby killing, but it was worth looking into. By their standards, all the tips were.

Malaniak called the Flint PD, and was referred to King. He left a message for King, left another, left several more. "I kept leaving messages, leaving messages. He never called me back," says Malaniak. "Finally I got him."

He told him about the Ludwig killing and the tip and asked if there were any similarities, enough to be of interest. There certainly were similarities, King agreed.

"We've got a blood grouping. We're looking for a guy who's type A," said Malaniak. "Do you have any serological evidence on your case?"

No, King told him, everything they had was degraded. (The semen was too degraded for the technology available in 1987 but it held secrets, stored in ice at the State Police Crime Lab in Bridgeport that might one day be unlocked.)

King told Malaniak they knew who'd killed Eby, they just couldn't prove it. But they'd get him eventually. Their guy in the Flint case was type O. They weren't looking for the same killer. Had he been the punning type, King might have told him it was a stone-cold certainty.

"Well, thanks anyway." Malaniak hung up and filed away his report on the result of the tip. It was another dead end.

Eventually, some 2,300 tips would be phoned in. Months later, after the flow had dried up, they were reorganized and renumbered. For no particular reason, just happenstance, the call from Mark Eby was designated as Tip Number 1.

## 50
## MARATHONS, DESERT STORM AND BINGO!

The People Who Run and Walk Downtown was a creation of Detroit's Central Business District Association in 1983. The pro-business group thought it might be able to use the running boom to create cash flow and profits for downtown restaurants and bars on what was traditionally one of the slowest nights in town.

The CBDA ran a small ad in a weekly shopper asking if there were runners out there interested in getting together after work on Tuesdays. About thirty showed up for the first organizational meeting and the group had been meeting at a different downtown bar or restaurant after work every Tuesday since.

On summer Tuesdays, as many as 200 would show up. On cold winter nights, as few as thirty. It was an eclectic mix of old and young, black and white, blue collar and white collar, suburbanite and Detroiter. Though many of the group were single, it wasn't a typical singles-bar scene with people hitting on each other frenetically. People were more likely to talk about track workouts or recent 10K times than their signs of the zodiac.

In 1989, Michael Flynn started showing up on Tuesdays and made a big first impression. He was charming and gregarious, the kind of guy to walk up to strangers, thrust out a hand and offer a big smile. He was a pilot for Northwest Airlines. He'd often arrive in his pilot's uniform, either just getting in from a flight or on his way out of town. He'd change in the bar restaurant into his running clothes, go out for a six-mile run, then return. If he had to catch a flight, he'd change back into his uniform and leave. If he was just in from a flight, he'd have a few beers and chat up the women.

He was one of the group's nice guys. So much so, in fact, that at the club's annual Super Bowl party in 1990, when he was scheduled to make an afternoon flight to the West Coast, he made up a huge batch of chili and dropped it off at the party for others to enjoy during the game while he was heading west.

One of the women he chatted up was a pretty, young engineer named Patricia Bosch. She was a triathlete, very attractive, rather bosomy for a very good female runner. And she was single and the obvious object of attention of many of the single men in the group.

It wasn't long before Michael and Patricia were dating. The gregarious pilot and the curvaceous engineer made quite a match.

There was one odd thing the better runners in the club noticed, though. On Tuesdays, Michael would tell about his latest PR over the weekend—PR being running lingo for a personal record at one distance or another. Each Tuesday, Michael would tell of having run yet another 10K (6.2 miles) at yet another record pace. He soon was breaking the forty-minute mark in the 10K that many runners consider the benchmark for qualifying as a very good recreational runner.

Except that when Michael went out to run each Tuesday night with the other runners in the club who could also break forty minutes, he could never come close to keeping up. He'd be with them for a mile or two, gasping furiously, then fall quickly off the pace, ending up running the last few miles by himself. And this all happened at a pace of maybe seven minutes and thirty seconds a mile versus the 6:15 he claimed he could do at races.

A bullshit artist, the other good runners quickly decided about him. No way could he break forty minutes on Saturday and die like a dog on Tuesday.

Another of his claims? He was divorced and carried around a picture of his young boy, dressed in his hockey uniform. Flynn said he got to be best friends with Bill Ford Jr., of the famous Fords who dominate Detroit business and cultural circles. Seems Flynn was at a local hockey rink to watch his son play and had gone to the concession stand. On his way back he saw a tot falling off the back of the bleachers lining the rink and had made a miraculous catch just before the child slammed into the concrete. It was Bill Ford's child and he and Flynn had since grown close.

A third claim? That his background was diverse. He introduced himself to another single young woman in the group one night, Julie Hamilton, a psychotherapist at Eastwood Clinic. Hey, small world, Flynn said. He'd worked there for years as a therapist, too.

After a month or so of dating, Patricia found out that Michael's running wasn't the only thing he inflated. Somehow word got to her that he wasn't a pilot with Northwest, that he was a fireman in East Detroit. And apparently not a very good one, either. Word was he was afraid of heights, not recommended in that line of ladder-aided work, and on disability.

She confronted him with it and at first he denied it. He was angry, demanded that they not break up. He called incessantly, came over, pleaded his case, didn't want to give up on the relationship. Later, Patricia noticed clothing disappearing from her house and suspected Michael was sneaking in and taking things.

Word about all of that went through the club like wildfire. Interestingly enough, though, the club members tolerated his deceptions about running and flying. No one ever called him on them to his face. He kept coming out on Tuesdays in his pilot's uniform, and he kept telling about improbable times at weekend races, and people kept telling stories about him behind his back.

In October of 1990, fellow club members turned him in for cheating at the *Detroit Free Press* International Marathon. He'd finished in three hours and fifteen minutes and qualified for the Boston Marathon, and in the process had beaten out several of the runners he couldn't keep up with on Tuesdays.

In a review of film from various cameras set up along the way to catch cheaters, he was nowhere to be seen until after the midpoint in the race, when suddenly he appeared. Ridiculously enough, in his first appearance on film, he was wearing a nylon jacket on a hot day and hadn't started sweating, yet, though he was supposed to be more than thirteen miles into his run. Later shots of him show the nylon jacket tied around his waist and sweat pouring down. Late in the race he was walking.

He requested a hearing with race officials to dispute the charges, but didn't show and was disqualified.

Late February or early March of 1991, Mike O'Hara, a sports reporter who covered the Detroit Lions for *The Detroit News*, Wally Poupore, a computer specialist at Ford, and two other members of the downtown runners had separated themselves from their fellow club members for a tête-à-tête.

Tonight, the talk wasn't of training pace or race times, it was of murder. And of the suspect in their midst. Someone wanted to throw out something for comment, but only to a small circle of trusted friends.

"You guys been following the murder of that Northwest stewardess?"

"Sure," they said, or nodded. Who hadn't?

"Anything jump out at you?"

"Michael Flynn," said O'Hara.

"You got it," said the first speaker.

"Flynn? Why?" someone asked.

Speculation was rife in the media that, since there were no signs of violence outside Ludwig's hotel room and no signs of forced entry, perhaps the killer was someone who had gained her trust. Between the lines there seemed to be a bit of blaming the victim, that she'd maybe been picked up in the hotel bar. Hey, she was a flight attendant, right?

"They're saying it might have been someone she knew, or someone she might have met that she had reason to trust," said the first speaker. "A fellow employee. Maybe a pilot. Know anyone who hangs around bars in a pilot's uniform?"

Again, someone said: "Michael Flynn."

"What should we do?"

"There's an 800 number to call. A tip line. Should we call it?"

"We've got to."

"What if he didn't do it?"

"What if he did?"

Flynn's deceptions no longer seemed humorous.

What's more, it was widely reported that Ludwig's clothes were missing, and hadn't Patricia suspected Flynn of taking some of her things?

Someone volunteered to call the tip line.

On succeeding Tuesdays, the small group of People Who Ran Downtown would continue to speculate about Flynn and the Ludwig murder. No one from the Romulus PD ever acknowledged getting the tip, or mentioned whether or not they followed up on it. The group of runners never knew if Flynn was investigated and, if so, if he had been cleared.

Whenever Flynn came up to them over the following years, grinning his big grin, glad-handing them, they pictured a raped and mutilated flight attendant in a hotel room at the airport. They avoided him—and the image—whenever they could.

What O'Hara and the others wouldn't find out for eleven years was that the cops had, indeed, acted on the tip. That it had been the second best one they'd get out of the 2,300.

Concurrently, Flynn's name had come up by way of the Macomb County Sheriff's Department, which called Snyder on March 8. They were holding Flynn at the county jail and thought the Romulus PD ought to hustle their way up there.

Flynn had shown up in a Navy uniform at an elementary school, claiming to be a pilot just back from Desert Storm. He wanted to arrange a speech before an assembly. Suspicious school officials called the sheriff's department.

He agreed voluntarily to a search of his car, and sheriff's deputies found ID for Northwest Airlines and a Northwest captain's uniform in his trunk.

Snyder raced up I-94 to Mt. Clemens and interviewed Flynn in the county jail. He told them that he was, in fact, a lieutenant with the East Detroit Fire Department and had been a cop in East Detroit, too.

Flynn told them the last time he had been to the airport was in October, to fly to a marathon in Minneapolis, and that he had never been to the Hilton.

His former girlfriend, Patricia Bosch, was cooperative. She still had one of Flynn's coats, which she turned over to

Snyder and Malaniak. It was a Navy pea coat, bearing the tag "Lt. Flynn, U.S.S. Midway."

In the pocket of the coat—this got their hearts going—was a letter Flynn had written to Bosch just days after Ludwig's murder. In the letter, Flynn said he knew Ludwig, that she was a fine person, and that it made him sick to think about what had been done to her.

Bingo! "This is our guy," thought Snyder.

Flynn readily agreed to give Malaniak and Gorton a saliva sample for a DNA test. When it came back weeks later, bingo turned into bust. His DNA didn't match the semen at the scene. He wasn't the killer. He was just an odd duck with a good line and nice uniforms.

## 51
# THE PROFILERS

Snyder found out that profilers from the FBI and various police agencies around the country were having a convention in Iowa in March. Northwest offered free flights and Kraus sprung money from the budget for a hotel and food, and sent Malaniak and Snyder went to see what they could come up with.

Malaniak thought it was a bunch of hooey. Snyder thought it'd be like chicken soup, couldn't hurt. Besides, who wants to pass up a trip to Iowa in March?

"They told us the killer was a white male," says Malaniak. "Big deal. Aren't they all? It was pretty useless."

One profiler told them the killer may have been mentally disturbed, which, given what he'd done to the body before and after death, including just about sawing off her head with a serrated knife, struck Malaniak as "No shit, Sherlock."

The profilers also told them the killer surely lived within five miles of the airport and had likely taken Ludwig's belongings to build a shrine to her and her murder in the basement of his house. If it was typical of a Romulus house, the horror of the shrine would be hidden behind the normal exterior of a small, aluminum-sided bungalow.

The shrine would include her panties, brassiere, panty

hose, wallet, purse, diamond earrings, three pieces of burgundy Northwest flight attendant luggage, credit cards, uniform and ID tag.

The killer was certainly single, probably did not have a girlfriend, likely had been dominated by his mother and may still live with her. He was probably no taller than 5'10", probably changes jobs frequently, probably never served in the military. His car was likely an old junker, and filled with just about everything he owns.

Another conclusion: The killer was an organized rapist and a disorganized murderer. He had planned the rape, but hadn't planned the murder. It was something that just got out of hand.

Snyder was skeptical. This was no accidental murder, no disorganized killer. He had gone to the Hilton to rape and kill, he had raped and killed, and so far he had gotten away with it.

"Hey, you've seen those films from gas station cameras where a guy goes in to rob the place, the robbery goes bad, he ends up shooting the clerk. What does he do?" asks Snyder. "He freaks out. He runs out of there as fast as he can. That's an accidental killer. If Nancy's killer didn't intend to kill her, he wouldn't have stuck around and cleaned up."

Unlike the Flint PD, Snyder and Malaniak took what the profilers had to say with a grain of salt. A good thing, too, since most of it would many years later prove to be dead wrong. About the only thing they believed was that the killer might very well be in their midst, living in one of those Romulus bungalows they drove by every day. It wasn't much of a return on the investment of plane tickets to Iowa.

The profilers hadn't helped. They were no closer to solving the case.

As had the Eby murder, the Ludwig murder faded into one of those filler stories editors assign on slow news days, or on anniversaries or year-end round-ups.

"There was so much interest in the case, there wasn't a year that went by when, on the anniversary, someone in the media didn't call to ask about it," says Snyder.

"Clues Scarce in Death of Flight Attendant," read a *Free Press* headline six months after the murder. "Flight Attendant Slaying Still Unsolved," read the non-newsy headline in the December 28, 1991, edition.

By then, all the leads had hit dead ends. The case had long gone cold.

## 52
## OTHER BINGOS!

Michael Flynn wasn't the only good suspect. Not the first "Bingo!" Not the first bust. The first had been the shuttle-bus driver fired for screaming at a Northwest flight attendant. Another early suspect was a violent crack cocaine addict who was picked up on drug charges and, during routine questioning, said he couldn't remember what he'd been doing Sunday night, but he might have done it. He was cleared, too.

Not long after the murder, a former manager at the Hilton called in a tip. Six months earlier, he'd been working the desk when a white male came up to him and said his key card wouldn't open his door and he wanted a replacement.

The manager recognized it as a missing master key for another floor. He called police and stalled the guy till they could arrive. Stalling meant, in this case, listening to the guy—with the unlikely last name of Straight—talking about his Satanic cult and how he was going to Atlanta to chop off some arms and heads.

Extremely disoriented, he told police he was the Antichrist and wanted to find someone in the hotel to have sex with so he could rid himself of his evil spirit. His mother was called and he wasn't charged.

Pretty hot tip, a guy known for possessing stolen key cards wanting to have sex to purge his demons and hoping to cut off heads? Malaniak and Snyder paid him a visit, tracking him down at a Papa Romano's pizza joint nearby, where he was a delivery man. He said he was on medication these days, and had been in church with his parents the night of Ludwig's murder. He gave a saliva sample and was cleared.

Waitresses at the Wheat and Rye restaurant near the airport fingered a waiter at the Holiday Inn. His girlfriend was a Northwest flight attendant and he liked to beat her up. He was cleared.

Blood and saliva tests cleared some sixty suspects in the first few months. Eventually saliva, blood or DNA tests would clear two hundred persons, including Art Ludwig, who Snyder reluctantly asked to take a test about six months after the murder, as a formality.

Periodically, some sicko, having read about room 354, would show up at the front desk and specifically ask for that room, looking for some thrill in spending a night where Ludwig had died. Police were called each time. Each time the suspect was cleared.

For years room 354 was taken out of circulation, stripped of furniture and carpeting and used as a storage area, even after the hotel was sold and became the Royce Hotel. Today, the hotel is a Doubletree Hotel and the room is back in service, with the same number.

In May 1992, it looked, again, as if police might have their man. Leslie Allen Williams, 38, had been arrested for four rape-murders and other assaults in Oakland County. Ludwig had been killed on a Sunday, and Williams' last six known assaults had come on weekends. His blood type was A positive. He had bound his victims' hands. All of his assaults were spontaneous, unpremeditated crimes of opportunity.

In June, though, police announced he was not the killer. Further lab tests showed he had the wrong enzymes in his blood.

The year 1995 was a busy year for hot leads.

Ann Arbor police called Snyder to tell them they'd arrested James Klepinger for raping and murdering his girlfriend. Of interest was his MO—he'd used ligatures to bind her hands. And he lived just down Merriman Road from the airport.

But Snyder determined he'd been in Ohio when Ludwig died.

Glen Rogers was arrested in Kentucky in connection with a cross-country killing spree that claimed the lives of women in Mississippi, Florida, California and Louisiana. Rogers' sister told police her brother might have killed more than fifty women nationwide.

Charles Rathbun, a free-lance photographer who had once worked in Michigan, admitted that he had killed Linda Sobek, a cheerleader for the Los Angeles Raiders, but he said it was accidental. He was suspected of killing a second woman and had been charged with rape in 1979.

Romulus police investigated both men. Blood samples cleared them of Ludwig's murder.

Then they got word of a mirror-image killing in Minneapolis, of all places, which sent their hearts racing. James Luther Carlton, a 40-year-old construction laborer and crackhead, had been arrested for the torture, rape and murder of a 26-year-old office worker named Judy Lee Dover. Her hands had been bound and she'd been gagged. There were seven puncture wounds on her right shoulder and three above her right breast. A slashing wound to her neck had severed all major arteries and vessels. And she'd been raped.

Blood tests cleared him in the Ludwig case.

Three years later, another heart-thumping "bingo" started with a teletype out of a small police department in Minnesota, telling the Romulus PD they'd arrested a former Michigan resident from the affluent Detroit suburb of Grosse Pointe.

Two women get in their van at a Wal-Mart. The driver hears something, turns, sees this guy in the back holding a hunting knife. She jumps out screaming. He panics, jumps out, runs to a pick-up and squeals out of there. She gets the license plate and calls the cops.

The cops find him in a motel. The knife is wrapped in a towel in the truck, next to a large bottle of bleach. Like he was planning to clean up a mess.

They ran his name, found out he'd been arrested in Michigan in 1986, went to jail and got out in December of 1990, just in time to murder Ludwig.

His blood work in Michigan showed he was A positive, just what they were looking for, though his PGM grouping wasn't known. Malaniak wanted him to submit to another sample, this time to find his PGM, but he refused. Fourteen months later he finally agreed to another blood test.

Wrong PGM grouping. He was clear on Ludwig.

The next hot suspect wouldn't surface until 2002.

# 53

# ART ON THE ATTACK

Art Ludwig wasn't a passive victim. Anything but. He decided early on to do what he did best. He was a media guy. He'd work the media. He'd keep the story alive. He'd keep the heat on. He'd do what he could to get Nancy's killer one way or another, sooner or later.

Early on, there was a delay getting the 800-number tip line started, something with budget problems in the police department. Ludwig told Ken Kraus he'd pay for the tip line if he had to, but he wanted a line up and running, ASAP. Kraus called him back. His bosses had okayed the line and Romulus would pay for it.

Ludwig kept coming back to Detroit to do radio and TV interviews. He was accessible to the reporters at *The Detroit News* and *Detroit Free Press*, and they were happy to keep the story alive.

Everything he did, he made sure he told his growing number of media contacts about.

A month after the murder, he videotaped an appeal for information and had it disseminated to Detroit media outlets. "Victim's Husband Tapes an Appeal" read the headline in *The Detroit News*.

Two months after the murder, Art flew into town and met with a psychic from Brighton and a clairvoyant from Farmington Hills in room 354 at the Airport Hilton. They told him they were able to pick up the same image of the killer and that their image didn't match Arcia's description or the composite in the newspapers. But they couldn't actually describe what they thought they were seeing. Privately, Ludwig thought they were useless. Nonetheless, it was fodder for headlines, a way to keep the story alive. "Grieving Husband Calls on Psychics to Find Wife's Killer."

"At first, Snyder and I felt they'd solve this fairly fast," says Ludwig. "But then, I felt the more we kept it on the front burner, the better off we'd be. One, there was less chance the Romulus police would go on to something else if there was a lot of hue and cry. Second, it would generate leads."

Ludwig got the Teamsters—Nancy was a member of local 2747—to kick in $30,000 to the reward fund. Headlines. "Teamsters Join Hunt for Killer: Truckers to Circulate Fliers About Slain Flight Attendant," read the headline in *The Detroit News* of August 21, 1991. Art's picture accompanied the story with a cutline: "Art Ludwig: He wants answers."

The award announcement coincided with a big campaign to splash WANTED posters all over town, with details of Nancy's slaying and photos of the composite drawings of the killer. Art held a press conference at the Airport Marriott Hotel on August 26 to announce that there would be a barrage of posters. The next day papers prominently carried the story. "I'm frustrated," Ludwig was quoted as saying in the *News*. "My mission is to raise public awareness." He also took out big display ads featuring the poster in all the dailies and suburban weeklies in the Detroit area.

The Teamsters said they would run the reward poster in their union magazine and their 1.6 million members nationwide would distribute the bright yellow flyers at hotels, restaurants and airports nationwide. Teamsters members and Art and his daughters taped posters up on light poles around town.

On September 16, Advo Systems, a direct-mail company in suburban Livonia, began distributing copies of the poster to all households within five miles of the airport.

Art knew how to pull the media strings and he pulled them, with good timing and great effect. He'd mentored a lot of successful TV executives and reporters over the years. Now he would call in all favors, all chits, to get all the airtime he could. He got on the Maury Povich show out of New York. He made appearances on *A Current Affair* and *Inside Edition*. He let cameras follow him around to fill the B rolls of their feature stories. "I prostituted myself to the media," he says.

While in New York taping the Povich show, Ludwig met with an author he'd heard about who was writing a true-crime book on unsolved cases. His wife's murder ended up garnering a chapter in the book, titled *Rewards*.

On the first anniversary of his wife's death, Ludwig took out display ads in all the Detroit area papers.

"IN LOVING MEMORY OF MY WIFE," read the first line.

"Northwest Flight Attendant," read the second. In huge bold letters the third line read: "NANCY JEAN LUDWIG."

The body of the ad said, in part: "Nancy was RAPED and MURDERED at the Airport Hilton Hotel in Romulus on Sunday night, Feb. 17th, 1991. The person responsible for this horrible act is still free and probably still in the Detroit area. It is absolutely essential that we get this person off the streets and into treatment before he strikes again. The next victim could be someone you love . . . wife . . . mother . . . girlfriend . . . daughter or neighbor."

Tips poured in. Snyder and Malaniak ran them down. Nothing.

Each anniversary Art had something planned that would bring the story back to life for a day or two. Someone knew something, he was sure. If he kept the story alive, they might catch a break. If he let it die. . . . Well, that wasn't going to happen.

Just after the fourth anniversary of Nancy's death, Ludwig's forlorn visage peered out at readers from the cover of the *Free Press Magazine* of March 12, 1995, heralding a story by Ben Burns, a former editor of *The Detroit News* who was dean of journalism at Wayne State University. It was a story that grew out of a fifteen-week project he assigned his students in a class on investigative reporting.

Ludwig told Burns he was willing to "do anything, say anything, go anywhere to catch the killer. He killed two people that night. He killed Nancy and he killed me."

On the fifth anniversary of her murder, the *Free Press* carried a five-column story with the headline: "6 Sisters Search for Stepmother's Death."

The story announced that four of Ludwig's daughters were arriving at what had been the Airport Hilton—it had been sold since the murder and was then called the Royce Hotel—from Minneapolis that day to kick off a campaign to find their stepmother's killer. They'd be in for several days doing interviews, passing out new flyers and beating the drums.

The story said that the hotel had agreed to let them place flowers and light candles in room 354, which had not been used since the murder.

Snyder was quoted: "I've never had a case for this length

of time that has kept the attention of so many people. I don't know why that is."

A two-word explanation: Art Ludwig.

More tips poured in. Nothing.

Despite everything he did over the years, nothing stopped some people from thinking he had either killed his wife or, more likely, hired someone to do it. There were rumors that he had lost money in an investment in a failed bread bakery (true) and needed the insurance money (false). He felt the cold shoulder from some, the glances from others, faces quickly averted when he turned to them. Always he felt as though he were under a cloud of suspicion.

Seven or eight years after Nancy's death, Art got a call from a close friend, who wanted to alert him that a mutual acquaintance was spreading dirt about Art.

The mutual acquaintance was one of Art's closest child-hood friends, one of his fellow busboys during summers at the Land O'Lakes Bar and Café in Brainerd. On weekends, when they got out of work too late to avoid breaking curfew, they'd slept in the employee bunk room on the second floor of the restaurant.

The friend was much bigger than Art, but they'd wrestle and engage in typical horseplay. They were inseparable in high school and kept in touch over the years.

The friend had become a cop. He was telling people: "I'm a cop and I know Art did it. It's just a matter of time till they prove it."

"I was absolutely stunned," says Art. "We'd lived to-gether. We went to high school together. I've been in his home. When he got sick, I visited him in the hospital."

Art hasn't spoken with him since, their friendship an-other victim.

But for all of Art's working the media, for all of Snyder's and Malaniak's bulldog relentlessness, eventually they had to admit there was nothing more to be done. It was a cold case. They were at a dead end.

# PART FOUR

## Cold-Case Squad

# 54

# THE SQUAD FORMS

Bradford Barksdale has an unusual academic background for a chief of police, with an affinity and talent for biology, chemistry, calculus and physics.

He went to Cass Technical High School in Detroit, Margarette Eby's alma mater. In 1970, when Barksdale graduated, it was—and today, still is—an oasis of learning in a largely dysfunctional school system riddled with incompetence and indifference, where high school seniors routinely cannot read or calculate above second- or third-grade levels.

Cass Tech is where the smartest and most motivated of the city's kids go, often arriving by city bus from many miles, and several transfers, away.

Barksdale went to the University of Michigan–Flint and spent his first three years as a math major, switching to African-American studies as a senior. He switched over after an incident that proved for him that math was too theoretical to pursue as a life's occupation.

A professor one day went through a counterintuitive proof that if you take .9999 and extend the nines to infinity, the number became equivalent to one. For Barksdale it was hogwash. He didn't care how many nines there were. If you kept having one nine after another, to him you were approaching as close as you could get to one, but still weren't there.

Of such a tiny thing, the difference or lack thereof between one and a decimal point followed by an infinity of nines, would Flint's police chief ultimately be made.

Like many big cities in the mid-1970s, Flint was recruiting blacks to diversify its police force, and Barksdale thought he'd give it a shot. He started out working undercover narcotics because he was a fresh face no one would recognize. He made sergeant in 1984 and lieutenant in 1987, about the same time he was assigned to the Flint Area Narcotics Group (FANG), a multi-jurisdictional task force that included members of the state police.

In 1995, Barksdale was promoted to captain and on October 3, 2000, twenty-three years to the day after he started training at the police academy, he was named chief of police.

Coincidentally, in 1981, during a fifteen-month layoff from the PD during one of Flint's recurring economic slumps, Barksdale got to know Eby. He took a temporary job as director of safety and security at U-M–Flint and was in several meetings with her.

He was working vice and narcotics when Eby was murdered, and had no involvement with the case, though like everyone in Flint, he was well versed in its particulars.

While working with FANG, Barksdale had become friends with his supervisor on the task force, Captain Robert Bertee. They were both no-nonsense, straight-shooting cops with reputations for knowing how to get things done and done right.

Bertee had been a small-town kid, growing up in Michigan's Thumb. He graduated from high school in 1970, went to college for a year, didn't like it and dropped out.

In 1973, he took a part-time job as cop in his home town of North Branch, a job that came with not a minute of training. He just raised his right arm, took an oath and got his uniform. He fell in love with being a cop, joined the state police academy the next year and upon graduation became a road trooper for $4.82 an hour in Pontiac, a city very much like Flint in that its auto-factory economy was suffering through hard times as imports cut into the Big Three's market share.

Bertee worked undercover in Detroit three years, then worked on several multi-jurisdictional teams, in affluent Oakland County north of Detroit, in western Michigan and in Flint. In 1996, he was promoted to captain and placed in charge of the state police's criminal investigations division, where he oversaw covert operations, such as the installation of hidden cameras and microphones during investigations, and, reporting to the state's attorney general, investigated all allegations of corruption or malfeasance by the state's elected politicians.

By the time Barksdale was appointed chief, Bertee had become a lieutenant colonel with the state police and was its highest ranking career officer, reporting only to a political appointee who held the rank of colonel.

**LEFT:** Margarette Eby, with Dayle *(left)* and Lynn, after getting her Ph.D from the University of Michigan in 1971. *(courtesy Mark Eby)*

**BELOW:** The Eby kids join their mom in Cedar Falls, Iowa, for Thanksgiving in 1978. *(courtesy Mark Eby)*

**LEFT:** Nancy Ludwig, an avid fisherman, shows off a salmon caught on Lake Michigan. *(courtesy Art Ludwig)* **RIGHT:** Nancy helps out at a family picnic. *(courtesy Art Ludwig)*

**LEFT:** The composite, based on Ann Johnson's description of Ludwig's presumed killer, described later by veteran police as the most accurate composite they had ever seen. *(courtesy Dan Snyder)*

**RIGHT:** Jeff Gorton during his brief Navy Career, 1982-83. *(courtesy Michigan State Police)*

The Gorton house as it looked while under surveillance in February of 2002. To the left, half-hidden behind a snow bank and covered in a tarp, is Jeff's gold Monte Carlo. *(courtesy Michigan State Police)*

Proud Jeff in front of his beloved Monte Carlo. *(courtesy Michigan State Police)*

Underwear labeled "school teacher by Steve's house—pump job w/oil tank I hit." *(courtesy Michigan State Police)*

Jeff Gorton wearing women's undergarments in his home. *(courtesy Michigan State Police/Frame-grab by Jason Homler)*

**LEFT:** Marie Gagliano and Robert Greenburg—the victim who got away, the man who befriended her who later became her husband, and their home in the woods outside Jesup, Georgia. *(Tom Henderson)*

**BELOW:** Gate house at the Mott Estate, also known as Applewood. *(Tom Henderson)*

Lynne Helton, in her lab. She shot the photos at the Ludwig crime scene and later entered DNA from both cases into a data base that eventually linked the Ludwig murder to that of Margarette Eby. *(Tom Henderson)*

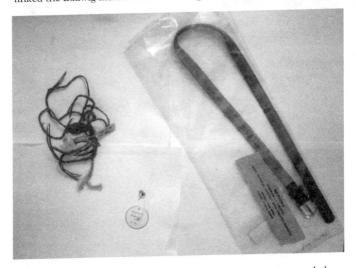

Some of the few things left behind of the Ludwig crime scene—a belt, a gold charm and some of the twine used to bind her arms. *(Tom Henderson)*

The Buckler Sprinkler Company, the Gorton family business. Jeff's truck was dispatched from here to the Mott Estate to flush out the lines and get ready for winter in November of 1986. *(Tom Henderson)*

Skateland Arena, where police grabbed Jeff Gorton's drinking cup to be tested for DNA. *(Tom Henderson)*

Michigan State Police Det. Lt. Mike Larsen outside Skateland. *(Tom Henderson)*

End of the hallway where Ludwig was killed. Her room, 354, was right next to the emergency exit, where the killer may have waited for her to arrive. *(Tom Henderson)*

Former Romulus detectives Gordie Malaniak *(left)* and Dan Snyder *(right)*. The third floor window behind them and between them is room 354, where Ludwig was killed. *(Tom Henderson)*

Greg Kilbourn's retirement party, April of 2002. Left to right are key members of the Michigan State Police cold-case squad that solved the Eby and Ludwig murders – Rudy Gonzalez, Greg Kilbourn, Dan Bohnett, Hal Zettle, and Mike Larsen. *(courtesy Mike Larsen)*

From left to right, former flight attendant and intern at Gorton's trial, Cori Reyes, Judge Maggie Drake, and prosecutor Betty Walker. *(Tom Henderson)*

In 2000, Flint was in another downturn, this one severe enough that Michigan's governor, John Engler, had repeatedly threatened to have the state take over the running of the city, and in fact a trustee was eventually appointed to oversee Flint's day-to-day operations and try to rein in its huge budget deficits, reducing the mayor to a figurehead.

The police department was going through layoffs, and in even more of a budget crunch than normal. Eventually the department would lose 100 positions, going from about 350 officers in the late 1990s to about 250 in 2002.

When he heard his old friend had made chief, Bertee gave Barksdale a call and suggested they get together. He thought there might be something the MSP could do to help his old friend battle the bad guys in Flint.

"I wanted us to be more fluid and flexible in our approach to crime-solving. If you see something, offer your assistance. Some police departments want your help, others don't," says Bertee. He figured Barksdale would.

"I've never found a chief of police that cared for his community more than Brad Barksdale cares for his," says Bertee, who was willing to be creative—and, more important, willing to allocate resources—to come to Flint's aid. Bertee even was willing to go so far as to pull in detectives or troopers from other districts.

Before the end of the year 2000, Bertee and Barksdale met for lunch. Having worked together in FANG, both were supporters of multi-jurisdictional task forces. Both were also big proponents of DNA technology and well versed in recent technological advances that might make it possible to solve old crimes.

They decided to form a cold-case task force that, so as not to step on any toes, would only target very old cases no longer being worked. That would also reduce the possibility of opposition, either from within the ranks of the Flint PD or from local politicians, Democrats all, who were very leery of perceived meddling by the state or its Republican governor.

They also decided to target cases where crime-scene evidence would lend itself to updated DNA analysis. There was one case that jumped out to Barksdale as fitting every criterion.

"The Eby case was at the top of the list," he says.

He asked Bertee if he was familiar with the case. He wasn't. Barksdale filled him in. "Nothing would impact our community more than solving this," he told him.

Bertee went back to his East Lansing office at the MSP's headquarters and told his assistant, Mark Dougovito, who supervised all the detectives in the state, to work on the nuts and bolts of putting a task force together. He told him there was no line-item amount in the budget for a task force.

"Just do it, and do it right and I'll get you the funding," said Bertee, with the full support of his boss, Colonel Mike Robinson.

On May 3, 2001, Dougovito met with Dan Bohnett and Lieutenant Gary Hagler of the Flint PD. Bohnett, a former hippie and Vietnam War protestor, was a detective lieutenant overseeing all the MSP detectives in ten posts stretching over thirteen counties in central and northern Michigan, and the idea of a cold-case task force struck a nerve with him. For one thing, he had worked at the Flint post from 1994–1999, "when it was the crime capital of the world," he says. For another, "An uncleared major crime is unacceptable. We didn't close cases," he says. "I didn't care if it was twenty years old. I told my people, 'Investigate crimes like they happened to your family.' "

Bohnett said Bertee had asked him before the meeting what he'd need to go into Flint with a major-crimes task force. His answer: ten detectives and a lot of funding. Flint had no money, so it would all have to come from the MSP.

Barksdale was back in Flint thinking maybe the MSP would offer up two or three detectives for the squad. Bertee offered ten. Flint would assign two or three officers. They would target the Eby case and one or two others.

It was decided that the squad would be housed in the Flint PD headquarters downtown and that Flint would provide some basic office necessities such as a room or two and mailboxes.

The MSP would provide most of the manpower, GPS surveillance devices when needed, computers, high-speed data lines and 800-megahertz radios.

Bohnett was told he could hand-pick his detectives. His first two choices were sergeants Greg Kilbourn and Mike

Larsen, according to Bohnett "the two best detectives working the state at the time, and to team them up . . ."

On May 16, Larsen and Officer Mark Reaves began the actual physical work of setting up a place to work. They rounded up old MSP file cabinets and other office equipment that weren't being used. They hauled in computers. They got the phone company to install high-speed lines to connect their computers and phones directly to the Flint MSP Post 35 west of town. "Bertee told me, 'Whatever you need to get it running. If you need to use my name, go ahead,' " recalls Reaves. "I was dropping his name like apples from a tree."

The Homicide Task Force was born. Even if it did have just one tiny room that would barely fit three officers, much less the planned twelve or thirteen. Even if the room, with dirty beige walls and scruffed, scratched linoleum floors was just across from the bathroom, and the sound of flushing toilets in the old plumbing came through the thin walls so clearly you could barely keep a phone conversation going.

But there were still obstacles to be overcome. Almost as soon as Larsen and Reaves started trucking in stuff, the Flint PD's sergeants' union filed a complaint with the Michigan Employment Relations Commission, alleging a violation of state labor laws and that the task force was an illegal outsourcing of Flint police work.

They went to Genesee County Circuit Court Judge Richard Yuille and asked him to grant an injunction to stop the state police from investigating any of Flint's old homicides.

"The city is outsourcing jobs that should be done by city sergeants," said the union president, Police Sergeant Rick Hetherington.

Barksdale had no comment for reporters.

## 55
## DEAD OR ALIVE?

Barksdale had no comment for reporters, but he had plenty of comments for the sergeants. He was mightily pissed off, to the point of apoplexy, and Brad Barksdale when mad is very, very mad.

"I told them they were embarrassing themselves. 'Don't let people think you are more concerned with your paycheck than putting murderers in jail,' " he told them.

Bohnett was equally ticked off, especially that the union was fighting them on the Eby case. "My God, I wanted to get that one solved. I mean, you're talking about a case lying down in the basement, just sitting there in a file. And all the detectives who worked it are retired and gone."

Barksdale knew some of it was just a rote response from a union sick of seeing officers laid off. Part of it was fear that this was the first step in the door of a state takeover of Flint. "They were getting paranoid. It was ridiculous. I thought it was ludicrous, but I understood what the paranoia was," said Barksdale.

There was also a fiasco involving the FBI that was still fresh in a lot of people's minds. In the mid-1990s, the FBI had offered the Flint PD help in setting up a crime task force. Flint provided office space in the police headquarters. "It was a damn scam," says Barksdale. "All they wanted to do was come in, wire the police building and City Hall [with bugs] and look for corruption."

The Feds got a quick boot when it was discovered what they were up to, says Barksdale.

Barksdale was worried that the brouhaha would cause Bertee to rethink his offer. "He was afraid we'd pull out, but I told him, 'We'll work it out. We'll get it done,' " says Bertee.

The union came to its senses. The issue was settled during negotiations. The union was promised that the task force would only work old cases, those at least a year old that had gone cold and were no longer being actively worked. The task force would be given the green light for a year and then its existence would be open to further negotiation. And, as a face-saving gesture, without much other significance, the union made—and was granted—another demand: The name of the task force would be changed from the Homicide Task Force to the Violent Crimes Task Force. The union thought the first name might imply that Flint cops didn't know how to solve homicides, though why the second name is any better is a matter of conjecture.

Pettiness prevailed, though. For example, the Flint cops

wouldn't let the state cops use their LEIN machine down-stairs, the computerized system for seeing who's got warrants out on them anywhere in the state.

The Eby case was at the top of the task force's list. It fit all the criteria, plus, if it could be solved, the PR impact would be enormous, both for showing the value of joint task forces and in getting more money from state legislators to fund DNA testing.

The task force would work two other cases, too, one involving a suspected serial murderer. "We had a lot of dead prostitutes. We had them falling over like flies," says Bohnett.

The other case was the killing of a GM worker, a guy who got his vacation check and started hitting the local bars, trying to find some cocaine. Police thought someone went out with him to his van, supposedly to make a sale. Instead, the killer shot him in the back of his head and took his money.

Detective Sergeant Kilbourn was put in charge of the Eby case. Detective Sergeant Larsen got the prostitutes.

## 56
## THE FACTS, MA'AM

Kilbourn, lanky, gray-haired, taciturn, has a Joe Friday air of "Just the facts, ma'am" about him. More than a few criminals have made the mistake of taking his quietness for dullness. He has a reputation for methodically pursuing leads and working evidence.

A criminal justice major at Michigan State, Kilbourn joined the state police in 1977 and spent seven years as a uniformed patrol officer before moving into undercover narcotics and stolen-property surveillance work. In 1986, he was promoted to detective sergeant and assigned to the Criminal Intelligence Division under the state's attorney general, working politically sensitive cases usually referred to the MSP by local cops leery of taking on local politicians accused of crimes and various chicanery.

Later, he worked undercover investigating murder for hire and prostitution, then was assigned to be part of an FBI task force investigating bookmaking in western Michigan.

Kilbourn worked more than his share of odd, high-profile cases, the most famous of which was that of Richard Davis, whose wife supposedly died in a suspicious horse-riding accident. Years after the murder, her body was exhumed and new lab tests were able to determine that she had been poisoned. By then, the wealthy Davis was long gone. Later, he was caught on his sailboat and returned to Michigan after the case was aired on *Unsolved Mysteries*.

Personally asked to join the task force by Bohnett and assigned to head up the Eby case early in June of 2001, he had been only vaguely aware of it. "It was just another murder case in Flint to me." He and Bohnett rounded up two large boxes of notes and scribbling gathered on the case over the years, as well as crime-scene photos and sketches.

The state police keep copious and well-organized notes during investigations. It was culture shock for Kilbourn and Bohnett when they first went through the Flint PD material. Almost none of it was in the neat, typed-up, dated narrative form they expected. Much of it was hand-written notes, not always dated, not always readable, often accompanied by the doodling and personal sort of shorthand one uses in making notes. It was chaos.

"It was a tactical decision to keep reports at a bare minimum," explains Kilbourn. The Flint PD hadn't wanted to have to hand over reports to the media under terms of the state's sunshine laws. So, no reports; problem solved. "They would go back and draft official reports when and if the case was solved."

It never had been, hence, no reports.

"For us, it was mind-boggling," says Bohnett. "The guys were saying, 'This is an impossible task you're giving us. What are you thinking?' "

"Don't complain and cry and jump up and down about what we don't have," Bohnett told his detectives. "We'll start with what we do have. We'll start the case over and build our own files. Start from the beginning. Yeah, we don't have a crime scene, but we've got pictures of a crime scene."

Bohnett told Kilbourn and Dennis Diggs, a bright rookie detective Bohnett had pulled in from the CID office in East Lansing, to take the boxes of stuff back to the Flint state police post, ensconce themselves in an office and take all the time they needed to make as much sense as they could of what was there.

Kilbourn read it all first, then Diggs read it all, and then they began to organize it, figured out what it had told them and what it hadn't. Dave King may not have been the most organized record-keeper—and much of the lack of formal reports was intentional—but he was happy to help them.

"He bent over backwards to meet with us and go over his notes. He gave me every tidbit of information that he could remember," says Kilbourn.

It helped, too, that Gary Elford, the Flint detective in charge of the original crime scene who had retired and become an investigator for the Genesee County prosecutor, Arthur Busch, was assigned to the task force. He helped smooth things out between the task force and members of the Flint PD.

About the time the MSP was forming its cold-case squad, Busch had asked the state for funding for his own cold-case unit. He had been turned down and would remain mightily miffed over what he perceived to be a slight to him and meddling by the state. He wanted to get his own guy on the squad; for their part, Bohnett and Kilbourn knew and respected Elford and were happy to have him. He would prove invaluable in helping sort out the old reports and give them insights into the various players.

More than two weeks after hauling the boxes of notes back to the state post, Kilbourn was ready to begin his own investigation, basically working the case from the beginning, starting with the arrival of Hyde and Smith at Eby's on that Sunday nearly fifteen years earlier, then moving on to the list of Eby's lovers and to the Mott employees.

A common response was, "I already talked to the cops."

But they hadn't talked to the state cops, and now they would.

Kilbourn began interviewing family members, too. He needed to clear them, of course, but he also wanted to get a feel for the person behind the headlines. Dayle, Eby's oldest child and an attorney, told him how she and her mother had remained close despite one living in Indianapolis and the other in Flint. She told of their talking by phone once or twice a week. Of the time her mother had concocted some

story to get her to visit her at the gatehouse in July of 1986,
and when she got there it turned out to be a surprise party for
her 35th birthday.

She told Kilbourn that her mother's house had been broken into several times. There was some sort of secret pas-
sageway or tunnel that led into the basement of the
gatehouse from the outside, and her mother had once found
a Mott employee in her basement and demanded that the
tunnel be locked.

Kilbourn also put out a description of the Eby killing on a
national law enforcement network called ViCAP, for Violent
Criminal Apprehension Program, where police can compare
MOs of various solved and unsolved crimes. They got numerous responses of similar crimes with known and unknown perps nationwide, and began trying to link those
killers to Flint.

Since the purpose of the task force was to see if new lab
techniques could be successfully applied to old cases, Kilbourn and Diggs went through the evidence to see if the
MSP's new state-of-the-art crime lab in Lansing could be of
assistance.

In the early days of the investigation, Kilbourn found a
lab report that said semen samples from the crime scene
likely had been degraded, but he couldn't find anything to
say conclusively that they were of no value. DNA testing
was in its infancy in 1986. Not a lot of cops knew much
about it. King and others on the Flint PD had assumed,
based on that lab report at the time, that the DNA was bad.
But was it? Or, could something that would have been considered degraded by the standards of 1986 now, with much
more refined techniques, be usable? More important, did
they even still have it?

Kilbourn learned that the blood and semen samples had,
indeed, been kept in cold storage at the Bridgeport lab by the
MSP, but that they had never been submitted for DNA analysis. He asked that the regional crime lab in Bridgeport,
which had been keeping the samples on ice, submit them for
testing to the DNA lab in Lansing. They arrived there on
June 19.

The first result came back on July 6. Charles Stone was
finally and officially cleared as a suspect. DNA technology

was light years ahead of where it had been when the original testing of samples taken from Eby was done early in 1987. Those tests couldn't tell anything about Eby's attacker's blood type or couldn't provide a DNA profile. Now, new tests were able to show a DNA profile for her killer, and Stone's profile didn't match.

That was news, but not big news. All it did was clear a suspect, which was something they were doing a lot of in the early days of the renewed investigation.

The big news came on Monday, August 6, about 3 p.m. when the director of the DNA lab, Charles Barna, paged Kilbourn, who immediately called him back.

It was about the Eby case, about the samples that had arrived on June 19. "There's been a case-to-case hit with the DNA," said Barna.

"Does that mean we've solved the case?" asked a stunned Kilbourn.

"No," said Barna, and then he explained it to him.

Sources of DNA can be collected at crime scenes from blood, semen, teeth, skin, hairs, urine, bones and muscles. The DNA is then entered into a national database of DNA samples known by the acronym CODIS, for COmbined DNA Index System. In February of 1995, Michigan hooked up to the nationwide CODIS system, which had begun with a pilot program in Minnesota in 1991.

There are two populations of samples in the database, those of convicted felons and those from unsolved crimes.

The match made on the samples from the Eby scene was to an unsolved crime in Romulus in 1991. When Michigan had hooked into CODIS, one of the first things Lynne Helton had done was to enter in the DNA from the Ludwig murder.

Now, CODIS had told them that the same person who had raped and murdered Margarette Eby in 1986 had raped and murdered Nancy Ludwig. They now knew they had a serial killer, but they still didn't know who it was.

The two highest-profile murders in the state in the last twenty years—in the last fifty years if you didn't count Jimmy Hoffa—were committed by the same person.

It was an energizing moment for all. As Kilbourn spread the word to the members of the task force, a surge went through them. It was the first real progress on the case since the FBI's profile had sent everyone down a dead end in 1986 and 1987.

They now had a focus—due south of Flint, about a ninety-minute drive south on I-75 to the airport-dominated city of Romulus.

The link between the two cases was good news, of course, but bad in a way. The task force members already had huge to-do lists involving tracking down old witnesses, old friends and acquaintances and old suspects. Now, there were literally **thou**sands of new names to deal with, and another cold case suddenly was theirs to solve, too.

At 3:45, Kilbourn called the Romulus PD. There, Commander David Early recounted details of the Ludwig case, which were chilling in their similarity to the case he was now familiar with. Kilbourn told him he'd be down to talk to him in person the next day.

## 57
## "THE BLOODING"

*The Blooding*, Joseph Wambaugh's 1989 best-seller, soon became required reading for task-force members. For them, the book, a recounting of a manhunt for a serial killer in England and the new technology that finally caught him, was both a primer on DNA, and an encouragement that their serial killer—who, like the villain of Wambaugh's book, had raped and murdered two women and had avoided capture for years despite intense publicity and ongoing investigations—could be caught.

DNA has become so much a part of the law-enforcement vocabulary—and a major part of the plot of crime novels, movie scripts and popular TV shows such as *CSI*—that it's often forgotten just how recent its application to solving crimes has been.

Lynda Mann, 15, was raped and murdered on November 21, 1983, on a dark, wooded footpath outside the quaint English village of Narborough.

Despite a massive investigation involving 150 police, thousands of man-hours of work, hundreds of interviews, numerous suspects, and intense media coverage on TV and radio and in the tabloids, the murder went unsolved.

In September of 1984, crime detection would change forever, though no one knew it at the time. That's when Alec Jeffries, a 34-year-old research scientist at England's Leicester University, looked at X-ray films that had just been developed and had his "Eureka!" moment.

He stared at clear, visual proof that his theory was correct—that if you identified regions of the DNA molecule that had the most variation from person to person and came up with a way to highlight those regions with a radioactive probe, you would have the equivalent of a genetic fingerprint.

Jeffries took DNA from blood cells and cut them into pieces by adding enzymes. The bits were dropped onto a gel and exposed to an electric field, which caused the larger fragments to separate from the smaller. Radioactive material was added and the sample then X-rayed.

The film, when developed, showed Jeffries that his theory was correct. The DNA separated into bands that looked much like a bar code, and each person's bar code, with the exception of identical twins, was distinct.

Jeffries immediately applied for a patent and his wife, Susan, drew up a list of commercial applications. At the top was settling immigration disputes, a very big issue then in Great Britain. Foreign citizens claimed to be blood relatives of British citizens. If their claim was true, they were entitled to enter into the country. But many of the claims were fraudulent and there was no easy way to prove the issue one way or another. Until now.

Another application was to determine the suitability of bone-marrow transplants.

A third was improved animal husbandry.

On July 31, 1986, another 15-year-old girl, Dawn Ashworth, went missing. Raped and then murdered, her body was discovered on another dark, wooded footpath just a few hundred yards from where Mann's body had been found.

This time police were quick to solve the murder. They arrested a porter at a nearby mental hospital, a misfit with a history of molesting young girls, and he quickly confessed to the murder. But although the two murders were nearly identical, the porter denied having killed the first girl.

Police, sure they could link him to both killings, asked Jeffries if he could analyze the semen collected from both victims and compare the DNA to that in a blood sample taken from the porter.

The results were conclusive, and shocking. The murders and rapes had, indeed, been committed by the same person. But that person was still at large. The porter hadn't done it. His confession was false.

On November 21, 1986, judicial history was made. DNA evidence was used for the first time in a murder case. Police and the court were convinced by the scientists that Jeffries' DNA tests were accurate and unassailable and charges were dropped against the porter.

The police, having lost one suspect because of DNA testing, decided to turn the technology to their advantage, and began taking blood samples and running DNA tests of all the young men in the Narborough area.

The killer, the improbably named Colin Pitchfork, a baker and cake decorator, was eventually caught and convicted. The irony was that he passed his blood test, by altering a passport and getting a friend to pass off his blood as Pitchfork's.

The friend eventually told other friends while out at a pub, and one of them called police. Pitchfork was picked up, readily confessed, submitted to a legitimate blood test and was linked conclusively to both murders.

In 1987, Jeffries' technology went commercial, when the chemical company ICI opened up a blood-testing center in Cheshire, England. And law enforcement—at least that portion of it dealing with murder or rape—would never be the same.

## 58
## MR. YANG

Mike Larsen is Mr. Yang to Kilbourn's Mr. Yin. Where one is taciturn and by-the-book, the other is brash, outgoing, quick to laugh, play-it-by-the-seat-of-his-pants.

When asked to cooperate for a book on the Eby and Lud-

wig murders, Kilbourn, by then retired from the state police
and an investigator with the state gaming commission, said
he'd been asked by the Flint prosecutor not to comment until after a trial. Larsen, still with the MSP, invited a reporter
to his office, engaged in several long and detailed interviews, providing plenty of material both on and off the
record, and had begun making photocopies of MSP reports
when it dawned on him:

"You know," he said after a third interview, "I probably
ought to go through channels. There's a media guy in Lansing you probably should contact."

Larsen looks as if he hasn't gained an ounce since graduating from Muskegon High School in 1973. Even though a
grandfather, he still plays pick-up hockey once a week in the
winter, keeping his bag of equipment and sticks on the back
seat of his state-issue car.

After high school, Larsen joined the Army and did a
four-year stint at the super hush-hush National Security
Agency. For years its existence was officially denied; it was
the Agency That Dare Not Speak Its Name. Larsen was a
computer specialist at its Fort Meade, Md., headquarters,
which contained more computing power than any organization or business in the world, more than most of them
combined.

Larsen was a technician, installing programs, doing
maintenance, changing magnetic tapes on the giant main-
frames at the world's most secretive intelligence organization.

He also moonlighted with a Maryland moving company,
and because he had a top-secret security clearance, got the
jobs that involved places like the White House and the CIA.

Larsen then returned to Muskegon in western Michigan,
attended community college, refereed high-school athletics
and got a job in a factory to support his young family. His
wife's uncle was a state cop and Larsen had been intrigued
by that. One day a recruiter visited campus, signed him up
for a Civil Service test and in 1979 Larsen joined the Michigan State Police's ninety-sixth recruiting class.

At the time of the Eby murder, Larsen worked out of the
Bridgeport post, across the driveway from the crime lab,
whose crew had worked the crime scene.

Larsen was the second member Bohnett hand-picked for the task force in May of 2001. "Larsen, you just let go of the leash and let him go," says Bohnett. "If he interviewed someone, we'd get everything we needed to know. He never left anything out."

While Kilbourn dug into the Eby case, Larsen took on the string of dead prostitutes who'd started showing up in 1998. Eventually he and Reaves would give DNA swabs to more than 400 persons.

They'd soon discover that there were at least two different and unrelated serial murderers involved, and stumble across a serial rapist of prostitutes, as well. Things moved fairly smoothly, and eventually one murderer of two prostitutes would be caught and convicted, as would the rapist.

But Larsen wouldn't be involved in the denouement of those cases. On August 6 came the case-to-case-hit on CODIS. That same day, Bohnett pulled Larsen off the prostitute case and onto the Eby–Ludwig murders.

Yin and Yang would be working together, now.

## 59
## FURIOUS IN ROMULUS

It was the morning of August 7, 2001, and Gordie Malaniak was, as usual in a very foul mood, a mood that was about to get much fouler.

Malaniak had grown up on Detroit's southwest side, an old, tired neighborhood of frame houses, many still with the original asphalt shingle siding, sagging front porches and tiny yards. It's a neighborhood that's long been home to immigrants and auto workers. Just up Michigan Avenue is Dearborn, Henry Ford's birthplace and now home to the largest Arab population outside the Middle East, where there was dancing in the streets in the spring of 2003 at the fall of the giant statue of Saddam Hussein.

Malaniak's dad was the son of Ukrainian immigrants. His mom, who still lives in his old childhood house despite pleas over the years from her family to move to the suburbs, is the daughter of Lithuanian immigrants.

Malaniak went to school at the St. John the Baptist Ukrainian Catholic Church, a parish founded by Slavic immigrants and the only Ukrainian Catholic church in metropolitan Detroit. Malaniak was raised "old school," and he's still "old school." He still won't eat meat on Fridays.

Malaniak started his police career in Detroit in 1978, but in one of the city's recurrent economic downturns, was laid off in 1980. He worked part-time in suburban Royal Oak Township and as a security guard at inner-city Detroit's Receiving Hospital, where mayhem was the rule and security guards earned every penny.

He was a hard-nosed cop and could play bad cop with the best of them. His bad cop paired with Dan Snyder's good cop was a work of art. Malaniak is taciturn to the point of seeming to simmer even when he's not, of looking gloomy when he's not, of seeming pissed when he's happy. When he's pissed, you know it.

He had a reputation around the Romulus PD for hard work, for a bulldogged approach to detective work that was both respected and irritating. He *liked* working long days, carrying a heavy case load that made some of his peers look like shirkers.

"He worked twice as hard and twice as long as anybody else. He'd work fourteen, fifteen hours a day, seven days a week," says Snyder today. "We didn't always get along, but he was a hell of a cop, the best cop I ever worked with."

The last thing Malaniak ever did was suffer fools. He was the one, when the department sent him and Snyder out to meet with FBI profilers at a convention a month after Ludwig's death, to proclaim early on that they were a bunch of assholes, didn't know shit. Said he was a white male? Big deal? Most serial killers were. Taking what they had to say with a grain of salt went against *his* grain. Ah, they're useless, he'd tell Dan or anyone who cared to listen.

In 1981, Malaniak became one of the original five hires of the new Romulus Police Department. In May of 1989, he was promoted to detective sergeant, working with Snyder. And in February of 1991 they got their biggest, nastiest case, the Ludwig murder.

Ten years later, in August of 2001, Malaniak had good reason to be pissed off.

The Romulus police force is riddled with politics, in a small town where politics were often down and dirty. You never knew who you might run afoul of or for what. The mayor didn't like you and the chief needed to curry favor with the mayor—well, of such things were demotions made.

Three months earlier, Malaniak's boss in the detective bureau, Commander Dave Early, had given him the word: Malaniak was keeping his rank of lieutenant, but being moved out of the DB and back into uniformed duty in a patrol car.

"You're back in uniform," said Early.

"That's fucking nice," said Malaniak, who admits, "I had a big chip on my shoulder."

Malaniak with a chip on his shoulder wasn't a pleasant thing to behold. They wanted him on patrol. Fine. He'd be on patrol. He came into the station as little as possible. He couldn't stand to see either Early or Kirby. One thing remained the same: He humped his butt.

"Even after his first run-in with Kirby and he was busted back to patrol, he'd work so hard, people'd say, 'What are you doing?' He'd do five times as much as anyone else," says Snyder.

For some reason or another, now forgotten, Malaniak was in the station, out doing something at the front desk behind the Plexiglas in the lobby when three guys walked in at 9:30 a.m., looking business-like, not like the usual Romulus residents wanting to file a report.

"Is Gordie Malaniak here?" one of them asked him, coincidentally.

"I'm Gordie Malaniak. Who are you?"

"I'm Greg Kilbourn. I'm with a Michigan State Police crime task force." With him were State Police Detective Jaime Corona and Gary Elford. Malaniak's blood pressure doubled. His heart raced. What in the world had he done—or did they think he'd done—to bring three plainclothes state cops to Romulus looking for him?

"What's this all about?"

"You don't know?"

"No."

"We came up with a link between a killing we've been investigating in Flint and the Nancy Ludwig case."

"You're shitting me."

They weren't, of course. They'd talked to Early and done some background checking with Lynne Helton, and now were here to get up to speed on the Ludwig case. Kilbourn needed to look at their reports, get copies, see what they had, how it was organized and how they could use it to get started on phase two of what was already an exhaustive reinvestigation.

And here they were, having driven down from Flint only to find out that one of the two guys they needed to talk to hadn't even been told they were coming, or that there had been a dramatic breakthrough in the Ludwig case.

"It fucking floored me," says Malaniak. "I was stunned. As soon as they told me, I said to myself, 'You gotta be fucking kidding me.' I was just fuming."

Kilbourn, Corona and Elford were buzzed in to see Early.

Malaniak called Snyder at home. Snyder had been promoted to lieutenant in the patrol division and was no longer in the DB. He had found out late the day before, but hadn't had a chance to call Malaniak. Barna had called Helton after he'd talked to Kilbourn, knowing she'd worked the Ludwig scene, and Helton had called Snyder at home. As soon as Helton had called him, Snyder called Kilbourn, saying he was no longer in the DB but wanted on the case and would make himself totally available. He was hoping to elicit Kilbourn's support.

Malaniak went into the room where all their voluminous files were stored. Snyder is a neatnik and, because they had been his files, they were meticulously organized and squared away. No more. Someone had been rummaging through them, spilling stuff on the floor, probably trying to get some background on the case and where it stood.

Snyder reported in and went to talk to Kirby. Snyder was head of the officers' union and he and Kirby had butted heads over union issues, contract negotiations and just about everything else. Snyder's disdain for his boss was well known. Snyder, unlike his partner, could suffer fools, but he refused to suffer Kirby.

As Snyder tells it, he told Kirby he'd work the case with the state police on his own time, on weekends, at nights, taking vacation time, whatever it took.

"No. You're not to be involved at all," said Kirby.

Snyder was stunned. Kirby had gotten word that Snyder had talked to Kilbourn the day before and was ticked off. "What right do you have to call them?"

"It's my case."

Kirby told him emphatically that it wasn't his case. It was Early's case. And he ordered him to have no contact with the state police whatsoever.

"It was the dumbest thing I ever heard of," says Malaniak.

Later, Malaniak heard scuttlebutt that the Romulus PD was going to turn everything over to Kilbourn and Larsen. Not just the files, which was understandable, but the case itself. "They were going to give up our case and not assign anyone to work with the MSP. I said, 'This is fucked up!' " says Malaniak. "There was bad blood right from the beginning."

Kirby might have told Snyder not to have any contact with the state police, but he hadn't given Malaniak any orders. He called Kilbourn and left a message: "There's a lot of internal bickering going on here. You need to contact Dan Snyder. He knows this case better than anyone."

But Kilbourn needed Kirby's cooperation, and Early's. He wasn't about to get embroiled in office politics if he could avoid it. "I decided right away I wasn't going to be involved in all that," he says. "I didn't sneak around Early's back. That wasn't going to help anyone."

It was Early's case, and so it was Early he'd work with.

On Thursday, the 9th, Early met with Kilbourn and Dan Bohnett at the Michigan State Police 2nd District Headquarters in Northville. They wanted to set the ground work for a joint investigation. The meeting wasn't promising. Early said his department was overworked, was down to just three detectives and that he wouldn't be able to spare anyone full-time. He was willing, though, to offer clerical help to assist in entering tips or other computer work.

so ... er so ... on weekends, all nights, take ...

## 60
# HER BLOOD BOILS

When Barna got word of the case-to-case hit, he tracked Helton down to say there'd been a breakthrough, that they were on the track of a serial killer and that she needed to meet with Kilbourn ASAP. He'd need to know things like, what evidence did they have stored? What kind of samples were still viable? What was the scene like?

Barna found her on vacation in the small Upper Peninsula town of Garden. He reached her through the land-line number and she agreed to come to a meeting at the Flint post as soon as she was back, in a couple of days. At the Flint meeting, from what Kilbourn said, "I had inklings or tidbits that Dan would not be in the loop."

She was, and is, a big fan of Snyder's, having worked several bad scenes with him. "You'll never find another more dedicated individual than Dan. Never. What you see is what you get. He's sincere and genuine. Easily one of the finest detectives I've ever worked with. If this had to happen to Nancy, then thank God it happened in a place where there would be someone like Dan," she says.

None of her cases ever hit Helton the way the Ludwig case did. Nothing pumped her up more than finding that they'd made a breakthrough on it. And nothing irritated her more than finding out that politics were going to keep the one guy off the case who absolutely had to be there.

Not one to normally have an agenda, after the first meeting with Kilbourn, she says, "My only goal was to get Dan back involved. He was the investigation embodied. He had every detail, big or small, physically and mentally organized. You could ask him any question about any aspect of the case, and he could respond. He *was* the investigation."

Her second meeting on the case was with Larsen, Kilbourn and Early at the Northville crime lab. Early again said he and Romulus were swamped, and that maybe it would be best if they just turned the case and the renewed investigation over to the MSP. And tips that came into Romulus, how about they just forward them on?

Early also told them he had brought himself up to speed

by reading the file, but Helton was dubious. She thought: "There's no way you can learn what you need to know by reading from a file."

She'd try to be fair, give him a chance. But almost from the start, it was apparent to her that "Dave Early didn't know a hill of beans about this case. I would tell him things about the case he didn't know. I was appalled. It was a disaster."

It was about to get worse. Helton finished her line of conversation at some point and Early chimed in with his theory of events in the Hilton hotel room. It was his considered opinion that the killer had, in fact, killed Ludwig by hanging her over the curtain rod in the bathroom.

There was a heavy silence. Helton looked at him as if he had a twitching rat's tail sticking out between his closed lips.

"I was stunned. Stunned," says Helton. "I thought, 'That's the stupidest thing I ever heard.' I thought, 'This guy has no investigative skills at all. He's got no experience with crime scenes. It's a mindless comment from a dumb bureaucrat.' "

She didn't show anger. Her skills honed by years of precise testimony at trial, she went point by point, through a demolition of Early's theory. "I told him flat-out, 'There's no way. No way.' There would have been entirely different bloodstain patterns at the scene. I was quiet and professional. I laid out the factual information, why the evidence was clear. It didn't take long to slam-dunk him and put the kibosh on that whole harebrained theory."

The meeting soon ended. Early didn't try to contribute anything else.

As soon as he left, Helton says, "I had a hissy fit to get Dan involved. Early pissed me off. It was stupid politics and no one was going to use politics to cause this case to keep from being solved."

She told Kilbourn she was not going to stand for it, that it was unconscionable for him to conduct an investigation without going to the source, and the source was Dan Snyder. "I was standing in for the victim and I was not going to stand for this. I was fit to be tied. It was shameful. Was Romulus at all interested in Nancy's interests? Absolutely not. It was shameful and almost another violation of the victim."

Things are hazy at this point, the reticent team-guy Kilbourn not wanting to claim credit for calling Kirby or Early and laying out what had to be done. Somehow, the message was delivered, though.

By the end of August, Early was off the case and Snyder was back on. Romulus was *not* going to turn over responsibility for the renewed investigation to the state police. Snyder would be part of the task force. He was going to work this thing as hard as he had ten years earlier.

In November, a Romulus police patrolman named Al Lambert, with a long history in local politics—in addition to being a cop, over the years he had also been a city councilman and a member of the school board—and a direct descendant of the old-boy network that had long run the city, won the election for mayor.

Lambert reportedly didn't like Early. Early was out of the DB and back in uniform. On December 1, Snyder was named to head up the DB and promoted to executive lieutenant. Snyder pulled Malaniak out of his patrol car and out of uniform and put him back in the DB. Malaniak was assigned to the task force, too.

## 61
## THE DOG-DNA THEORY

Shit happens, Malaniak knew that. You make mistakes. But the more he thought about it, the more it ticked him off that Dave King had blown him off so readily more than ten years earlier when he'd called to follow up on Mark Eby's tip that the two murders seemed related. Malaniak had a blood type, but it didn't match Stone's, and so the cases were unrelated, said King. And Malaniak had filed Eby's tip away as just another of many that were dead ends.

"Out of all the tips you work, you hope you don't screw something up or miss something," says Malaniak. "I was happier than hell to get the cases linked, but I'll always wish I'd taken the extra step in '91. I never went to Flint. I never interviewed King directly. In hindsight, I wish I'd worked it harder. I don't know, if I'd have had the experience I have now, I'd like to think I wouldn't just have taken his word for it. But he was so sure."

In 1991, Malaniak was a young, inexperienced homicide detective in a small town. King was the veteran big-city detective.

Sometime shortly after CODIS linked the two cases, Snyder ran into King at a police convention and they exchanged introductions. King was still sure Stone was the murderer.

When Snyder said something about the two cases being linked, after all—making that point having been the reason he'd wanted to meet him—King replied:

"How do you know Stone didn't do it?"

"He's got the wrong DNA."

"You know he had a dog, don't you?" said King, referring to a dog Stone had always traveled with and who accompanied him to Flint for his 1986 visit.

Snyder looked at King, stunned, taking a moment to digest the implication. What was he saying? That Stone took semen from his dog and put it into Margarette Eby's vagina when he killed her, and five years later took more of the dog's semen and put it in Nancy Ludwig's vagina? Yep, that's what he was saying.

"At that point, I knew there was nothing I could say," says Snyder.

It's an exchange King acknowledges. "I still held out the chance we'd been manipulated by Stone, because he was such a strange fellow and because of his knowledge," he says. "In my mind, I wondered if it was something from an animal. He was that bizarre."

**62**

## ARMED WITH COTTON SWABS

DNA told them the Eby and Ludwig cases were linked.

So, too, did the crime-scene photos.

Kilbourn had fixed the Eby scene photos in his memory, not that you could forget them, having seen them. As soon as he saw the Ludwig photos, it was clear the same killer had committed both crimes. The photos were almost like duplicate prints, the slashed throat, the torture marks, the body rolled over on its stomach.

The first thing Kilbourn did in August after filling in Romulus on the Eby link was to take the photos and all the boxes of information Snyder and Malaniak had amassed back to Flint. He, Larsen, Corona and Diggs then went through it all.

They started going through the tips, setting up a computer program and ranking the tips according to several parameters. "We could tell they'd done an excellent job on their tip sheets and follow-ups," said Kilbourn. "I could tell they'd spent a tremendous amount of time."

Kilbourn says Snyder—and Malaniak later, when he joined the task force—fit right in. They could have groused about an outside agency, in effect, critiquing their old work. They certainly could have groused when asked to help go back through 2,300 tips they'd already cleared.

But, "they were terrific. I got total cooperation from those two guys. I knew Dan knew his case. We were there to learn from them and get information out of them," says Kilbourn.

They quickly winnowed the 2,300 down to 100. That was the easy part. "You should see some of the crap people had called in," says Larsen. Scorned women, nut cases, angry next-door neighbors ticked off over long grass or broken fences.

The best 100 they looked at in detail, eliminating them one by one.

The task force also began reinterviewing principals and witnesses in the Eby case, trying to find a tie to someone in Romulus or the Detroit area.

It was always part of the philosophy of the task force that new or improved technologies would help solve cases once thought to be as dead as their victims.

Now, with a DNA link firmly established between two such prominent murders, it was time to work technology hard. The Flint PD didn't think they had serological evidence. Romulus had plenty of it, and more than ten years of technological advances since they'd gathered it to support their investigation. Many suspects and would-be suspects had been cleared by saliva or blood tests in Romulus. When they came across names in the Romulus case that hadn't been given saliva or blood tests at the time, they visited them armed with buccal swabs.

More important, it was past time to definitively clear people in Flint.

"We went to every male acquaintance of Eby's, in every shape or form, and asked for DNA swabs," says Larsen. Larsen or another state cop would vigorously rub the swab against the lining of the cheek; later the collected tissue would go to the crime lab in Lansing for a DNA profile.

Former lovers had been reluctant to talk when the case was new. Fifteen years later, they weren't happy, especially the ones who had been married and having an affair with Eby, to see police back at their door dredging up their sexual pasts, this time with swabs in hand. Nearly everyone cooperated. Those who did were cleared.

Kilbourn and Larsen flew to Milwaukee to swab one of Eby's former lovers. Soon, "the feeling was, the killer wasn't someone she was intimate with."

They took swabs of family and friends, of co-workers at U-M–Flint, of Mott employees. They tracked down William Renneckar, the organist at Eby's church, who had been at the dinner party with her the night she was killed, at the Cypress Retirement Home in Charlotte, N.C., and had the Charlotte–Mecklenburg Police Department swab him at the old folks' home on August 15, 2001.

That's the same day they went public with the information that the Eby and Ludwig cases were linked. They had wanted to sit on it awhile, keep it a secret from the killer, but news had leaked out of the Romulus PD. Channel 4 in Detroit had called *The Flint Journal* asking a reporter there what he knew. The reporter called the Flint PD. At 4:30 p.m., Chief Barksdale held a press conference and announced that DNA tests had linked the two unsolved murders.

They were back in the headlines, and a tip line was set up. The tips poured in.

Police swabbed Jonathan Eby in August and he, too, was cleared. He also told them how angry he was to find out the cases were linked, something he'd suspected and tried to alert police to in the days after Ludwig was killed.

Police compiled a list of hundreds of horticultural students from Michigan State who had worked at the estate during the summer. Over a period of several months, about 130 swabs were taken, and 130 persons cleared, including one would-be suspect they tracked down in the Pinellas County Jail in Florida.

Hal Zettle, who was pulled off the prostitute case, and Charles Diggs traveled the state, giving buccal swabs to former Flint residents who had moved. Other police agencies in Florida, Pennsylvania, Wisconsin, Texas, Ohio, Mississippi and Washington visited people from the to-clear list who lived in their states, and swabbed them.

If they couldn't get approvals, they resorted to other means to gather DNA. On August 18, they got the okay from the owners of the Heritage Food and Spirits Restaurant in nearby Fenton to take an empty bottle of Killian's Irish Red beer, water glass, napkin, dinner plate and utensils they'd watched a suspect use. On August 31, the lab reported that his DNA had cleared him.

The task force also began working through the population of people the Flint PD had overlooked—contractors and sub-contractors.

"Mott had the most unbelievable records I've ever seen," says Larsen. The police found meticulous records of who was on the estate, doing what, at what time of day. "We wanted to know what kind of contractors might have been affiliated with the Mott Estate that might have given them access to the gatehouse."

They came up with the names of thirty-two contractors who had done work at the estate in 1985 and 1986, including landscapers, electricians, architects, insulation companies, pavers, asphalt crews, excavators, painters and a lawn-sprinkler company.

They even swabbed a former journalism student at Wayne State University, whose professor, Ben Burns, had written the cover story in the *Detroit Free Press*' Sunday magazine about Ludwig's murder, and who had assigned the case to his students. But this student continued to hang around the Romulus PD asking about the case for years, even after dropping out of school, and seemed so preoccupied by it, that police finally thought they'd better clear him. They took his swab on December 17, 2001.

The task force subpoenaed records from U-M–Flint and compiled a list of 150 names and addresses of Eby's former pupils, and then drafted letters asking if they would submit to swabs. They put the letters in yellow manilla envelopes, but they would never be mailed.

The envelopes still sit at the MSP post in Flint, unstamped. Just before Zettle could run them through the postage meter, and before they could finish going through the list of employees of all the subcontractors, they got another dramatic break in the case.

## 63
## THE PARTIAL PRINT

Early on, Dan Bohnett was surprised to hear from Kilbourn that among the physical bits of evidence from the Eby crime was a color photo of a bloody fingerprint on the bathroom faucet.

It was, says Bohnett, one of those "lo and behold" moments. Nothing much had been made of the print at the time. It was too much of a partial, given the technology at the time, to be of value. In 1986, unless you had a perfect, full print, the Feds' computers were useless. The Michigan State Police wouldn't have a rudimentary computer fingerprint ID system until 1989, and the only way you could link a partial print to a killer was to already have a suspect in mind, take his prints and see how they compared. Even if the killer's prints were on file with the FBI, it would have taken thousands of man-hours to physically pull prints out of files and visually compare them to the partial.

But times had changed, eh? That was the whole point of the task force. One of Larsen's jobs was to work the fingerprint angle.

On August 27, Larsen asked Lieutenant Galvin Smith, the MSP's chief fingerprint examiner at the Bridgeport post, to enter the Eby partial into the automated fingerprint identification system, or AFIS. The results were immediate: nothing. No match.

Larsen assumed that was the end of it. He, and many other cops, thought the state computer system tied into the

Feds' national database. But he asked Smith if there was more they could do.

There might be, said Smith, though it wasn't standard operating procedure yet. The AFIS system in Michigan only tied in to Michigan cases and perps. The Michigan system had come on-line in 1989 and old cases were entered after that as time permitted. The Eby print was first entered into AFIS in 1992, without a match. And the lack of a match again in 2001 only meant that her killer had never run afoul of the law in Michigan, at least not enough to be fingerprinted.

A new AFIS system was supposed to allow the state databases to interface with the FBI's, but the system was behind schedule and not on-line yet. But perhaps the FBI's AFIS system was able to make the connection in reverse, to state databases.

He told Larsen he'd call the Feds and see what they could do. It was a long shot. That same day, Smith called FBI headquarters, asked them how to go about trying to get a match on a print he had on an old case. The Feds did have a more powerful computerized system for matching prints, with, of course, a more powerful acronym, IAFIS, the "I" standing for "integrated."

He was told to drop his print in the mail.

On September 4, the print arrived at the FBI and was routed to Heather Krohn, who had been a forensics examiner in the latent-print division of the FBI crime lab in Washington, D.C., for three years. Her job was to classify, compare and identify inked and latent fingerprints.

Inked prints are those taken by police of suspects, rolling their fingertips in ink and then rolling the fingers on a card. Latent prints are those left at a scene from the oils on a finger, usually invisible to the naked eye but which become visible by the use of lasers, chemicals or fingerprint powder.

There were other requests ahead of Smith's, but she would be able to get to it soon. She sent a letter to Smith acknowledging receipt of the prints and a quick response. If everything went well, she hoped to have an answer one way or another by mid-September.

Everything did not go well. Everything went to hell. On

September 11, a bunch of hijackers started crashing planes into the World Trade Center, the Pentagon and a field in Pennsylvania.

As "911" took on new meaning, suddenly a fifteen-year-old murder case in Flint was about as far off the beleaguered FBI's radar screen as it could get. No, that's not quite true. The subsequent anthrax mailings, murders and frenzy pushed the Flint cold-case even farther from the radar screen. Krohn would be kept busy on more pressing matters for months. For the rest of 2001 and into 2002.

Starting to run out of leads, and not wanting to leave any stone unturned, on October 17, Larsen wrote to the producers of *Unsolved Mysteries*, asking them to produce a show profiling the Eby and Ludwig murders.

## 64
## FRONT BURNER

On Jan. 24, 2002, Krohn called Galvin Smith to say his prints were about to go back on her front burner. Early in February, Krohn picked up the envelope she'd first glanced at five months earlier. She took the negative of a partial fingerprint to the lab's photographic unit and had it photographed. It was a small partial, about half an inch by half an inch, of the upper left quadrant of the right thumb. It showed a right slant loop pattern.

When the new photo came back to her, she scanned it into the IAFIS system. Though casual fans of TV crime dramas and even many police across the county think the Feds have long had all-knowing fingerprint capabilities, the partial print she scanned in would have been fruitless as recently as 1999.

The AFIS system that had just come on-line when Eby was killed in 1986 would not have been able to make a match of such a partial print. You would have needed an entire, pristine impression of a fingerprint to make an identification possible.

IAFIS works by searching its database and returning a top-20 list of possible matches, based on reference points to the print in question. The examiner, in this case Krohn, then pulls their cards and visually starts eliminating suspects.

By the time Krohn was done, one name remained.

On February 6, Krohn called Smith with the news. She had a match, to a guy who'd been convicted of assaulting a woman in Orlando, Fla., in the early 1980s and spent nearly two years in prison in northern Florida at the Lancaster Correctional Institution. His name was Jeffrey Wayne Gorton. He was still alive, age 39. And guess, what? He was living in Michigan, on Tuscola Road in the Flint suburb of Vienna.

Smith called Larsen, pretending to be as cool as a cucumber. "I didn't want to overly excite him," he says now. He was calm, understated, playing the thing for the drama he knew it would bring.

"It was one of those days you always remember where you were, and who you were with," says Larsen, who was working an afternoon shift that day, having driven over to Grand Rapids with his wife that morning to pick up his 3-year-old grandson, Griffin, whose parents were heading to Vegas on vacation.

Larsen was at the Flint PD, with Hal Zettle in the basement office that the task force had expanded into. The phone rang. It was Smith.

"We got the results of that partial print back from the FBI," said Smith quietly. Larsen could hear defeat in his voice. Shit. A dead end. Behind his sandbagging delivery, Smith was "very ecstatic. It was a big, big, big case, and we had no one to tie it to. These kinds of cases you dream of being involved in."

"And . . . ?" said Larsen, knowing the worst was coming.

"We got a match. Give me a pencil and I'll give you a name," said Smith. And then he gave him Jeffrey Wayne Gorton's name, his date of birth and his current address, just a few miles up I-475 from downtown Flint.

"My heart started racing," says Larsen. "It was like the God of policemen reaching his hand down and saying, 'You've worked long and hard and I'm going to give you a hand.' He said, 'Enough is enough.' "

Of all the thousands of names they'd seen and entered

into computers and cross-indexed and swabbed and cleared, it was the first time he'd seen or heard of Gorton.

Kilbourn was out on an interview and was due back at the Flint state police post soon. "I couldn't wait to get there and tell him," says Larsen. On the short drive over, Larsen called him on the car radio twice without answer. He pulled into his spot near the door to the post, ran inside and there was Kilbourn walking down the hall.

"Come on in here. I've got some real good news for you," said Larsen, leading him into a small office and closing the door.

Soon they were both zooming on nearly overdose-level rushes of adrenaline. A good thing, too, because they'd work thirty-five of the next forty-four hours.

On February 7, Krohn mailed out her official findings to Smith. It was FBI No. 54834CA3, case No. 95A-HQ-1347984, lab No. 610904028MX. In the calm, understated language of crime technicians, Krohn wrote: "One latent fingerprint, appearing in Q2, a negative, source not indicated, has been identified as a fingerprint of Jeffrey Wayne Gorton."

Gorton had been released from prison in Florida on December 24, 1985, after serving less than two years of his four-and-a-half-year sentence.

On October 9, 1984, prison psychologist H. V. Bartlett had reported that Gorton was attending group therapy up to three times a week and that "he has eagerly sought help and has been the most productive contributor to the group, and I believe in the inmate upon who I would be willing to wager for the future," he wrote, rather ungrammatically.

Yet, on April 10, 1985, Gorton was placed in administrative confinement for improper contact with a staff member. He admitted trying repeatedly to touch the employee, including reaching out with his toes to try to rearrange the employee's clothing, and said he felt he was losing control of his emotions.

Nonetheless, prison authorities decided to release Gorton eight months later. It was a Christmas present for him and for the extended Gorton clan back home. But had the Christmas carols Gorton heard on the 25th been a death knell for Margarette Eby?

# 65

# BOGEYMAN, APRIL 1983

*Replay:*
*Orlando, Fla., April 29.*

> Marie Gagliano got out, and as she walked behind her car, she noticed off to the right a man heading her way. She immediately thought: Guy walking his dog. She turned to face the rear of the car, put in the key, opened the hatchback and lifted the brown bag, and as she did, her subconscious mind flashed a warning: She wouldn't necessarily have seen a dog, given the cars in the lot, but something about the way the man was walking meant: <u>no dog</u>.
>
> A jolt of fear hit her and as she straightened up, the bag still in her arms, she turned to her left. By then, given his rate of speed, he would have been past her. Ten yards? Twenty yards? Somewhere to her left and receding. But the man wasn't walking, and he wasn't past her. He was standing <u>right there</u>, his face filling her vision, a foot from hers.
>
> In a slasher movie, it would have been one of those moments where the audience jumped. A tight shot of a woman and a car. Woman turns. Man's head enters shot from left. Audience gasps en masse.
>
> Marie screamed as the man reached down, lifted her skirt, grabbed her lower legs and flipped her over backwards. She landed on her left wrist and butt, groceries flying through the air and scattering across the pavement. He grabbed her ankles and lifted, and she went flat on her back.
>
> She screamed one long scream. And he held her tightly by each ankle and dragged her toward the nearby Dumpster.

The bogeyman never made it with her to the Dumpster. She screamed so loudly in the not-so-dark parking lot—"My God, I never knew it was in me to scream like that"—that the bogeyman went to plan B: After dragging her for ten or fifteen yards, he let go of her legs, reached up, grabbed her slip, ripped it off and ran to his car.

As she lay there, people started coming to their windows, hollering out to ask about what was going on, if she was okay. His car squealed out of the parking lot.

Two of the faces at a window above her were friends, a rare husband-and-wife couple in the singles complex. They came down, helped her gather her groceries and monitored her condition. Nothing broken. The bevy of heavy bracelets on her left arm all dented in, having taken the brunt of her fall. Her right elbow was cut and bleeding but not badly enough for stitches. Her skirt was ripped. The right cheek of her butt where she'd landed on it hurt like hell. It would later swell up like a grapefruit.

Back in their apartment, she couldn't stop shaking. What if she hadn't worn a slip? She usually didn't. What if he hadn't been able to get an easy trophy? The cops arrived just ten minutes after her neighbors called them and took a report. She told them, "He struck me as clean-cut, a Joe College type." Nice slacks, a Polo shirt, brown glasses, maybe six foot, 165 pounds. They asked her if she needed medical attention, and left when she said no.

A few days later, two detectives stopped by Burdines to see her. They had a composite sketch. Another woman, Bettye *CQ* Dixon, had been attacked in broad daylight the day after Gagliano. Same MO. She was reaching into the back seat of her car at her apartment complex when she was attacked from behind, knocked to the ground and hit and kicked while the man pulled on her half-slip, eventually ripping it off her. He got away, but this woman had clearly seen his face and had helped with a composite sketch. And she'd ID'd his car, a Buick Regal.

Gagliano said it looked like her assailant.

One other thing. There'd been another assault that they were linking to this guy, a woman named Ghita Fisher who also worked at Burdines and had been grabbed in the store parking lot on April 8.

On Friday night, May 6, two female Navy recruits were walking on the grounds of the Naval Training Center. A male came up behind them, dropped to his knees, reached up under one of the recruits' skirts and ripped off her slip.

Both women started fighting with him. They could hear his dog-tags clanging, so they knew he was in the military. Meanwhile, two patrolling base police cars had seen the commotion, and when the man ran to his car and drove off, they pursued him.

Unfortunately, the two police cars collided with each other and the assailant got away.

The guy the Navy police lost was, it was thought, the guy responsible for a one-man crime spree of perversion and assault. In addition to this most recent incident, there had been numerous reports on the base of some guy running up to women and pulling off their panties as they stood at phone booths or on street corners. The Naval Investigative Service was hot on his trail, and there had been numerous news stories and TV and radio reports of the various incidents.

On May 18, police caught a break. Earl Deimund, the manager of the small, forty-trailer Conway Shores Mobile Home Park in Orlando, not far from Marie Gagliano's apartment complex, afraid an impending rain storm would cause a leak, had gone into one of the trailers to fix a window in need of repair. The trailer stood on lot 18, where a young family lived—Jeffrey Gorton, 20, his 18-year-old wife, Dawn, and their little baby, Jeff Jr. Dawn was out of town at the time, having caught a cheap military flight back to Michigan to visit her folks.

They had seemed like nice kids at first, not your cliché of trailer tenants. Gorton was in the Navy, stationed at the Orlando Naval Training Center, studying high-tech stuff at the nuclear power school. Sharp guy, going places, but something about him rubbed Deimund the wrong way. They'd even had a confrontation recently when the manager asked him about a missing canoe. The sailor denied any involvement, but Deimund wasn't so sure. And lately some residents had begun to complain that the young man seemed to be prowling around and was giving them the creeps. Others had complained that some of their underwear had gone missing off clotheslines.

Anyway, Deimund goes in the trailer and what does he see in one of the bedrooms? He'd tell police later that it was two grocery bags filled with panties, bras and pantyhose. He pulled some out and could readily tell they'd never fit Dawn.

Among the first things he saw, to his shock, were some of his young daughter's underwear.

Not that the tale needed embellishing, but Deimund would later seem to embellish it. Instead of finding them in grocery bags, he was quoted as telling an Orlando reporter: "It was spread out on the bed like he had been counting it and organizing it. There were panties, bras and other things all laid out neatly."

Deimund called the Orange County Sheriff's Department and alarms went off when he told them Gorton drove a Buick Regal. The Navy then gave Orlando police a photo of Gorton as well as photos of other similar-looking Naval personnel to be used in a photo line-up for the assault victims. The photo of Gorton was of poor quality and neither Gagliano, Dixon nor Fisher could identify him as their attacker.

On May 23, Orlando police visited the trailer park to interview Gorton. He had been evicted by Deimund in the meantime and left no forwarding address. So they went to look for him at the base.

That same day, Dawn had worked the midnight shift at Taco Bell. They'd found a nice apartment, but it was out of their price range, so she'd taken a part-time job to help make ends meet. Jeff was supposed to pick her up at 5 a.m. but never showed. She called home and got no answer. She walked the quarter mile home, finding Jeff gone and their infant son locked in a closet.

A little while later, Jeff walked in. He said he'd been out for a morning run, which seemed odd since he'd never done any running or been involved in any physical exercise as far as she knew. He changed into his uniform and left for work.

There, Orlando police, in cooperation with Navy investigators, pulled him in for questioning. He first asked for an attorney, then waived his rights, said he had some psychological problems and admitted to assaulting Gagliano and Dixon.

When asked about the assault on Gagliano, Gorton said: "I think I saw her at Albertson's. I stopped there to get something to eat."

"Did you think she was attractive and decided to follow her from that point, or what?"

"Well, no, no, I just, she probably was just bending over or something, I could tell she had a slip on. Then something came over me, I probably decided I wanted it."

He said he followed her to her apartment complex, then "I just walked up behind her and grabbed her slip." He was hazy on details, explaining: "I don't pay enough attention to things I do to keep it in my memory, I guess."

Gorton agreed to let police search his new apartment. There, he went into the attic and came out with a cardboard box filled with undergarments and one pair of women's shoes. Dawn was sitting there when Jeff and the Navy police walked in. Though Orlando police reports don't mention it, Dawn would say that police also took out a large military duffel so stuffed with women's clothes it couldn't be zipped.

Jeff left, under arrest, and was arraigned the next day in Orange County Circuit Court. Included in the haul were a black slip taken from Dixon, a beige slip taken from Gagliano and a green slip that had belonged to Mrs. Deimund.

Soon, detectives were back at Burdines, showing Marie Jeff's arrest photos. It was definitely the same guy who attacked her. They told her they'd be in touch regarding any court proceedings. Seeing the photos brought back fresh memories of him. She lasted out her shift, barely holding it together inside, trying to sell cosmetics as if nothing were wrong.

At least he was behind bars.

A week, maybe ten days, later, Marie was back in the same Albertson's near her apartment doing some light shopping. Waiting in line, she glanced over at the line next to her. And there he was. Her attacker, standing with a young woman who was holding a baby. She was young, 18, and looked younger.

"My first inclination was to run up to him and scream at him. But fear took over," says Gagliano. "Then I wanted to say to her, 'What's your problem, being with that guy?' But I saw the baby. It was real young and I felt so bad."

She ran with her groceries to her car. "I freaked out," she says. She raced home and called the police to tell them Jeff had gotten out, somehow. They knew, of course. He'd posted a $2,500 bond on May 26 and was released. (Jeff's grandparents lived in nearby Leesburg, and Dawn had borrowed the money from them.)

"Out on bond?" she screamed into the phone. "Couldn't you at least have told me? He was just at my grocery store. He lives in the neighborhood."

The cop told her: "You didn't hear me say this, but get a gun, and if he bothers you again, do us all a favor."

It would have been a favor for a 26-year-old woman named Kristi Walker. While out on bond, on September 16, Gorton would strike again. It was the same day the Navy gave him a "less-than-honorable" discharge, though it's hard to imagine what you'd have to do to get a dishonorable discharge if knocking down Navy women and ripping off their slips isn't enough. About 11 p.m., Walker was sitting in her ground-floor apartment in Orlando when she heard her front-room curtains rustling. She looked over and saw a white arm reaching through the window. She screamed and the arm pulled back. Police found that the screen had been pried out of its frame. They also found prints which were quickly matched to Jeff. His bond was revoked and he was charged with breaking and entering. This time, Dawn borrowed $5,000 from Jeff's parents for bond, getting the money via Western Union. But instead of getting Jeff out of jail, she used some of the money to hire United Van Lines to move her things back to Michigan. When she got back, she returned the rest of the money to the Gortons.

Marie slipped into a deep depression in the weeks and months after her assault, a gradual slide that she didn't notice, but her roommate, friends and co-workers did. She could still go to work and function normally in that she did her shopping, banking, bill paying and the like.

But if she wasn't doing chores or off at work, she found it impossible to leave the apartment. "I was afraid to go out, I was worried someone would follow me."

Nights weren't so bad, only the occasional nightmare.

One Saturday afternoon she got a call. It was her roommate's boss, Robert Greenburg, who ran the jewelry department at a catalog showroom. Marie had met Greenburg before. He had a reputation as a nice guy, a great boss. He was always having cookouts for his employees. An avid fisherman, if he caught a mess of fish, he'd call folks up and invite them over to his apartment on Lake Frederica, a nice one with a big pool, for a fish fry. Donna had told him she was worried about Marie and he had told her he'd try to work some charm on her, but he kept the reason for calling a secret.

"Hey, come on over," he said. "I'm having some friends over to go swimming."

"No. Thanks, anyway, but I'm going to just hang around the apartment."

"Well, then I'm coming over to get you. You don't have any choice. I'll be there in twenty minutes."

They now describe that swim as their first date, but as first dates go, it was unusual to say the least. Trying to engage her in some horseplay in the pool, Greenburg splashed her. She splashed back. A good sign. He splashed harder. She splashed harder. He grabbed her and started twirling her around in the water. And she hit her foot on the side of the pool and broke her little toe.

Surprisingly enough, the first date led to a second and a third.

Though she was at least getting out of the apartment, had taken up tae kwon do, and was interacting with people, she was still troubled, and told Greenburg about her fears.

"My uncle up in Georgia has got some clay pits. That's where we all learned to shoot when we were kids. Come on up with me and I'll teach you to shoot," he said.

So they took some vacation days and went up to his uncle's place near Jesup, not far from Savannah, out in pine forests and swamps, crocodiles in the water, mosquitoes filling the air, armadillos ruling the land.

And Marie shot, and shot, and shot. Never got tired of it. "All I had to do was pretend the target was that guy, and I hit it every time."

"My God, Bob, you got you a regular Annie Oakley there," said his uncle.

Back from Jesup, she attended Gorton's trial, which ended up as a plea bargain. "I had my eyes fixed on him but he wouldn't look at me," she says. Several serious charges, including assault, were knocked down to two counts each of robbery and one of burglary.

Gorton gave the judge this unadulterated crap, to Marie's thinking, about his remorse. Hell, he ended up sounding like the damn victim. He had compulsions he needed help fighting, if only someone would help him. "I know I did something wrong and I want to get help," he told the judge. He wanted to get better. "I just hope I can have a chance to prove that I can."

At sentencing, in February of 1984, the judge gave him the statutory maximum of four and a half years.

Marie was livid that someone so obviously unbalanced and dangerous, who could do what he did to her and all those others, who could fill her with the fear she'd been battling ever since, would get off so lightly.

Marie and Bob were married a year later. A year after that, Gorton was paroled.

In 1992, Marie and Bob moved to Jesup and bought twenty acres out in the country. Marie hand-planted 1,387 slash-pine trees, a hybrid, hearty fast grower favored by the logging industry. Just to say he helped out, Bob planted one. It was her project, maybe a lingering bit of therapy, she figures.

Today, Bob is retired from the jewelry business, but works part-time in a friend's store in town when it doesn't interfere with his hunting and fishing. Marie never got tired of shooting, or of guns.

She works at the nearby Wal-Mart, selling guns and ammo. And when the armadillos get to overrunning the property, she picks up the loaded .22 she keeps handy and goes out in the clearing in front of their house and, surrounded by already-towering slash pines, picks those armadillos off one by one.

If she's out there shooting and Bob's off fishing, a caller gets a message that says: "We're probably out fighting mosquitoes or shooting armadillos. Leave a message at the tone."

They were a rare happy ending in the bogeyman's odyssey. She was one who got away.

# 66

# A DREAM COLLAPSES

Dawn Gorton eventually had a happy ending, too.

Be careful of what you wish for, is one maxim that applied to her. Another was the Chinese curse, May you lead an interesting life.

Since getting pregnant, Dawn had wished, prayed and dreamed for Jeff to love her the way she loved him, to marry her, to be the proper father of their baby. In June of 1982, that dream came true.

In September, back in Orlando after a stint in Chicago, they settled into a seemingly typical life for a young Navy couple, her helping ends meet working in a fast-food restaurant.

"I was young, he was young. There was nothing out of the ordinary," she would tell reporters later.

Well, there was *something* out of the ordinary. Just before their eviction from the trailer park, Deimund had told her Jeff was stealing women's undergarments from his tenants. Soon after, she'd caught Jeff removing undergarments from behind paneling in the wall of their bathroom. He denied stealing them, though, saying he'd bought them for himself and wore them to keep warm.

Then, just a week or so later, in their new apartment, she had the displeasure of watching someone from the Navy haul out a large duffel bag filled with women's undergarments.

Following Jeff's next arrest in October, Dawn and young Jeff left Florida to return home to Flint. While United Van Lines moved her things back to Michigan, she drove back with Dawn Gach. In September, she had called her old friend to ask her if she'd come to Florida and help out her and Jeff. Gach moved in with the couple, got a job at Taco Bell, too, and shared child-care duties. She was in the shower when the cops had shown up and arrested Jeff. It had only been two and a half years since she'd introduced Jeff and Dawn. It seemed more like a million.

While Jeff was out on bond awaiting sentencing and back in Michigan over the Christmas holidays of 1983—his parents paid for his airline tickets—Dawn got pregnant for a second time.

While home, Dawn says Jeff admitted everything to her—knocking down women to steal their slips, breaking into houses, stealing things from clotheslines. When asked why, he said he didn't know. He knew it was wrong, he just couldn't stop himself. But he seemed to have no remorse. It didn't seem to bother him.

Jeff wrote her from prison every ten days or so. One letter said there were some black guys who wanted to rape him.

Dawn briefly entertained ideas of a reconcilement when Jeff returned to Michigan after getting out of prison. But those ideas ended the day Jeff told her and her mother that he'd had a boyfriend during much of his prison stay. "I was looking for sensation," he told them. The other stuff—pulling panties off women, stealing from their homes—she could have dealt with. He could have gotten counseling, could have promised to stop and tried to. She still loved him. But the image of her husband enjoying sex with a man·in prison was not something she cared to re-sign herself to.

Dawn eventually filed for divorce, which was granted on March 8, 1988.

Though she would tell people later that she'd written Jeff off early in 1984, a month after their divorce was final, she wrote him a one-page letter, saying, in part:

> *I don't know what I can do to reach you. I'm sitting here with Jeffery and he's asking a lot of questions lately. He even tried calling you . . . I really need for us to always be friends . . . I hope that I didn't do anything to upset you . . . I hope you're all right and everything's okay. I'm really worried. Please call. Take care.*
> 
> *Always in my thoughts,*
> *Dawn.*

In December of 1988, Dawn married Fred Hemingway, a GM employee she'd been dating for two years, and they re-main married today. Jeffery retained his last name of Gor-ton. Her second son was born on September 7, 1984. She told people then, and she told state police in 2002, that he was Jeff's child. Jeff told everyone that he was not. Dawn would later tell police that a DNA test proved Jeff's paternity, but that Fred adopted him and Jeff signed off on any paternal rights. Brenda, though, would say the reason the Hemingways never sought child support for the boy was that the test showed Jeff *wasn't* the father.

The second son was given the last name of Hemingway. A son born in 1986 was also given Fred's last name. They had a daughter of their own in 1990.

Jeff paid child support until Jeffery's eighteenth birthday. The only thing other than a child support check Jeffery ever got from his father was a birthday card when he was 16. Dawn says Jeff's parents wanted nothing to do with their grandson.

## 67
## GETTING A PAGE

Dan Bohnett, who is now retired, describes his former job of overseeing the twenty-seven detectives in the ten far-flung posts and thirteen counties of central and northern Michigan as a "divorce-maker." He didn't end up divorced, but it was a lot of sixteen-hour days, long drives and getting called back on duty any time of day or night if something broke.

He'd been up in Tawas, a tourist town on Lake Huron, helping a detective work an old case, that of a bow hunter intentionally shot while he was up in a tree.

He was driving home the afternoon of February 6, battling traffic and droopy eyes, though it was just early afternoon, on I-75 north of Bay City when his pager went off. "I was dead tired," he recalls.

The page was from Kilbourn. Bohnett called him on his cell phone. Protocol was to be pretty nondescript on the non-secured wireless phones, and Kilbourn was nothing if not a dedicated follower of protocol.

"How you doing?" asked Kilbourn.

"Man, I'm tired today. I'm going home and get some sleep."

"I think you need to come to Flint."

"Is it important?"

"It's real important."

Bohnett wasn't involved day to day with the task force, but he knew things had been heating up on the dead-prostitute case. Was that it? Nope. More union trouble?

"It's nothing like that. We got some case things going on you need to know about. RIGHT NOW!!"

Bohnett knew if Kilbourn was speaking in capitals and exclamation points, it was *important*. "I had other guys, if they said it was important, it was, 'Okay, I'll be there in a little while.' If Kilbourn said it was important . . ." He put the gas pedal to the floor. "Man, what's going on?" he thought, no longer droopy-eyed.

He was in an unmarked car, without flashers. On I-75, you don't draw attention at 80, but you do at 95, which is what he hit on the way south. He was glad he didn't get pulled over by a local cop on patrol.

Bohnett whipped into the Flint post and hurried inside. Kilbourn was placid, his normal cautious, play-it-close-to-the-vest self. He didn't want the news getting out, even to his fellow cops. He led Bohnett to a small office and closed the door.

"We got a match on the Eby fingerprint, and the guy lives in Clio. His name is Jeff Gorton," he said.

Bohnett knew what fingerprint he was talking about, the partial bloody print left by the faucet in Eby's bathroom. The one they'd sent out to the FBI when the world was a different place, pre–9/11.

"Oh, boy, we're going to have a long night," Bohnett said to himself. To Kilbourn, he said: "We gotta get DNA. We gotta put a surveillance crew together and get DNA. Get on him twenty-four/seven."

Though there were members of the Flint PD officially on the task force, the reality was, the Flint cops were too busy working their own cases and hadn't been involved much at all in the Eby or Ludwig investigations.

Now, though, out of courtesy, Bohnett called Chief Barksdale. He had to keep it on the QT, but it looked like they had their guy. Something was going to go down and go down soon.

Kilbourn and Larsen had already done a drive-by of Gorton's home on Tuscola Road in Vienna. Had scouted out the neighborhood, looking for places to put members of a surveillance crew. There might be a perfectly good and innocent explanation for why the guy would leave a bloody partial in Eby's bathroom—maybe he was a boyfriend whose name hadn't come up who'd spent the night and cut himself shaving in the morning.

"Does one fingerprint make a guy guilty? No. She'd had a lot of visitors," says Larsen. Nonetheless, they liked their chances that the print had led them to their killer.

By 5 p.m., they had a surveillance crew in place. Had it been a typical subdivision, surveillance would have been a piece of cake: Park someone down the street in sight of the house—on the eye, as they called it—and have others out of sight on various streets both ways from the house. As soon as the suspect leaves, the eye calls others on the crew and tells them which way he's moving.

The house on Tuscola presented logistical problems. It was on a busy two-lane county road without any parking lanes. The lots were huge, which meant not many nearby neighbors you could pretend to be visiting. And it had snowed a lot that month, with snow piled up high both in front of the Gorton house and along both sides of his driveway, making visual contact difficult.

Larsen sat surveillance with them awhile. He pulled into a driveway of a neighbor down the road, at a house with the lights out and no cars in the driveway. But two minutes later, the neighbor pulled into the driveway, too, and Larsen, not wanting to give the game away, just started his car and left without explanation.

One car was able to park along the road far enough from the house not to be suspicious, but able to see the front door. A van left the house and was followed to a nearby party store before returning. Around 10 p.m., the Gorton house went dark and surveillance was pulled.

"We were better served at that point by being organized, getting some sleep and then starting twenty-four-hour surveillance," says Larsen.

Meanwhile, Bohnett had assigned duties. They needed to find out Gorton's criminal record, his work history, his friends, his family. They needed to draw up a list of people to interview as soon as possible in case they got a DNA match and made an arrest. That would mean his wife, if he had one. Ex-wives, siblings, parents, co-workers. Who were they and where did they live? When and if they brought Gorton in, they'd need to have things coordinated so they could bring in or visit as many as they could at the same time, so there'd be no coordinating of stories.

They'd need to do records searches, looking for marriage certificates, divorce decrees, mortgage filings, traffic tickets, arrest warrants, if any.

"It was controlled chaos, but it was chaos," says Bohnett. "We had people running everywhere."

His afternoon had begun with droopy eyes and thoughts of bed. Now, wired on adrenaline and caffeine, there was no thought of rest. Bohnett and some of his detectives would be going non-stop through the night and into the next day. Others would try to grab a few fitful hours of sleep.

The next morning, Thursday, the 7th, Bohnett and the task-force members gathered at the Flint post at 7 a.m. for a strategy session. Kilbourn called down to the Romulus PD and got Malaniak, who had a habit of coming in early.

"Hey, Gordie, it's Greg."

Malaniak could tell from Kilbourn's voice that something was up. Mr. Calm, wasn't.

"We got our guy."

"You gotta fucking be kidding me."

"Not only that, but he's living here in the Flint area."

"There's no doubt?"

"There's no doubt."

Snyder walked in about 9 and Malaniak told him the good news.

"Come on," said Snyder. "We're going to Flint."

## 68
## WORKING AT THE GATEHOUSE

Everything the police dug up seemed to scream: *This is the guy!*

They found out that Gorton had a conviction in Florida in 1983 for assaulting women and stealing their underwear.

He'd been released on Christmas Eve of 1985 and returned to Flint.

He'd had more than his share of contacts with state police, but had for the most part avoided trouble—a traffic ticket in 1979, possession of open alcohol in 1981, another traffic ticket in 1981. Computer records show numerous instances of his name being run through the system to check for warrants, but there were no explanations.

His name had been run by computer through the National Crime Information Center seven times over the last ten years, by Grand Blanc police in May of 1992, by the Flint PD in September of 1992, by the Jackson County Sheriff's Department in May of 1993, by Genesee County in November of 1994 and June of 1995, by the Flint post of the state police in June of 1998 and by Bay County in September of 2000.

The checks could have been innocuous, a result of being pulled over for a warning about burned-out taillights, for example, but likely for something more serious, like a call about a suspicious person in the neighborhood.

His most serious contact with the Michigan judicial system had been in 1995, a disorderly conduct charge. But it wasn't your ordinary disorderly conduct. He'd been shopping in a Pamida department store just around the corner from his house at 5 p.m. on August 16 when a female security guard monitoring surveillance cameras spotted Gorton lifting a woman's skirt and staring at her panties as she bent over in front of him to look at something.

Amazingly enough, he had been so light of touch that the woman hadn't even noticed it. The security guard called the Genesee County Sheriff's Department, and by the time Gorton had finished his shopping and gone through the checkout line, deputies were at the scene. They pulled his white van over before it could leave the parking lot and eventually arrested him.

At first Gorton denied it, but when told the incident was captured on videotape, he said, according to the police report, that he was "sorry for the incident and he did not know why he did it . . . he had just looked under her skirt a little bit."

He was charged with fourth-degree criminal sexual conduct, but pleaded to disorderly conduct and was sentenced to 90 days, a sentence held in abeyance in lieu of a fine of $205, six months' probation and a psychological evaluation.

The charge was only a 90-day misdemeanor. Gorton caught a break. Had the crime carried any sentence longer than that, under procedures then in place, his fingerprints would have been taken and entered into the AFIS system. When Larsen had asked Galvin Smith to run the bloody print at the Eby scene through AFIS the previous summer, Gorton's name would have popped up then.

But better late than never.

Gorton had also caught a break in 1993. A terrified woman came into the Flint state police post on August 4, 1993, and said a man had been stalking her for months, following her nearly every morning on Tuscola Road and then southbound on I-75 as she drove to work at the J B Supply Company, and that he often followed her home from work, too. He lived near her and used to attend her church, Colonial Hills Baptist, but she switched to another church to get away from him.

He had come into her work place several times and just stared at her. He had followed her to Wal-Mart, he had even followed her into the parking lot of her attorney one day. He had never said a word to her, just stared.

She had tried to get police to do something earlier, but they said there was nothing to do. But she had read the day before about Michigan's new stalking law and since she was being stalked . . .

She had the license-plate number of his van, a work van with the name "Buckler Lawn Sprinkler Inc." prominently displayed. Trooper Greg Campbell drove to Gorton's house and told him about the complaint. Gorton denied stalking her. He said it was just a coincidence that they left home the same time each day and headed in the same directions. As for the attorney's office, that was a coincidence, too. Gorton said he'd gotten lost and just pulled in there to turn around.

Campbell warned him about the state's new stalking laws, and that he didn't want to hear any more about this. The woman declined to press charges and the stalking stopped.

Campbell's report ended inexplicably, "There was no identifiable criminal history on Jeffrey Wayne Gorton."

Police were quickly able to find out that Gorton was still employed by his parents in the family business, the Buckler Automatic Lawn Sprinkler Co. in suburban Flint, and had been since April of 1986. Mott's meticulous records would later reveal that Buckler had been working at the estate on November 5, 1986, just two days before Eby's murder, turning off the automatic sprinkler system before winter hit. To keep the underground pipes from freezing and cracking, the water inside them had to be blown out with a powerful air compressor, and that's what a Buckler crew was doing at the estate early in November of 1986. The estate was billed $162 on November 11 and Buckler was paid on November 17.

Buckler employees weren't just at the estate, but at the gatehouse. In the basement of the gatehouse, in something called the potting room, were the controls for the estate's automatic sprinkler system, and some Buckler employee either would have been given a key to the ground-floor exterior door that led to the basement, or would have been let in by some Mott employee.

There might yet be a legitimate explanation for Gorton's bloody print in Eby's upstairs bathroom. Maybe he'd cut himself while working on the pipes and Eby had let him into the house to wash off the cut and put on a Band-Aid. Likely? No. But it was possible. They needed his DNA. They'd keep him under surveillance as long as it took to get it.

If his DNA matched the DNA in the semen left on Eby and Ludwig, case closed.

## 69
## SURVEILLANCE RESUMING

Larsen got to the Flint post at 6:30 a.m. on the 7th. It had the early makings of a zoo. The word had gone out around the post that they were about to take down the guy who'd killed Eby and Ludwig, and everyone wanted to be there when and if he was brought in.

Soon Snyder and Malaniak arrived. In the afternoon, Snyder sent for four more of them, to help draw up warrants and work surveillance.

Kilbourn called Jeff Nye at the crime lab in Lansing and

told him they had a suspect and were putting him under surveillance.

Nye gave him some tips. If he eats anything, try to get the silverware. If he smokes, get the butt. If he drinks out of a glass, get it. Keep your eyes peeled for napkins. Hard surfaces like metal and glass are much better than Styrofoam or paper, but grab what you can. Nye told him if they got any evidence that might yield some DNA, to rush it to Lansing, any time of the day or night. Just call him on his cell and he'd run the tests.

Surveillance was resumed. A crew of state police from Lansing was brought in to work the first shift. Curiously, no Flint PD were involved, or maybe not so curiously, given the ongoing animus toward the presence of the task force.

It was a dull day for the first. There are few slower ways to pass the time than to sit in a car and watch a house, or to wait for word from someone watching the house. You drink coffee. You read and reread the paper with one eye. You look at your watch and see that only twenty minutes have passed. You get cold. You turn on the car and crank up the heater. You turn the car off before you die of carbon monoxide poisoning and slowly start getting cold again. You look at your watch.

While the surveillance crew twiddled, the cops back at the post added to their intelligence. They knew where Gorton's first wife and current wife worked. They began compiling names and addresses of his neighbors. They began drafting search warrants for the Gorton home, for Buckler Sprinkler and for his parents' home, which sat next door, a path leading out the back door of the house and across the back lawn to the company parking lot and office entrance.

It was already dark by 5:45 p.m. when the Lansing surveillance crew was relieved. Nothing had happened all day. Kids had gone to school and returned. Gorton, who collected unemployment during the winter months, was home, but had stayed tight.

The night crew was mostly Romulus—Mike St. Andre and John Hlinak in separate unmarked cars, Malaniak and Greg Brandemihl sharing a third, and State Police Sergeant Mark Reaves in a fourth. Reaves had done odds and ends on the Eby case for Kilbourn, but most of his task-force work had been on the prostitute murders. Since Reaves knew the area, his job was to be the lead tail on Gorton if and when he left the house. One of the Romulus guys was on the eye. Reaves was in the parking lot of a party store up Tuscola. The eye would radio him, he'd fall in behind Gorton, and the others would follow.

They were just settling in, no time to be bored, when at 6:07 p.m., Gorton, his wife and two kids came out of the house, loaded into the Pontiac station wagon and pulled out onto the highway. The eye radioed Reaves, told him which way Gorton was moving and off they went.

Along the way, Gorton accelerated through a yellow and Reaves had no chance to make it. He sat there at the red watching Gorton's taillights recede into the night. It was one of those lights that seemed would never change. Finally, Reaves hit the accelerator and blew through the red.

St. Andre, sitting behind him in an unmarked Pontiac Grand Prix, watched as a driver coming through the green slammed on his brakes, hit the horn, swerved to avoid an accident and raised a middle finger, all at once. "Man, don't have an accident, now," thought St. Andre.

Reaves accelerated, closing the gap on the taillights ahead. The light changed to green and the other cops hit their accelerators, too.

Reaves thought he would follow Gorton into the rink. He had a hand-held 800-megahertz radio. The Romulus guys had walkie-talkie Nextels. In the meantime, they'd come up with a plan of their own.

As part of being a smart tail, Reaves kept going straight when Gorton pulled into the parking lot at Skateland on N. Dort Highway at 6:20. He circled back and parked in a church lot across the street. In the meantime, the Romulus cops had pulled into the Skateland lot and St. Andre and Brandemihl had already gone inside.

Reaves and Malaniak waited, wondering if they were going to hit pay dirt inside.

They did. At 7:28, Brandemihl came out of the rink, walked over to Malaniak and handed him a bag and a cup-inside-a-cup. Malaniak went to Reaves' car and passed them on to him. Reaves dumped out the pop left inside the crucial cup, put the two cups in another evidence bag and headed off for the Flint post, arriving at 8:05.

The rest stayed on the Gortons, who left the arena at 8:15, arrived home seven minutes later and had lights out by 10:30.

Hal Zettle drove the evidence west on I-69 in his rattle-trap state-issued Corsica to the town of Perry and passed it on to Jeff Nye, the state police chemist and DNA whiz. By 9:15 he was at the state crime lab.

By midnight, Nye had reached a preliminary conclusion. The tiny amount of DNA he'd been able to remove from the napkins and Styrofoam cup didn't look anywhere near what they'd need to make a match with Ludwig and Eby's killer. He called Greg Kilbourn to give him the bad news. Kilbourn passed the word on to Snyder.

Malaniak, after a short, fitful sleep, called Snyder early in the morning. "You hear anything on the DNA?"

"It doesn't look like there's enough."

"Fuck."

Nye wasn't through yet, though. Down, maybe, but not out. The small sample he'd collected had to be run through the equipment and matched against their known sample, the killer's, which would take three or four hours. He guessed he had half a nanogram of Gorton's DNA out of the fifteen to twenty microliters of solution that he'd distilled from the evidence. Half a billionth of a gram. Half of a billionth of one twenty-eighth of an ounce.

DNA is a monstrously big molecule, with six billion pairs of proteins in its long double helix. Just a few years earlier, Nye would have had to hope for strands of DNA as long as 10,000 base pairs in a sample to get a match. Now, he could get by if there were as few as 100. He had so little to work with, even that seemed doubtful. But the lab equipment was state of the art and it had to be given a chance.

## 70
## THE BRASS POURS IN

Nye got lucky. There are thirteen different genetic markers to link DNA samples. By the end of the night of computerized chemistry, the printout showed seven markers linking Gorton's DNA to the killer's. The more links, the greater the chance the two were one and the same. A result of seven links wasn't conclusive, but it was persuasive. Most important, it would be enough to satisfy the probable-cause standard needed to get a search warrant to get a buccal swab from Gorton and run a conclusive test.

It was now 6 a.m. There was just one more thing to do before he called Kilbourn with the good news. To prove that the equipment wasn't screwing up or running out of spec, he needed to check the instrumentation by running a control sample. If those results came out okay, they were home free.

By 8:30, the i's were dotted and the t's crossed. The control sample tested fine. The machinery was working. He could officially say that Gorton's DNA was "associated" with the rapist who'd murdered Nancy Ludwig and Margarette Eby.

Nye called Kilbourn about 9, gave him the good-morning news. They started high-fiving at the Flint post. "Oh, man, what a feeling," says Larsen.

Nye went back to work. By 10:30 he had a written report ready for Genesee County Prosecutor Arthur Busch's office, a report they'd use to seek a warrant to take Gorton's DNA. His boss, Charles Barna, looked his work over, agreed with its conclusions and would call Flint at 12:45 p.m. to tell him he agreed with Nye.

All morning, the brass poured into the Flint post "coming in like gangbusters," thought Mike St. Andre. All the way up the state police chain-of-command, word had gone out the night before that they had Gorton under surveillance and had snatched some evidence for a DNA test.

By use of an urgent-voice-mail system the state police used to deliver hot news via pager, the brass had been updated, first that there didn't seem to be enough DNA, then that there was, and that it showed a match.

Not wanting to miss out on the big day, anyone who was anyone had piled into the parking lot from Saginaw or Lansing and wedged into the post to await Gorton's arrest and the inevitable press conference, including Inspector Mark Dougovito, who oversaw all the detectives in the state; Captain Dan Miller, Bohnett's boss in the Saginaw district, which included Flint; Lieutenant Colonel Bertee, who had given birth to the cold-case squad, and some PR staff to handle the expected chaos with the media.

Bertee had been at his home in De Witt, outside Lansing, when Dougovito gave him the word via voice mail. "You take a job like mine, where do you get your job satisfaction from?" he'd say later. "Troopers or undercover narcotics guys get their reward on a daily basis. But something like this? That gives me my reward."

You could hardly expect him to go to his office in East Lansing. He drove to Flint.

"Solving these two cases, short of solving the Jimmy Hoffa murder, well, there weren't two higher profile cases in the state of Michigan," explains Mike Larsen.

By 10 a.m., Bohnett, Kilbourn's and Larsen's immediate supervisor, knew he'd be treading a fine line today. In a perfect world, the brass would keep away, and out of their hair. But they'd put up a lot of money and taken a lot of political flak to fund the cold-case squad. "How do you tell a lieutenant colonel to stay home? How do you say, 'Captain, Inspector, just stay home and let us do our job'? It don't work that way," explains Bohnett.

He was trying to keep things under wraps, keep the news from leaking out to the media that there was a suspect. "I didn't want him knowing we're on him," says Bohnett. "He might have trophies in the house he can destroy."

And listening to brass. "You got the command guys saying, 'When are we going to do this? I thought you had it wrapped up?' "

So, he went to Larsen. "When you going to get him?"

"In a bit, Dan. I have a few things to do first."

"I got the brass on my ass."

"I understand."

He had his best detectives on the guy, they were about to make a collar on a case that was more than fifteen years old, and here people were, in Bohnett's words, "worrying about making the noon news. Holy Christ."

Bohnett literally herded the brass into a large conference office in the front of the station. He put his detectives and the Romulus guys as far in the back of the station as he could.

"I was going from one end of the post saying, 'Soon,' to the other end, saying 'What do you have? When are we going to have it?' "

Malaniak couldn't believe how packed the place was

when he got there at 10:30. Thinking they didn't have enough for a match, his wife had gone to work at a local bank, leaving him to care for their handicapped daughter. Then Dan got him on the Nextel and told him the good news. "Shit," Malaniak thought. "What if my wife can't get out of work? Biggest goddamn day of my career and I'm going to miss it babysitting."

But his wife was able to leave, come home and relieve him. He made it to Flint in fifty minutes, some sort of modern-day record.

They had enough for arrest and search warrants, but before they got them, Larsen and Kilbourn wanted a crack at Gorton first, to see if they could get him to talk, catch him off guard. If their first contact with him was with an arrest or search warrant in hand, their chances of getting anything good out of him diminished considerably.

Contrary to what you see on the TV cop shows, police aren't required to read a suspect his Miranda rights immediately. Courts have generally interpreted Miranda to mean that until someone is no longer free to leave a police interview of his own accord, the police don't have to read him his rights. They'd see what Gorton had to say willingly, if anything.

But no matter what he said or did, they knew they'd be arresting him before the day was out.

Larsen called FBI profiler Bob Morton at Quantico to ask his advice. Larsen explained the situation and said they wanted to see what they could get voluntarily.

While Larsen was on the phone with Morton, about noon, Bohnett stuck his head in the doorway of his tiny office. Larsen told Morton "Just a second," and looked at Bohnett.

"What time do you think we can do the press conference?"

Larsen blew up. "SHUT UP! GET THE HELL OUT OF MY OFFICE! I'M ON THE PHONE, GODDAMN IT!"

Bohnett took Larsen's blow-up in stride. "He barked at me. I'd have barked, too, if I'd have been him. Man, he blew. He blew *up*. I almost chuckled, to be honest. I knew the stress he was under," says Bohnett today.

Morton advised they play it cool, introduce themselves politely, tell Gorton his name had come up as part of an old investigation and ask if he would mind talking to them. Be quiet. No shows of force. No handcuffs.

"More than likely he'll be very interested in what you know and will want to hear what you have to say," said Morton.

Kilbourn and Larsen put on their coats. Snyder asked if he could come. Larsen felt bad telling him no. Three cops on the porch would give the game away.

It was an eighteen-mile drive to the Gorton residence, where a surveillance crew was already stationed. They'd seen his wife leave for work and his kids get on the school bus, but Gorton hadn't gone anywhere.

On the way over, Kilbourn and Larsen got another call from Nye, saying the data looked even better, that he was even more certain Gorton was their killer. They also worked out how they'd play it.

At 1:15 p.m., they pulled into the driveway, went up to the door and knocked. Gorton opened the door. Kilbourn made introductions, then Larsen took over.

"Mr. Gorton, your name came up in an old assault case and we have a few questions to ask you. Do you mind if we come in?"

Gorton stepped back and let them in. As the door was closing, other troopers were already in action, putting a well-rehearsed plan in place. One went to Genesys hospital, where Brenda worked, to pick her up. Another went to the home of Fred and Dawn Hemingway, to pick up Gorton's first wife.

Inside the house, they chatted briefly, then Larsen said they were hoping they could go back to the post for the interview, that they'd be happy to drive him home when they were done.

"Sure, let me get my shoes and jacket," said Gorton.

"Outwardly he was quiet. He was cool," says Larsen. "But looking into his eye, you could see the gears moving a million miles an hour."

Gorton didn't know it, but he had no choice. Larsen and Kilbourn had talked it over. If Gorton didn't come voluntarily, they were going to bring him in in handcuffs, put him in jail and then go out and get an arrest warrant. "We weren't leaving the house without him," says Larsen.

They walked out of the house in single file, Gorton closing up the house and trailing them. Inside the house, they'd patted him down for weapons, so they weren't worried about turning their backs on him. They didn't cuff him. Greg got in the front. Larsen got in the back with Gorton.

Greg Brandemihl was sitting surveillance in an unmarked Romulus police car. He couldn't believe it when Larsen and Kilbourn came out with Gorton trailing. No way he'd let that scumbag have any chance to surprise him from behind. "I wouldn't turn my back on him," he thought.

They were acting pleasant and friendly, "like they were all going out for breakfast," says Brandemihl.

The profiler might have said don't go busting in the door, but if this had been Brandemihl's arrest, no fucking way Gorton would be sauntering down the driveway. Working undercover drugs, "we do hard arrests," says Brandemihl. Knock down doors, knock down perps, introduce yourself while they're eating carpet and wondering who the fuck just unloaded on them. Cuff 'em tight, throw 'em in the back seat of the car.

But it wasn't his arrest. He watched them drive off and then he sat there, securing the scene, waiting for what he assumed would be an imminent search warrant. He'd be waiting for hours, though, getting cold of hand and foot and hot under the collar as morning turned into afternoon and afternoon turned into night and still no warrant and still no search.

## 71
## BOTH SIDES FUMING

Genesee County Prosecutor Arthur Busch leaned back in his big black leather chair late Friday morning, taking a breather, and thought, "This is going to be a long day." Today, he was going to earn his weekend.

Little did he know just how long the day would be, or how much he'd earn his Saturday and Sunday.

It was a work day, but instead of suit and tie he was dressed in blue jeans, hiking boots and a black T-shirt. The historic, stately courthouse in downtown Flint was undergo-

ing a major renovation, and today was moving day for his
staff, across the street to temporary offices in a small low-
slung office building.

He'd been nursing a bad back and had put off the move as
long as possible, but he was out of time. He had to clear out
to make room for the contractors. He'd been carrying boxes
to the moving trucks and was taking a short break for a
meeting he and Randy Petrides, chief of the trial division,
had scheduled with Flint police and senior staff to discuss a
felony case. Busch's cell phone rang, he took the call, put
down the phone and tersely asked the police to leave.

It was Captain Dan Miller of the Michigan State Police,
calling to let him know there had been a DNA match on the
Eby case, that they were about to pick up a local guy for
Eby's murder after some undercover surveillance work, and
they'd be coming over for search and arrest warrants.

Busch almost popped his spleen. The biggest case in Flint
in decades was about to become the biggest arrest and prosecution of his career, and they were letting him know *now*?
Clearly they had intentionally kept him out of the loop. He'd
been kept in the frickin' dark with the mushrooms while it
all went down. That was, to him, an intolerable lack of eti-
quette, courtesy and even common sense.

Just the courtesy of a call the night before and he could
have alerted his staff to forgo the casual clothes and forget
about moving. He was steaming. He'd be steaming all day.

"I was pissed they did it on purpose, to minimize my involvement because we'd had our run-ins over the years," he
says. And pissed that "I was not involved or consulted in this
whole sting operation."

Nor in the Gorton interview. Wouldn't it have made sense
to ask the prosecutor for advice on questions that might elicit
the kind of answers they could use in court?

"It's a team play, but the state police don't play a team
game. They're Lone Rangers," says Busch.

Bohnett, though, says there was good reason to keep him
in the dark, that both the Flint PD and the prosecutor's office
were notorious for leaks. "You'd go in for a search warrant,
and when you went to serve it, you didn't know if they were
going to greet you with milk and cookies. You never knew
where the leaks were coming from."

"In Wayne County, we would have got the warrants to the prosecutor the night before," says Snyder. "But the state police wouldn't consider faxing them to Busch the night before because they didn't trust him or his office. Buckler Sprinkler was a business, and you never knew if Gorton's dad was a campaign contributor and might get a call tipping him off."

While Gorton was being interviewed by Kilbourn and Larsen, other state police and Romulus cops drove downtown to meet with Busch. They thought getting warrants would be a slam-dunk, a mere formality. They thought wrong. Busch wasn't the only one who was going to be in for a long day.

Busch, baby-faced and looking more like a recent law-school grad than the chief prosecutor of a major and dangerous city, is a liberal Democrat who grew up three blocks from the site of the historic Flint sit-down strikes of the 1930s, which gave birth to the United Auto Workers. As a boy he delivered *The Flint Journal* to Fisher Body plant No. 1, and hung out at the nearby union hall, "where I learned most of my politics."

He has outlined a book he hopes to find a publisher for, with the working title of *Declaring War on Everything*, about how, in his words, "ten years of right-wing justice have filled our prisons," how ill-served as a society we are by the military analogies politicians use to declare war on terrorism or war on drugs, and how we need to stop warehousing criminals and start rehabilitating them.

"There's no delivery system for rehabilitation. Do we believe only in retribution?" he asks.

Busch had several big scenes in Michael Moore's *Bowling for Columbine*, bemoaning, as befitting a Michael Moore movie, racism and its effect on the poor of Flint. What he didn't tell Moore's audience is what he brags about to visitors to his office, that he has almost single-handedly taken on the gangs in Flint, getting their butts off the streets and into prison. The gangs, of course, being made up generally of the same poor minorities he accuses the system of warehousing.

Busch is eloquent, quotable and loves the limelight. He showed all three qualities in 2000, when the national media descended on Flint after a 6-year-old first-grader, Kayla

Rolland, was intentionally shot and killed by a classmate, who had found a .32-caliber semi-automatic in his house and brought it to school. His mom was at work as part of the state's work-to-collect-welfare laws, and a 19-year-old staying at her house had neglected to hide or unload the weapon.

The story touched any number of media hot buttons, and Busch's, too.

For days, the camera crews lined up in a row outside the school, filing their reports. Busch would walk the line, doing one stand-up after another. As much as he savored the national attention, he knew when and how to play a local game, too. One day he was just about to do a lengthy interview for a local TV news show, when a national producer pulled him aside and asked him if they could grab him now.

"I can't. I'm busy," said Busch.

"But it's Katie Couric," said the producer.

"I don't get elected in Manhattan," said Busch.

April of 2003 was an interesting month for Busch, to say the least. He started it out in Hollywood, accompanying Moore to a round of Oscar bashes. And he finished it in Washington, arguing before the Supreme Court that a conviction years earlier in a murder case in Genesee County did not amount to double jeopardy, even though the judge had originally decided that the facts in the case did not merit a charge of premeditation, then later reversed himself. (The Oscar voters agreed with his friend Moore, and the Supreme Court later unanimously agreed with him.)

Fresh back from Hollywood and about to leave for Washington for his appearance before the Supreme Court, Busch was blunt and shot from the hip when interviewed about the events on the day Gorton was picked up.

He admitted he was angry from the start about a state police task force being established in Flint, and he admitted he didn't have much use, in general, for the cops who ran it.

Busch had applied for funding to set up his own cold-case squad when word came that the state police would be running one, instead, and that no funds would be forthcoming for his staff. He said the decision was made by then–Michigan Governor John Engler, something state police brass dismiss as preposterous.

Busch said he met at one of his favorite spots in Flint, the Sunrise Coney Island—"I like to hide in the corner there, and people don't know my business"—to discuss a cold-case squad with his chief investigator, Gary Elford, who had run the Eby crime scene and later joined Busch's staff after retiring from the Flint PD.

"I had Gary meet me there to have coffee and I told him I wanted to work on the Eby case. It bugged me we couldn't solve it after all those years. I thought DNA had gotten cheap enough we could afford to run tests without a lot of time and expense."

Busch said he even had meetings with King and former members of the Flint PD to learn about the case and that he was planning to take a hands-on approach to interviewing their chief suspect, Charles Stone, who was reported to be living in Maryland.

"I was planning a trip to Maryland with golf clubs in hand," said Busch. "I was going to show up there all these years later and have a chat with him."

But, "Within a couple of days of meeting with Gary, the state police came in. Maybe my paranoia is running wild, but . . . My idea wasn't popular with the Engler administration because they didn't want a Democratic prosecutor to get the kind of publicity this thing would develop," says Busch, who got his law degree with Engler in the 1983 class of Lansing's Cooley Law School. "As soon as they figured out what I was up to, they sent in ten state police officers with the sum total of one homicide investigation between them."

He also admitted, "I was pretty upset with [Chief Barksdale] that he agreed to it without consulting me."

The state police and Busch had clashed several times during the cold-case investigations, once when he refused to issue a warrant to arrest a truck driver in the serial raping of prostitutes, another when he refused a search warrant for Hal Zettle, who was investigating the serial murders of prostitutes. It didn't seem to mollify him that Elford was eventually appointed to the task force.

Of Zettle, Busch said: "Basically this traffic cop who has been given a white horse to ride, comes in and wants a search warrant to go to a suspect's house. I told him 'You know, you need probable cause. What makes you think you have something?'

"And he said, 'I know it in my heart.' My group of veteran prosecutors and I looked at each other and rolled our eyes. 'I know it in my heart' turned into 'No.' " (Keith Cummings was eventually arrested and convicted in 2001 for killing two of the prostitutes; the murders of the others remain unsolved.)

Regarding others in the state police chain of command, he said Captain Dan Miller, Dan Bohnett's supervisor, was "a dickhead," and that in his view Bohnett "was a command officer with very little experience. He was very good with radar guns and that's about it."

As for declining a warrant for the rapist, Busch said the state police thought a warrant would help them link the guy to Eby's death. "I wasn't too impressed with that approach." And that most of the acts seemed to have occurred in Tuscola County, anyway.

Barksdale said his relationship with Busch was irreparably damaged when Busch refused to issue a warrant for the trucker. He said the Flint police had arrested him, he had confessed to the forcible rape of eleven prostitutes, either at gunpoint or knifepoint, had served time in Colorado for previous rape convictions and told police he was willing to plead guilty to felonious assault.

"We went to Busch for a warrant and he flat-out refused us," said Barksdale. "He said we had no authority to accept a plea. He said it sounded like a failure to pay and that the prostitutes should sue him in civil court for their money. Can you believe that shit?"

Barksdale then turned to federal prosecutors. Luckily, one of the rapes involved a gun, and a federal prosecutor in Bay County charged the trucker, Clyde William Haire, with violating federal gun laws. In September of 2002, Haire was sentenced to 327 months in prison.

So, when Busch got the call well into moving day that a suspect was about to be taken into custody for killing Margarette Eby, there was a long history of animosity between him, the Flint PD and the state police. Relations weren't about to get any better.

# 72

# AN OVERDUE CALL

Back at the Flint post, as Larsen and Kilbourn pulled out to go to Gorton's, Snyder made a phone call. Some of the state cops thought he was rushing things, ought to wait for an arrest. Snyder had waited long enough.

It was a call he'd promised Art Ludwig that one day, one year, sooner or later he'd make. This was going to be news they were going to have a hard time keeping a lid on. He didn't want Art Ludwig to hear about it on the news or from some reporter on the phone, so it was a call he was going to make *now*, procedure be damned.

In Minnesota, Art was sitting in the blue rocker in the living room, reading the morning paper, half-watching CNN when the phone rang.

"Art? Hi, Dan Snyder. This is something you've been waiting to hear and something I've been waiting to tell you for eleven years. We've got Nancy's killer. The state police are on their way to pick him up right now."

Art broke down on the phone.

"It was like an emotional ax in the head," recalls Art. "It's the call you've been waiting for for eleven years. It was so emotional. You're reading the paper and the last thing you expect is a call from Dan Snyder."

Dan told him to sit tight with it, to keep it quiet for an hour. They were making an arrest, but wanted to interview the suspect first.

Half an hour later, someone at his old station, KARE, phoned. Word was leaking somewhere. Art did as Dan had asked and stalled. "Something's going on in Flint, but I don't know what it is, yet."

Half an hour later, another station called. By then, "the cat was out of the bag," says Art. He told them the good news, then got on the phone and started calling all the family and friends he could think of.

Later, tough-guy cop Brandemihl would say of Snyder's call: "That was truly touching. It was probably the most touching moment in Dan Snyder's career. I was happy for him."

Later, Snyder would go through the list of 20,000 names he and his investigators had compiled. Gorton's wasn't on there. He wasn't someone they had been told about, or heard about, and overlooked. Snyder was relieved. "It meant I hadn't missed anything. Or screwed up."

## 73
## "IS IT MY MOM?"

At Genesys hospital south of Flint, the police searched the huge parking lot until they found Brenda Gorton's car. Sergeant Rudy Gonzalez stayed with it in case she should drive off while his partner was inside.

Coincidentally, Brenda, a records clerk, was on the phone, trying to reach Jeff—someone from the TV antenna company was coming today and she wanted to remind him to stick around the house, but for some reason he wasn't answering—when her boss came up to her and told her, "Brenda, you gotta go down to personnel."

The way she said it, it reminded Brenda of being in school and being called down to the principal's office.

Her immediate thought: Mom's been hurt in a car wreck.

She went down to personnel.

"Brenda, there's somebody for you in that room," said the woman at the front desk, pointing to a small room off the main office area.

Sure now it was bad news, her mom must be dead, not just hurt, Brenda said, "I'm not going in that room by myself."

"No, you have to."

"Is everyone okay? I'm not going in that room until I know my mom's okay."

"Your mom's okay. Everyone's okay."

Brenda went in.

Sergeant Allan Ogg stood up and introduced himself.

He had a few questions.

"How long have you been married to your husband?"

"Twelve years. What's this all about?"

"I can't tell you."

"You can't tell me what this is about?"

"No. We need to get you home so you can make arrangements to take care of your kids. Won't they be coming home on the bus?"

Before she left, she called her kids' school and left a message for a friend who worked in the school office, to take her kids home with her after school and she'd pick them up there.

Brenda insisted on driving her own car. The police were reluctant to let her, but had no choice. A little while later, Brenda pulled up to a house that had seemed so normal just a few hours ago. The driveway was now filled with five unmarked police SUVs and yellow police tape cordoned everything off.

"Is Jeff here?" she asked.

"No."

"Where is he?"

"I can't tell you."

She asked if she could go in the house. No. She had to go to the bathroom. No. She insisted. Finally, they had no choice. They didn't have warrants yet. No one had been charged. It was her house.

As she walked in, the phone rang. It was someone else from school. It turned out the friend she had left a message with had gone home early and wouldn't be able to take the kids.

Brenda called her mom and asked her to pick them up.

"Don't take them home. Do not come here. Take the kids to your house."

"Why? What's up?"

"I don't know, but believe me, *take the kids to your house. Do not bring them here!*"

Brenda came back outside, this time determined. She started screaming, *"Where's Jeff?"*

Finally someone said: "He's been arrested."

"What for?"

"I can't tell you right now."

Brenda pictured a speeding ticket gone awry, Jeff pulled over going ten over with a warrant out for his arrest for unpaid parking tickets. Or something.

Having sat there for hours with nothing to do but watch the scene, Brandemihl had noticed what looked to be a car covered by a tarp hidden behind a berm of snow piled up from the driveway.

At some point, he went over to Brenda and asked her what was under the tarp.

"That's Jeff's car. That car never moves. He's had it since before we were married." She didn't tell him, but it was the first car Jeff had ever financed on his own and he had a fantasy of some day putting its engine into a 1968 Chevy.

"Can you show it to me?"

"Sure."

They walked gingerly through the snow at the side of the garage. Brenda lifted an edge of the tarp. It was a gold Monte Carlo.

## 74
## A VIDEOTAPED CHAT

On the drive back to the police station, Larsen and Kilbourn engaged Gorton in small talk, wanting to keep him calm. He would respond quietly and politely, but with one exception, he never initiated any talk of his own. That exception? He told them he'd been in charge of the crew that had installed the sprinkler system at the state police post they were now heading to.

One thing struck Larsen: "He never asked one question. Not, 'What does this case you're investigating involve?' Nothing. It was a strange trip. I don't know whose mind was going faster, his or mine. I know we've got the right guy and he doesn't know we know."

They led Gorton into the station, the brass and local cops having been banished to offices and out of the hallway so things wouldn't seem too out of the ordinary.

They took Gorton to a room usually used by the polygraph unit. Hidden audio and video had been set up, so Gorton wouldn't be aware he was being filmed and taped. Then they left him alone for a few minutes.

*Videotape, date in upper left corner, 2-08-02. Time in upper left corner, 1:40 p.m.*

*Gorton sits in a chair just to right of center screen, wearing blue jeans, cuffs rolled up about four inches, gray T-shirt. Screen left is a small table. He vigorously rubs his right hand with his left. He rocks back and forth. He looks around the room, up at the ceiling, tilts forward and tries to read the top page of a packet of papers Larsen has left on the table.*

*1:44 p.m. Noise of a door opening screen left. Kilbourn reintroduces his partner.* "I'm Mike Larsen," *says Larsen, reaching across the table to shake Gorton's hand.* "People sometimes forget names real quickly."

*Kilbourn leans over and shakes his hand, too.*

*They're all friends in this room.*

*Gorton leans back, right leg crossed over left, arms folded across his chest. Larsen and Kilbourn are just off screen to the left. Larsen's left hand can be seen taking notes.*

Larsen: "Jeff, let us explain to you. We're part of a task force that's assisting the Flint Police Department. We're working on a couple of different cases and your name came up in one of our cases, specifically the assault on a woman by the name of Margarette Eby. You're probably wondering, 'Jeez, why am I here?' and the bottom line is, at one point you worked at the Mott Estate. I don't know what year you worked there, but your company, Buckler Sprinkler . . ."

Gorton: "I don't think I ever worked there."

"Okay, we'll get to that. But you can obviously see why we'd have to talk to you, just like we had to talk to—what, probably a hundred other people so far? This is a real shot in the dark for us because this is a case that's gone unsolved for a long time. There's a great big pool of people we have to contact, and we're just slowly working our way through it."

*Larsen tells him that he and Kilbourn are square shooters, that while they are not required to at this point, for their sake and for his, they want him to read his Miranda rights and sign an acknowledgment that he has read them.*

*Gorton takes the form, glances at it, picks up the pen, asks for the date and signs and dates it.*

"Maybe you're a speed reader, Jeff," *says Larsen.* "Did you in fact have a chance to look it over?"

"Mm-hmm."

*Gorton confirms the spelling of his name, his date of birth (11/1/62), his height (6 foot), his weight (185), his home address and phone number, his employment history at Buckler. They go over his military history (enlisted summer of 1981, just after high school) and what he did in the Navy (electrician). All the while, Gorton rocks slightly, arms crossed, speaking very quietly, face betraying no emotion.*

*"Where were you lucky enough to get stationed at?" asks good cop Larsen.* Orlando for boot camp, then Chicago, then back to Orlando.

*What about his parents? Laurence and Shirley are alive, still married. Deborah is the oldest sibling, Steve is the next oldest, then Dan, who's dead, then Bryan, then Jeff, then Greg. All the boys work in the family business.*

Gorton doesn't give details about Dan's death, just says it matter-of-factly. It was anything but. Dan, who had a history of depression and heavy alcohol use, committed suicide in the driveway of his suburban Flint home at the age of 37 on October 10, 1997. He had been hoping for a reconciliation with his ex-wife, but had just found out she had a new boyfriend. He started an air compressor in the back of his red Chevy work van, the compressor normally being used to blow water out of sprinkler lines. He then went and sat down in the front seat with the windows rolled up and waited to die of carbon-monoxide poisoning. His ex-wife found his body two days later.

*What about a first marriage?*

*"We got married, but it wasn't the right thing. We got married right after I went into the Navy."*

*Was she a high-school sweetheart? "I guess you can call her an old sweetheart," he says reluctantly. "She got pregnant just before I graduated from high school. She's remarried. I'm not sure of her last name."*

*What happened to their child, a boy? "I'm not sure."*

*"What's his name?"*

*"Jeffery. But spelled different. I know he graduated from high school."*

*"When did you last have contact with him?"*

"1986. Dawn told him he had a different father, her boyfriend at the time."

"So, even though she played those mind games with you, saying he had a different dad, did she stick you with child support?"

"Yeah."

"All through high school?"

"Yeah."

Jeff is vague about divorce details. Says she came back without him to Flint. They tried to reconcile in 1986, but it didn't work out.


2:02 p.m.

Larsen: "Do you recall doing any work at the Mott Estate?"

"I might have been there once. My brother did some install work there. Greg."

"So, you were at the Mott Estate once?"

"I was there when he put an addition down. I forget what they call the building. But he put an addition down."

To refresh his memory, Larsen, surprising Jeff, pulls out a sheaf of blueprints for the sprinkler system at the estate, dated 1984, drafted by Jeff's dad. Where did he work?

"It was a little building down in a lower area. A chicken coop or something. With some flowers around it."

"To the best of your knowledge, that is the only time you were ever at the Mott Estate?"

"I was there one other time, for two minutes. This fall. Me and my brother Steve. Bryan had left some tools there."

"And the other time you were there. Do you recall when that was?"

"I don't know. Four or five years ago."

"It's easy to understand not being sure, unless you're carrying around a diary with you," says still-good-cop Larsen.


2:07 p.m.

Larsen: "Jeff, again, one of the reasons we called

*you here is, you're one of the employees of Buckler, and Buckler was a contractor at the Mott Estate during the time frame this woman was assaulted. As I told you earlier, we've contacted quite a number of people. Thanks to modern technology, we don't have to spend a lot of time with people. We can do DNA analysis that enables us to totally eliminate somebody in a very short period of time. We don't have to take up much of their time and it saves us a lot of time.*

*"We're just slowly working our way through. We've already worked through all the former employees of the Mott Estate. And now we're working our way through the contractors. God knows there are a lot of them, so we've got a lot of work cut out for us. Obviously, at some point we'd like you to provide a DNA buccal swab so we can eliminate you. Is that something you'd be interested in providing to us?"*

*Jeff, arms crossed, says, almost inaudibly, "I don't have no problem with it, but I don't know if I should or not."*

*"You don't have to. I gotta tell you, we've contacted over one hundred people who are basically in the same position as you, and we have had some people who said no. This is America. You have a right to say no. We're not going to lay you down on a floor and take it," says Larsen, good-copping to the max. "If you choose not to, that's your decision and we'll respect it. Up till now, four or five people out of more than one hundred have refused to."*

*Bring it up, gloss over it, move on to other business, like it's no big deal. Which it isn't, since they already have a sample and fully expect a search warrant to be back soon allowing them to take a swab without need of permission.*

*"So, you don't want to take it?"*

*"Not right now."*

*"Want to think about it?"*

*"I want to think about it."*

*Kilbourn, his question having an edge to it, particularly since he's been so quiet so far: "Did you ever have a reason to go into one of the Mott Estate houses?"*

*"I do know there's a [sprinkler] controller in the main building, but I don't know where."*

*"I just want to clarify: There's no reason for you to go in the houses, right?"*

*"No."*

So much for having an excuse ready to explain the bloody print in Eby's bathroom when the time comes to bring it up.

*"Jeff, I've mentioned the sexual assault of Margarette Eby. Have you ever heard about this case?"* asks Larsen.

*"I've heard something."*

Larsen pulls out a black piece of paper, pushes it across the table to Gorton and asks him to diagram the Mott Estate the best he can from his two trips there.

Gorton puts in the main house, a greenhouse, mentions a garage, puts in an outbuilding at the bottom of a hill at the back of the estate. No gatehouse.

*"Is this the way the Mott Estate looks to the best of your recollection?"* asks Larsen.

*"Yeah."* Nods his head. *"My brother would know more. Greg does ninety percent of the work there, and Bryan does the rest."*

*"Jeff, you mentioned vaguely remembering this case. When I mentioned the Eby assault, what immediately came to mind to you?"*

*"I didn't recall remembering the name but I remember reading in the paper something happening there."*

*"Any specific recollections of what you read?"*

*"No."*

*"When was the last time you read about it?"*

*"Not too long ago. There was someone from Detroit or something."*

*"Do you remember what you read?"*

*"No. Something about they figured out it was the same person who did it or something."*

2:16 p.m.
Kilbourn: *"What do you think should happen to the person responsible?"*

*"He should probably go to jail,"* Gorton says, almost in a whisper.

*Larsen:* "*Having been there on the estate there, Jeff, when you read about this, what kind of person do you think could be responsible for something like this?*"

"*Not sure.*" Shrugs. "*It's a good question. I don't really know all the details, so I can't say what kind of person. Not a good person.*"

*Larsen:* "*Maybe a good person who had some problems. I mean, there's any number of reasons. In this line of work, we try to avoid strictly judging anybody.*"

"*Mm-hmm.*"

"*We may have a situation where people have problems and sometimes mistakes happen and they truly are mistakes.*"

"*Mm-hmm.*" Arms still crossed. Left leg over right. Rocking more perceptibly.

2:18 p.m.

*Larsen:* "*Is there any reason somebody would mention your name as a suspect in this case?*"

*Gorton, shaking his head side to side:* "*No.*"

*Larsen, pushing Gorton's diagram of the Mott Estate back in front of him:* "*Jeff, I want to go back to this diagram you made of your recollections of the Mott Estate.*"

*Gorton leans forward.*

*Larsen:* "*This is a circular driveway and actually, there is a small house the Mott family calls 'the gatehouse.' Do you have any recollection of that?*"

"*Not really. I've driven by the front of it, but the Cultural Center. I think I might have seen a gate here or something.*"

"*I'm not talking about a mansion. It's much smaller. Do you recall it?*"

"*I've never paid much attention.*"

"*No recollection of a house down here?*"

"*I'm not saying there isn't. I might have seen it.*"

"*Any chance you might have gone into that house at one time?*"

*Gorton shakes his head side to side.* "*No. I don't know whose house that is.*"

"*Well, let me ask you this: You're on the job. You*

*work outside. Is there ever a time when nature calls and you have to knock on a door and say, 'Hey, can I use the bathroom?'"*

"*Usually we use the trucks or go behind a tree or something.*"

"*Do you recall any instances in the two times you were at the Mott Estate that you may have gone into the main house, or this smaller house?*"

"*To use the facilities?*"

"*Yes.*"

"*It was so long ago. I don't remember everything I did when I was there.*"

*Kilbourn:* "*Did you ever hear anything personally about Margarette Eby? What kind of a woman she was?*"

"*No. A teacher or something.*"

*They ask him if he ever took any classes at U-M–Flint. Yes, the summer after high school. College prep stuff to see if he was up to college. Did he ever have her as a teacher? Not sure. Ever take music classes? No.*

*Why did he quit school?*

"*When I found out my girlfriend was pregnant. We'd been broken up for some time. I was just looking for a way to get away. That's when I joined the Navy.*"

*Larsen:* "*You said Greg did ninety percent of the work at the Mott Estate. Did Greg ever mention Margarette Eby to you? The reason I say this, Jeff, is apparently Mrs. Eby had some peculiar activities. She apparently used to go back of this gatehouse and sunbathe nude. And the other thing is, she didn't have any curtains on most of the windows and she'd often walk around the house nude. This information was obtained in conversations we had with employees on the grounds. Did your brother ever mention any of that to you?*"

"*No.*"

*2:27 p.m.*

*Larsen:* "*Jeff, can you give us a couple of minutes? We've got a document we're waiting on and I want to*

*see if it's here. Can I get you a glass of water or a cup
of coffee while you're waiting?"*

*"Maybe a glass of water."*

*Larsen gets him the water and they get up and leave.
They go to the video monitor and look in at him. His
face seems to be relaxed, but his body? Caught on a spy
cam, the guy looks as if he's going to come out of his
skin. He leans forward, leans back. Looks skyward,
looks around the room. Hands are clasped, unclasped,
clasped. Resumes rocking. Right hand rubs vigorously
on right knee. Back and forth and back and forth. Left
hand rubs left thigh. Hard, like smoke's gonna start
coming up from those blue jeans any second. Rubbing
like he's Lady Mac-Freaking-beth.*

*2:35 p.m. Noise of door opening screen left. Cops
are back. For nearly all the next hour, Gorton has his
arms crossed, and one leg, then the other, crossed over
the opposite knee, constantly rocking back and forth,
only a couple of inches, but non-stop.*

*Larsen:* "We'll try not to keep you here too much
longer, but we still have some questions for you. Jeff, I'd
like you to clarify for us your military record . . . For
some reason, you kind of glazed over everything that
happened in your military career. I gotta tell you, we
got some idea of what happened to you."

"Mm-hmm."

"I can understand and appreciate that could be a
sensitive subject to you. And it sounds like, for the trouble you got in, you obviously paid your dues."

*Larsen tells him it wasn't the fall of 1981 he joined
the Navy, but later. When?*

"February or March. It was a crazy time. Like I said,
I was trying to get away from a kid. Just that she was
pregnant and trying to make me think it was mine."

"Was she a promiscuous person?"

"Not really. But we'd been broken up for three or four
months when she came to me and said she was pregnant."

"So, anyone would question that. Did you ever have
a test done?"

"No."

"So that's why you went into the military, to escape that?"

"Basically. I told her I didn't think it was mine. It didn't think that was right, because, for her to come to me three or four months later and say it was mine."

He says he joined the Navy under the buddy program with Joe Contreras, a friend from high school. They went to boot camp in Florida together and then their separate ways, Gorton off to Chicago for advanced training as an electrician and then to Orlando for the nuclear-power school.

Jeff found out in boot camp that he could run, but he couldn't hide. "She came down and found me in boot camp. Finally I agreed to marry her. It was the right thing to do," he tells them.

Larsen: "The nuclear school—how long did that training last?"

"It was supposed to last two years."

"What happened? Didn't you complete the program?"

"I got into some trouble and left the Navy."

"As I mentioned to you before, Jeff, good people get in trouble. In our work, there isn't anything that surprises us. We're not judgmental. Different people have different wants and desires." Pause. "What drove you to get into trouble in Orlando?"

"I stole some things I shouldn't have."

"What in particular?"

"Personal stuff."

"Belonging to . . . ?"

"Other people."

"Men? Women? Children?"

"Women."

"What in particular? Was it jewelry? Something valuable? Clothing?"

"Clothing."

"Anything else?"

"No."

"The original charge we saw said burglary. In my mind, burglary is forcibly entering someone's home and taking something. Is that what you did?"

"I climbed in through a window and stole a couple of things."

"Did you ever do anything like that in Michigan prior to getting caught in Orlando?"

"No. That was the first time I thought about breaking into someone's house."

"But you thought about women's clothing. When did that first surface for you?"

"Seems like most of my life."

"As I say, we're not judgmental. To me, it doesn't matter if you're heterosexual. If you're gay. If you like cats or dogs or women's clothing. Basically, it doesn't matter. We all have our own personal desires. Was it in high school when you had your first attraction to women's clothing?"

"More like junior high."

"Did you have trouble getting girlfriends?"

"Not really."

"Were you sexually active?"

"Not a lot."

"Did you experience sexual intercourse in high school?"

"Not really. Until I was with Dawn."

"Was she the first time?"

Pause. Then, "As far as I can remember."

"Did you start with your mother's clothing?"

"Right." [In a subsequent interview, he would say he started cross-dressing when he was five.]

"And did that progress to the point, perhaps, where you went over to a neighbor's house, perhaps entering through an unlocked door or a window, or taking clothes hanging from a line?"

"Not really. I think I might have got a couple of things from my friends' parents. You know, not breaking in, because I was already there."

"Is there any particular item of clothing you are particularly fond of, be it panties, bras or panties of sleepwear, you're attracted to?"

"Hose, I guess."

"Do you still have strong fetish desires to this day?"

"Yeah. I've seen a psychiatrist for it, after I got back to Michigan."

"*After you served time in prison?*"

"*Mm-hmm.*"

"*Did you spend all twenty-two months of your time in the same facility in northern Florida?*"

"*Mm-hmm.*"

"*What was that like for you? How were you treated?*"

"*Okay, I guess. It was just a place to stay. You didn't get no help or anything.*"

"*Did you feel you could have used some help?*"

"*Yeah, I could have used some help. I knew that wanting those things was wrong.*"

"*It's not wrong. There's nothing in the world that says wanting those things is wrong. You just have to go into any pornographic store and find there's just about anything for any particular person. And just because a person has a fetish, that's not wrong. Perhaps in your childhood it was instilled in you that what was different was wrong. I grew up a strong Catholic and it was instilled in you: 'Masturbation is wrong, you're going to hell.' Was your home environment similar? Was your mother or father like that?*"

"*They didn't really talk about it.*"

"*Sex was never brought up?*"

"*No.*"

"*You never had the birds and the bees talk with your dad?*"

"*No. Definitely not with my dad.*"

"*What about your mother?*"

"*I must not have, because I got a girl pregnant.*"

"*Was there a dominant parent in the house?*"

"*Well, my mom raised the kids, but my dad was the dominant one. If he said this, that's the way it was.*"

"*Just going over to your house, it's obvious you're a clean and meticulous person. That probably is a carry-over from the way your mother brought you up?*"

"*Probably.*"

Kilbourn has been quiet this second session. Larsen says: "*Greg, is there anything you want to ask about Orlando?*"

Kilbourn: "*Quite frankly, you've been very cordial to us since you've been here. Apparently you skipped over that stuff the first time you told us about it. Were you simply embarrassed, or were you hoping we didn't know about it?"*

"It's not something you're proud of."

*"Is there anything else—be honest, now—is there anything else you've not told us, especially about that time period, that you think we should know?"*

"Well, there were two or three things that got me in jail."

*"What were the others?"*

"One is, I did try to pull a slip off one lady."

*"Where did that occur?"*

"Some apartments. It seemed a way to get something else."

*"Was there anything else of that nature?"*

"There was one where I tried to get something. I tried to break in another place but didn't get in."

*"Any other incidents in Florida?"*

"There was one on the base that got me in trouble. It was the same thing. I tried to pull a slip off a girl."

*"Were you successful?"*

"No. It all happened right together. The one I broke into was when we were in the trailer park and it was the manager of the trailer park. He must have turned my name in. It was his daughter. His daughter was like twelve or something."

*Kilbourn, still:* "You were married. That can't be a good thing for your marriage."

"Right. That's why she came back to Michigan."

*"Your sentence was supposed to be four and a half years. You got out early. Do you know why?"*

"If you go to classes and stuff, you get out early."

*"Did you hurt any of the women, or was it strictly just trying to take articles of clothes?"*

"Just take articles of clothes."

*"Did the women get accidentally injured? I'm trying to think how you'd get a slip off."*

"I knocked them down, but I don't think they really got hurt. One was in a group of people and I didn't re-ally get anywhere. It was just an attempt. The other one," *she fell down. I didn't really push her down. She must have stepped back and fell."*

*"Did you have an attorney?"*

*"I had one. I don't think I had a good one."*

*Kilbourn laughs heartily.*

*" 'Cause people doing the same time as me had thirty or forty car thefts."*

*"So you think your sentence was out of line?"*

*"It was out of line compared to some people who were there."*

*Larsen: "Did that make you bitter toward the criminal justice system?"*

*"No. I just wished they'd have had something there. They tried to have a program, because there were more people like me there, but it just never was much. They couldn't get funding for it. When I came home, I went to a psychiatrist on my own."*

*Kilbourn: "When you got out of prison, did you immediately return to Michigan? Or did you work in Florida?"*

*"They took me to the airport."*

*"What about this girl in the trailer?"*

*"I'd met her. Seen her a few times. Pretty good-looking. I'd actually never planned on breaking in there, but I was mad at the manager, so I thought I'd get even. Someone had stolen a canoe and I had no reason to steal a canoe, but he'd come over and accused me of stealing it. So I was mad at him."*

*Larsen: "Do you feel any anger at the system as a whole?"*

*"I wish I'd have gotten more counseling, yeah, but I'm not mad at anyone."*

*"Where you're at in your life right now—do you feel as if you could use some counseling?"*

*"I still get some urges and stuff, I'm not perfect."*

*"None of us are. Compared to the alcoholic, a guy with a fetish is like a pebble compared to a boulder, the drunk driving his car and could potentially kill someone."*

*Gorton halts his rocking and stares at Larsen.*

*Larsen: "Do you have any particular issues with*

women? Do you have a hard time relating to women?"

"Not really."

"Do you get mad real easy at women?"

"No."

"Any desire to hit a woman?"

"No."

"Were you teased in school?"

"We were poor, so wore poor people's clothes. I got teased about that. And I had a bad complexion and stuff."

"Is there any fantasies that you have in regard to women and stealing their clothing that you still feel inside you?"

"It's always probably going to be there. Yeah."

"Is there anything specific, like bondage, where you'd tie someone up?"

"Nah." Shakes head.

"Sadistic? Where someone's tortured or whipped? Anything of that nature?"

Shakes heads side to side.

It is 3:00 p.m. Across town, the press conference is about to begin.

Kilbourn: "When you got back to Michigan, you still had these desires. Were there any similar incidents to those down in Florida?"

"Since I been back? Not really. It's been a couple of years, now, but I did get in a little trouble in Clio. I got probation. I did try to look up a girl's skirt. I didn't try to take anything. I was just looking. The girl was wearing a short skirt and she bent over and I just . . ." He makes an upward motion with his right hand.

Kilbourn: "What led up to it?"

"I was there to shop. My wife's birthday or some holiday was coming up. I was looking to get something for my wife and I seen her there and I don't know why I did it—I'd never done that before. She had a short black skirt on. I remember she was good-looking, but I can't describe her."

"That's the only thing you can recall happening to you in Michigan?"

*"Not since I seen the psychiatrist. He said I had to learn to control it myself. I still get the desires for women's things. It's usually my wife's things."*

*"Do you wear her clothes?"*

*"I have a couple of times."*

*Larsen: "Is she aware of your fetish?"*

*"Yeah, she kinda knows."*

*"Is it okay with her?"*

*"Okay? I don't know about okay. She'd prefer I didn't have any thoughts like that at all."*

*"Does that cause an issue with your wife?"*

*"Not really. 'Cause, I don't do it much, anymore."*

*Kilbourn: "You have a pretty good marriage other than that?"*

*"Yeah." Nods.*

*"Do you ever hit your wife?"*

*"Do I ever hit her? No."*

*"Ever had any police contact of a domestic nature?"*

*"No."*

*"Sounds like you have a good marriage."*

*"Mm-hmm." Nods.*

*3:15 p.m.*

*Larsen: "Jeff, other than your arrest in Florida, what's the worst thing that ever happened to you that you regret?"*

*Larsen is thinking about Eby and Ludwig, hoping they may have Gorton ready to confess. But instead, Gorton says, "I remember one time I was upset I didn't get a job in the shop. Down in Detroit? Where's the Chrysler plant? Not Detroit, but down there somewhere. It was skilled trades."*

*Larsen: "Why did you choose Detroit?"*

*"I didn't choose Detroit. I was on unemployment and they did it. Everything was done here. All the skills tests. So then I passed that and went down, not to Detroit, but to wherever their main facility is. So I went down and did some more testing."*

*"Anything else you might regret?"*

*"No. Mostly it's been kind of blasé."*

*"We're all kind of disappointed in ourselves because*

*we didn't meet our expectations. Anything else in your life that sticks out for you? You ever spend any time down in southeast Michigan?"*

*"Not really."*

*" 'Not really' means 'Once in a while'?"*

*"I flew out of the airport once."*

*"When was that?"*

*"I don't remember what year. My wife and I went through the company. Flew to Vegas one time. And to Cancún. Costa Rica once. It was all with my wife. Oh, and I went to Florida once. Me, my wife and my kids."*

*"Four times you have flown out of Metro Airport in Detroit?"*

Nods yes.

*"Ever spend the night in any of the hotels down there?"*

*"We did once."*

*"Remember where you stayed?"*

*"No. I remember the planes flew over the top of us. Me and my wife and kids. About four years ago."*


3:20 p.m.

Larsen: *"Ever been to the Romulus Hilton?"*

A pause. Left eyebrow raises. That's about it. Gorton gives nothing away. *"Hilton? I don't think so."* Shakes his head. *"I'm sure we could never afford to stay at the Hilton. One of the trips we stayed someplace, it wasn't the Hilton. It was the cheapest place we could find."*

*"Ever been in the Hilton at any time?"*

*"Not that I know of. Probably like a Holiday Inn. Something like that."*

*"From reading the newspaper accounts of what happened to Margarette Eby and the woman in Detroit, what do you remember?"*

*"I just remember that they were killed or something, and it was by the same person or something. I don't know if I actually read it. It was on TV. I might have read some of it. I don't read too much."*

*"Did they describe how these women were killed?"*

Long, long pause. Arms crossed. Left leg over right

knee. Rocking pauses, too. "*Probably did, but I wasn't paying much attention.*"

"*Did it mention a sexual assault to both?*"

Long pause. "*It might have. Just that he did it. I didn't pay that much attention to it.*"

"*Are you an avid TV watcher?*"

"*Not a whole lot.*"

"*What are your favorite channels?*"

"*We don't get too many channels.*"

"*You don't get cable?*"

"*Just have an antenna. Usually we like to watch the comedies. That's all I have time for, if I have time to watch 'em.*"

Larsen is smooth. Lull him with TV habits, then, Boom! "*When was the last time you were down in the area of Metropolitan Airport?*"

"*The airport?*" Left eyebrow raises. "*This fall we drove by an airport. Don't know which one.*"

"*Are there any other incidents that might have happened?*"

"*No.*" Shakes head.

"*Reported or unreported?*"

"*No.*" Shakes head.

"*Any other incidents?*"

"*No. I'm trying to keep myself clean.*"

3:29 p.m. A long pause by Larsen. A sigh. And, then, "*Okay.*" Said pregnantly, with the second syllable stretched out: "*O-Kaaay.*" And said as he squares off the papers in front of him and picks them up. Gorton's got to be thinking: "Holy shit, they're done!"

Across town, questions are being asked in a much more frenzied manner, people shouting out to get the floor.

Larsen turns to Kilbourn. You can't see him turn on screen, but you can see his hands rotating to the right, holding the papers. You can almost picture his body half rising from the chair. "*Greg, you got anything?*"

If Greg doesn't, they'll be done. Greg does. "Did these problems ever escalate beyond theft?"

Gorton shakes his head no. "Just used to take 'em and try 'em on and stuff."

Long pause.

Kilbourn: "How do you feel about being here? You feel good about it? Sounds like you're kinda cleansing your soul here. Mike and I are both pretty decent guys. You feel okay about this?"

Gorton shrugs. "I don't like to talk about my problems. Problems I could probably be having."

Long pause. Gorton takes a big gulp of water.

Kilbourn: "Anything else? We'll try to get you out of here in a timely basis if possible. But we need to go a little further here, get a little more information, so we'll get through this situation here." Gorton's blood pressure must be spiking, but he's stoic. "Anything else you need, like water? Or are you all set?"

"I'm all set. How long do you think this will take? I know my wife wants to go out tonight."

Kilbourn: "I'm not sure. She's obviously been contacted, and if you're concerned about your kids, she was notified. That situation has been resolved."

"We had plans, to go out. I think it was tonight."

He's rocking again. Arms crossed.

"We'll give you a few minutes to relax. We'll be back and go from there."

And he and Larsen get up and walk out of the room.

This time they let him stew for twelve minutes. He sighs. He leans back and stares at the ceiling. He rubs his hands and rocks and rubs his hand and rocks. Gotta be the longest twelve minutes of his life.

3:43 p.m. They return.

Kilbourn: "You've been very patient. We appreciate that. We haven't really talked about your cars. What kind of cars do you like to drive? Are you a car guy?"

"Not really, no."

"What kind of cars do you own?"

"An old convertible, a 1964 Dodge Dart. And a van. A brown conversion van. And I got one that's rotting away. An old Monte Carlo."

"When did you get that vehicle?"

"I got it about '87, '88. I drove it until a few years ago. I still drive it once in a while."

"What year is it?"

"An '82. It's under a cover."

Larsen: "Are you all straight with your water?"

Nods yes.

"Jeff, up to this point I think we've got through some issues. You weren't being totally honest with us, but I think we worked through that. We're going to be totally honest with you. We've given you a chance to share with us some events that have happened in your life. It's time for us to share some things with you."

Larsen says this louder, more forcefully than he's said anything thus far. He pauses. A long pause, and he reaches down to some papers in front of him and shuffles through them. Gorton watches him shuffling, arms crossed, rocking slightly, face impassive.

"If I can find it, I'll be happy to share it," says Larsen. "In the meantime, do you have any questions for us? I don't want this to be a one-sided conversation. Feel free. There's nothing we have to hide."

"No. As I said earlier, I wonder how long this is going to take? We're supposed to go out tonight."

"Well, Jeff"—Larsen has found the paper he was looking for, pulls it out and hands it across the table to Gorton—"I want you to take a look at this."

Gorton takes hold of it, stares at it. You can't see it on screen, but it's on FBI letterhead. "I'm not sure what this is."

"Flip it over. What does it say? That sentence near the top."

Gorton begins reading. " 'Two latent fingerprints of value appear in Q1 and Q2, two negatives . . . One latent fingerprint appearing in Q2, a negative, source not indicated, has been identified . . . ' apparently as me."

What it had gone on to say, and which he didn't read,

*was*, "*has been identified as a fingerprint of Jeffrey Wayne Gorton, FBI #54834CA3.*"

"*Is that your name?*"

"*Mm-hmm.*" Nodding.

4:38 p.m.

*Larsen:* "*Jeff, you told us things that have troubled you, and it's very evident to us that you'd like to get some help. You're the only one who can answer this. The problem with the underwear escalated and ultimately resulted in the assault on Margarette Eby.*"

Gorton shakes his head, face impassive. "*I don't think so.*"

"*I absolutely, positively know you did. Do you know where the print came from?*"

"*No.*"

"*The upstairs bathroom of a house you said you'd never been in. There is no question you're the person who's responsible. The question is why? And what can we do for you?*"

"*There's no why, because I didn't do it.*" Voice quiet, uninflected.

"*You did. You can continue to say you didn't do it and I'll continue to say you did it, because I absolutely positively know you did. I'm not here to say you're a bad person, because I don't think you are. I think you had some issues in your life and some problems, and there were many times people could have helped you and didn't. Wouldn't you agree?*"

"*I could have used some help, yeah, but not with this.*"

"*The question is, why did it happen, Jeff?*"

*Kilbourn:* "*We need to go to the prosecutor with a reason, if we're going to be able to help you. We can't help you if you don't help us.*"

"*I just need to see an attorney, now, because I know I didn't do anything.*"

*Larsen:* "*If we're going to get you help, this is your opportunity. This*"—waving the FBI report—"*is not the final report, okay? The DNA analysis from you came back today and it's a perfect match. We're going to afford you the opportunity to explain this. Your family is out there in the lobby now, and I've got to go out and talk to your wife. I'm not going to give her all the details. And then I gotta go talk to your parents and your brothers and your sister.*

*"I'm not here to judge you. This isn't the first case like this we've worked on. But I've done enough of them to know there's a reason why things happen. I know I'm sitting here talking to a guy who's cried out for help.*

*"The prosecutor already has the evidence, the fingerprint, the DNA analysis. There's no one else with that DNA on the face of the earth. I surely would like to walk out there to your family and explain it to them that you were remorseful and wanted to take responsibility and set an example to your wife and, more important, to your children."*

*"Well, I didn't do anything."*

*"You can deny it and deny it and deny it, but we know you did it. This isn't a matter of 'Jeez, he may have done it.' This is absolutely, beyond a shadow of doubt, one hundred percent positive you did it. Were you expecting this? It's been almost sixteen years. Were you looking over your shoulder for us?"*

*"I don't know what you're talking about. I want to talk to my lawyer." Still quiet, arms still crossed.*

*"Okay."*

*3:57 p.m.*
*Kilbourn: "At this point, we have to tell you you're under arrest."*
*Larsen: "You're under arrest for two counts of homicide. Just sit tight. I'll be right back." Larsen leaves, Kilbourn remains.*

*3:59. Larsen returns.*
*"Stand up, Jeff. Come here."*
*Gorton stands and walks toward the camera, turns screen left and walks off screen. The sound of handcuffs snicking shut can be heard.*

*Also off camera, this from Larsen: "This interview is over. Anything you want me to say to your wife? Any messages?"*

> *"Not now." The door opens, they leave, it snaps shut. The camera continues to focus on Gorton's empty chair.*
>
> *Across town, the press conference ends.*

If Margarette Eby were still alive, this day would have been her 70th birthday.

Later, Larsen would muse, All these years the Flint PD was looking for a monster. They should have been looking for the guy next door.

## 75
# WAITING AND WAITING

Mike Ondejko was considered Romulus PD's warrant wizard. His specialty was drafting them on a computer template, knowing how best to describe the chain of events and evidence that would readily win approval of prosecutors and judges.

While other Romulus officers worked surveillance and state police gathered evidence and background information on Gorton, Ondejko crafted warrants the day and night before. The day of the arrest, he was en route to the Bahamas for the start of a long-planned vacation, which Snyder saw no reason to cancel or delay. After all, the warrants would be a slam-dunk, right? Snyder was used to faxing Ondejko's requests to Wayne County prosecutors and having them readily approved, and then faxing them to judges who signed them just as readily.

With Snyder, Larsen and Kilbourn conducting a series of interviews, it fell to Malaniak to deliver Ondejko's warrants to Busch's office. Petrides, the trial-division chief, would be the one to sign off on them.

To him and Busch, Malaniak's arrival was part of the problem. If they had questions, the lead investigators, Larsen and Kilbourn, were the ones they wanted to ask them of. And where were they? Doing interviews. Unavailable. The Flint PD sent a detective over, but immediately it was clear he had been kept out of the loop, too, and couldn't answer any questions.

Second, what was a cop from Wayne County doing there? Third, what Ondejko might or might not be good at and the way he did things in Wayne County were irrelevant in Genesee County. Fourth, there was this time pressure that wasn't helping anyone.

"My first concern was, the state police were very anxious to have a press conference," says Busch. "I wasn't so interested in having a press conference as I was in positioning the investigation so we didn't have issues that would relate to suppression of evidence. I wasn't going to allow my case to get hijacked so someone could be on TV for a minute or thirty seconds."

State police brass had hoped for a noon press conference, which made no sense to anyone except those well up the chain of command. It made no sense to Kilbourn or Larsen, who had taken their time getting their ducks in a row before heading out to get Gorton; it made no sense to Snyder; it certainly made no sense to Busch. Being a politician and being that this was the biggest case in decades, he wasn't about to pass up a press conference, but there was no way they could have one that soon.

He got it pushed back to 3. Bohnett says Busch delayed the press conference till then because he wanted to take it over. "He tried to control it," Bohnett says.

Busch says he had it delayed because he didn't understand why the state police were in such a hurry for such an old case. Let's get organized, and then have a press conference. As it was, they still held it before warrants were even issued, much less executed. "The idea we'd make press statements before we executed search warrants . . ." bemoans Busch.

The press conference was held across the street from the courthouse, in the City Hall office of Mayor Woodrow Stanley. "It was a weird place to be," says Busch. "I remember walking in thinking there was more brass in that room than I'd ever seen in my life, and there I was standing there in a black T-shirt and blue jeans and going on TV."

Busch asked that no mention of DNA be made. He says it was a tactical request. A search warrant would allow them to get a buccal swab from Gorton, and that would make any match to the Eby murder conclusive. Bohnett and others say it was a tactical decision, all right, believing that Busch wanted to control the release of information over the coming days and to keep his name in as many headlines as possible.

"He wanted to steal the thunder," says Bohnett.

Bull, says Busch. In addition to it being good tactics, he wanted to avoid mentioning DNA because "the prosecution is prohibited by law from disclosing any results of tests until we get in court. It is unethical," he says.

The Flint and Detroit media were there in swarms. Photographers, reporters with notebooks, radio guys with mikes, TV trucks out front with their antennas raised high. Politicians and police brass filled a large podium. Even Charles Barna, Jeff Nye's boss, had been summoned, wearing his white lab uniform to add to the visuals.

"The state police had invested ten million dollars in a crime lab. When I looked at the guy behind me in the lab coat, I knew he wasn't there to run tests at the mayor's office," says Busch. "He was there to show the public the ten million dollars was well spent. He was show and tell."

Busch took some satisfaction from noting an absence of national TV media, saying afterward, on one hand, "Convicting him on Channel Four doesn't meet our goal of taking this character off the street." On the other hand, Busch would say: "I knew national. I had been on national. If they had let me, I could have used my contacts at CNN and other places. In order to make it a national story, you gotta do a lot of massaging.

"I didn't have any time to work the magic I usually do."

In response to the inevitable question about DNA, instead of giving the answer Busch had requested, that details be kept to a minimum pending arraignment, Bohnett says he "accidentally on purpose let it slip that DNA was a factor. If Busch would have had a gun, he would have shot me. I didn't care. What was he going to do to me?"

# 76

# FINALLY

Before, during and after the press conference—neither Larsen, Kilbourn, Snyder nor Malaniak attended—Petrides worked on the warrants. His staff wasn't about to accept Ondejko's template work. They were going to start over from scratch and do them their way.

They wanted a lot of background information. Who was Gorton? How and why did his name come up? When? "We needed to know what kind of evidence they'd collected," says Busch.

To this day, some police believe Petrides slowed things down on orders from Busch, that Busch was going to pay them back for keeping him out of the loop by keeping them out in the cold, literally. Keep them waiting outside the Gorton house in the cold and wind of February as a short day gave way to a long night.

Petrides, a Flint native and Notre Dame Law School grad, joined the prosecutor's office in 1979. Prior to the Gorton case, the biggest case he'd worked on was using racketeering laws to break up the Spanish Cobra street gang.

After Busch dismissed the police from the meeting they were holding during the break in moving, he told Petrides that the Eby case was breaking wide open and assigned it to him and assistant prosecutor David Newblatt. Where Busch was angry, Petrides' emotion was "excitement. I don't know any other word for it. Coming out of the blue, we had our man. We'd had rumors over the years and suddenly—Boom!—it's a reality.

"The feeling was almost like mission control waiting for blastoff."

If the day seemed to drag for the cops waiting to go into Gorton's house, it seemed to fly for Petrides, a surge of adrenaline rushing the hours by.

Once Gorton was arrested, they had forty-eight hours to charge him, but the real need for speed was to get search warrants executed, for his house, his parents' house and the family business. Newblatt was in charge of draw-

ing up the arrest warrant and Petrides of writing the search
warrants.

The information in Ondejko's warrants was useful, but
they weren't about to delegate the writing of warrants to some
cop from another county they'd never met. They needed to
confirm his information with Elford and state police. They
needed updates on Gorton's interrogation, with the final
word being he hadn't confessed and had asked for an attorney.

The search warrants were more complicated than an arrest warrant. They needed to figure out what kind of information they might need and where to find it. Time-card
records, for example, of the day Eby died. Invoices sent to
the Mott Estate. Could they link Gorton to the estate?

Petrides, one of the last Americans without a cell phone,
needed to keep Busch apprised of developments as the press
conference approached, and after. He used an old-fashioned
land line.

Meanwhile, Snyder was fuming. At a deli across the
street from the Flint post, during one break in a very long
day, he'd been warned about Busch. "They were telling me,
'This guy is going to be a problem.' " As the day went on, he
got madder and madder. He called St. Andre on the Nextel to
warn him that the search warrants might be delayed. "You
won't believe what's going on down here."

"Dan, we don't need them. This is a Romulus case, too.
We'll get our own warrants," said St. Andre.

Snyder told Bohnett if it went on much longer, he'd go to
the state attorney general if he had to. Or to the Wayne
County prosecutor. They had a house they needed to secure.
The press was starting to show up at the Gorton residence
and at the police post.

"We should have had them by noon," says Snyder. "We
were sitting and sitting and sitting."

Petrides says any allegation of a deliberate slowdown
"are preposterous. I'm living proof of that. I was there when
Art got the call and shortly after that we started churning out
the warrants. There were several hours of work to do and it
took several hours to do it. If anything, there was pressure
from Art to get it done fast."

Busch says part of the perception by the cops that things went too slowly is their exuberance over the DNA results. But, he says, it was simple naïveté by the police that DNA results and DNA results, alone, would mean a quick warrant. "They thought DNA was enough. I can't blame them for that, because any traffic cop would think that. You get someone on radar and that's it, it's cut and dried," he says, working in another dig at the task-force investigators.

"But a prosecutor looking at DNA, alone, would be malpractice. I knew from my own experience that DNA off Styrofoam cups and napkins doesn't always turn into gold. We needed other evidence. We wanted to prove he was at that guest house. We needed to execute search warrants at the family business and the parents' home, and drawing all that up took time."

Ultimately, Nye's written report made the difference.

Busch got it and called him back to question him about the sample.

"Is this adequate?" he asked Nye. "How close is this?"

"Barely close enough," said Nye.

"In horseshoes, close is good enough. And in getting this warrant, that's going to be enough, too."

Busch gave his go-ahead.

Petrides wanted 68th District Court Judge Michael McAra, one of Flint's best judges, to sign the warrants, and the judge agreed to do so and to stay at the office past his normal departure time of 5 p.m. if necessary. McAra got the paperwork about 7, read it, got sworn statements in his courtroom from Elford and State Police Trooper Dennis Diggs attesting to the accuracy of the information claimed in the warrants and, about 7:45 p.m., signed them.

Elford by then had left the task force to take the job of captain of the Grand Blanc police, but out of courtesy for his past work, Kilbourn had asked him if he wanted to help out. He'd sat surveillance awhile, then helped out with the warrants.

Finally, long after nightfall, Malaniak called Snyder to say the warrants were done and he was on the way with them. They could go in the house.

# 77

# FAMILY REUNION

While awaiting warrants, Hal Zettle drove over to Dawn Hemingway's. They would need to talk to Gorton's first wife, especially since she'd been in Florida with him when he'd first run afoul of the law.

She wasn't home, but their son, Jeffery, was. Zettle talked to him briefly, gave him a business card and left. Half an hour later, Dawn called back, and she and Jeffery were picked up and driven to the Flint post.

She recounted to Zettle and Dan Snyder her background with Jeff, his arrest, their separation and divorce. She said she hadn't kept in contact with him, and that Jeffery hadn't seen his dad since he was about two. The Gortons had paid child support, and if there were any issues in that regard, she talked to Brenda, not Jeff.

She told police that both before and after she married Jeff, she'd had almost no interaction with his parents. They were very private, she said. Kept to themselves.

While Dawn was being interviewed, Brenda was briefly visiting the Tuscola Road house, then following state police to the Flint post. Just after she got there, about 4, Mike Larsen came out to the small lobby, introduced himself, said he'd be busy for a bit and asked her to wait there for a few minutes till he could come back and get her.

She sat down. She rocked back and forth. She kept saying to herself, "What am I here for? What am I here for?"

An ex-smoker, she probably had never wanted—or needed—a cigarette more. She went over to the desk sergeant and asked if she could borrow a smoke. Sympathetically, he said he didn't smoke but would ask around.

He came back a minute later with a cigarette and matches. The post, like all Michigan government buildings, is smoke-free, so she went outside.

She came back in and sat down, resuming her rocking. There was a teen-ager sitting near her on one of the few lobby chairs. She'd had barely registered his presence, assumed he was there on other business.

At one point, he leaned toward her and said: "You must be Brenda."

She turned. "Who are you?" And as she was saying it, she knew.

"Jeff Junior."

They stood up and gave each other a big hug. Though they lived in the same metropolitan area—and one of the reasons Brenda needed to work part-time was to pay the child support that had recently ended on Jeff Jr.'s eighteenth birthday—they had never met. Jeff Jr. had sent his dad a prom picture and an invitation to his graduation, but had never heard back.

"Oh my God. You look just like my son."

And she pulled pictures of her kids out of her wallet to show Jeff his half-sister and half-brother.

Larsen came out finally and led her back to an interview room.

She asked if she could call her sister-in-law, Jeff's sister Sarah, and her husband, Greg, who lived just a block away from their house on Tuscola.

Larsen said no.

Snyder led the interview. Brenda wanted to know what was happening. He said he'd tell her in a bit, but needed to ask some questions.

And he led her through a brief history of their relationship. Where had they met? At a bar.

What kind of guy was he? A good husband and good father. He worked long hours in the summer. In the winter, he was unemployed and put the kids on the school bus, picked them up after school, helped them with their homework every day, went to church on Sunday, kept the house clean while she worked.

Did he have a temper? No. He had never raised his voice in all their years of marriage. One time, while pushing a car stuck in the snow in their driveway, he swore.

What was their relationship like with her in-laws? The only contact she ever had with his parents was on Christmas Eve. Despite the fact they all worked together and lived near each other, they hardly ever saw each other outside of the context of water pipes. Brenda could only recall two times in their entire marriage, including holidays, that Jeff's parents had even been in their house.

Did they have a lot of friends? She did. She was outgoing. Jeff was quiet, didn't have many friends. He hadn't talked to his best friend, Kevin Bosh, a buddy of his from high school and the best man at their wedding, in at least two years.

Snyder asked Brenda if Jeff got along with her family. Absolutely. Everyone thought the world of him.

Did Jeff have any kinky habits? Well, he did like her to wear nylons to work, so he could rub her feet when she got home. He liked the feel of the nylons when he massaged her. (In a follow-up interview with Larsen nearly two weeks later, Brenda would come clean. She'd first caught him with nylons in their bed just a few days before their son was born. Jeff said he'd been out to a girly bar with Bosh, and a stripper had dropped them on their table. Then, three or four years ago, she'd found a pair of panty hose tucked between the box springs and the mattress, and she'd confronted him. He admitted to having had a fetish for women's clothes since he was a kid, and had been told in counseling it was something you were born with. She'd made him promise not to let the kids see him wearing such things, and she'd been so disgusted, she'd taken to sleeping on the couch a lot.)

Did she know about an incident at a Pamida store? No.

Did she know Jeff had gotten in trouble in Florida? No.

Did she know Margarette Eby or Nancy Ludwig? No and no. Not only didn't she know them, she'd never even heard of them. In fact, she thought they were asking about a woman with the last name of Evy.

Snyder was disbelieving. She'd never heard of Margarette Eby? It certainly seemed hard to believe, given that Brenda had been living in Flint in 1986 and the murder had been the biggest thing to hit town since the internal-combustion engine.

With unknowing irony, today she explains her lack of knowledge: "I'm not a news person. We weren't raised to watch the news or read the paper. We couldn't care less about the news in our family. We go on with our lives and when the news hits us in the face, we deal with it."

It hit her square in the face then.

It wasn't until mention of the Mott Estate that some of it finally came back to her: Every Mother's Day the Mott Estate has a big public to-do, and the previous Mother's Day, Brenda had gone there with her sister-in-law Sarah, and Jeff's mother. Jeff's sister had pointed out the gatehouse and told her about the mysterious murder of long ago. It was the first and only time Brenda had heard about it.

So, she asked again, what did this have to do with her husband?

"We think he did it," said Snyder.

It didn't register. "Yeah, right. What are you telling me?"

"We think Jeff killed Margarette Eby and Nancy Ludwig."

She wanted to tell them they were nuts, her husband hadn't done any such thing. She was on the verge of losing it. "Can I speak to Jeff?"

"No. I'm sorry."

She asked Snyder if he'd call her pastor, Doug Klein. He did. It would turn out he was not yet back from getting a tooth pulled, and Snyder left a message on the machine. Brenda asked if he would call her sister. Snyder did and a few minutes later Dan Loga's wife showed up and led Brenda out of the post.

They drove to their mother's house. Meantime, Brenda's pastor had gotten word and was there, as was Dan. Dan had been laying some hardwood flooring down at his house when his wife had called and said something horrible was up, but she had no idea what. Her mother, fearing the worst and not wanting to hear it, had gone upstairs and literally put her head under the covers. Getting to the point about Jeff, Brenda said, "He's been arrested for a terrible, terrible thing." She couldn't say the word.

Patty leaned in toward Dan and whispered, "Murder."

"What did you tell me?" he said, in shock.

She repeated it. He went upstairs. He couldn't find words to tell his mother-in-law what had happened. He said it was serious and they'd be back, and then he and Brenda drove over to the house on Tuscola to see what the police were up to there.

Dan heard on the news the name "Margarette Eby." And he heard the other name: "Nancy Ludwig." Dan kept abreast of the news. He read the papers. He immediately recalled the murder at the airport. He remembered seeing stories about the reward and the composite drawing. He remembered, too, reading about the car that had been seen in the Hilton parking lot and saying to his wife, "Jeff's got a gold Monte Carlo." And then, of course, thinking nothing more about it. It was just an item of interest, a mild coincidence.

At some point, Brenda called a friend. The two couples had plans for Saturday night, a mystery–dinner theater package.

"We won't be able to make the dinner," said Brenda.

"Yeah, I know," said the friend.

"You know?"

"Yeah, I saw it on the TV news." Jeff wouldn't be ar- raigned till the next day, and that's when his name would be officially released, but leaks had sprung from the time he was picked up, flowing from any number of sources to trusted re- porters, and from there to the TV and radio air waves, and from there by word of mouth to just about everyone in Flint.

Kitty Knapp, one of the Gortons' neighbors, was shocked when she heard the news racing through the neighborhood. They'd been friends a dozen years. Jeff and Brenda had been at their daughter's wedding.

"He's always doing things with the kids. I can't say any- thing bad about the man. I've never seen the man lose his temper. I've never heard the man swear. He's just been a good guy," she told reporters.

Her husband, Elsworth, said: "He doesn't do much talk- ing and he doesn't do much smiling."

**78**

## LOOKIE HERE

When Malaniak called to say he was on the way with the warrants, that was all the cops at the house needed. They didn't wait for the warrant to physically arrive at the scene, they went in—St. Andre, Brandemihl, Malaniak, Snyder and State Trooper Jaime Corona.

Before they were done, another ten state troopers would arrive to help out, including Galvin Smith, the fingerprint specialist who had helped break the case open.

At 8:10 p.m. just as officers were setting up in Gorton's house, Larsen did a buccal swab of Gorton, vigorously rub- bing a cotton swab back and forth against the lining of his cheek. Nye's results might very well not stand up in court, but they wouldn't need to. The buccal swab would either clear Gorton, or nail his hide to the wall.

At the house, they set up the command center in the kitchen, where they'd photograph and log whatever they came across that was of interest.

A tow truck came and hauled the Monte Carlo back to the Flint post, where technicians would go through it looking for bloodstains and bits of hair. (Nothing of evidentiary value was ever found.)

Meanwhile, Snyder and Brandemihl took the master bedroom, which was rather small and cramped. First thing Snyder did was raise up a corner of the top mattress. It was a hair-raising moment, literally, one that sent chills through Brandemihl. There, on Jeff's side of the bed were a bunch of women's undergarments, bras, panty hose, panties. "The comfort zone of a psychotic," thought Brandemihl.

Flint cops had been looking for a trophy-keeper since 1986. Romulus cops had been looking for one since Ludwig had been found in 1991 with her luggage and belongings missing. Were these trophies of other murders?

They found a church flyer. In it was a picture of the Gorton family.

Brandemihl opened a drawer in the nightstand on Jeff's side of the bed. It was filled with undergarments.

The bed was in the corner of the room, just far enough from the wall to allow a large entertainment center to be fit in, with a narrow pathway between it and the bed. Near the entertainment center was a small closet, with several shelves built in, and a ladder that connected to a small entry portal into the attic above. They'd send someone up there later.

Opposite the entertainment center was a large walk-in closet, both its doors covered with mirrors to give the room an illusion of space. Brandemihl looked in the entertainment center, saw a video camera aiming out into the room, toward the mirrored doors opposite, and a VCR.

In the closet, his wife's clothes were jammed on hangers on the pole that ran its length. Boxes were stacked on and behind each other, filling up all the available space. Some held household appliances, such as mixers and coffee pots, extras gathered over the years. There was a plastic storage tub, too. They pulled it out and opened it. Inside were bundles of underwear, some with names and street addresses attached. Jackpot!

Rummaging through the underwear, Brandemihl found a videotape and popped it into the VCR. He and Snyder saw enough in a few minutes to convince them this was their guy, and that he was one sick puppy—not that they needed much convincing on either count:

*Opening scene: a spy cam has been hidden near ground level, to the front and left of a toilet. Past the toilet, high on an opposite wall, is a window. It is daylight out. A plant dangles down from a pot beneath the window. Nothing happens. Nothing happens.*

*Then, a woman in a fancy, long red dress walks in, pulls down her underpants, holds her dress in one hand, squats 8–10 inches above the toilet seat and defecates. She wipes herself, flushes the toilet and leaves.*

*Seconds later, a younger woman in a blue dress walks in, sits down and urinates.*

*Scene Two: a long shot, zoomed in on a neighbor cutting her lawn on a riding mower, dressed in blue shorts and a bathing suit top. Back and forth she goes as the camera follows her for several minutes.*

*Scenes in rapid order:*
*Bits from* America's Funniest Home Videos, *maybe. An old lady gets off a bus and her pants slip down, revealing her underwear. Another woman is dancing, her skirt slips down, revealing the cheeks of her butt. A woman gets out of a car. The car takes off. Her dress is caught in the door and rips off, revealing her underwear.*

*Montage of several bits of movies follow quickly, none lasting more than a few seconds, including a love scene, with a man holding a woman from behind as they fall on a bed, and a rape scene.*

*Home video, perhaps the Gorton house: Christmas tree in the corner, brightly lit. Adults and kids and presents fill the front room. Camera zooms in on a woman in a chair, knees slightly apart, the focus on her crotch.*

*Pan to tree, pan back to woman and zoom in on her crotch.*

*Scene from a movie: Young man holds a woman. "Please let me go," she says. There is a long silent pause. Perhaps he will. But then he throws her on the bed, grips her hands over her head with one hand, rips off her panties with the other hand and rapes her while she cries. When he finishes, he says: "So, how was it?"*

*Payless Shoe Source ad, close-up of a woman's foot and an empty shoe, then a few seconds from a Leggs pantyhose ad.*

*A scene from* Home Improvement: *Tim Allen is driving a car. His wife is changing clothes in the back seat, lying down, her legs visible above the front seat. Tim Allen turns his head around to sneak a peak.*

*More movie scenes: Cut to Sharon Stone getting raped in an elevator. Cut to the voyeur in* Body Double *window-peeping on Melanie Griffith. A hijacker jumps up, puts his gun to the head of a female flight attendant and drags her into the cockpit.*

## 79
## AND LOOKIE HERE

Meanwhile, Zettle had finished writing up reports on Dawn and Brenda at the Flint post and joined the search of the house. Romulus had the bedroom, so he and fellow trooper Eric Shroeder took the large metal storage shed out back of the garage. In it were fifteen or thirty large containers. They thought they'd struck gold, too, but it was just Halloween and Christmas decorations and other harmless stuff.

Next was the garage. The first thing that struck them was the absolute meticulousness. Everything was just so. Tools hanging on nails. Labels on everything. They'd open up a drawer at a work bench and see labels for finishing nails, for long nails, for medium nails, for short nails, for washers of one size, washers of another, for screws of one sort or another, for nuts and bolts. A place for everything and everything in its place, and labeled in a neat hand.

They did strike gold in the garage. Among the storage boxes were four or five large, eighteen-gallon, hinge-topped plastic Rubbermaid containers, and police, when they pried off the lids, found that what had been placed there was an almost unimaginable assortment of every conceivable size, color and type of women's undergarment.

Many of them were labeled in the same neat hand, tagged with bits of paper detailing names, dates and location.

One of the smaller troopers climbed up into the attic through the bedroom closet, popping open the small square in the closet ceiling that served as the entryway. There were 2-×-10 boards covering the rafters and blown insulation. He lifted up the boards, prodded the insulation, found nothing.

At some point, Brenda returned to the house with her brother-in-law Dan Loga, who had a video camera of his own. In the kitchen Brenda denied at first knowing anything about the undergarments in the bedroom. Finally, though, she admitted to knowing her husband had a fetish.

They'd been hoping to find a few items of Ludwig's clothing. Instead, they found seven or eight hundred items, a cataloging and processing nightmare. St. Andre was thrilled it was the Michigan State Police, and not Romulus, in charge of shooting the photos and entering all that stuff, item by item, into a computer database.

They'd be busy for days. "You guys are doing a great job," he teased the cops in the kitchen as more and more stuff was brought in for them to deal with.

Reaves, who executed the search at Gorton's parents' house on Linden Road in Flint, ended up spending a week logging all of Jeff's trophies into a computer. "I never thought I'd get tired of looking at women's underwear, but let me tell you, I got tired of looking at it," he says. That wasn't the end of it. Worried they'd missed something, police returned months later and Brenda voluntarily let them do another search. They spent more time in the attic this time, and found hidden behind the chimney, a spot they'd missed the first time, hundreds more articles, bringing the total haul to somewhere around 1,200 items in all.

They'd collect and catalog other stuff, too, mundane items that showed their suspected serial killer lived a life not always too dissimilar from their own—he shopped at Sears with his Sears Premier Card, he belonged to the Bonus Savings Club at Farmer Jack, he had a Genesee District library card, his family health coverage was through HealthPlus of Michigan, he had a credit card for Lowe's Home Improvement Warehouse, and he liked fireworks enough to have a membership card for fireworks.com.

Finally, early in the morning, their long day over, the police headed back to the Flint post.

At some point earlier, someone had been sent out to a party store before it closed to pick up some beer. Too tired to move, too elated not to celebrate, Malaniak and Brandemihl violated one of Michigan's drinking laws. They broke out a six pack and had a couple of beers each in a car in the parking lot of the state police post, and then they made the long drive back down I-75.

## 80
## PROFESSING IGNORANCE

Hours earlier, about 4:25 p.m., police had called Gorton's parents, Laurence and Shirley, but they weren't home.

About 6:10 p.m., Sergeant Reaves and Sergeant Mike Davis went in person and found them there this time. The officers told them their son had been arrested. Reaves said that Gorton's mother was badly shaken and seemed surprised, but that, oddly, the father seemed to take it in stride, as if it didn't come as that much of a shock.

They wanted to interview the parents separately, but Mrs. Gorton insisted on staying with her husband, and so a joint interview was conducted in the kitchen.

They said they'd founded Buckler Automatic Lawn Sprinkler Co. in 1980 and had been contractors for the Mott Estate since 1982. Before founding the company, Laurence had worked for another company at the estate. He chose the name "Buckler" he told them, because there was an established irrigation supply company called Buckner and he thought it might help if people thought his new company was the old established one.

As for Jeff's trouble in Florida, they professed remarkable ignorance. They knew he had gotten in some sort of trouble, and they had sent him money—reportedly about $5,000—to pay his legal fees. And they knew he had gone to prison, but they claimed they had no idea what it was all about, what he'd done or been charged with. Jeff, they said, had kept it quiet.

What they didn't tell police was that one of Jeff's grandmothers had spoken at his sentencing in Florida on his behalf, and surely had heard the charges recounted, the litany of assaults and B&Es. Hard to imagine she hadn't told his parents, or that they hadn't asked her.

The Gortons also said they never observed or suspected abnormal behavior by Jeff and had never received any complaints from clients.

Mr. Gorton remembered seeing Margarette Eby around the estate, and one time she'd asked the guys on one of his crews to help her unload her car. He didn't know her, had only said hi to her once, didn't find her attractive.

At 6:45, Mrs. Gorton told them she felt as if she was about to be sick and asked if she could go outside.

At 7:10, Mr. Gorton authorized a search of the house, but Mrs. Gorton refused. She told them she'd been on the phone to the Flint post and was mad they wouldn't let her talk to her son or see him.

At 7:35, their daughter, Debbie Ross, and one of their other sons, Greg, and his wife, Sarah, arrived and police allowed them in.

At 7:50, the Gortons were told a search warrant for the house and business next door had been signed and a few minutes later, Reaves and four other officers searched the house and the business in the presence of Mrs. Gorton.

There were several large storage buildings on the property and six officers searched those as Mr. Gorton and Greg looked on. They contained nothing of value.

Mrs. Gorton kept the company books. Included in items taken from the house were eight file cards showing work done on the Mott Estate since Buckler was founded, and W-2 forms and time sheets for all employees. In addition to the Mott Estate, the company did the sprinkler work for all the McDonald's, Burger Kings and Taco Bells in the Flint area.

Jeff may have been a foreman in the family business, but his W-2 forms would show that if he were ever to get rich, it would be by inheritance, or the lottery, not from his labors. His base pay in 1997 was $12,160. It was the same in 1998. Counting overtime and a modest bonus, he made nearly $23,000 a year. In 1999, he made $10 an hour. Thanks to overtime—generally 12–14 hours weekly—he took home $375–$385 a week.

Some other things caught the cops' eyes and were confiscated—ten porno magazines.

Later, company employees would tell police that at least some of Jeff's brothers, usually behind his back, referred to him as "the panty sniffer."

Bryan Gorton felt like he'd been hit in the stomach when he heard a news account late Friday afternoon that his younger brother had been arrested for the murder at the Mott Estate.

He was willing to talk when State Police Sergeant Daniel Pekrul and trooper Jason Teddy knocked on the door of his Flint house just after 5 p.m. He invited them in and over the next hour and a half told them that Jeff had always been the good son. Dan had been a heavy drinker and committed suicide, and the other brothers had their weaknesses, but Jeff had always done the right thing.

He was the A student at Southwestern. He'd been the star chess player. He didn't abuse drugs, rarely drank, never raised his voice with his wife and kids. In nearly forty years, Bryan had never seen him lose his temper. He'd never owned a gun, didn't like to hunt, seemed a gentle soul.

Occasionally, Buckler would get assignments that took a crew or two out of the Flint area, particularly jobs for McDonald's and the Proclean chain of laundry centers. It was pretty common if a crew was out of town on an overnight assignment to go out hitting the bars at night or find a topless joint. He remembered being in the Detroit area in November of 2000 and the four Gorton brothers all going out to a topless bar.

Jeff always had an eye for the women and would make

comments about women he'd see, but, said Bryan, he always seemed to prefer "classy" women who were dressed up.

He knew Jeff had been in trouble in Florida, for window-peeping, he'd thought. And he said that as far as he could remember, the last time he'd seen Jeff other than at work had been the previous Fourth of July. Except for his younger brother Greg, Jeff wasn't very close to any of his family.

Detective Gonzalez and Sergeant Allan Ogg went to Steve Gorton's house in nearby Linden. He said Jeff had been in some kind of trouble in Florida involving a woman, but didn't know any details other than that he'd gone to jail.

He said Jeff was known for his meticulousness but added that he was "always a little bit perverted." When asked to explain, Steve said Jeff and his buddy, Kevin Bosh, used to always go to topless bars together, but that he thought Jeff had settled down since.

He was shocked at the charges against Jeff, of course, but said that several years earlier a customer had complained that Jeff had gone through a woman's dresser drawers, a charge Jeff denied.

Dan Gorton's ex-wife, Tammy, was originally reluctant to meet with police. She was remarried and was afraid that in all the hubbub over Jeff, her kids would find out that their dad had died as a suicide, and not of accidental causes.

Eventually she agreed to meet with Larsen at her house. She'd married Dan a year after the Eby murder and divorced him ten years later. Just after the divorce, he'd gone out to his company van and turned on the air compressor. She was well familiar with the Eby case, because at the time she and Dan had been living just two blocks away and the murder had creeped her out.

Jeff's immediate family claimed to be in the dark about his past, but Tammy knew all about it. She knew he'd spent time in prison in Florida for stealing women's clothes and had always considered him a "pervert."

She said Dan used to come home from work and tell her about Jeff's antics, that he'd follow women while on the job and would be so obsessed by them that he'd miss turns on the road.

She told Larsen there was little love in the Gorton family. She did stay in touch with Greg's wife, Sarah, by phone, but since her divorce, Mr. and Mrs. Gorton had had no contact whatsoever with her kids, their grandkids, who then were 16 and 18.

She told Larsen that Sarah had talked to her quite a bit about the news. Mrs. Gorton had asked Sarah to visit Jeff in jail, but Sarah had told her she would quit the family business or they could fire her before she'd go see him.

Tammy also told Larsen that in the past, Sarah had asked her not to tell Brenda Gorton anything about her husband's troubled past, that Jeff had asked her to relay this message to her. Tammy and others had kept Jeff's past a secret from Brenda, who she said was a very nice woman.

And she said that she was aware of at least one complaint filed against Jeff during his employment at Buckler. She said Sarah had told her some woman had called to say that Jeff had been going through some boxes in her house, but she didn't know if anyone had ever followed up on the complaint, or if Jeff had been disciplined.


Greg and Sarah Gorton's former next-door neighbor, Laurie Tafoya, also found it hard to believe the family had little or no inkling of Jeff's dark side.

After hearing the news of Jeff's arrest, she called the Flint PD, and they referred her to the state police.

She told Greg Kilbourn that she had had numerous run-ins with Jeff from 1986–1989, beginning when her daughter had seen Jeff peeping in through her bedroom window one morning when she was getting ready for school. She screamed and mom came running.

Laurie didn't see Jeff, herself, but she went next door to tell Greg about what his brother had been doing. Greg said he'd settle it, and asked her not to call police.

The next incident occurred at a birthday party for Greg and Sarah's daughter after the Gortons had moved to another house, less than a mile away. Laurie drove her three daughters to the house. Jeff was there, and shortly after they arrived, Jeff said he had to leave to pick up his girlfriend, Brenda.

Laurie then realized she'd forgotten the birthday present and she drove back home to get it. Jeff's Monte Carlo was in her driveway. She entered and found Jeff in the rear of the house, in the laundry room, scaring him half to death in the process. He closed the door as she approached and held it shut while she and her daughters tried to force it open, screaming at him all the while.

Again she told Greg. Again he told her he'd take care of it, and to please not call police.

In April of 1988, Laurie moved to another house, just three blocks from Greg and Sarah. Not long after, she saw someone peeping into her bathroom window about 5:30 a.m., but because of the distortions in the glass, couldn't identify who it was. She was sure it was Jeff. She called Flint police and they came out and followed footprints from the window to the parking lot of a nearby business.

In 1989, she was looking out a window one night when suddenly Jeff came face-to-face with her. She ran out and turned on a deck light. He froze in his tracks, then took off running to the same nearby parking lot and got into his Monte Carlo. She found a cement block he had placed under her window to give him a better view.

She called Flint police but they said her brief look at the peeping Tom in the dark was not enough to make an arrest.

In 1990, she purchased a big black dog. For the first few weeks, it would bark hysterically during the early morning hours, frantic, as if someone was in the yard. After a while, his barking stopped and Jeff was never seen there again.

Gone missing during the three years were a lot of under-garments—including a long white slip, a long black slip with a matching chemise, a red teddy, a red wool dress and a royal blue dress.

Another of Greg and Sarah's former neighbors, Toni Trombley, told of a different series of encounters with Jeff in the summer of 1986.

She had rented a room from her cousin next door to Greg and Sarah Gorton. It still freaked her out more than fifteen years later when she recounted for police how she'd come home one day and discovered that Jeff was something more than the quiet, gentle guy who had been stopping by lately to engage her in conversation. That he was also a guy capable of sneaking in her house to leave her a bouquet of flowers and a note. And, while he was at it, completely cleaning the house, including washing the laundry, folding it and putting it away.

She'd ordered him to say away. She bought a padlock for her bedroom. She came home one day to find the padlock broken off, and she'd moved away soon after.

## 81
## BUSCH BLOWS UP

The day after his arrest, Gorton was arraigned on a battery of charges before Judge McAra. The arraignment is the legal step of officially notifying a defendant of the charges against him, and setting bail, if any. Gorton asked for a court-appointed attorney and was held without bail.

Things got ugly the morning of Gorton's scheduled pre-trial hearing—where the state lays out the bare bones of its case to show that there was a crime and that there is probable cause to think the defendant committed it. Before going before McAra, Busch met with some of the police involved, including Larsen, Malaniak and Kilbourn. Though Malaniak had been with Petrides all afternoon the day the warrants were issued, it was the first time he'd met Busch.

Busch walked in and without so much as a "Congratulations," or "Good morning," erupted at them. He started yelling about leaks to the media, demanding to know why was he reading stuff in the paper, saying they were jeopardizing his case, etc.

"Let's get this straight right now. Anything that comes out about this case will come out of my office," he said.

Or, as Larsen recounts Busch's spiel: " 'Everything's got to go through me and blah, blah, blah.' He's just a media hound."

"What a total asshole," thought Malaniak.

"He just ripped us up one side and down the other," says Larsen. "Here we had a hundred and fifty years of police experience in that room and he was screaming at us. We were

all offended. It was embarrassing. I mean, you've got guys
up from Romulus and they're hearing that?"

Kilbourn cut Busch short. He forcefully informed him
that nothing had been leaked. "I told him everything he was
talking about had come out in open court. Somehow, he
wasn't aware of it," says Kilbourn. Everything in the papers
or on TV had been disclosed at the arraignment or was else-
where in the public record.

And then they all went out ànd put on the happy team face
before the judge, Gorton, his attorney, Philip Beauvais, and
the multitudes of media. Beauvais asked for a continuance
so the client could be evaluated for his competence to stand
trial.

Gorton was taken back to the county jail in handcuffs.

Late in May, the report from the state's Center for Forensic Psychiatry came back, finding Gorton sane and compe-
tent. On June 12, the preliminary examination was finally
held, the evidence was laid out, and McAra bound him over
to the county Circuit Court for trial.

## 82
## KEEPING THE STORY

Bryn Mickle, the talented young police reporter for *The
Flint Journal*, hadn't been around when Eby was murdered,
but he was well aware of the case from stories he'd written
about the state police task force after joining the paper to
take the night police beat when that job opened up in October of 1999.

If you're a young reporter and you want to work on your
chops, there aren't many better places to cover than the night
police beat in Flint, Michigan.

Mickle has an unlikely background for an up-and-coming
hard-news reporter. He was a 1994 graduate of the University of Michigan, studying sports medicine of all things. He
was a trainer on the school's hockey and football teams and
got to work with the legendary Bo Schembechler, traveling
with the football teams to the Rose Bowls of 1989 and 1992.

He found himself bored with spoiled athletes, complain-
ing about nagging problems, most of them pretty minor. One

night, at a downtown Ann Arbor pub, he was drinking with the editor of the school paper, *The Michigan Daily*. Mickle thought the paper was a rag (though, in truth, it is one of the finest college newspapers in the country).

Fortified by drink, he expressed his opinion. "You think you can do better? Try it," was the response.

To his surprise, a couple of days later, without the fortification of alcohol, Mickle went into the paper's offices and asked for an assignment. He had fun, they ran his story with his by-line, they didn't butcher it much in the editing and he had an epiphany: "Hey, you can get paid for this!"

He started his career in 1995 at *The Brighton Argus*, a weekly half an hour north of Ann Arbor. Then he followed it up with a series of jobs at small dailies on the East Coast before he joined the *Journal*.

The *Journal* is a Booth Newspaper, a chain not known for loose purse strings. When the press conference broke the Gorton story wide open, Mickle made a call to the *Orlando Sentinel*, to see what sort of arrangements could be made to get the *Journal* as good a story as inexpensively as possible.

He talked to a reporter named Doris Bloodsworth. The deal was: Mickle gave her what he got, filling her in on who Gorton was, the Eby and Ludwig murders and what he knew of his Florida past, which wasn't much. She'd go through the *Sentinel* files and go over to the courthouse to get whatever records she could get her hands on about Gorton's crimes there and get back to him ASAP.

That night, February 12, he called Bloodsworth. As Mickle recalls it, he asked her: "Were you able to get the records?"

He said there was a pregnant pause, followed by a hesitant "Yeah."

"How do you want to work it? Do you want to dictate them? Fax them?"

"Well, we've decided this is a pretty good story and we're going to hold on to it." They would, she said, pass on what they had to Mickle after the *Sentinel* published.

It took a moment to sink in. They weren't going to tell him what the court documents had to say. They weren't going to follow up on their end of the deal, at least for a while. Shit! Livid, he hung up and went to his editor. Mickle had

made the deal and he was going to catch the flak for having
it go bad.

The editor told him to get his butt to Orlando, ASAP, forget the cost. Mickle got on the phone, scrambling for last-
minute connections. He was able to get on the first flight out
before daybreak the next morning, but he had to fly out of
Detroit, not Flint's Bishop Airport just down the road from
where he lived. The *Journal* had to pay a premium for the
last-minute seat, and it was a lousy trip with lousy connections. Mickle left at 5 a.m. and didn't get into Orlando till
3:30, in a bad mood and stressed out.

Mickle got a cab to the courthouse downtown, arriving
just before it closed. The clerk went to get the file, but came
back without it. It was around but misplaced. They'd have to
find it. Come back tomorrow.

Saving the *Journal* a few bucks, Mickle took a cab to his
grandparents' house in Orlando to spend the night. Next day,
he got an early edition of the *Sentinel.* Bloodsworth's piece
was headlined: "Former Orlando Resident Is Suspect in
Michigan Death."

The story told of Gorton's arrest in Michigan for Eby's
murder, and recounted his arrest and imprisonment for two
years in Florida. Bloodsworth quoted one victim, Betty
Dixon, who testified that, as Gorton had attacked her from
behind, she turned around and got a "look into the eyes of
Mr. Gorton, who had much anger on his face and very
pursed lips."

Gorton had told police he needed mental counseling for a
compulsion he had to forcibly take articles of feminine apparel. At one point Gorton said he would claim an insanity
defense, but later pleaded guilty when assault and other
more serious charges were reduced to two counts of robbery
and one of burglary. James Valerino asked that the court give
Gorton counseling, and Bloodsworth wrote that it was un-
clear if he had, in fact, received any. (He did, briefly.)

Ironically, an italic line of attribution at the end of her
story told readers that wire-service reports had contributed
to the story, wire-service reports *The Flint Journal* may very
well have generated. Mickle steamed.

She'd mentioned Earl Deimund, the manager of the
trailer park, but it looked like what she had came out of the

court files, that she hadn't interviewed him anew. Mickle found a phone book, looked in the D's and—voila!—Deimund was listed. Got lucky there. He gave him a call. Got luckier. Deimund answered and was willing to be interviewed, providing valuable nuggets the *Sentinel* didn't have.

Deimund had had numerous reports from residents of underwear missing, but after word went out about Gorton's arrest, "people came out of the woodwork to report underwear thefts," Deimund said. At some point during the investigation, Orlando police decided they didn't need all the underwear as evidence and laid it out on a table in the park's laundry room for residents to claim. Some of it was his wife's and daughter's.

The only way Gorton could have gotten into his trailer was through a bathroom window, a window that cranked open from the inside and was six feet off the ground. How Gorton was able to open it from the outside and pull himself up and in was a mystery, said Deimund. "It couldn't have been easy."

Mickle went to the courthouse first thing in the morning. They had found the files. He paid for copies, read them furiously, highlighting passages. The records told a compelling tale, part of which was the seeming indifference by the Florida court system to Gorton's brief, but very busy history of assault and depravity in the Sunshine State.

The records showed that Gorton pleaded guilty on October 3, 1983, to three felony counts in the attacks on Gagliano and Dixon and the B&E of Deimund's trailer. The very next day, he was arrested by Orlando police for the B&E two weeks earlier of Kristi Walker's apartment, the same day as his discharge from the Navy. On December 12, he was allowed to post bond so he could return to Michigan for the holidays. On January 31, 1984, he was sentenced to four and a half years, without parole. On February 14, he pleaded guilty to the Walker B&E. On February 15, bearing the ID number 094833 he started serving his first prison sentence. On March 9, he was sentenced to three years without parole on the Walker case, to be served concurrently with his first sentence. And on December 24, 1985, having served just 22 months, he was released from jail and driven to the airport, and flew home in time to have a Merry Christmas.

There was no time for Mickle to craft all of that into a polished story before his plane left at 4 p.m. Mickle would, in the parlance of old-time journalism, be the leg man on this story. He called his desk, and Ken Palmer played the old role of re-write man. Mickle dictated a ton of stuff, Palmer crafted it into a fine piece bearing Mickle's by-line and they made deadline. It was headache-inducing, old-style newspaper reporting. All in all, two days to remember. The *Journal* had gotten lucky over the *Sentinel*'s reneging on their deal to share the story. Mickle's pieces in the *Journal* were far more compelling and complete.

Just one thing wrong: It was Mickle's first Valentine's Day as a married man. His wife had to settle for a Winnie the Pooh chocolate square and an airport greeting card.

Five days later, the *Sentinel* followed up with another story. The headline read: "Orlando Judge Does Not Regret a 'No' to Counseling."

Orlando Circuit Judge Ted Coleman said he didn't remember details of the Gorton case, did not regret not ordering counseling and that there was no guarantee counseling would have worked. Valerino and others would, in light of Gorton's arrest in Michigan, criticize the judge for not having ordered counseling, but in fact, Valerino had asked for counseling *and probation* in lieu of a prison sentence, something the judge rightly dismissed out of hand.

One footnote regarding Mickle: When news broke the previous August linking the Eby and Ludwig cases, Mickle started getting e-mails and phone calls from some guy out of state. Some guy named Charles Stone. He claimed to be an investigative reporter with the CIA and needed details on the case. He sent Mickle an unpublished article he wrote claiming that the Eby murder and murders at the VA hospital in Ann Arbor were the work of the same man. Mickle thought Stone was Looney Tunes, but politely continued to exchange e-mails with him.

A letter Stone wrote him on September 4, 2001, was the first intimation Mickle had that Stone had been linked directly to the Eby murder himself. Up to that point, his name had never been in any Flint PD reports released on the case, and had not shown up in any old articles from the paper's morgue.

"The Eby case was led astray by the attempted frame-up of the investigative writer [Stone] by the FBI and local police . . . I have asked the U.S. Senate Judiciary Committee to investigate the FBI conduct," wrote Stone, who said he'd asked the FBI for copies of its files on the Eby case. "But nothing has been sent on the Eby case. Almost certainly the file has disappeared."

It wasn't until after Gorton's arrest, when the state police turned over copies of their files to Mickle, that he saw that Stone hadn't merely been fantasizing. There hadn't been a frame-up, but the FBI had sent the investigation astray. Local police *had* mistakenly targeted him as the killer.

Stone had resurfaced in Flint several years earlier, and years after that, he had been visited in Delaware by King and DeKatch.

One day Stone just showed up on King's porch, ringing the doorbell. That alarmed King, because he'd just moved to a new condominium and had an unlisted phone number. How did Stone know where to come knocking? It reinforced his opinion of Stone's resourcefulness. King had recently retired. He called Elford to tell him Stone had paid a visit.

Elford thought it might be Stone taunting him, the audacious killer they couldn't catch coming back to wave it in their face. He put a tail on Stone. The last the tail, or anyone else in Flint, saw of him he was heading south out of town on I-75.

Stone had also initiated contact with the Ebys, writing a letter to Dayle in Indianapolis in 1992. Though he was delivering pizzas, the letter came on letterhead reading "Stone and Associates" in big letters across the top, and listing an address in Silver Spring, Md.

He told Dayle he'd been framed for her mother's murder because he'd been digging into a conspiracy at the VA Hospital in Ann Arbor.

"In my opinion, because I had stumbled upon a really hot situation . . . I think something may have been trumped up in your mother's case to frame me. You know the old saying, 'Take care of two birds with one stone.' I was the Stone. It was abuse of the Justice Dept. of the worst kind. The government would do anything to keep all of this quiet."

Dayle immediately called King, who scared the bejesus out of her when he told her Stone was attracted to her. She asked King for a picture of the pizza deliverer so she'd know what he looked like if he ever started following her around or showed up at her door. He never did.

## 83
## THE PANTY COP

Police catalogued 833 items of women's apparel taken from the Gorton home that night. Some of those items were boxes and bags filled with stuff. In all, there were upwards of 3,000 pieces of one kind or another. Police knew they didn't have 833 bodies to account for, but they were worried there were more—perhaps a lot more—than the two they knew about. In the days after Gorton's arrest, police flew over the property, looking for depressions in the ground that might show where other bodies were buried. They didn't see anything.

On July 20, police would return, and find and catalog hundreds of other things that had been well hidden and overlooked in the attic on the first search.

Dan Loga, who was there at both searches, says, "I couldn't believe the stuff they took out on the first search. It was absolutely mind-boggling. And they took just as much out the second time."

Today, the stuff takes up half the space in the narrow evidence room at the Flint post, waiting for requests from other agencies to possibly help clear their unsolved rapes or murders.

The undergarments fill fifty-eight large cardboard boxes literally stacked to the ceiling. They fill four large Rubbermaid storage tubs. They fill three suitcases. They fill thirteen giant brown bags, the kind you use to fill with leaves in the fall.

After the first haul, Gonzalez was given the task of trying to track down as many women as he could from the labels that were affixed to many of the undergarments.

Some of the items were tagged with full names, some just

first or last names, some with street names or business names. Some read:

"Linda, Holloween 96."
"Brewerington pump job."
"Older daughter, black pack, younger daughter, brown pack, Mom, grey pack plus other boxes."
"Citizens Bank back lot in car."
"Pioneer Insurance."
"Clothesline RR track."
"Flushing doctor installed system for him."
"Cindy, Brenda's cousin."
"Steve's Deb."
"Brenda's mom."
"Shaheen, Flushing, about got caught."
"Randy's wife."
"Sweetie from across the street."

The main concern was that they were dealing with a serial killer and collector. Were there more than two victims? Did any of these clothes belong to women who were missing? Or who might be unsolved homicides somewhere? Or who had been assaulted or raped by an until-now-unknown assailant?

Gonzalez had earlier helped in the surveillance of Gorton's house, had interviewed one of his brothers and had helped execute the warrant at his parents'. He eventually reached about fifty girls or women in the Flint area and brought them into the Flint post for interviews and to ID their belongings. They ranged from girls not yet in their teens to 70-year-olds.

It turned out Gorton had stolen from his mother-in-law and had stolen at least seven packets of stuff over the years from Dan Loga's wife and daughter—Jeff's sister-in-law and niece—including nylons, pantyhose, tights and a bra. He stole from the wives and girlfriends of his friends. He committed a slew of neighborhood B&E's. He stole from many clients, often more than once as he came back each spring to get the system up and running and each fall to shut it down.

Controls for a sprinkler system were generally located in a basement, if there was one, or a laundry room, if there wasn't. With Gorton's crew, the procedure was for Jeff to always do the inside work, and his partners worked outside at the sprinkler heads.

Often, since Buckler had been servicing their houses for years and had built up trust, customers would let Gorton in, then leave for work or other duties, giving the fox the run of the henhouse.

"He'd come in the morning and have coffee and talk with them before they'd leave for work," says Gonzalez. "A lot of them said he was the nicest guy in the world. He had two faces. The good family man, good with kids. Not a stereotypical predator."

A lot of the women hadn't noticed anything missing. Some took the news calmly. Some freaked out. One woman, in her early twenties, broke down and started sobbing. She'd just moved out from her parents' and a few weeks into her new independent life, Gorton had struck.

Gonzalez's fellow cops started calling him "the Panty Cop."

"The guys were teasing him," recalls Larsen. "It was 'Hey, how you get that assignment?' He had a parade of women coming into the post for two weeks."

One woman named Toni told Gonzalez that Buckler had installed their system fifteen years earlier, and that Jeff always serviced their house. He was always courteous and never displayed inappropriate behavior.

Toni recognized three of her things.

A woman named Holly said Gorton had been coming to her house for nine years. She ID'd seven things taken either from her or her daughter.

A woman named Renee had noticed one of her things missing, but didn't suspect Jeff—it was a pair of panties decorated with lemons and limes.

The attorney who got Gorton probation in his 1995 arrest for lifting a woman's skirt in the Pamida store was paid, in part, by Gorton installing a system. While he was at the attorney's house, Gorton stole some of his wife's things. He stole from other attorneys and even local judges.

The wife of a local politician, John Cherry, was robbed, too. In November of 2002, Cherry was elected Michigan's lieutenant governor.

Loga's daughter was an adult, an X-ray technician living

in Grand Rapids, when she came into the post to ID her stuff. One of the items she recognized was her first training bra.

Odd things that had happened over the years—things you don't think much of at the time—began making sense to Loga. On Easter of 2001, Loga and his wife had hosted the family dinner. Loga had to leave that afternoon for a business trip to Ohio. At one point, he went to find his kids to say goodbye to them and saw Jeff walking out of the laundry room. Another time, his daughter had seen Jeff walking out of her bedroom.

Loga, who continued to visit Jeff in jail, thinking it the Christian thing to do, asked him how he could steal from his family, of all people. "Jeff, we're people who have taken you in and loved you."

"Well, Dan, I treated your wife and daughter like every other woman in my life," he said. As if Dan should be happy his family hadn't been discriminated against.

Larsen remembers one particularly embarrassing moment. He needed to speak to Gonzalez about something, and didn't know he was in the middle of an interview with one of Gorton's victims. Larsen walked into Gonzalez's cubicle just as he was holding up a white slip that had what seemed to be semen stains all over it.

"Oops, bad timing, sorry," said Larsen, backing out into the hallway, red-faced.

None of the women wanted their things back.

## 84
## FINISHING THE VIDEOS

Another task for the cops in the days following the search of the house was to watch the videotapes. Some of them were harmless, containing either clips or entire episodes of *Mad TV*, *Spin City*, *Frasier*, *Grounded for Life*, *The Bernie Mac Show*, and *Malcolm in the Middle*.

Another, titled "Wally's Play 2nd Grade," was of Gorton's son's performance in the gymnasium at school. "Xmas 2000" was of a large Christmas celebration in a hall. "Xmas 2000 Pt. II" was of the Gortons in their home Christmas morning. "Star is born 2001, Wally's B-Day 2001, Jenny's 2nd grade play, ASST Stuff FULL" contained a children's play at church, a birthday party at the Gortons' and a children's play at school. "Costa Rica 2001" showed the Gortons and Jeff's brother, Greg, and his wife, Sarah, on vacation.

"Jenny Gymnastics, Roller Skating, Bowling, Wally, Wheels Inn Canada" showed such typical family fare as gymnastics practice, kids roller-skating, kids bowling and a large hotel outside Windsor, Canada, that is popular with American families because it has a pool and a small amusement park.

But the seemingly typical family home videos included much that was atypical, too, including numerous zoom shots of the buttocks and panty lines of teenage gymnastics instructors and zoom shots of women's crotches at family and school functions.

One tape contained part of an episode of *CSI*, the popular show about crime-scene investigators. The tape had been rewound to a particular point in the episode. When police started the tape at that point, the TV investigators were at a crime scene, looking at a bathroom stall. No writing was evident on the wall, but when they lit it with special lights, a message popped up, giving the real investigators watching it a particular chill: "I killed five women."

Dan Snyder thanked God for the fast-forward button when he watched one no-soundtrack video shot in the Gorton bedroom:

> *Jeff Gorton is lying on the bed, staring into the camera in the entertainment center. He has on large round glasses, looking a bit professorial but for the white bra, panty hose and women's panties he is also wearing.*
>
> *He removes the panty hose, places them to the side, off camera, picks up another pair and puts them on. He crawls forward on the bed and rises up on his knees, his hairy, slightly fleshy belly filling the screen. He rubs his belly above his crotch in a circular motion for a few seconds, lies back, pulls off those panty hose and puts on a third pair. There is a gaping hole in the right thigh. He rubs his belly with the same circular motion for a moment, pulls those hose off and puts on a fourth pair.*
>
> *He rubs his belly with the same motion, extends a leg and shows the bottom of his foot to the camera, waves,*

*then takes the hose off. He puts on a fifth pair, solid
black, rubs his belly, takes them off, takes off his panties, puts on white panty hose, gets up, walks toward the
camera, pulls the hose well above his belly button,
walks back, lies down, takes them off.*

*Picks up another pair of hose, looks at them, puts
them down. Picks up another pair, looks at them, puts
them on. These have a huge hole in the left calf. They
have a hole in the crotch. He pulls his limp penis out
through the hole, walks over to the camera, adjusts the
zoom, goes back, lies down, his groin area now filling
the screen.*

*He begins to masturbate.*

It continued for some fifteen minutes of Gorton masturbating
an unwilling, shriveled-up penis. The best he could accomplish was a drop of preseminal fluid, which he dabbed up with
his index finger and put in his mouth. He went at it for another
fifteen minutes. Finally, he got a semi-erection and climaxed.

He then put on black panties, exchanged them right away
for black bikini bottoms, put on another bra, padded the bra
with rolled-up nylons, stood sideways to the TV monitor to
admire his profile, put on panty hose, put on a skin-tight
camisole he could hardly get over his shoulders, stood up on
a chair, kept one leg on the chair, put the other leg on a
dresser and, facing the camera, rubbed his belly. He stepped
down, took off the camisole, put on a black teddy, put a
white slip over the teddy, got back up on the chair, put one
leg back on the dresser, rubbed his belly and got down. He
put on a pink, frilly negligee and resumed masturbating.

State police watched, and made a time-line log of the first
tape Brandemihl had found hidden among the underwear. It
went on for several hours and was a disturbing mix of the neu-
rotic and banal. It began with quick montage of rape scenes,
peeping scenes, flight attendants with guns at their heads and
commercials with women's feet and panty hose, and ended
with a series of long passages of Gorton and his wife in their
bedroom. Usually she was naked, having come out of the
shower in the bathroom across the hall, and the camera cap-
tures much of the dull and ordinary stuff—and occasionally
the sweet and touching, too—that makes up a married life.

The first bedroom scenes were shot from a camera hidden under the bed, aiming at the mirrored doors of the closet. Later, the scenes were shot from the entertainment center, still aiming at the mirrored doors.

Gorton seems to take great pleasure in helping Brenda pick out her clothes from the closet, or hanging them back up. Brenda was what might be politely described as Rubenesque. A common interaction for the couple is for her to find a hole in a pair of panty hose she is putting on, and for Jeff to go off in search of nail polish, returning when he finds it to dab it on the hole to stop it from expanding.

He drops to his knees in one scene and applies the polish meticulously, painstakingly.

The bedroom scenes are interspersed sporadically with other scenes—a bit from a porno movie of a naked woman lathering her breasts; of part of an ABC news story on saline implants where a woman talks of going from a 34B to a 36D; of a school function at the Gorton kids' elementary school, with Jeff zooming in on the crotches of various parents, including one woman who sat down on her heels to help clean up a spill of some kind, exposing a peek of her underwear to the zooming camera; and, most disturbing, what police think was Gorton out on a neighborhood prowl one summer night, shooting, through a screen door or window, a naked woman sleeping on a couch.

The shot of him peeping on the neighbor is followed seconds later by Brenda and Jeff discussing a home improvement project while she towels off.

"You? It'd take you a year to do this one room," she says. "I'd like to get it all done in one shot."

While most of the scenes are post-shower scenes, others are Jeff, alone, getting dressed. In each, he pulls on women's panties, pulls panty hose on over them, pulls the waist line far up over his belly button, rolls the elastic back down, then pulls on his blue jeans or khakis and puts on a shirt and ends up looking like the guy next door.

*February 11, 2001, says the date on the screen. Brenda walks in naked, drying her hair. "I've got a heck of a headache. I don't know why."*

*She talks about possible summer trips. "We could go*

*to Mackinaw Crossings. They got a mirror maze and fudge and a laser light show every night."*

Then, *"My head hurts so bad."*

He, fully dressed, comes up behind her and cups her breasts from behind.

She smiles. *"We're going to get those kids to bed at eight tonight."*

A moment later, Jeff says, *"I hear there's a mall going in. That should bring some business."*

Then Brenda is back talking vacation. *"We could go to Jellystone [Campground]. That's a nice place. This July. It's not far from home. It'd be a weekend thing. There's lots of activities. That'd be a nice place to do a weekend. In the summer. Hayrides and activities."*

February 17, 2001:

She walks in from the bathroom, naked. Jeff picks a dress up off the bed. *"Want to hang that with this?"* he asks. She does. He puts the dress on the hanger with the other item and puts them both in the closet.

He grabs her side.

*"Get out of town. It tickles,"* she says good-naturedly. He touches her again.

*"Stop it,"* she says, laughing. Then, *"Hurry."* And runs over and turns off the light. Screen goes dark.

March 11, 2001:

She towels off.

*"That bill's due March fifteenth,"* he says. *"It's gotta be in the mailbox by eight in the morning."*

She reaches in the closet, comes out with clothes.

*"Nylons, please,"* she says to him.

*"Color, please,"* he responds.

*"Blue or white."*

*"Here's tan. I don't think you have blue, do you?"*

*"I don't know."*

*"You got black."*

*"Black? I don't think so."*

She leaves the room. He puts on a pair of panty hose and slips into his blue jeans.

*She reenters the room. They discuss a fund-raising cookie drive for school and she tells him to put a box in her car for one of her friends, so she won't forget.*

*Their son comes to the door. Jeff opens it and looks out. The boy, off camera, says, "Can we get some honey from the trees?"*

"Those are maple trees," *says Jeff gently.* "It's syrup. Honey comes from bees."

*He closes the door. She pulls off a bra she has been putting on.* "Look at this. The whole hook is gone. Give me the bra I wore last night."

"I think you can sew it."

"I don't think so."

"I do."

*He comes up to her again and hugs her from behind. He kisses her, turns her around, pushes her back on the bed. They enjoy a moment of tenderness, then stand up. He picks a dress up off the floor, zips it and folds it. He picks up a broken hanger.* "This was a good hanger, too," *he says.* "It had that spongy thing on it that kept the clothes from slipping."

*She leaves the room.*

*He pulls down his blue jeans and adjusts his panty hose.*

*November 30, 2001:*

*She has found another hole in her hose and sends him off to look for clear nail polish. He comes back with the wrong kind.*

"I wanted clear, but . . ." *It'll do.*

*She leaves the room. He follows her to the door, peeks down the hall after her, closes the door, walks over the camera and makes an adjustment to his panty hose.*

*December 1, 2001:*

*Jeff does up her zipper, then kisses her, pushes her back on the bed, lifts up a leg and looks at her foot. She has on dark panty hose.*

"You've picked up a whole lot of cat hair there," *he says.*

They lie on the bed together, just off camera. She talks about her work schedule, shifts she hates, shifts she likes. She says they need something from the store.

Then, out of the blue: "I wish I was sexier for you, Jeff. I wish I could wear sexier things so you wouldn't want to wear them so much."

He kisses her, takes his shirt off on camera. Kissing sounds are heard off camera. "Let's do it," she says. He stands, crosses in front of the camera to the dresser, picks up a pair of scissors and goes back. What he does with the scissors can't be seen, but she doesn't take any time to take her panties off, so presumably he cuts a hole in the crotch.

They make love. When they are done, he massages her feet.

She gets up, looks at the hole in her panty hose and tosses them aside. "That's why we don't spend a lot of money on these things," she says. "That's why we buy them by the bulk, eh?"

*December 2, 2001:*
Darkness, the sound of a door opening and suddenly light. The camera seems to be sound-activated. Jeff and Brenda are entering the bedroom.

"What did you think of it?" he asks.

"I loved it."

"Should I go up the driveway with the rest of it?" Jeff always goes hog wild with holiday decorations and that's what he's talking about, how he's done the yard. Plus, they're having Christmas this year. With everyone coming over, he'll want it extra special.

"Yeah, I guess."

"I thought about just going along the road, but I thought that don't look right."

"We don't have enough, do we?"

"I need to buy some more candy canes. A few."

They talk about a church pageant that's coming up. "Do I have to go on Saturday, too? Or just Sunday?" asks Jeff.

*December 3, 2001:*

*"I'm supposed to get the Game Boy tomorrow, right?" says Brenda.*

*Jeff grabs her breasts.*

*"Stop it. You act like I'm a play doll. I'm not. I'm your wife." But she says it like she's joking, good-natured.*

*"Shouldn't I love you?"*

*"Stop, I said." Then she laughs.*

*He cups her breasts, again.*

*"I want to get him that Game Boy. And then there's the Nintendo Sixty-four. That's like thirty-nine dollars. That'd make him happy," she says.*

## 85
## "UNCLE PERV"

Police talked to as many of Gorton's current or former co-workers as they could, people who might have seen or heard about his collecting while on the job.

Zettle interviewed Kevin Bosh, Jeff's best man at his wedding to Brenda, a former high-school buddy who also worked with him during two stints of employment at Buckler.

He said that Jeff had told him he'd been imprisoned in Florida for getting into a fight over money. His wife had made him quit working for Buckler because he was drinking too much. Whenever it would rain, Jeff would head for a bar to shoot pool, and it rained a lot in Flint in the summer. Jeff would nurse a drink, Kevin would pound them down.

If they didn't feel like shooting pool, they'd go to strip joints, Vosko's on Grand Traverse Street or Cloud Nine on Saginaw Street.

Kevin never saw Jeff steal clothes, but once saw an undergarment in their work van. Jeff had called him once and said that if Brenda ever asked him about any items of women's clothing, he was supposed to say they were from some woman Kevin had been with. Jeff was always making comments about girls or women they'd pass on the street and would pull over and strike up conversations with women in neighborhoods they were working in. His attraction to two of those women was so strong that he wouldn't stop talking about them. And one time Jeff had infuriated Bosh by driving past their exit ramp at the end of a work day because he insisted on following a car driven by some woman who had caught his eye.

Bosh's wife said that after she had made Kevin quit, Jeff had come by the house and gotten into a heated argument with her husband, telling him he knew how to handle his wife and Kevin ought to learn how to handle his. His wife told police she'd been at the Gortons' house one time when Jeff got mad over how much Brenda had spent on the kids and cut up her credit cards. And Jeff had told both Kevin and his wife that he did all the cooking, cleaning and outside work at his house.

A lot of days, the brothers and their crews would congregate at a place called Terri's Lounge. They'd spend a lot of time there if it was raining, just lunch hour if it wasn't. They'd cash their checks there on Friday. One former Buckler employee said he regarded Jeff as a pervert because of the rude things he'd say, not just about women, but to them. One time at the lounge, he told Jeff's brothers about some particularly bold thing Jeff had said to some woman that day. One of them told Jeff, "Your perverseness is going to get you in trouble."

One former employee, Ken Wirebaugh, told police it was common knowledge among Jeff's family that he was odd. Wirebaugh was aware that Greg, Steve and even Greg's wife, Sarah, used to refer to Jeff as "the panty sniffer."

Joe Watson told police it was common knowledge when he worked for Buckler in the mid-1990s that Jeff was stealing underwear, and that some of the other employees, not just his relatives, also called him "a panty sniffer."

One former high school buddy and roommate of Greg's who'd worked on a Buckler crew with Jeff told police that Jeff was very intimidated by men, but would go into a trance over women. He told them Jeff was a genius, but a goof, unable to carry on a meaningful conversation. Greg had told him Jeff went to prison for robbing a trailer with the wrong crowd. One time, on the way home from a job, Jeff had followed a van past their exit, driving an extra six miles out of their way.

Frederick Babcock, one of Brenda Gorton's cousins, worked with Jeff the summer of 1999. He thought Jeff was "a pretty big creep," and his pet name for him behind Jeff's back was "Uncle Perv." He said Jeff would drive the van "like he was in a daze" as he followed women, often missing turns and bypassing freeway exits.

One Buckler employee said that in 2001, Jeff had started making comments at lunch in the Scenic Inn restaurant about what underwear the waitress might be wearing, loud enough that she had to have heard. His guess was that she was wearing a lacy bra. Another said Jeff kept pictures of women in G-strings above the sun visor in his van.

A common refrain from workers, many of them college students, was that Jeff was unfailingly polite and quiet. All of the brothers seemed quiet. They never seemed to raise their voices or get angry about anything. When employees worked with the other brothers, it was always Steve or Greg or Bryan who would work outside, that generally being considered more important, demanding work. Working the controls inside was usually for someone with less experience. But on Jeff's crews, it was always the other way around.

Another common refrain was Jeff's compulsion at red lights of ogling whatever woman happened to be nearby and asking his co-workers their judgment of her looks; or of his constant tales at lunch of which hot women he'd seen at which customers' houses over the years.

Jeff was known for always being at work on time and for having a neat, meticulous van. It was routine for whoever was doing the outside work to be finished way ahead of Jeff, the inside guy, and having to sit around waiting for him to come out. One co-worker said he was struck by the fact that Jeff always had a rag or handkerchief in his back pocket and was forever wiping his hands.

## 86
## ONE IN 97 QUADRILLION

At 11:14 a.m. on February 11, state police chemist Jeffrey Nye received a sealed medium-sized white envelope containing two buccal swabs from Jeffrey Wayne Gorton.

Two days later, his tests were done and Nye's report was submitted to Larsen.

In very dry language, Nye wrote: "The DNA results shown

above confirm the association between evidentiary sample 2040.01F-M and an investigative sample 535.02A."

There were thirteen points of DNA reference to be compared between the unknown semen sample deposited by the killer in Eby's vagina and the sample from Gorton's cheek. All thirteen matched perfectly.

In a brief chart on page three of his report, Nye noted that the odds of finding another white male, other than Gorton, with the same DNA found in the semen were 1 in 97 quadrillion. The odds of finding a black male with the same DNA were 1 in 3.5 quintillion. The odds of finding a Hispanic match were 1 in 49.6 quadrillion.

On March 14, another DNA report came back from Lynne Helton, confirming that Gorton was a perfect match with the DNA in the semen deposited in and on Nancy Ludwig, too. Her report contained the same mathematical figures as Nye's.

Since there haven't been anywhere near a quadrillion males in all the time since homo sapiens evolved, the chances of two males with matching DNA, who aren't identical twins, being on the Mott Estate in the same week in 1986 were as close as you can get to zero.

So close, in fact, that one of Chief Barksdale's old math professors probably could prove, even to him, that such a small number is the same as zero, itself.

## 87
## TAKING IMAGINARY AIM

Late on February 17, Gorton was driven from Flint to Romulus, where he was put into cell three at the Romulus PD at 12:45 a.m.

The next morning, eleven years to the day after Nancy Ludwig's body had been found in the Hilton, Dan Snyder read Gorton his rights on that case and tried to question him.

"If you're going to ask questions about the case, I'm not going to say anything. I want a lawyer," said Gorton.

Later that day, he was arraigned before 34th District Judge Virginia Sobotka, who set a preliminary exam for February 27.

Art Ludwig flew in for this big moment. Snyder picked

him up at this hotel and took him to the courthouse. He led Ludwig in through the cops' entrance, bypassing security and metal detectors.

Ludwig helped Snyder carry some stuff into the anteroom, where he, the prosecutor and Snyder traded small talk until someone told them Gorton was on his way over from the jail, to get into the court.

It was a small room. Ludwig sat in the back. Gorton was led in, hands cuffed. Ludwig, a crack shot with a handgun since his days in the Army, fantasized about what he could do with a .45. He stared at Gorton and wanted him dead, wanted him dead by his hands, wanted him to die violently.

The hearing was brief. Gorton was led back out.

Snyder and Ludwig went out for breakfast and Ludwig told him about his fantasy with the .45. Picturing it, picturing him taking Ludwig in through the cops' entrance and then Ludwig shooting his prisoner dead, Snyder said, "That would've been embarrassing."

# PART FIVE

# Trial and Punishment

# 88

# HIS OTHER FACE

Jeff Gorton wrote a letter of apology to Dan's wife, Brenda's sister, shortly after being arrested. He wanted to know how she was doing, and he reported on how things were for him. It read, in part:

*"This is a really hard letter for me to write, but it's one that I want to write, one that I need to write . . .*

*"I have absolutely no good excuse for what I did to you guys. After all the years of love, all the years of caring, after accepting me into your family as one of your own, after all you have done for me, for Brenda, for the kids—after all that, I had to go and do what I did. No amount of sorries can make it go away."*

He then said he hoped he could get the help he needed to cure him of his problems, and to get some understanding into why he did what he did.

*"I do know that it's time for all the deceit, all the hiding, all the lies, all the hurt to go away . . . I've spent many nights asking God to forgive me for all I've done. I've been reading the Bible, studying it, getting myself right with God. I can't get better without him. I know he forgives me for my sins (the Bible says so). I only hope that you can forgive me, too."*

But nowhere in this letter, or subsequent letters to his wife, would he admit to any problems other than wanting to wear, or take, women's undergarments. As for the more pressing issues of near-decapitation and rape, he made no mention. And no apology.

*"There is one part of me that needs work,"* he closed, *"but I'm mostly the man you always knew.*

*"Thanks,*

*"Jeff Gorton"*

At Easter of 2002, he sent a card to his family, and wrote in a brief note in the card that he wished them a happy Easter, that they were in his prayers, to please forgive him, and to decorate an egg for him.

He wrote a two-page letter to accompany the card. In it, he stated that he knew he was going to Heaven *"because I've asked Jesus to forgive my sins and have accepted him into*

*my life—even more so than before. I'm just glad in my heart
that all you guys are God's children, too, so I know we will
all be in Heaven together, forever."*

He told them things were going as best as they could. He
was eating three meals a day, got clean clothes once a week
and things to read. He said he didn't get to watch TV often
enough and when he did, it was too loud. Twice a week he
went to church, and on Fridays, a pastor came in and they
spent half an hour singing songs of praise and half an hour
reading scriptures.

He concluded that he hadn't received any letters from
home on a regular basis and that he didn't know why this
might be: *"I'm hoping to start getting weekly letters to update me on your lives. There shouldn't be any reason not to
get at least one letter per week."*

Another letter to Brenda and the kids:

*"I miss you guys so much—probably more than you will
ever know. All I can do is think about us as a family—all the
great times we have had together. Times like the circus, Dis-
neyland, Canada . . ."*

He told them he missed tucking his daughter into bed,
putting the blanket over his boy and holding his wife while
they slept. He told Wally to be the man of the house while he
was gone and told Jenny to help Mom by doing as she was
told and working hard in school.

*"Brenda, I can't say enough 'I love yous' and 'I miss you'
and 'sorries' to express myself and make up for all of this . . .
I, believe it or not, have cried so much I'm surprised I got
this all down on paper. As you know, I've never been a crying type person, but nothing has ever hurt as much as this
before."*

He wrote another letter to Brenda, nine anguished, touching pages. Anguish about his cross-dressing, anguish about
his stealing underwear. Again, not a mention about the
things that were causing *her* the most anguish, that the man
she'd loved and married might be capable of nearly sawing
off a woman's head with a serrated knife, of carving symbols into her breast, or of raping her both before and after
death.

He didn't know where to start, or how many apologies she would accept or would believe, but he wanted her to know that he meant every word.

He told her he knew he hadn't been Mr. Romantic. He blamed his dad for his inability to show much emotion. He stated that his dad *"never showed any love to my mom (or us kids), never spent any time with us as a family."*

He told his wife that *"I really loved to see the joy on your face when I got you things. It really made me feel like you knew that I loved you—the jewelry, the bedroom suite, the leather coat, all the many things I got for you for your birthday or Christmas, our anniversary and Mother's Day and any other reason to buy you things . . ."*

*"From the time they were born, I loved our kids with all my heart, they are the part of what completed my dream. A wife I loved, two great kids, a house, a future—everything I wanted and thought I'd never find,"* he continued. *"It tears my heart apart to see what I've done to your heart, your life. You're the last person in the world I ever wanted to hurt . . . I pray that you never hate me, that maybe there will be the smallest amount of love left in your heart for me."*

He likened his need for women's clothes to *"a gambling addiction or drug addiction, or more like a shoplifting addiction. People get hooked on taking things, even things they don't need . . ."*

And then he closed with the rationalization of all rationalizations, passing off his need for women's clothes, no matter how they were obtained, as:

*"It's like it brought out the feminine side of me—and you know females are more loving and giving and understanding than men. Yes, there was one part of me that the Devil had a hold of, but the rest of me loved you with everything in the world . . .*

*"Well, please know that I'm with you with all my heart. And I love you with all my heart. I just can't believe my life without you. It's something I never imagined could ever happen. Sorry for all I've done.*

*"Love forever,*
*"Jeff*
*"XOXOXO"*

# 89

# LIKE HIS HAIR WAS ON FIRE

Philip Beauvais, Jeffrey Gorton's court-appointed attorney in Flint, wanted to catch some of his client's trial in Detroit, so he cleared his schedule for Friday, August 23, 2002 and Monday, August 26. He thought two days of sitting in would give him a feel for how things were going, and how they were being handled by Craig Tank, a 30-year-old court-appointed attorney in Wayne County.

He needn't have bothered.

What Beauvais thought would be a two-week trial starting with jury selection on Monday, August 19, was over three days later. The only way they could have tried Gorton faster would have been to do it the way they used to do it with accused witches: tie him up, throw him in the water and see if he floated.

As Tank let everyone know during the trial, this was his last case as a public defender. He was about to embark on a lucrative career, he hoped, in private practice.

He didn't argue this case as if it were his last as a PD, he argued it as if his hair were on fire and they wouldn't bring out the extinguisher until the jury came back with a verdict. His very brief pre-trial witness list provided a clue—two men who shared an office in downtown Detroit named Joseph Bruce and David Kleefuss, and Gorton's ex-wife, Dawn Hemingway. It wasn't clear what Bruce and Kleefuss would testify to, but neither seemed to be experts on DNA or fingerprints. And what Dawn could do to get Jeff off—unless it was to provide an alibi for the dates of the murders in question—was dubious.

Jury selection easily could have gone two days on a case like this, which had had such publicity over the years. But the jury was seated on Monday, in time for opening arguments and the first witness, Joann Sweet, the maid who had discovered Nancy Ludwig's body in 1991.

Except that Tank—a squat, broad-shouldered man who looked like his name—didn't offer an opening argument. It was his right, and he claimed it, to reserve it for later in the trial.

Tuesday, the pace speeded up. Prosecutor Elizabeth Walker was able to get through ten witnesses—Paul Janiga, the chief engineer at the Hilton, who had gone to room 354 after getting a call from the maid; Lynn Nelms, Frederick Roybal, Phil Arcia and Ann Johnson, the Northwest flight attendants who had seen a suspicious man at the hotel the day Ludwig was murdered; Michael Giroux, the first cop to the scene; David Bennett, the clerk who checked Nancy in; Gary Elford, the Flint detective who had worked the Eby crime scene; Greg Kilbourn of the violent-crimes task force; and Heather Krohn, the FBI fingerprint expert.

Nelms was a trouble spot for Walker. She was the second witness of the day, following Janiga to the stand. Nelms testified about the angry, glaring man who got on the Hilton shuttle at the airport and sat next to Nancy, staring at her oddly. But in 1991, she had described the man as 40 to 45 years of age, with a weathered, lined face. Gorton was only 39 now, more than eleven years later, and his face was still unlined.

Tank's cross-examination of Nelms, in its entirety, was:

> "Ma'am, at the time this took place, you described this person as being in their forties?"
>
> "Probably."
>
> "Probably. And that was ten years ago, correct?"
>
> "Correct."
>
> "So that person would be in their fifties, now, correct, if they were still with us?"

Tank had no further questions of her. Eight witnesses would follow her. He would have questions for only one of them. He didn't ask a single question of the other eight witnesses.

Of Janiga: "Your Honor, I have no cross." He was a minor witness and there was no need to refute his testimony. A body had been found.

Of Roybal, who testified that he heard a scream at 9 p.m., looked out his peephole on room 353, didn't see anything and went to bed: "Your Honor, I have no questions for the witness." Again, no need to cross. Ludwig had been attacked, she probably screamed. That wasn't the issue.

Then came Arcia, a crucial witness. He had gone over to

his window to turn off the heat and watched for many minutes as someone carried luggage and belongings to the trunk of the gold Monte Carlo. It was his precise description that helped put a composite drawing of the killer together. He was the one who described the man in such detail, the police doubted he could be so accurate, from the ungroomed hair to the width of his rolled-up cuffs. Who had told police eleven years earlier that it couldn't be an attendant or pilot or other airline employee. And who recounted all of that for the jury, but then was only able to give a so-so identification of Gorton as the man he'd seen so many years earlier.

WALKER: "When the police asked you about your observations and you gave the description, did they also ask you whether or not you thought you could identify the individual again if you saw him again?"

ARCIA: "Yeah, they asked me."

WALKER: "Okay. And do you see anyone in the courtroom who resembles, given the ten-, eleven-year age span, the individual that you saw coming out of the hotel carrying the flight attendant's luggage?"

ARCIA: "Sort of, yes, ma'am."

And then he pointed to Gorton.

Sort of? Of such ambiguities are defense attorneys born, or at least trained, to leap on. You can't *sort of* convict someone. You can't *sort of* recognize someone. Moreover, Arcia had described a clean-shaven man. But the man in the courtroom he pointed at had a mustache.

TANK: "I have no questions, Your Honor."

Courtroom observers were stunned. How could he not cross-examine this witness? There were obvious questions to ask to impeach his testimony of eleven years earlier. Had he been in the hotel bar before he went to his room? Were the lights on in his room? If so, wouldn't they have reflected off the glass at the window? Did he cup his hands to the window and put his forehead to his hands to block out the light in the room? What kind of light was there in the parking lot? How come you think a guy in a mustache looks like a guy who didn't have a mustache? What do you mean "sort of?" "Sort of" isn't 100 percent. How strong is your "sort of"? Ninety percent? Sixty?

David Bennett took the stand at 11:15 a.m. and told of check-in procedures, that there were sign-in sheets at the front desk detailing flight numbers, projected arrival times and job descriptions. The sheets would say "FA" for "flight attendant," but not give a name. If you were able to see the sheet, you could see that a room was reserved for a flight attendant who was due in at a particular time, but you would have no way of knowing if it was a male or female.

No need for a cross-examination, said Tank.

Ann Johnson testified that her room's sign-in sheet was sitting on the counter, in plain sight, when her crew arrived. And not only that, the keys were sitting there, too. She also testified to going out to run in the hallways and stairways the afternoon of Ludwig's murder, and being scared by a young man with sandy hair who was hanging around. Johnson's recollections helped in the composite drawing put out by Romulus police.

She was linking, in the jury's mind, lax practices at the front desk with the stranger in the halls. But had this stranger actually done or said anything to her? Did she see him holding a card key? Had she seen keys on the counter other than hers? Since she was checking in with a group, isn't it possible the clerk had seen the group coming in and knew the room had to be theirs, and put the key there just as they were arriving?

TANK: "Your Honor, I have no questions for the witness."

Giroux described the crime scene when he arrived on the scene early on the afternoon of February 18, 2001. None of that was in dispute, so there was no need of a cross-examination.

Elford was called to the stand at 12:15 p.m. Normally, evidence about other crimes or alleged crimes by a defendant would be inadmissible, but a Michigan case in 1993, *People* vs. *Vandervliet*, established an exception in Michigan. *Vandervliet* allows testimony about other crimes to be allowed in if there are extraordinary similarities in modus operandi.

In a pre-trial motion made to Judge Maggie Drake, Walker was able to convince her that the M.O. in the Flint case and the Romulus case—both women were middle-aged, slim, attractive, had brown hair, had been raped, had been stabbed in their breasts, had had their necks nearly severed, and had been left face down on beds—allowed the jurors to hear details of the Eby murder.

Though Gorton had only been charged in the Flint case and could still be found not guilty of that murder, Elford would tell the Detroit jurors all he knew about the Eby murder, and then Greg Kilbourn would take the stand to tell why they thought Gorton had committed that one, too.

Elford had testified in hundreds of trials. Defense attorneys always start the day by opening up their big briefcases and pulling out relevant documents they'll need during the course of the proceedings—transcripts of interviews given police by witnesses, files of one kind or another. Elford was struck by the fact that Tank had a single sheet of paper in front of him, and seemed to be doing nothing with it. He took no notes. Elford wondered if he was even listening to the proceedings.

Elford testified at length. When he was done, Tank said: "Your Honor, I have nothing."

"I've never seen anything like it," Elford would say later. Philip Beauvais is a friend of his, though they have been adversaries in the courtroom. Back in Grand Blanc that night, he called Beauvais to tell him about Tank's performance. Though the trial was only two days old, Elford assumed there would be two outcomes: Gorton would be found guilty, and Walker would one day have to retry the case when an appeals court threw out the conviction because of an incompetent defense. "I figured it was going to be kicked back on appeal, no question," he'd say.

Court recessed for lunch at 12:50 p.m. The jury came back at 2:43 and Kilbourn was called to the stand. He told jurors the brief history of the violent-crimes task force in Flint, that it had begun in May of 2001 by reopening the investigation into Margaret Eby's murder, that DNA had linked it to the Ludwig murder in Romulus, that a fingerprint from Eby's bathroom had been linked by the FBI to Gorton.

He told of the surveillance of the Gorton residence, that

Gorton worked for Buckler Sprinkler, which had worked at the Mott Estate just before Eby's murder, that Gorton owned a gold Monte Carlo.

Kibourn told of the similarity of the photos from the two crime scenes—"they were so similar, it was really scary, in my opinion. The brutality, the overall injuries, the slashing, all that was the same."

Kilbourn was a crucial witness. He'd evoked powerful language. Tank, at least, finally arose from his chair. His cross-examination was hardly that. He did nothing to impeach anything Kilbourn said. He basically just introduced a few more undisputed facts into the record:

"Officer, when did you retire?"

"April twenty-seventh of this year."

"This year. And Detective Larsen—he worked with you on this task force?"

"Yes, he did."

"When did he begin to work with you on the task force, if you recall?"

"Actually, he joined—He was part of the task force from the very beginning."

"With you?"

"No."

"Okay."

"We had two separate divisions. We were working on two different cases. He joined my task force when we got the CODIS hit between the Eby case and the Ludwig case in Romulus."

"Okay. And he worked with you in conjunction from that point in time forward?"

"That's correct."

"I have no further questions."

"It was an embarrassment. It was outrageous," said Kilbourn later of Tank's defense, thus setting the modern-day record of two for most homicide cops mad at a defense attorney for *not* challenging more vigorously the case against the guy they'd arrested and put behind bars.

Krohn was the last witness that day, another crucial witness who would recount for the jury the hows and whys behind linking the tiny bit of a partial bloody print found at the Eby scene in 1986 to the defendant now sitting before them.

By all accounts this partial print was a very bad print to work with. How could she be so sure? She scanned it into a computer? Aren't scanners capable of making errors? How infallible is the software program that makes matches? What is the percentage of false positives? Of false negatives? The scanning system has only been in place at the FBI since 1999 and just had an upgrade before the alleged Gorton print? Well, we all know about the bugs when Microsoft does a Windows update. What kinds of bugs or fixes has your upgrade needed?

Krohn's testimony runs to twenty-six pages in the trial transcript.

Tank's response runs to one line: "Your Honor, I have no questions for the witness."

By now it wasn't just cops—Elizabeth Walker was looking askance at the defense attorney, too. She was doing more than that. She was steaming. Tank's performance was so clearly, demonstrably bad that she thought it might be a tactic, that he was putting up such a bad defense, his client could get a retrial. Perhaps doing nothing more than delaying the inevitable, but also, under that state system that grants an automatic appeal to all those convicted of murder—appeals that are carried out by appeals specialists who have a reputation for being very skilled, professional advocates—eventually getting Gorton an attorney with more passion and ability.

Walker had gone up against Tank twice before. Both times he'd accounted himself well, getting charges reduced when it didn't look like he had a chance, and getting clients less jail time than they'd expected. She had even tried to recruit him for the prosecutor's office, so his behavior was puzzling, at best.

Or, maybe this was all part of Tank being a sharp operator. Maybe he had something up his sleeve, was sandbagging her and everyone else.

"There was just as many files, so many documents, so much information—it was just so voluminous—I was afraid

I'd missed something," she said later. "That Tank had found something in there, and there was a *Perry Mason* moment coming, and I'd look like a fool."

That night, Walker did something extraordinary—she called a defense attorney at home to plead with him to do a better job against her. She called to chastise him for his lack of effort, to tell him he'd better start busting his butt, because she wasn't going to have issues of an incompetent defense louse up her conviction.

Tank reassured her. He was on top of things. He had a defense planned. He was going to put his client on the stand and offer Gorton's side of the story, that a bisexual friend of his now serving time in jail for murder—for tying up, raping and stabbing his victim—did the deed. Gorton was guilty only of helping him cover it all up.

Tank hadn't thrown in the towel, he insisted. Walker had won the first round. The bell was about to ring for round two. She and the state would have a fight on their hands. She'd see.

## 90
## A PIECE OF WORK

If Tank had to sell another killer to the jury, he couldn't have come up with a better person than James Warren Klepinger, a white-trash, seriously disturbed killer already serving life without parole in Michigan's Riverside Correctional Facility in Ionia, a place where they lock away the hardest of hard cases.

According to Tank, Gorton had told him before the trial that he had been there in room 354 the night Ludwig was killed, but his involvement was minimal. He and his bisexual buddy Klepinger had gone to the Hilton in search of flight attendants—not to kill, but to pick up and have sex with, a threesome if possible, or regular sex if it wasn't. Picking up attendants was something they'd done in the past.

Tank was going to put Gorton on the stand, and he was going to testify that he'd met Ludwig at the Hilton after she checked in, successfully laid on some sweet talk, went back to her room without Klepinger and had consensual sex with her. When they were done, Gorton had gone in to take a shower.

Meanwhile, Klepinger had struck out with the ladies, himself, and had gone up to see what his partner was up to. Ludwig let him in and Klepinger must have flipped out when he realized Gorton had gotten lucky and he had not.

For when Gorton came out of the shower, there was Ludwig, dead, and there was the room, a bloody mess.

Gorton and Klepinger decided to make it look like a robbery gone bad. They took all of Ludwig's things and got the hell out of there.

There was more than just Gorton's version of events to sell, however. There was also Klepinger, himself.

At the time of Ludwig's murder, Klepinger was 28 and living in Englewood, Ohio, but he was a Michigan native. At the time of his arrest for murder in Ann Arbor in 1995, he was living on Merriman Road, just a mile or so from Metro Airport.

He had a long and twisted history of exposing himself to women, stalking, window-peeping, assault, rape and murder. And he'd undergone counseling for an addiction to pornography.

Tank needed to draw attention away from his client, and Klepinger certainly seemed capable of grabbing attention.

He had first attracted the notice of the Romulus PD on April 11, when Ann Arbor police contacted them to say they needed assistance finding a guy suspected of killing his girlfriend.

The M.O. certainly resonated with Malaniak and Snyder. Klepinger had bound his girlfriend's wrists with rope, he'd gagged her, he'd raped her, he'd tortured her and he'd slit her throat. And there he was, just down the road from the airport.

On April 17, Malaniak searched Klepinger's apartment. He found a book titled *Hand-Me-Down Genes and Second-Hand Emotions*, which contained highlighted passages concerning emotional problems and homicidal tendencies. But Klepinger wasn't there.

He was eventually arrested, confessed to the Ann Arbor murder and was convicted. But Snyder cleared him on involvement in Ludwig's murder. His alibi—that he was in Ohio at the time—seemed airtight. But, Tank could point out, Ohio is just thirty-five minutes south on I-75 from Romulus, and who's to say a crazed guy like Klepinger wasn't capable of making a mad dash up a freeway to commit mayhem?

Tank could tell the jury about what Klepinger was up to in Ohio in 1991. He could tell them what sort of madness and mayhem he was up to on February 20, the same week Ludwig died. He could say, "Ladies and gentlemen of the jury, yes, Mr. Klepinger was living in Ohio in 1991. And here's what he was up to. Here's what he was doing behind the back of his wife. You listen to this tale and then you tell me if it is out of the question—if it is beyond reasonable doubt—that Mr. Klepinger was also in Romulus on February eighteenth, engaging in other madness behind his wife's back. Madness that, unlike what he did on February twentieth, he got away with. We can't trust Mr. Klepinger, nor should we trust his old alibi."

And then Tank could tell the jury this story, corroborated by police reports:

At 8 p.m. on February 20, Theresa Klepinger, James' wife, called police to tell them about a suspected sexual assault. One of her best friends had called, but as soon as she started talking, the friend suddenly stopped. Theresa could hear screams, and then, "Please don't kill me!" Ironically, she wouldn't find out for hours that it was her own husband whom her friend was screaming at.

Police raced to the scene, found the front door to the apartment unlocked, and entered. They announced their presence. A woman hollered out for help. James Klepinger walked out of an upstairs bedroom and told them that the woman had asked him to come over and have sex with her and that's what they were about to do when they were interrupted by police.

The woman told another story, that he had come knocking at her door saying his car had broken down and he needed to use her phone. He pretended to call his wife and said she wasn't home. Suspicious, the woman called Theresa herself. They began to talk and that's when Klepinger hit her on the head, dragged her away from the phone and began choking her.

He then half-carried, half-dragged her up the stairs and pulled off her clothes. That's when police arrived.

"Yes, ladies and gentlemen of the jury, my client was in room 354 the night Nancy Ludwig was killed. Yes, he had sex with her. Yes, he was an accessory after the fact in covering up this hideous murder. But the man who did the killing is a man who has killed before and killed in exactly the same fashion."

Never mind that Mike Larsen had interviewed Klepinger in jail and believed the convict when he said he didn't know Gorton and hadn't killed Ludwig. That he had offered to take a lie-detector test and had voluntarily taken a buccal swab and been cleared of having sex with Ludwig. And it certainly seemed unlikely that a man with Klepinger's history would have done all of the killing and had none of the sex. But it wasn't up to Tank to *prove* Klepinger had done it, only to raise reasonable doubt about his own client.

(Coincidentally, the results of Klepinger's swab were received in the mail by Larsen the same day the FBI called to say they'd identified the print in Eby's bathroom as Gorton's.)

So, that's what Tank could have told the jury. That's what he planned to tell them. But he says something happened Wednesday night that changed all of that. Something that made it impossible to put his client on the stand. Something that made it impossible to blame James Klepinger. Something that would remain a mystery for months.

Gorton wouldn't tell his tale to the jury. Tank couldn't tell his side of the mystery to anyone, barred by rules of attorney–client privilege, until an unusual legal proceeding many months after the trial would free him to talk.

In June of 2003, Tank would tell of a strange encounter on a sweltering summer night in the Wayne County jail—brought on by his client's angry meltdown over the active presence of so many women in the trial. It was a night Tank says dramatically changed his tactics and left him so shaken—freaked out, he would say, terrified—that afterwards, as he stumbled out of the jail onto Clinton Street and hit fresh air, he threw up on the pavement.

# 91

# A BOOK OF HER OWN

If Jeffrey Gorton had a meltdown because of the number of women involved in his trial, if he was guilty as charged and had what were obviously severe issues with women, well, it was ironic at the least that his fate would be settled in a courtroom dominated by strong females.

If he thought he might be able to intimidate them with his stare, or his alleged deeds, he was wrong. Especially Judge Maggie Drake, a pioneer and a powerhouse of a woman. Her story is one of those you just couldn't make up, her truth being better than any fiction.

Wayne County courts have been known over the years for judges who start late, enjoy long lunches and leave early, who couldn't care less about the length of their docket. Friday is motion day, but lawyers learn if they want to get ahead, it's best not to make too many of them. Friday afternoons are still reserved for golf or getting an early start on the drive north for a weekend at the summer cabin. It's not as bad as it once was, thanks to attempted crackdowns by the state's Supreme Court to bring at least some order to the local court, but there have been times in the past when a terrorist could have blown up the Frank Murphy Hall of Justice on a Friday and killed nary a judge.

One Wayne County judge spent a career being referred to behind his back as "Half-a-day Hathaway," and that was being generous.

Judge Maggie Drake of the state's Third Circuit Court starts on time, makes sure lunch is long enough, and no longer, for jurors to be able to walk the two blocks to Greektown for a hot dog or souvlaki and back, and if an attorney thinks he or she might be able to get a late-afternoon tee-time, it's only because he or she hasn't appeared in her court before.

She also—a rarity in any court—treats jurors as if they are intelligent beings with equal rights in the judicial process. If the lawyers haven't asked a witness a question she wants answered, she'll ask it herself. And then she'll ask the jurors if they have any questions they'd like to ask. If they do, they write them down and pass them to her, and she in turn passes them to the attorneys. At the end of the trial, she goes through a debriefing with the jurors to see what they liked or didn't like about the process, and to answer questions they might have.

Jurors like her. But they'd better pay attention. One dozes at one's extreme risk. On a lunch break, this is a typical instruction: "Ladies and gentlemen, you will get your belongings. You will go to lunch at this juncture. Again, you know where lunch may be found. Let me again remind you that you are not to discuss this case. You are not to talk to anyone associated with this case, even if you're talking about the weather. There will be no talking, no discussion, no 'Hello, how are you?' None of that. Is that clear?"

Heaven protect the person in her courtroom she catches chewing gum, when she'll stop proceedings cold, lecture the perpetrator and pretty much frighten anyone who's even sitting next to someone with gum in their pocket.

She doesn't favor prosecutors or defense attorneys. She's tough on both. She expects them to be on time and prepared. Of prosecutor Betty Walker, she'll say, for example: "She is extremely verbal, very energetic, very thorough. A great prosecutor. I like her a lot. But she talks a lot. Sometimes I have to shut her up."

During a morning recess on the second day of the Gorton trial, Drake addressed the prosecutor:

"Ms. Walker."

"Yes?"

"I need you to coordinate making sure those exhibits are marked. I don't want that done during the trial."

"I understand that, Judge. But the problem is, we just . . ."

"Just get it done. I don't want to hear the reasons. I just want it done."

"I understand fully."

"Okay."

But she's not above a little levity to ease a courtroom situation. When David Bennett, the Hilton room clerk, was called to the stand Tuesday morning, Drake said:

"Good morning. Good morning."

"Good morning."

"How are you?

"Oh, all right. Little nervous."

"Are you?"

"A little nervous."

"It's okay. You can relax here. You've got the best judge in the state in front of you."

She was being facetious, of course, but she is highly respected—enough so that the Michigan Democratic Party would announce at its state party convention later that month that it would run Drake for the state Supreme Court in the November election, a first for a black woman.

The state has an odd method of choosing Supreme Court judges. The election is supposed to be non-partisan and ballots don't list the candidates' party affiliation. But they are selected to run at state party conventions. In 2002, two strong Republican incumbents meant that Democratic challengers had no chance of being elected. The Democrats had little budget for a lost-cause election and asked Drake to be a good trouper and help the party out. It would be good for the party that champions diversity to run her, and it would help her in future re-election bids in Wayne County to say she'd once run for Supreme Court.

On a shoestring budget, she would run an effective campaign, get a ton of endorsements, including that of the *Detroit Free Press*, the Michigan Trial Lawyers and a batch of unions, win the vote in Wayne County and finish with more than 600,000 votes statewide, a losing effort, but far better than expected. She'd tally 14 percent of the vote in finishing third, with the two winners getting about 31 percent each.

At the end of the day Tuesday, after excusing the jury— "Enjoy your evening, drive carefully, no bungee-jumping, no sky-diving"—Drake said:

"Ms. Walker?"

"Yes?"

"Please make sure that you will have everything that you want to have admitted tomorrow."

"I hope so, Judge."

"We are not going to go with any hope tomorrow."
"I . . ."
"We are going with what's factual."
"Okay. We will."

No one in the courtroom would have suspected that this iron-willed judge started her career as a nurse. Or that her tale began in Selma, Alabama, where the civil-rights marches of the early 1960s set her on the path that would intersect with Jeffrey Gorton's in 2001. She left Selma in fear. She hasn't been afraid of much since.

Maggie Williams, the fourth of eleven children, was born and grew up in Orrville, Ala., a small, unincorporated town of 1,500 on the outskirts of Selma.

Her dad, Arthur, farmed a little bit of everything on his 600 acres—cotton, corn, pigs and chickens. He raised all the family's food and sold the rest at her grandfather's general store, which serviced the black community. Her mother, Margaret, taught at the local junior high. Unlike Drake, who stands 5 foot 8, her mother was a tiny bit of a woman. Like Drake, she was iron-willed. Powerful.

"I had the most fantastic mother. My mother was a strong believer in education. She used to preach daily: 'You *will* get your education. One thing they can never take away from you is an education and a strong mind.' We went to church and we went to school and we worked. And you had to read in my mother's house."

The Williams clan firmly believed and actively participated in the civil-rights movement that swept through Selma, one of the defining places in the fight for racial equality. Her grandparents, parents, uncles, aunts and siblings took part.

The protests came at a cost. There were threats of violence and economic repercussions. The white suppliers stopped delivering produce and other goods to her grandfather's store. The white gasoline wholesaler wouldn't deliver gasoline for the pumps in front of the store. There were more threats in a place and time where lynchings weren't necessarily still common, but common enough.

As have several generations of southern blacks, many in her family decided to make their way north. They may have been wrong in thinking the north was more enlightened, but they were right that it offered economic advantages. There were jobs, union jobs, and they paid well.

An older brother got hired as a Detroit cop, became a real-estate broker and ended up as the vice-president of the teachers' union at Wayne County Community College. Another brother went to dental school and is now a lieutenant colonel in the Air Force. Two brothers, one of them a church deacon, got jobs as mechanics at GM. One sister became a high-school counselor and dance instructor, another became a nurse and teacher in New York, a third became a teacher and model in New York.

Only one brother, Curtis, remained in Selma, where he survived the troubles of the '60s and became a county commissioner and radio minister.

Some left for Detroit before her. Maggie waited for the spring of 1965, until she graduated from high school, before heading north with one of her aunts.

Maggie got her nursing degree from Mercy College in Detroit, went to work at Detroit Receiving Hospital downtown, got married and had two kids.

She worked odd shifts, and long, twelve-hour shifts, at Receiving. Working days one week, midnights the next wasn't conducive to raising a young family. She yearned for more regular hours. Her brother Art, the Detroit cop, told her she ought to join him on the force. The pay wasn't bad and the benefits were great.

In 1970 she applied. "They told me they wouldn't hire me because I was a woman," she recalls. In those days, there were only a few women on the force, in a small department dealing with family issues. It was deemed the only police work suitable for women, and openings were rare, usually as a result of deaths or retirement.

"I had a college degree and Detroit cops had GEDs," she says dismissively, referring to tests taken by high-school dropouts to prove they know the equivalent of a high school graduate. "They were only police officers because they had gonads. It was the last bastion of male employment in the county."

In 1971, Drake and a handful of other women joined a federal class-action lawsuit against the Detroit police force, which they won in 1973. She and a handful of others became the first female patrol officers in the history of the department.

Drake was assigned to the tough 12th Precinct at Seven Mile and Woodward, known for its drug-dealing and prostitution. Seven Mile is a mile away from Eight Mile, the road made famous by Eminem, and the dividing line between the city and its suburbs.

Her fellow cops at the precinct didn't greet her in an enlightened fashion, or with open arms. Routinely, she'd enter a room to find men's undershorts or jock straps hanging from doorknobs or crudely made phallic symbols sitting on desks or hanging on walls.

There was only one bathroom at the precinct, and it was for the men. There were no lockers for women. She had to dress at home.

"They were going to make sure all the women resigned. None of us did."

Drake says she had a mouth on her, stuck up for herself, went in and used the men's bathroom, ticked people off, got put on a midnight shift and was told to walk a beat. Never mind there'd never been midnight beat officers in that neighborhood.

In 1976, Drake was accepted to medical school at Detroit's Wayne State University. She applied for and was granted a leave of absence from the police force. On her last day of work before leaving for school, she and her partner— by then she was off the foot beat and working a patrol car— took a call about a man on a roof at Seven Mile and Outer Drive. Her partner was driving. He hit his lights and siren and off they went.

They rolled through a red light and were broadsided at full speed by a car whose driver hadn't heard or seen them. Drake woke up days later in the hospital. She didn't know where she was, or who she was. She had a closed-head injury and no memory. She had spinal-cord injuries and couldn't walk for a year. She couldn't start her classes at Wayne and lost her spot in medical school.

In 1977, a year after her accident, and not wanting to reapply to medical school, she enrolled in law school at the

University of Detroit and got her degree three years later. And then, in 1982, she went back to being a cop, though not by her own choice.

She was fresh out of law school and mulling options when word filtered back to someone in the police department that she had graduated from law school. She was still on disability from the department, and someone in management figured if she was healthy enough to go to school and healthy enough to be a lawyer, she was healthy enough to be a cop.

Still raising her two kids, she couldn't afford to lose her disability pay, so she rejoined the 12th Precinct. She was working the desk one day when in walked John Conyer, a long-time U.S. congressman. He knew her and knew she had gone to law school and wondered why someone with a law degree was working the front desk of the 12th Precinct.

A couple of days later, word came down. Conyers had made a call or two. She would still be a cop, but in a position that would take advantage of her skills. Ironically, given her rude early treatment as a female cop, she was assigned to the city's Law Department, defending cops accused of misconduct. She was a cop and a lawyer both.

In 1992, she ran for county judge. She started her war chest with $300. At her first fund-raiser, no one came except members of her family. Yet on election day, she upset Dominic Carnovale, a judge who'd held office for eighteen years, who was considered a shoo-in when the race began. In 1998 she was re-elected with the highest vote total of any judge in the county.

A month before the Gorton trial, and six weeks before she was tapped to run for the state Supreme Court, Drake made a dramatic return to Selma. There, she married Nathaniel Riddle, a wealthy retired businessman from Chicago, in the city's historic St. James Hotel. In a courtyard where once only black servants or maids would have been allowed, her siblings, son, grandkids and in-laws gathered for a family portrait.

# 92

# SPEAKING THE LANGUAGE

Maggie Drake ruled the courtroom. But ruling the attention of the jury and spectators was Betty Walker, a short fireplug of a woman whose passion and eloquence have made her the star homicide prosecutor in the large Wayne County Prosecutor's Department.

Walker was in her mid-50s at trial but looked fifteen years younger. Ask around about her with her colleagues and you invariably hear two phrases: "I love Betty Walker," or, "Isn't she great?"

An African-American, she was born in Black Bottom, a legendary black neighborhood known generations ago for its after-hours jazz and blues joints, numbers runners, hard men and easy women.

Black Bottom was bounded to the west by downtown, to the east by the historic Elmwood Cemetery, which was designed by Frederick Law Olmsted, the father of landscape architecture, who also designed Central Park in New York and Golden Gate Park in San Francisco, and who gets the credit (or blame, depending on how you view cutting the grass) for inventing the front lawn in a neighborhood in Chicago.

As urban renewal displaced Black Bottom's inhabitants, Walker and her single mom, Elvetta, moved to nearby public housing. "I grew up in the projects," she says.

But her family life wasn't typical of the projects. Education was stressed. Her father—though her parents were divorced, he was an influence—taught at Wayne State University and her mother was the first black psychiatric nurse at Ypsilanti State Hospital, a sprawling state mental hospital, where she eventually became director of nursing education.

In 1989, Walker graduated from Western Michigan University with a teaching degree and fluency in Spanish and French.

Today, Walker feels as if she were born to take down killers and bad guys. The killers and bad guys she's sent off to prison would be surprised to find out she spent the first eleven years of her career teaching Spanish and French to Detroit Public School kids, quitting only because she could no longer stomach uninvolved parents who didn't seem to care about raising their kids, or incompetent administrators who didn't seem to care about teaching them.

A friend in law school at Wayne State, knowing she was fed up with teaching, told her she ought to sit in on one of his classes.

She started law school in the summer of 1977, going part time at night the first two years while she continued to teach. After graduation in December of 1980, she was named by Wayne State as its assistant dean for supportive services as part of the school's affirmative action team. She did that for three and a half years while picking up assignments here and there as a defense attorney.

But from her first class in summer school in 1977 on, she had wanted to be a prosecutor. In that class, they studied a case that was overturned on appeal because of prosecutorial error. "I said, 'That's not right.' I wanted to be a prosecutor and do it right so a defendant goes to jail and does *not* get out."

She applied at the prosecutor's office in Wayne County, but was turned down. The prosecutor's department in the early 1980s was very much an old-boys club. There were few women, and they rarely, if ever, tried cases. They certainly never worked homicides. They did research, handled some preliminary exams, were allowed to do paperwork on appellate cases.

In March of 1985, a new prosecutor, John O'Hair, a liberal Democrat determined to open up the department to women, blacks and Hispanics, hired her, telling her, as she recalls it: "You're going to bring the criminal-law revolution to Wayne County.

O'Hair assigned her to what is referred to as "out-county," the county courts outside Detroit.

Judges and cops out-county saw few enough blacks in their day-to-day life, and they'd never seen a black female prosecutor. Walker took a lot of grief at first, ignored or worse by the cops. She was often mistaken for either a secretary or a defendant.

To her surprise, she quickly grew to love the work and the

atmosphere. Her talent quickly won her the respect of judges and cops. And the work load was night-and-day different from what prosecutors faced downtown. Mostly she handled arraignments and pre-trial hearings. Many days, she was done and out the door by 1 or 2 p.m. Stardom was at a minimum, but so too was stress.

In 1989, she was brought back downtown and assigned the misdemeanor jury docket so she could rack up some trial experience. In 1990, O'Hair moved her to felony court, where she worked on the repeat offender's bureau, prosecuting serial rapists and felons specializing in carjackings and home invasions.

The prosecutor's office was restructured after a new prosecutor, Mike Duggan, was elected in 2001. A homicide unit was put together and she was ordained as its star, based in part on her prosecution the previous April of John Eric Armstrong, a serial murderer who had murdered five prostitutes in Detroit and tried to kill three others.

Star or not, the life of a public prosecutor is a far cry from that of the highly paid defense attorneys she is often up against. She shares a small office, maybe 14 by 9 feet, with two other prosecutors. "The big deal is getting a window," she jokes. And that she has, a sliver of a window that looks toward downtown. Straight ahead in her view is one of Detroit's best metaphors, the once-elegant Sheraton Cadillac Hotel, which has been shuttered for two decades.

Detroit is no longer Murder City and in 2003 had just over 300 murders, its lowest total in thirty-five years. But "just" is a funny word to apply to 300 homicides, and the prosecutors are still overworked. The first week of 2003, there were twelve homicides on the county docket, and only six prosecutors to handle them. They tried to get judges to grant continuances or they had subordinates do jury selection on one case while they scrambled to wrap up another.

Missing out on jury selection is something Walker does only as a last resort. She knows firsthand in the racially charged Wayne County court system how easy it is for black jurors to acquit black defendants, even in the face of strong evidence, especially if their accusers are white suburban cops. "I try to keep young women off a jury," says Walker. "Especially if it's a good-looking defendant. They're, 'Oh, I don't want to send him to jail.' And I'm 'I tell you what, bimbette . . .' "

One of many ironies in the Gorton case was that as Walker was trying to keep women off the jury, Tank was trying to keep them on, and very successfully. So much so, that their presence, combined with so many other women in the court, threw Gorton into a rage, and brought on the meltdown that changed Tank's planned defense.

## 93
## A FLIGHT ATTENDANT'S REVENGE

In this courtroom filled and run by women, which his lawyer would later say drove Gorton nuts, there was one who had a vested interest in seeing that Ludwig's killer was brought to justice.

Cori Reyes was an intern with the Wayne County Prosecutor's Office, a third-year law student set to graduate from Wayne State the following spring and take her bar exam nearly a year after the start of Gorton's trial.

Reyes was also a former flight attendant, and after being hired at both of her airline jobs—first with the Detroit no-frills carrier Spirit Airlines and then with American—she'd been trained in security measures in classes that used the murder of Nancy Ludwig as their prime example.

"Her murder was something that affected the entire airline industry," says Reyes. "They told us, 'There's someone out there preying on flight attendants. He's on the loose.' "

Reyes had been a University of Michigan grad, majoring in comparative literature, who decided she wanted to see the world for a few years before she got serious about her adulthood. After flying for four years, she took a leave of absence from American to start law school.

She was interning at the prosecutor's office in February of 2002 when a buzz went around that there was going to be a big press conference, that the state police had caught Ludwig's murderer.

Reyes didn't know Walker, but when she found out she'd been assigned the case, she introduced herself and said that as a former flight attendant, perhaps she could be of assistance.

"Great," said Walker, who immediately began grilling her on procedures and precautions attendants are trained to take.

Reyes did research on case law—Walker wanted to get details of the Eby killing into evidence and was able to do so thanks to a precedent Reyes researched known as *People* vs. *Vandervliet*—and grunt work like making photocopies and helping organize exhibits.

If Gorton felt the eyes of the various women boring his way, he wasn't imagining it, especially in Reyes' case. During jury selection on Monday, particularly, she kept an eye on him. She thought it interesting that each time a slender, dark-haired attractive woman was questioned—there were three of them in all—"he had a physical reaction. His lip curled up. He looked like he was ready to jump out of his seat. There was just a totally different reaction to them from the other women or men. It was like a metamorphosizing scene from a movie. He looked so normal, and then suddenly he didn't look normal at all."

On Wednesday night, defense attorney Tank would later claim to have seen a similar metamorphosis, and say that it had momentous impact on the trial.

Walker, to Reyes' surprise, let her participate in the prosecution itself, and she handled Wednesday afternoon's examination of Mike St. Andre, the Romulus undercover cop who had played the key role of snatching Gorton's cup from the roller rink. Until then, Reyes had only worked some forfeiture hearings, where the worst thing that could happen from her point of view was that the judge would let a defendant get his car back.

(Months after the trial, Reyes took her bar exam and Walker was her sponsor for admission into the state bar.)

Feeling nervous, but acting cool, Reyes led St. Andre through his history as a cop, the night at the rink and the capture of the cup. He was a key witness, obviously. Reyes had prepared herself for her big moment by rehearsing any number of possible objections Tank could make, so she'd have a response ready. To her surprise, Tank had none.

Surely, though, he'd have a vigorous cross-examination and she'd need to be ready to counter with a redirect to undo whatever damage Tank might inflict. There had been a big crowd at the rink. Lots of kids drinking lots of pop. Lots of people at Gorton's table in the course of the night. Surely there would be questions trying to shake St. Andre's testimony that he had grabbed the right cup, or had handled it properly after he grabbed it. The cup had passed through a lot of hands in a brief period.

When Reyes told the court: "I have no further questions," Drake said, "Mr. Tank?"

"Can I just hold on a second?" asked Tank. And then, to Reyes' further surprise, he said, "I have nothing, Your Honor."

Reyes' moment in the spotlight was over.

She had done the best she could to fulfill one of the goals of hers since she'd heard there was going to be a press conference announcing an arrest in Ludwig's murder. She'd wanted Art Ludwig to be able to tell the world that a former flight attendant helped put his wife's killer away.

## 94
## MEDICAL TESTIMONY

Wednesday was another busy, fast-paced day in the trial of Jeffrey Gorton.

To begin the morning, Mike Larsen took the stand. He went over some of the same ground Kilbourn covered and told of personally giving Gorton the buccal swab the night of his arrest.

Tank did cross-examine Larsen, finally starting to set up his Klepinger defense.

"Officer, it's your testimony today that you investigated over a hundred people in reference to what took place?"

"Yes."

"Most of them by way of buccal swabs, correct?"

"Most of them. Some were interviews."

"Okay. And when you did this, one of the ways that you did it, you based some of it on geographic location in relationship to the scene at Romulus, correct?"

"I'm not sure I understand the question."

"You found out where the people lived and worked and that gave you a way to get started with respect to suspects, didn't it?"

"Well, there were a number of suspects in both police reports when we started this investigation."

"Well, the geographic location of where these people resided and worked gave you a start, didn't it? If someone lived close to the scene at Romulus, or someone lived close to the scene in Flint and they have a violent history, you started looking at them, didn't you?"

"Not necessarily."

"No, okay. You remember, officer, don't you, getting a DNA swab from a James Klepinger?"

"Yes."

"Okay."

"I personally didn't. I sent a request out to a detective sergeant by the name of Mike Morey at the state police post in Ionia."

"And you did that for a very specific reason, didn't you?"

"Yes."

"And the reason that you did it was that you were aware of Mr. Klepinger's background, weren't you?"

"Yes."

"You were aware of the fact that he murdered a woman in Ann Arbor, weren't you?"

Tank then wrapped up by asking Larsen if he was aware of the original crime-scene composites, that Klepinger's height of 5'10" and weight of 150 fit into the description of the stranger hanging around the Hilton, and that he once lived 1.1 miles from the airport.

Walker on cross-examination was able to elicit that Klepinger's fingerprints did not match the Eby crime-scene prints and that his DNA did not match the DNA at the Eby scene or the Ludwig scene.

It would be Tank's one and only relatively vigorous cross-examination of the trial. It hadn't helped that Klepinger hadn't been linked to either scene by DNA or fingerprints, but he had established that the state police had been interested in him as a suspect, that he matched the description of the eyewitnesses in Ludwig, that he was a convicted murderer and that he had once lived near the airport.

All in all, he had accomplished what he'd set out to accomplish.

Tank had rubbed Larsen the wrong way at the preliminary hearing months earlier. "We thought he was a big shot the way he was passing out business cards." Tank had instilled, well, not fear, but the sense they would be in for a good battle. "We thought, 'Well, okay, we've got a good case.' "

At trial, Larsen made it three for three—another homicide cop surprised by how inept Tank seemed to be. Like Elford, he thought Wayne County hadn't seen its last trial of Jeff Gorton. "At the time, we said, 'Betty Walker will be retrying that one,' " Larsen would say months later.

He, too, couldn't recall seeing Tank take any notes during the trial.

If there is a better prosecution witness than Lynne Helton, Elizabeth Walker has yet to find one. Helton took the stand at 10:25. She was seething with a rage she'd kept bottled up since working the Ludwig crime scene, but her calm demeanor would keep that rage well hidden.

She would do everything in her power—including describing the horror of the crime scene—so there could be no doubt about the enormity of what had happened in room 354. She has developed a style over the years, of keeping science jargon to a minimum and imagining the jurors are friends she's sitting with at a table in her kitchen having coffee.

"I want to come across as the girl next door," she admits.

Before she was done, one of the jurors was crying, "and that's never happened before. I laid it on pretty thick as far as my descriptions," she would acknowledge later. "The violence [at the scene] shouted at you, and I wanted the jury to appreciate it."

She didn't want the jury to see her glaring at Gorton, nothing as obvious as that. But she kept sneaking peeks at him, trying to make eye contact.

"I wanted my eyes to tell his eyes that I *know*. The DNA doesn't lie, it doesn't matter what his story is." Just briefly their eyes met, and Gorton quickly averted his. But there was satisfaction for her in that second.

She described the wounds to Ludwig in stark, graphic detail, about the wounds to the face, the jagged, gaping slashes to the neck with a serrated knife, the controlling pinprick wounds that had been part of the murderer's play, the symbol cut into her breast, the semen evidence of acts of sex both before and after her death. And then she told the jury in plain, understandable language the science behind DNA evidence, and why it pointed clearly and unmistakably—with ratios like 97 quadrillion to one—to Jeffrey Gorton.

Helton was on the stand for two hours and ten minutes, sandwiched around a recess and a lunch hour.

Helton's last bit of testimony was:

"The DNA profiles belonging to the semen donor on all three of the evidence samples matched exactly the DNA profile provided to me as being from Jeffrey Gorton."

WALKER: "I have nothing further."
JUDGE DRAKE: "Mr. Tank."
TANK: "Real briefly."

His cross-exam lasted two minutes. He asked nine questions about the math behind getting to 97 quadrillion to one. There were thirteen factors in matching DNA samples. Matching one factor had a certain probability. Matching a second had another. A third another. Multiply the probability of each separate factor by the probability of each other factor and you get the final answer.

Walker couldn't have led Helton through the process any better if she had tried. There could be no doubt in the jury's mind. This wasn't voodoo, it was simple multiplication.

Jeff Nye was next. He recounted for the jury how he'd worked with the napkins and cup taken from the roller rink, which provided enough of a link to Gorton to get search warrants and arrest him.

Tank had nothing to ask him.

Cori Reyes took over for Walker. She walked Mike St. Andre through the night they'd followed Gorton into the rink and snatched his napkins and cup. Obviously an important event in this long chain of events, and a key witness.

Tank had nothing to ask him.

Yung Chung, a forensic pathologist in the Wayne County

Medical Examiner's Office, was the last witness of the day. He had done the autopsy on Nancy Ludwig's body and described in a clinical, almost detached manner—the jury having to strain to understand him at times through his thickly accented English—the injuries he found when he did his examination on February 19, 1991.

"She had lots of scratches and superficial cuts almost to entire face. Her neck was sliced deep enough to cut the airway and both sides of major blood vessels. There were several stab wounds to the left parietal scalp and also left forehead. There are some slicing wounds on the right palm that indicate she had a struggle for this incident. And a lot of abrasions and puncture mark on the left upper chest area, and the left eye was blue swelling."

He then described all the various wounds in detail, the length and depth of her defensive wounds, the severing of her windpipe and carotid artery, the cutting deep into the esophagus, which he said was very elastic, very tough, very hard to cut, the many and varied puncture wounds with the tip of the knife to her head and chest.

Wounds of this nature were "unlikely sustained by one slice there, probably over and over many times to make this. And also the edge of the neck wound would indicate there is many times knife back and forth."

Graphic photos were passed around to the jury. Some of them looked close to being ill.

Chung was on the stand for thirty-two minutes of horrific, detailed testimony.

When he was done, Tank said, "I have no questions, Your Honor."

Months later, Tank would say Chung's testimony was a turning point in the trial, that hearing Chung recount in detail one wound after another, and the effort expended to make it, made him doubt his client's version of events—that he'd had consensual sex with Ludwig and that Klepinger, in a rage while he was in the shower, had killed her.

Tank would say later that Chung's testimony made him realize he needed to ask his client some tough, pointed questions. Those questions—and the terrifying response—would change the course of the trial.

# 95

# CLOSING ARGUMENTS

The three rows of spectator pews in Judge Drake's court-room are arranged like the bottom three segments of an octagon. By sitting at the far left, as he had throughout the trial, Arthur Ludwig could get a good look at Gorton. He stared at him throughout, hoping to catch eye contact that never came.

Thursday morning he took the stand and recounted the last sad days of his marriage. He had nothing to add, really, to the facts at issue. But he certainly put another face on the tragedy for the jury.

Tank had no cross-examination. At 10:04 a.m., Tank said he had some matters to discuss outside the jury's presence, and they were led out. He then asked the judge to dismiss all charges, a so-called directed verdict.

"Clearly your motion for directed verdict is denied, counsel," said Drake.

Tank's original plan, or so he said, was to put Gorton on the stand. Instead, he had Gorton stand and tell the court that he understood his right to testify but wanted to waive it. And then Tank rested his case.

Or tried to.

"Mr. Tank, remember that you must rest in front of the jury when they come back," the judge chided him.

They were brought back and he rested again. He hadn't made an opening argument. He hadn't cross-examined most of the prosecution witnesses. And he hadn't called a single witness.

Walker presented her closing argument. She briefly walked the jury through the testimony and concluded, "Ladies and gentlemen, the proofs in this case are really quite overwhelming. There can't be any serious doubt as to the identity of Nancy Ludwig's attacker, rapist and murderer. His name then and now is Jeffrey Wayne Gorton."

And then Craig Tank, in his last case as a public defender, gave his closing argument, the likes of which those present may never hear again.

"Before I get started," he began, "I want to take a moment to thank each and every one of you for the time that you spent over the last four days and that you sat as jurors. The way that you conducted yourself and the time that you spent, it was obvious how attentive you were with respect to what took place."

At that point a juror's cell phone rang, with a loud and spirited rendition of "Take Me Out to the Ball Game." The courtroom erupted in laughter. The judge glared at the jury box.

"You need to shut the phone off."

JUROR NUMBER NINE: "Sorry."

JUDGE DRAKE: "You may resume."

TANK: "And so I want to thank you in advance for that. But over and above that, there are some specific things that I want to talk about, some specific things that are going to relate to the jury instructions that the judge is going to give that I ask you that you take into consideration when you begin your deliberations.

"You will be asked to take the facts that have been elicited at trial, to take them, to put them up next to the instructions that have been set forth and to compare whether or not each element has been met and whether or not it's been met beyond a reasonable doubt.

"The judge will instruct you on the meaning of reasonable doubt, and the fact that each element has to in fact be proven beyond a reasonable doubt. You will see and hear her instructions that reasonable doubt can be attached to. In referencing that, I want to take a few specific moments to talk about some specific elements associated with each one of the offenses.

"The judge will instruct you first on the offense and will instruct you at some point in time on the offense of felony murder. Felony murder as it pertains to a larceny.

"When you begin to talk about that larceny, one of the things that has to be established by the prosecutor's office is that items were in fact taken. That the goods and property were taken by another. I submit to you that there hasn't been any evidence in terms of what's been taken at this point in time. In addition to that, we talk about credit cards, money, things along those lines.

There is no evidence of those things being used in the future.

"In addition to that, and what I want to have or put some particular emphasis on with respect to the—with respect to the criminal sexual misconduct count as it relates to the felony murder is, again we see a situation there where, although there was trauma that was described at the scene in Flint or vaginal trauma, there is no trauma that's been described at the scene at the Romulus Airport. Again, it's something that you can attach doubt to and there is a reason that's obviously there for.

"Over and above that, when we begin to look at the crime scene and what's associated with it, when you think of it in terms of the way that a crime scene should be thought of, there is some very, very significant questions that need to be thought about with respect to premeditation. When you talk about and once you hear about what's been involved in terms of those things happening, there are issues with respect to premeditation.

"When you take all of those things and when you take them and put them together in the jury room and apply them, they are clearly appropriately there as the judge will instruct you.

"Again, I'd like to thank you for the time that you spent and how patient you have been with me. Thank you."

Courtroom observers sat stunned. The jury appeared stunned, as well. Everyone thought they were hearing a rambling, nearly incoherent introduction to what would become the closing arguments, but that had been the closing arguments, themselves.

If you strip away Tank's preamble thanking the jury, and his talking about what the judge would or wouldn't do later, the actual arguments on behalf of Gorton amounted to four paragraphs of . . . of what? What argument had been made? Tank four times mentioned the word "specific" in reference to what he was about to say. But what specifically had he said? What was there for a juror to take back to the jury room and ponder?

Walker's closing arguments had lasted for forty-two minutes. Tank's lasted for three.

Tank's closing arguments, or lack thereof, would later form the heart of an appeal for a new trial, claiming an incompetent defense. "A neophyte had been handed a case he couldn't handle," Philip Beauvais, Gorton's attorney on the Eby case would later say about the appeal in the Ludwig case.

"The most amazing thing to me is, the closing argument is just three pages of transcript. Three! And even reading it I don't know what in the hell he was trying to say. I've tried some cases where I've had some pretty bad co-counsel for co-defendants, but I've never seen anything as bad as this. I tell everyone, 'My fifteen-year-old son could have done a better job.'

"It was funny. Jeff thought Tank walked on water. Jeff thought Tank would perform miracles for him, because he told him he worked miracles."

The jury went to lunch, then heard lengthy instructions from the judge about the five counts of criminal sexual assault and premeditated murder and what was required to prove them. At 2:25 p.m., the jury went into deliberations.

While they were out, Gorton read some of *False Memory*, by Dean Koontz. When a bailiff asked him what it was about, he replied, "Self-hatred."

Tank told one court official, loudly enough so anyone in the courtroom could hear him: "This is my last trial. I'm going to do tax-evasion work." And, "I anticipated testimony I didn't get. From him. He just shut down on me. I was left in the lurch."

Gorton didn't have long to read. The jury came back at 4. It was guilty on all counts. Sentencing—mandatory under Michigan law of life in prison without possibility of parole—was set for September 19.

# 96

# AN ANGRY EX-WIFE

On September 19, Judge Drake gave Gorton life on each of three counts and 40–80 on two others. He was credited for 152 days served, a funny kind of credit, since the math of life without parole minus 152 is still life without parole.

If the sentencing was anticlimactic, the appearance of his ex-wife, Dawn Hemingway, was not. She had been on the witness list, but wasn't called. She was accompanied by a slender man of about 35, dressed in a suit and claiming to represent Dawn. Was he her attorney? No. A relative? No. "I'm just representing her interests." And what was his name? "Let's keep names out of this."

When he found out one reporter was there to write a book, he asked how much Dawn would be paid for her participation. He was told that ethical standards prohibited paying for interviews.

"Well, then, how about if the book says by you 'and Dawn Hemingway'? You know, by both of you? She can share in the money that way."

No, that isn't going to work, either.

"Well, she should have something coming to her."

The man in the suit arranged a series of post-sentencing interviews with various media members in the dark, gloomy hallway outside Drake's courtroom, positioning people here and there to await their turn.

For the TV and radio people, lights glaring on her, Dawn said: "I feel a very, very deep sadness for the victim's family. I'm glad after so many years, with DNA being what it is today, that justice has finally been served. It was a long time coming. A lot of pain has been put to an end after a long haul."

In a solo interview, she told of Gorton catching her eye when she entered the court. "He looked directly at me and smiled and waved. He was thinking, 'You were there for me before and you're here for me, now.' If he only knew. I want him dead. An eye for an eye."

She said that when police came knocking on her door the previous February to ask about her ex-husband, "I was shocked, but it wasn't shocking. I just want to ask him, 'How many others, Jeff? No bullshit, just me and you. How many others?' "

After Gorton's arrest, she had briefly been in the limelight in Flint, doing newspaper interviews and allowing local TV crews into her house to talk about her first marriage.

After the first trial, when Mike West, a producer for Bill Kurtis Productions in Chicago, asked for an interview for an episode they were producing on the murders for *Cold Case Files* on the A&E cable network, Hemingway's "representative" told him the cost of an interview was $8,000.

West told him they wouldn't pay and would just get some footage from the local Flint stations, if need be.

At the sentencing, Dawn told the book reporter that she would cooperate in the project, but when he called to set up an interview, her husband, Fred, wanted to know what she would be paid.

The reporter explained, again, that he couldn't pay for interviews.

"He says he can't pay," Fred told Dawn on their end of the phone connection. Dawn started yelling in the background. "No one wants to give me anything! I can't even get a lunch at Bob Evans. You'd think I'd be able to get a weekend getaway! I'm the one who was sleeping with a maniac!"

"Fred, I just bought Dan Snyder and Gordie Malaniak lunch. I'd be happy to buy you guys lunch, too, if that will help," said the writer. "I'll buy you lunch and you can hear me out about how much time I need and decide then if you want to cooperate."

"He said he'd buy us lunch," Fred told Dawn. He told the reporter to call him back next week and they'd set up a time and place.

When the reporter called back, Fred said, "Here's the bottom line. We don't need to meet for lunch. We've decided on a price, and that's it. It's going to cost you $2,000 to talk to Dawn. That's it. Dawn's got to get something out of this. Everybody's getting rich but her."

As Mike West said, "She acted like finding out you used to be married to a serial killer was a lucky break. An opportunity."

# 97

# A MOVING SPEECH

Archie Hayman, a slight black man is one of the most popular judges in Flint, with prosecutors, defense attorneys and court employees. He is gracious, fair and affable.

He'll tell a defendant whom he has just sentenced to a year in jail, "I'm going to pray for you and your family."

Or recognize someone in court who once appeared before him and who is there to lend moral support to a relative about to be sent to jail:

"Mr. Thomas. I haven't seen you in a while."

"That's a good fact, Your Honor."

"He was surprised I remembered him," the judge would later tell his staff during a recess, genuinely happy that Mr. Thomas wasn't back in court on charges, himself.

Hayman was considered the perfect judge to handle Jeffrey Gorton's second trial, scheduled to start on Tuesday, January 7, 2003. Except that there would be no trial. In a surprise move, the day before, about 3 p.m., Philip Beauvais, unable to convince his client to change his mind, called over to the judge's court in the old, stately historic courthouse on Saginaw Street downtown and said his client wanted to enter a no-contest plea to the charges of first-degree criminal sexual conduct and first-degree premeditated murder.

The clerk said she didn't think Hayman would go along, but soon was back relaying word that the judge said to have sheriff's deputies from the nearby county jail bring Gorton over as soon as possible and they could enter the plea that afternoon.

In Michigan, that plea carries the weight, and the same sentence, as a guilty plea. The plea was a blessing to everyone except journalists, hoping for the job satisfaction that comes from writing front-page stories on one of the biggest murder cases in the city's history. The plea saved the time and expense of a trial, it saved Gorton's family and the Eby family from having to sit through the excruciating details of Margarette Eby's murder, and it ended the automatic right to an appeal Gorton would have had if found guilty at trial.

Beauvais had hoped to make the plea out of the glare of

the media light, but someone from the judge's office called local media, and they were there in force by the time Gorton was brought in in chains, cuffs and his green jailhouse jumpsuit.

Gorton told the judge he understood what the plea entailed and wanted to make it.

"I've been an attorney for twenty-four years and represented some people charged with the most heinous crimes, and never in my wildest dreams would I ever believe he would enter a plea on first-degree murder," said Beauvais outside the courtroom. Earlier Beauvais had been rebuffed by prosecutor Randy Petrides when he offered to have Gorton plead guilty to a charge of second-degree murder.

Gorton had first told him the previous Monday that he wanted to plead. Beauvais visited him in jail on Monday, Tuesday, Thursday and Friday, trying to talk him out of it. He even called Brenda on Thursday to tell her to get a nice suit ready for the trial, just in case.

Brenda said, "I didn't think he was going to trial. I thought he was going to plead no contest. He wrote me a letter and said that was what he was going to do."

"Brenda, is Jeff the kind of guy, once he makes up his mind, you can talk him out of it?"

"Once Jeff decides something, he's going to do it."

"I can't talk him out of it?"

"No way."

Beauvais said that Gorton wanted to spare his family the ordeal of a trial, but that in part, Gorton's wish to end proceedings as quickly as possible stemmed from his first trial, and Craig Tank's defense.

"He's so disillusioned by what happened there that he has lost faith in the criminal-justice system and did not believe he would get a fair shake," said Beauvais.

Dan Loga visited him in jail and asked Gorton why he was pleading. According to Loga, Jeff told him, "First of all, I didn't want to put my family through it. Second of all, I didn't want to put their family through it."

"That struck me," says Loga. "That was the first bit of remorse I've heard from him. I thanked him. He saved everyone a lot of pain."

Mark Eby said it was a blessing for his family. "We had

discussed how much of it we would listen to, and it's a blessing we don't have to relive it in that level of detail," he said.

Eby said when he was told about the plea, he wondered aloud why. His 7-year-old daughter replied, "God answered our prayers."

February 13, 2003. Judge Hayman's courtroom was filled by 8:45 a.m., the pews wedged shoulder to shoulder for Jeffrey Gorton's sentencing. The sentence, itself, was a foregone conclusion—under state law there was no option but life without parole—but the air was still heavy with drama.

Flint's most notorious case was about to come to a close.

Dan Snyder and Greg Kilbourn sat in front of the rail separating the spectators from the players. Mike Larsen sat with the spectators.

Dan Loga, Gorton's brother-in-law, passed out a statement to members of the media. It included two paragraphs of his own thoughts and a quote from Brenda, who was not in the court.

"Horrific event that brings us here today. Mrs. Eby's children and grandchildren have been denied the nurturing and love only a mother and grandmother can provide. Family and friends have been denied the pleasure of her company.

"In speaking for Mr. Gorton's wife and children, I sincerely wish to convey to Mrs. Eby's family our deepest sympathy. Her family is forever changed."

Brenda's quote read:

*When this crime took place, I had not yet met Mr. Gorton. Never was I aware of his past or dark side. I began a life with him that led to a family. A family that was hoping and working for all the things families need and enjoy. I can understand much of what the Eby family has gone through. One day all was normal for me, too. School, working, planning for vacation and the day-to-day business of family life. The next day, my children's lives and mine are never to be the same, again. The past year has been one of great hardship. My children have no father. Our income is half of what it was. And the hardest part is to realize each day, the one I thought I knew is something I never imagined.*

At 8:53 a.m., Gorton was led in, again in chains, cuffs and a green jumpsuit.

Beauvais did some housecleaning—getting on the record that the sentencing report gave Gorton credit for 363 days served when it should be 370, and he said for the record that the no-contest plea came over his strenuous objections.

At 8:59, the Eby siblings approached the attorney's podium and microphone. Gorton must have felt a sense of déjà vu. Dayle, the oldest, was a ringer for her mother, so similar in appearance, she looked like a miracle of cloning. Moments earlier, Beauvais had walked up to the siblings and said, based on Dayle's remarkable resemblance, "You must be the Ebys." Later he'd tell a reporter, "She looked just like Mrs. Eby. It was like Mrs. Eby came back from the grave and bit him."

The four stood together, Jonathan Eby closest to the mike, holding a sheet of paper. He turned to his left to face Gorton, who was standing with a sheriff's deputy against the railing of the empty jurors' box, and he began reading:

> *"When I was seventeen years old, I lost my father's car in a car-jacking in Detroit. It happened around Christmas, and many out-of-town relatives were in the area. I was brought to my uncle's home shaken and angry, and was dismayed by my grandmother's reaction to the news. She suggested we pray for the perpetrator, and we did. I was flabbergasted. Shouldn't we have prayed for me, for judgment, for justice?*
>
> *"But she understood something that I am working in my mind and heart to get around: Part of receiving God's grace and forgiveness for the wrongs we have committed requires a willingness to extend it to those who wrong us. Grandma chose a path of mercy toward the offender and faith in Jesus Christ, seeking an eternal perspective to the situation.*
>
> *"Today, we are arrived at a watershed of sorts for my family and me. The wrong committed against my mother and us by the defendant was enormous and the loss and injury we sustained cannot be overstated. Margarette Eby was a unique and gifted woman whose love, enthusiasm and talent brought life to many people. Her*

*determination, courage and discipline continue to inspire me to press on in the challenges I face. The selfishness and evil that drove the defendant to abuse her as he did defies humanity and God, Himself. It is altogether right that our laws exact justice for the acts he has committed, and I applaud the efforts of those responsible for this man's removal from society and to face this day in court.*

*"But I recognize the inadequacy of incarceration—or even capital punishment—in rectifying the wounds to our souls we received from this man. There is no undoing or evening the score. The damage is, on some levels, permanent. But there is an opportunity we have to redeem this moment. We believe God is able to bring good out of evil and we also believe that He has called us to be grace givers, to extend His influence through the grief we experience, to reflect Him.*

*"So, today I choose to forgive you, Jeff Gorton, for what you have done to my mother and to me. Accountability and consequence remain in the courts, and you certainly have business with God that I encourage you to deal with sooner rather than later. But I'm done with hating you or wanting evil to come to you, and pray instead that good will come of this, for you and especially for your wife and children."*

Prosecutor Petrides went to the podium as they returned to their pew. He thanked the detectives, the state police scientists and FBI agent Heather Krohn for their work in solving the case. And he thanked Gorton's parents for their cooperation.

"They were the first two people to return their acknowledgment cards that they were being subpoenaed in the case," he said.

The judge asked Gorton if he wished to make a statement. If observers thought Eby's eloquence and compassion might have been enough to move Gorton to apologize for the pain he had caused, they were mistaken. "I have nothing to say at this time," he said.

"Mr. Gorton, you weren't the first person who's committed this kind of crime to come before me. You, unfortunately, probably won't be the last. So I'm going to ask all of us to pray for all of us."

And then he sentenced Gorton to life in prison and fined him $60 for a crime-victim's fund.

## 98
# PUKING ON THE STREET

On May 16, 2003, Beauvais' motion for a new trial because of an inadequate defense brought Gorton back before Judge Drake for another day in court.

At the hearing, Gorton was finally allowed to testify. He said he and James Klepinger had gone to the Hilton "to pick up women. I used to have a good pick-up line when I was younger."

He met Ludwig and "We kept talking. It took a while to get her to agree to have sex," he said. "We had consensual sex, but I wasn't there when she was killed."

Klepinger called up to the room looking for him and came knocking on the door while Gorton was in the shower.

When he came out, Ludwig was dead. "I started freaking out," said Gorton. "I suggested calling an ambulance but Klepinger said it was too late."

So they made it look like a robbery gone bad, instead.

As expected, Drake denied the motion. "Based on the overwhelming evidence, even if he had F. Lee Bailey, he couldn't have avoided the outcome," she said.

Once that motion was heard, Tank was no longer bound by rules of attorney–client privilege. He and Gorton were officially adversaries.

Three weeks after the hearing, over lunch in the Big Boy restaurant just off the airport grounds and around the corner from the former Hilton, Tank told his side of the story. It was a tale he said would ultimately lead to Gorton's death by execution in a place like Ohio or Florida, some state where he had killed other women that had the death penalty.

Tank said Gorton had told him before the trial that Klepinger had done the killing, and Tank said he believed the story. "A lot of it was corroborated by the facts." Such as Klepinger's criminal history, his proximity to the airport.

He said he believed Gorton's story well into the trial, and still thought he had a good chance of selling it to the jury, but that Chung's testimony about the autopsy convinced him his client must have had an active part.

"I'm kind of dumb. I didn't actually read the medical examiner's report," Tank admitted. Hearing Chung's detailed accounting of the wounds, Tank said that he said to himself, " 'You gotta fucking be kidding me.' It was overkill. It was different from my theory that he was in the shower. Forty-five wounds would take too long."

Wednesday night, Tank went to the county jail to talk to his client. It was a hot, stifling summer night.

When he pressed him on the contradictions between the testimony and his story, Gorton blew up.

"He went crazy. I pressed him on the amount of damage to her. I said, 'What you described to me isn't checking out with the testimony.' He flipped out and went into a diatribe. He was pissed off at all the women in the court. He was going on that these women weren't going to take him down. He'd killed all kinds of women just like he'd killed these two. He told me he had done the killing."

Tank says the mild-mannered Jeffrey Gorton he had come to know had a transformation in front of him, that he feared for his life. "When I was in a ten-foot-by-twelve-foot cage with him, what you are meant to see and what is underneath that and I *have seen*, they're different things. His eyes, the way they looked at me, I'll never forget it. It was like he was focused on the wall behind me and seeing through me."

Tank says that before Gorton was through ranting, he'd told him he'd killed women in Ohio and Florida and that he'd made up code names for the underwear he'd stolen from his murder victims. No one had ever found any of Nancy Ludwig's clothing. Gorton had some, though, said Tank, labeled "Nell North," the "N" and "L" of Nell standing for Nancy Ludwig and the "North" for Northwest Airlines.

(Later, Mike Larsen would go through his master list of names compiled from the boxes and bags of underwear hauled out of the Gorton house. He found "Mell North" listed, corresponding to a purple pair of underpants. That was on the computer printout. He then went to the hand-written originals. Sure enough, there was "Nell North." The "N" had been transcribed as an "M" by mistake. The underpants were tested for DNA, but results were inconclusive.)

Tank said he wanted nothing more than to get out of that cell and away from Gorton. He called for the guard, hurried out of the jail and onto Clinton Street. He was so upset, he leaned over and vomited.

The next day, as an officer of the court, ethics prevented him from putting Gorton on the stand and committing perjury. He knew that the case was lost. He would have to wrap things up without calling a witness.

Today, Tank says he still believes some of Gorton's tale, that it wasn't a planned killing, that he had in fact picked up Ludwig and had consensual sex before the two men went wild.

Remarkably enough, he said he still thinks he might have gotten his client off had they not had their jailhouse confrontation. "It would have been interesting to see how this would have turned out if I could have argued it. It would have been a wild one. I wonder what would have happened if I hadn't gone the extra mile and hired a jury consultant who had me load the jury up with women. If that hadn't have happened, he might not have had his meltdown. I'm still pissed I didn't get to try it. It would have been a hell of a trial."

The press got on him pretty good over the Gorton trial, but don't feel sorry for him, he says. He's rolling in dough, now, representing drug dealers and for-hire killers who can afford his fees, instead of the $36,400 he was pulling down at the public defender's office. He wears expensive, tailored suits, has bought a condo in Mt. Clemens and drives a Jaguar and a Toyota 4Runner.

He said it's his belief that the FBI will crack the codes on Gorton's cache of clothing and eventually link him to unsolved crimes in Ohio and Florida, that his former client will eventually be executed. But Tank says he will refuse to cooperate with police if he can avoid it.

"I don't have any moral obligations. My duties as a defense attorney supercede any moral issues. I don't believe in the death penalty. I'm very liberal. I don't want to see Jeff get it."

Tank's story still leaves major questions about his defense strategy—such as, if it wasn't till late Wednesday afternoon at the trial, during the medical examiner's testimony, that he began to have doubts, and if he planned on putting on a vigorous defense up till then, why didn't he cross-examine Arcia, or St. Andre or the other witnesses? Why didn't he present an opening argument? Why didn't he at least pretend to take notes? Why wouldn't he have read the medical examiner's report of the autopsy? Why would he believe Gorton's alleged tale that it was Klepinger, given that Ludwig didn't get to the hotel till 9 and numerous hotel employees gave statements during the investigation that she wasn't seen in any of the hotel bars and restaurants but had gone straight to her room? Where would Gorton have chatted her up? How could he have met her after 9, picked her up, had consensual sex, been there while she was tortured at length, washed up, cleaned up the room, packed his car and left, all by 10:30?

Two things do ring entirely true when talking to Tank: his belief that Gorton left other dead victims out there, crimes yet to be solved; and that something happened in the Wayne County Jail Wednesday night that left him shaken. Nothing he said had a greater ring of truth than recounting how he threw up on Clinton Street as soon as he was out of there.

# EPILOGUE

At the end of 2003, Jeffrey Gorton's conviction in Wayne County was under appeal by Beauvais to the Michigan Court of Appeals. The attorney has no hope of ultimately setting his client free for those crimes, but he does want to hold Tank's feet to the fire.

Dave King continues to teach young cops. He is a good cop. Elford, Larsen and Kilbourn—cops who know good from bad—all respect King. It was his misfortune to have made major mistakes on the biggest case of his career, compounded by the arrogance of the pseudoscientists at the FBI and the coincidence of an old childhood friend turning out to be the chief suspect, and a very good one, at that.

"After I retired, I have to confess, I thought, 'Dave, I hope I didn't screw up on that.' Having said that, I feel pretty comfortable with it right now . . . If you look at the number of cases I worked on after Eby happened, and all the open investigations I'd done beforehand, you get quite a few cases. There was only so much we could do.

"Some of the reporters I've spoken with persist in the idea that since we had a suspect, we closed all the other doors. That's not really true. Trust me, we weren't that simplistic. I don't believe the odds favored us getting anywhere with Gorton, had our investigation revealed him. A confession was a long shot at best . . .

"A community like Flint, with shrinking resources, trying to keep up with what was then a record high murder rate—a case like this comes along and it requires a team of good investigators to stay on it, full-time, for a long, long time. How do you justify it? What about the other unsolved cases?"

He is polite enough not to take pot shots at the profilers, but does say, betraying some pique, "You get these FBI guys bragging, 'I've made one hundred arrests in my career.' In a career? I was making one hundred arrests a month."

Eleven of the seventeen command officers of the Romulus Police Department were forced into retirement two weeks

after Gorton's sentencing. Their choice was to take a demo-
tion, which would affect their pension, or to take a buyout
and retire. For ten of them, the last day of work was Friday,
September 27, the end of the pay period. Malaniak, being
Malaniak, came in on Monday the 30th, to officially finish
out the month.

He put in his day, went over to a local park, drank a beer
with the guys, then they went to downtown Detroit to a
casino. It wasn't much of an end to a career. Anticlimactic.

"I didn't know what to expect. I guess I expected a little
more than that," he says. Both he and Snyder got plaques
from the Romulus PD for their years of service. Snyder un-
wrapped his. Malaniak's is still wrapped. It'll never hang
anywhere.

"I don't think I'll ever get over it," he says of his forced
retirement. "If I ever see Kirby, I'll tell him to kiss my
ass."

He's thinking of getting his private investigator's license.
"Not to do it full-time, but to pick up a job here and there.
Pay for my golf and beer and get me out of the house." He
works security for the Detroit Red Wings, a good gig for a
hockey fan, since it gets you in free to see a team that has
been sold out for years. He was in line for a job as an investigator for the state's gaming commission, but a hiring freeze
put everything on hold.


Dan Snyder bought a fifth-wheel trailer and a truck to pull it,
and a new house closer to his grandkids. He's enjoying his
forced retirement, and he and his wife spent part of their
summer vacation of 2003 visiting Art Ludwig up at
Voyageurs National Park in the boundary waters region of
northern Minnesota.

"We rented a little cabin a short distance from Art's
place, we ate too much, talked too much and told stories,
laughed a lot," said Dan's wife, Jean. "We met some of his
and Nancy's friends and spoiled his fishing. Dan can't sit
still long enough to fish."

Judge Maggie Drake and Prosecutor Betty Walker both
describe Snyder as the best cop they've ever come across.
Drake describes him as "an old-fashioned gumshoe."

Not one to pass out praise indiscriminately, Drake says,

"I thought he was the most fantastic police officer. I've been singing his praises. He did everything right. He had a noose around [Gorton's] neck and had him standing on a box ready for a push. Betty Walker didn't have much to do. Officer Snyder laid out a blueprint for her. Stevie Wonder could have tried that case."

"To appreciate the quality of the work he did, you'd have to have worked on the inside in other homicide cases," says Walker.

It's hard to imagine how the Romulus PD is better off without him and Malaniak. Snyder, not just content to work his way through the ranks, was in school much of his career working on one degree or another, first getting his bachelor's in criminal justice and then a master's in technology management from Eastern Michigan University.

Numerous attempts to ask Kirby about the situation failed. He canceled meetings, did not respond to numerous messages and e-mails, responded to others by saying he was just too busy. He was the only law enforcement officer who didn't find time for an interview of the many I set out trying to contact when the project first began.

The Gorton case has had a lasting effect on Walker. "He is the only man I've ever been afraid of," she says. "To this day, now, when I go home, I pull my shades. I never used to. I figured, 'I catch you peeping, too bad for you.' But no more. Now, as soon as I come home, the shades get pulled."

Greg Kilbourn remains an investigator for the state's gaming commission, doing background checks on suppliers and contractors for the gaming industry in Michigan.

Mike Larsen was promoted to detective lieutenant, replacing Dan Bohnett as boss of the Flint–Saginaw region's cadre of state police detectives. He put in a year and retired at the end of July 2003. "I just wasn't meant to be an administrator. I'm more of a hands-on guy." In October, he became a contractor for the state police, working undercover narcotics.

The next day, he and his wife, Mary Kay, hosted 100 persons at their son's wedding on the back deck of their house, overlooking a river in the mid-Michigan town of Owosso.

They then took off on an extended camping trip in northern Michigan.

Margarette Eby's children are suing the Mott Estate for its allegedly lax security practices at the time of their mother's death, and they are suing Laurence and Shirley Gorton for hiring Jeff and putting him in a position where he had access to people's houses—including Margarette Eby's just two days before her death—when they knew he'd been imprisoned in Florida.

"Let's see, he's just been released from prison on sexual assault. This is a good idea: Let's send him into people's homes," says the Ebys' attorney, David Binkley, who attends Bible study at Faith Evangelical Presbyterian Church in the affluent Detroit suburb of Rochester with Mark Eby.

The Mott and Gorton cases have been assigned to a Flint judge notorious for his glacial pace and long docket backlog. "I hope to get it settled in my lifetime," jokes David Binkley, who perhaps wishes he could also sue the State of Florida. It was in Florida that the judge sentenced Gorton to only four and a half years—this felony offender who'd been repeatedly climbing into trailers and apartments, stealing underwear by the dozens and running around viciously assaulting women, knocking them down like ten-pins. And it was in Florida that he was released on Christmas Eve, after serving just 22 months, even though he'd been in trouble in jail for repeatedly grabbing an employee's clothes and telling authorities afterwards he felt he was losing control. Had Gorton been made to serve his full term, he would still have been in prison in Florida, and not at the Mott Estate in Michigan, in November 1986.

Flint Prosecutor Art Busch continues to spar with the state police, creating front-page headlines in *The Flint Journal* over the continued presence of the violent-crimes task force. "Quite frankly, I'm disappointed with the results," he told Bryn Mickle, saying the task force had spent $2 million in two years but had only put two killers in jail. "They're well meaning, but they operate outside the prosecutor's office and hope to throw touchdown passes."

The fiscal year of 2003 was very tough on the state budget in Michigan, as it was tough on most state governments. The state police suspended its training academy for an indefinite period, and speculation was that the Flint task force might be scaled back or eliminated if budget woes got worse.

The state now has more than a ten-year backlog of some 30,000 samples of DNA tests to be done, largely because of a state law that went into effect in January of 2002 mandating all felons in state prisons be tested and their DNA entered into the CODIS system. State crime-lab folks used to run 3,500 DNA tests a year, on homicides and serious assaults. In 2002, they took in 50,000 samples, many of them from inmates. Publicity over the Gorton case helped the state police win a $1.4 million federal grant to help cut into the backlog a bit, but it was more like plugging a hole in the dyke.

Lieutenant Colonel Bertee says if he could get $1 million more a year for the state police, he'd put it all into scientists to test DNA and none of it into cops in uniform. "You talk about a bang for the buck." But the state legislature had nothing to give.

The law mandating the taking of prisoner samples paid off almost immediately. One of the first prisoners to be sampled, Magyar Hernandez, was out on parole when his DNA was tested and run into the CODIS system. An unsolved murder of a Frito-Lay driver in San Antonio, a woman who'd been raped and stuffed into a garbage can on a playground, popped up.

Hernandez was picked up and interviewed. He confessed to the crime and was sent to Texas for trial.

Nationally, the lack of funding for DNA testing, despite its promise in solving new and old crimes, is staggering. The most recent FBI survey, in 1998, showed a national backlog of 250,000 samples waiting to be tested for just the most serious of crimes, such as rape and murder.

In October of 2002, Phil Arcia, the Northwest flight attendant whose eyewitness account of Gorton's behavior in the parking lot was instrumental in putting together a physical description of the killer and his car, received $30,000 in reward money from the Teamsters.

Jeff's mother, Shirley, chastised Brenda when she was

granted her divorce in May of 2003. It was not the Christian thing to do, she said, it went against scripture. Brenda had felt guilt, but Dan Loga, ever there for her, had told her that the Gortons' refusal to tell her about Jeff's background and prison record, in his mind, made their marriage null and void. It was entered into under false pretenses.

He says he confronted Jeff's father about how in the world he could keep such a secret from a prospective daughter-in-law?

Laurence Gorton told him what he'd told police, that he didn't know what Jeff's troubles in Florida amounted to.

According to Loga, Jeff's father said, "It was a slap on the hand," and slapped his left wrist with his right palm. "We thought it was a slap on the hand." Jeff's punishment was minor, so they thought the crime must have been minor, too.

Loga didn't believe it any more than the police had.

Jeff's mother told Dan she still didn't believe Jeff had killed anyone. "I don't care what anyone says."

"What's not to believe?" Dan asked incredulously. "The DNA's there. Everything's there. Is it a mother thing, or do you really believe it didn't happen?"

"Maybe both."

They have had little contact with their grandchildren since the divorce. Buckler Automatic Sprinkler System continues in business.

Brenda's co-workers have stood by her, as have her neighbors, friends and relatives, such is their impression of her innate kindness and generosity. Her co-workers covered for her at work when circumstances forced her absence, donating vacation time and picking up hours, and they held fundraisers for her in the trying first year after her husband's arrest.

"Brenda is an open book," says Loga. "She loves people. She doesn't study people. She doesn't make them validate themselves. She takes them at face value. What you see with Brenda is what you get. She's the same person now as when she was ten years old. People love her. Her co-workers love her. There aren't many people who meet Brenda and forget her."

Loga has become something of a surrogate father for her two kids, taking them boating and fishing, playing catch with Wally, something his dad was interested in, taking them to the movies, explaining in words he hopes aren't too devastating when asked what it was their dad had done. After Gorton was first arrested, Loga was with Brenda and the kids at least every other day.

To help cover for a late shift Brenda had to work in the spring of 2003, Loga babysat with Wally and Jenny every Thursday after his day shift as a power-house engineer at GM's Flint North plant ended. He'd take them to the library to work on their homework, then cook them dinner. When Brenda's work schedule changed, he told her he'd grown so attached to her kids, he still wanted to come by every Thursday.

"They're going to be okay. Those kids are going to be fine," he says. Mercifully, their friends at school and at church and in the neighborhood haven't abandoned them, and teasing has been at a minimum. Wally continues to get all A's. Jenny gets A's and B's and is a cheerleader. Both stood up in the wedding party for Dan's daughter when she was married in October of 2003.

Jenny Gorton tells her friends her dad died in an accident. Wally keeps things to himself, but Dan does his best to draw him out.

Loga and his wife attended one day of Gorton's trial in Wayne County, the day of all the forensic testimony. They have no doubt what was done to those women, no doubt that Jeff did it. "But we can't reconcile that with the Jeff we know. Those good memories of him are hard to fade away," says Dan.

Though Jeff stole underwear from his wife and daughter, Dan remains in contact, through letters and visits to prison. Jeff always greets him with the same line he's greeted Loga with since they met at Christmas of 1986. "How you doing?"

"He's a human being," says Loga when asked about maintaining a relationship with Gorton. "Every time I visit Jeff, we start it with a prayer and end it with a prayer. I catch him up on the kids. I don't talk about Brenda. I've told him, 'I'll take care of your kids and keep you up to date on them.

And if they get to the point where they want to visit, I'll try to help with that, too.' "

During one visit, Jeff suddenly said: "Ohmigod, I've got nails," and he held them up to show Dan. Sure enough, a guy who'd bitten his nails non-stop as long as anyone can remember, no longer does.

He no longer rocks, either. He seems to have found peace in his punishment. "He rocked twenty-four-seven, and he bit his nails twenty-four-seven," says Brenda. "He has not rocked or bit his nails since this happened."

Gorton has refused interview requests, but told Loga the same story he told Tank, that Klepinger did the killing. Loga has pleaded with him to tell where he hid Nancy Ludwig's belongings and jewelry, to no avail. He's repeatedly tried to question him about the murders. "We'll talk about the kids and everything will be fine, and then I'll ask a question trying to get back to the why of all this and it's like a stone wall goes up. His facial expression changes. His eyes go glassy. And then I'll mention something about the family and he'll relax and be the Jeff I knew."

Loga was given the Distinguished Citizen Award by the Michigan State Police in July of 2003 when those involved in the case were honored. He was the lone civilian. Members of the violent-crimes task force who were honored included Bohnett, Kilbourn and Larsen. Lynne Helton and Jeff Nye were also honored for their roles in managing the science that eventually put Jeffrey Gorton in jail for life.


Art Ludwig, Snyder, Larsen, Helton—all are frustrated that Gorton never admitted to the murders, never filled in the blanks that remain. They wish they understood more about the why behind what he did.

Chasing the why is pointless. It's a question rational people ask. Gorton's actions were irrational and insane, though not in a legal sense. How else to describe someone who can compartmentalize things so well that he can rape, torture and murder a woman at the Airport Hilton, and four days later stroll through the airport concourses, happily planning his four-day Las Vegas itinerary with his just-pregnant wife? Who can nearly decapitate a woman at 9:30 p.m., immersing himself in a flood of blood spatter, then be home in Flint two hours later asking his wife how her day went when she gets home from working the afternoon shift?

There remains an impression of Gorton as some sort of criminal mastermind, having eluded capture for such high-profile crimes for so long.

But as Mickle says, "He was no mastermind, he was just incredibly lucky. He did everything wrong and should have been arrested in fifteen minutes."

This was a killer who spent much of Sunday, February 17, 1991, scouting out his killing ground. Walking the halls of the Hilton, checking out which rooms were by the fire escapes, likely taking a peek at the roster sheets at the front desk to find out which rooms would be assigned to flight attendants, carrying around a small bag containing his serrated knife for killing, twine for binding and a tube sock for gagging. Who, instead of parking his car right next to the emergency-exit door, which he could have done, parked it at the far reaches of the parking lot, 150 yards away, so he had to repeatedly make that long walk through a well-lit lot carrying bloody clothes and treasures to a car with the trunk open that stood out like a sore thumb.

Who didn't even have enough sense to at some point get rid of the car.

With his arrest, Jeff Gorton suddenly became the lead suspect for every unsolved rape and murder in Michigan, including that of another state police task-force case involving the murder of Ann Paetz, a 23-year-old whose body was found not far from Gorton's house in 1999.

On May 21, 2002, Sergeant Reaves and Sergeant Pekrul interviewed Gorton in the Genesee County Jail about Paetz's murder.

He looked them in the eyes and said, "I never directly said I was not involved in the other two cases, but I am saying that I was not involved in this case. When the other guys asked me questions, I did not talk. But I am talking to you today and will answer any questions you want."

Later, one of Paetz's rings was resubmitted for lab tests. Improvements in DNA testing since the ring was first tested revealed a tiny bit of blood that was not hers. It wasn't Gorton's, either.

Guests are still being checked into room 354 at the old Hilton, now a Double Tree, presumably with better security precautions.

The gatehouse at the Mott Estate is still there and looks in better shape than it did when Eby lived there. Presumably there are better security precautions there, too.

Flint continues to be a city in decline. Romulus is still—Well, feel free to call it Romutucky.